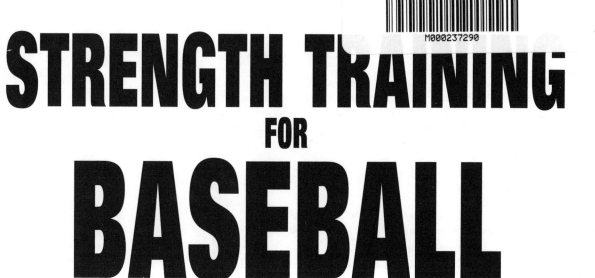

STRENGTH TRAINING
FOR
BASEBALL

Library of Congress Cataloging-in-Publication Data

Names: Coleman, A. Eugene, editor. | Szymanski, David John, 1951- editor. |
National Strength & Conditioning Association (U.S.)
Title: Strength training for baseball / A. Eugene Coleman, David J.
Szymanski, editors.
Description: Champaign, IL : Human Kinetics, 2022. | "National Strength and
Conditioning Association." | Includes bibliographical references and
index.
Identifiers: LCCN 2021006360 (print) | LCCN 2021006361 (ebook) | ISBN
9781492598251 (paperback) | ISBN 9781492598268 (epub) | ISBN
9781492598282 (pdf)
Subjects: LCSH: Baseball--Training. | Muscle strength.
Classification: LCC GV875.6 .S77 2022 (print) | LCC GV875.6 (ebook) | DDC
796.35707/7--dc23
LC record available at https://lccn.loc.gov/2021006360
LC ebook record available at https://lccn.loc.gov/2021006361

ISBN: 978-1-4925-9825-1 (print)

Senior Acquisitions Editor: Roger W. Earle; **Managing Editor:** Miranda K. Baur; **Copyeditor:** Heather Gauen Hutches; **Indexer:** Michael Ferreira; **Permissions Manager:** Martha Gullo; **Graphic Designer:** Dawn Sills; **Cover Designer:** Keri Evans; **Cover Design Associate:** Susan Rothermel Allen; **Photograph (cover):** Victor Decolongon / Getty Images; **Photographs (interior):** © Human Kinetics, unless otherwise noted; **Photo Asset Manager:** Laura Fitch; **Photo Production Coordinator:** Amy M. Rose; **Photo Production Manager:** Jason Allen; **Senior Art Manager:** Kelly Hendren; **Illustrations:** © Human Kinetics, unless otherwise noted; **Printer:** Sheridan Books

We thank Matthew Sandstead, NSCA-CPT,*D and Mel Herl, MS, CSCS,*D, RSCC at the National Strength and Conditioning Association in Colorado Springs, Colorado, for overseeing the photo shoot for this book.

Human Kinetics books are available at special discounts for bulk purchase. Special editions or book excerpts can also be created to specification. For details, contact the Special Sales Manager at Human Kinetics.

Printed in the United States of America   10 9 8 7 6 5 4 3 2 1

The paper in this book is certified under a sustainable forestry program.

Human Kinetics
P.O. Box 5076
Champaign, IL 61825-5076
Website: www.HumanKinetics.com

In the United States, email info@hkusa.com or call 800-747-4457.
In Canada, email info@hkcanada.com.
In the United Kingdom/Europe, email hk@hkeurope.com.

For information about Human Kinetics' coverage in other areas of the world,
please visit our website: **www.HumanKinetics.com**   E8076

STRENGTH TRAINING
FOR
BASEBALL

NSCA®
**NATIONAL STRENGTH AND
CONDITIONING ASSOCIATION**

A. Eugene Coleman, EdD, RSCC*E

David J. Szymanski, PhD, CSCS,*D, RSCC*E, FNSCA

EDITORS

HUMAN KINETICS

PART I: PRINCIPLES OF SPORT-SPECIFIC RESISTANCE TRAINING

PART II: EXERCISE TECHNIQUE

PART III: PROGRAM DESIGN GUIDELINES AND SAMPLE PROGRAMS

NOLAN RYAN

In 1965, I was the 226th player selected in the MLB draft. The New York Mets took me in the 12th round out of Alvin High School, a small school located about 20 miles south of Houston. One year later I pitched in my first MLB game, and four years later I pitched in the World Series. I was in the big leagues, but I wasn't having much success. I threw hard, but often I didn't have a clue as to where the ball was going. If you look back on those early years, there was nothing to suggest that I would go on to pitch for 27 years, win 324 games, and end up in the Hall of Fame. I had 29 wins and 37 losses and an ERA of almost 4.00 in my first four years in MLB.

Things started to look up in 1972 when I was traded to the California Angels. In my first season with the Angels, I started 39 games, finished 20, pitched 284 innings, recorded 329 strikeouts, and had an ERA of 2.28. My mechanics came together, which resulted in a significant improvement, but something more important happened that season that would affect my performance for the rest of my career: I discovered the weight room in Anaheim Stadium. It contained a Universal Gym that had been installed for some other sports team, which we were told to avoid because "lifting weights would make you muscle bound." Without my pitching coach or manager knowing, I began to sneak in workouts on my own. I had no previous experience with lifting weights, but I was careful not to do things that would make me sore or keep me from making my next start. After a few weeks, I noticed that working out did not have any negative effects on my pitching ability and my arm bounced back quicker between starts. I also found that my velocity actually got better in the later innings and that I was able to go deeper into games.

My pitching coach attributed my success to my improved mechanics—I was able to establish a rhythm and get into a groove. This surely had something to do with it, but I believe that my conditioning program made all of this possible by increasing my stamina. Fatigue causes your mechanics to break down, and once your mechanics break down, you can no longer pitch with the precise timing required for a smooth, compact motion. I was so pleased with my results that I bought a Universal Gym for my home, and it paid off. During my first three years with the Angels and my new conditioning program, I pitched 942 innings, had 1,079 strikeouts, and posted an ERA of 2.70. In my second and third years, I pitched over 325 innings, finished 26 games, and recorded over 360 strikeouts. There is no way that I could have recovered as quickly, or been as durable, without a sound fitness base developed through strength training. Strength training didn't add velocity to my fastball, but it allowed me to be more consistent from inning to inning and game to game.

I had established a strong fitness base during my years with the Angels, but it wasn't until I joined the Astros in 1980 that I learned how to fine-tune my program to properly address my needs as a power pitcher. I learned the importance of ground-based exercise and core strength. I learned how to train so that I could better transfer power up the kinetic chain to my shoulder and arm. I also learned the importance of performing daily exercises for the muscles of my arm, shoulder, and rotator cuff. I discovered that long distance running took velocity off my fastball, whereas doing short sprints in the outfield and running inclines added to it. I learned the importance of medicine ball drills and how riding a bike and running in water could help me stay in shape, avoid the pounding of outdoor running, and recover faster. My time with Houston was the turning point in my career.

I took the things that I learned in Houston to Arlington, and with a few modifications and adjustments, I was able to stay in shape and be effective until my mid-40s. At the end of my career, I felt the effects of my age. My back and knee bothered me. I got stiff sooner, and it took longer to get loose and to recover after workouts and between games. I couldn't run as fast or as often, but I learned how to work smarter. I worked hard almost every day and devoted a lot of time to recovery and preparation for my next start. There is no doubt that if it had not been for my weight room and conditioning work, I would have been out of the game many years earlier. Not only did it help me reduce the risk of injury, but it also kept me strong. Without strength training and conditioning, there is no way that I would have been able to pitch for 27 years and throw a sixth no-hitter at age 43 and a seventh a year later.

I have been very fortunate to know and work with several excellent strength and conditioning professionals during my 50-plus years in MLB as a player, owner, CEO, and special assistant. I have also had the good fortune of being involved with the Professional Baseball Strength and Conditioning Coaches Society, and I respect the excellent work that they do. I have tremendous respect for strength and conditioning professionals at every level and their knowledge, dedication, and willingness to go the extra mile to provide every player at every level—not just the superstars, number-one draft picks, or future Hall of Famers—the best chance of achieving their true potential and successful performances. I strongly believe that the principles, exercises, and programs presented in this book can help every athlete, regardless of their position or level of play, and can improve performance and reduce the risk of injury.

INTRODUCTION

DAVID J. SZYMANSKI

The understanding and implementation of resistance training for the sport of baseball has evolved. Prior to the 1970s, the prevailing thought was that resistance training would cause an athlete to become muscle bound and unable to perform well. Most training was restricted to conditioning, using medicine balls, calisthenics, or simply playing the game to get into shape during spring training. However, in the early 1970s, some athletes started doing their own resistance training in secret, without manager approval.

In 1976, the Houston Astros hired Dr. Gene Coleman—a university professor, strength and conditioning professional, and scientist with NASA—to train their athletes. At that time, the effectiveness of resistance training was still unknown, so only the A and AA minor-league players were tested and trained. The Astros did not have well-equipped facilities to perform resistance training, so minor-league players simply performed body-weight exercises. The results of athlete testing during the following spring training in 1977 showed marked physiologic improvements. This led the entire Astros front office personnel and coaching staff to begin to discuss the implementation of strength and conditioning for the major-league club. In the latter part of the 1977 baseball season, the Houston Astros major-league team began resistance training to prepare for the off-season leading into the following year's spring training. During the 1978 spring training, those athletes were tested using similar tests as those in this book. Based on the testing, individual strength and conditioning programs were created.

In the early 1980s, baseball strength and conditioning, especially for the Astros, continued to progress. Nolan Ryan, the highest paid player in Major League Baseball, joined the team and wanted to train routinely between starts. At the time, baseball players did not use free weight exercises because general managers, managers, and coaches still thought it would make athletes too muscular and impede performance. The starting pitchers completed a total body resistance training workout once between starts and the position players completed three total body resistance training sessions per week, using Nautilus machines, dumbbells, bands, and body weight for resistance. All athletes did 3 sets of 10 repetitions for seven to nine total body exercises. Besides the Astros, the only other professional baseball teams that incorporated resistance training during the early 1980s were the Phillies and Reds.

During the mid- to late 1980s, some teams began using free weights, in part due to the influence of the National Strength and Conditioning Association (NSCA), as well as the addition of young athletes to the major leagues who had experience in resistance training with their college programs. However, according to Dr. Coleman, it was Nolan Ryan who had a particular impact on athletes' thoughts about resistance training in baseball. Earlier in his career with the California Angels, Ryan found that his independent resistance training did not negatively affect his pitching. In fact, he believed that it provided greater stamina while pitching in a game in addition to helping his throwing arm recover more quickly between starts throughout the season.

In the 1990s, resistance training in baseball grew more common. More major-league teams were hiring full-time strength and conditioning professionals from numerous backgrounds and incorporating a mixture of free weight and machine programming. Strength and conditioning professionals like Bob Alejo (Oakland A's), Fernando Montes (Cleveland Indians), and Steve Odgers (Chicago White Sox) had a large influence on the way baseball players were trained and how Major League Baseball looked at the strength and conditioning profession. In 1993, these coaches created the Society of Professional Baseball Strength and Conditioning Coaches. Their goal was to unite the profession and to make sure that evidence-based best practices were implemented. In 1995, the Professional Baseball Strength and Conditioning Coaches Society was formalized. They worked with the Professional Baseball Athletic Training Society and the NSCA to host conferences and provide information to enhance the knowledge of those in the profession. Facility size and equipment at major-league stadiums differed widely, and exercise selection was based on what type of equipment was available. Position players learned that using heavier loads for fewer repetitions with free weight produced significant gains in strength and did not decrease performance. Pitchers, in general, were using lighter loads and a combination of free weights, machines, and dumbbells for their programs.

By the 2000s, all MLB teams had full-time strength and conditioning professionals with coaches or interns at most minor-league levels. Exercises were selected based on the coach's training philosophy and the equipment at the training facilities, which varied among stadiums or the local fitness club facility available when traveling. At the collegiate level, top NCAA Division I baseball programs began hiring dedicated strength and conditioning professionals.

In 2000, Auburn University hired David Szymanski—a strength and conditioning professional and, at the time, an exercise physiology doctoral student—as the exercise physiologist for the baseball team. His role included strength and conditioning, baseball coaching, and team researcher. The head baseball coach, Steve Renfroe, was interested in developing the complete baseball player, and strength and conditioning was part of that plan. Szymanski and Renfroe were also interested in monitoring the athletes to make sure they were healthy, strong, powerful, and conditioned. Athletes were reassessed each year to see if their athletic performance and sport-specific skills changed (i.e., improved, stayed the same, or worsened).

Today, every MLB team has a full-time head strength and conditioning professional, and most also have an assistant strength and conditioning professional with a full-time minor-league coordinator and additional strength and conditioning professionals at each level of play. Most top 25 ranked college baseball teams also have a full-time strength and conditioning professional; those that do not generally share an assistant who has had college baseball experience. High schools, depending on the level and size, may have a full-time strength and conditioning professional or staff for the entire school or may not have anyone specifically hired in that type of position. They may have a sport coach with strength and conditioning experience train the baseball players. Ultimately, resistance training for baseball has come a long way since the mid-1970s and will continue to develop as new equipment, technology, and training methodologies are created.

The purpose of this book is to provide information on how high school, college, and professional baseball players are trained using current best practices that have been developed from practical experience, evidence-based training methodologies, and research. Strength and conditioning professionals from high school, college, and professional levels were asked to provide their insight and write a thorough book about the importance of resistance training; analysis of the sport and positions; testing; sport-specific program design; most appropriate exercises; and program design guidelines for off-season, preseason, in-season, and postseason training. We sincerely hope that readers will find this book to be an excellent resource and an important part of their library.

PART I

PRINCIPLES OF SPORT-SPECIFIC RESISTANCE TRAINING

1

IMPORTANCE OF RESISTANCE TRAINING

DAVID J. SZYMANSKI AND BRAD LAWSON

Prior to the 1970s, resistance training was considered taboo among high school, college, and professional baseball players. The prevailing thought of the time was that resistance training would cause athletes to become too big and muscle bound, which was believed to impair throwing, hitting, and running performance. However, since the mid-1970s, when three Major League Baseball teams hired professionals specifically for training their athletes, practical experience and evidence-based research has slowly changed attitudes about resistance training in baseball.

THE ROLE OF RESISTANCE TRAINING

Baseball is an anaerobic sport that requires explosive, multi-planar movements. Therefore, one of the major goals of a well-designed periodized resistance training program is to develop maximum strength, which improves power, velocity, speed, and agility as well as positively affects body composition and helps reduce the chances of injury. Those who train high school, college, or professional baseball players should understand that to develop strength, they must apply the principles of overload, progression, and specificity of training (23). With the right training, the athlete should be healthy, strong, powerful, and able to perform optimally on the field.

MUSCULAR STRENGTH: THE FOUNDATION

The foundation of a resistance training program for baseball is muscular strength. Muscular strength can be categorized three different ways; general strength, special strength, and specific strength (1, 5, 12, 21, 23). **General strength** incorporates traditional weight training exercises, such as the back squat and bench press, as well as body-weight exercises that do not mimic sport-specific skills. The main purpose of general strength is to maximize strength gains. **Special strength** incorporates resistance training movements that include joint dynamics of a skill at higher speeds than traditional resistance training exercises, such as Olympic-style lifts, medicine ball exercises, and plyometric exercises. **Specific strength** incorporates movements with resistance or assistance that mimic the joint actions and speed of sport-specific skills, such as training with overweighted and underweighted implements, like bats or balls, that replicate the mechanics of swinging a bat or throwing a ball at speeds that are similar to, at, or greater than game speeds to enhance the velocity of swinging a player's normal bat or throwing the 5-ounce baseball, both of which are the desired outcomes.

When designing a resistance training program, it is important to think of muscular strength as a continuum of function from general to special to specific (12). This continuum will evolve relative to the athlete's maturation status, development level, and skill level, as well as the needs of the position. If functional strength is fully developed through general, special, and specific multi-planar (including rotation), multi-joint exercises, then the athlete's specific needs should be met.

In addition to developing muscular strength, athletes must develop power, velocity, speed, and agility. **Power** is defined as the rate of doing work (16), force multiplied by velocity, or the product of speed and strength (8). What this means to the coach or athlete is the ability to produce the greatest amount of force in the shortest amount of time. Developing and improving power is one of the main goals for anyone training power athletes such as baseball players. Used with proper mechanics, enhanced power means improved running speed and higher throwing and swinging velocities.

Velocity, which is technically a vector quantity that indicates displacement, time, and direction, represents how fast an object (e.g., a ball or a bat) is moving (6). The velocities of pitching and batting differ among professional, college, and high school athletes. When scouts evaluate a baseball player's ability, they look for five tools: arm strength, hit for power, hit for average, speed, and fielding. Two of these five tools—arm strength and hitting for power—directly relate to throwing velocity and bat swing velocity. Bat swing velocity directly relates to batted-ball exit velocity (23).

Speed can be described as the ability to accelerate to maximum velocity or to move the body through a range of motion in the least amount of time (6). Typically, speed is divided into two phases: acceleration and maximum velocity. For the baseball player, acceleration can begin from a standing position, such as a defensive position prior to a pitched ball or a leadoff stance before advancing to the next base. In general, the maximum velocity phase is rarely reached in baseball because athletes do not typically have an opportunity to run in a straight line at maximum speed for more than 90 feet (27 m) due to changing directions as they run around the bases or as they attempt to make a defensive play.

Agility has traditionally been defined as the ability to change body direction and position quickly (7). Over time, the definition of agility has evolved to also include the factors of perception and decision making (26). In sports, this change of direction often occurs in response to a stimulus— therefore, agility can be called a "rapid whole-body movement with change of velocity or direction in response to a stimulus" (19). In baseball, the stimulus is usually a thrown or hit ball.

INCREASE STRENGTH

Muscular strength is the foundational quality that many athletic skills are dependent upon for proper and efficient execution at all levels of play. Sufficient levels of general, special, and specific strength will support an athlete's ability to produce greater bat swing, batted-ball exit, and throwing velocities; accelerate out of the batter's box; and execute a quick defensive play before making a strong throw to first base. Not only does increasing an athlete's strength improve skill development and performance, but research has also shown it to reduce injury rates (11). The importance of maximum strength should not be underestimated or neglected during an athlete's long-term physical development plan as it plays a major role in many of the physical attributes and sport skills required to be a successful baseball player.

Strength is defined as the ability to exert force (16), but a more detailed definition would be the ability of a given muscle or group of muscles to generate muscular force under specific conditions (25). There are several factors that can influence the strength of an athlete; however, for the scope of this book, the focus will be on modifiable factors, such as exercise selection, training frequency, exercise order, training load, repetitions, sets, volume, and training phases. Instead of describing what happens at the cellular level in detail (except for certain topics), the emphasis will be on the neural and muscular adaptations that allow for improved strength, power, and velocity that occur as a result of general, special, and specific training (18).

These neural and muscular adaptations occur after performing traditional exercises such as the back squat, bench press, and dumbbell pullover (12). Over shorter periods of training time, lasting less than 20 weeks, gains in strength are usually related to neural adaptations associated with learning, coordination, and the ability to recruit primary muscles (18). These adaptations are related to an increased ability to activate motor units of the required muscle groups. Over longer periods of time (>20 weeks), an increase in muscular size, particularly in fast-twitch (type II) fibers, plays a larger role in maximal strength development (18). Long-term resistance training develops muscle **hypertrophy** (an increase in skeletal muscle mass) due to an increase in the size (diameter) in the microscopic thin (actin) and thick (myosin) contractile proteins (myofilaments) (18). The increase in contractile proteins increases the number of myosin that can attach to actin (called *cross-bridges*) in the muscle fiber, which contributes to the muscle group's ability to produce greater force (18).

For the untrained beginner or novice, implementing a consistent training method with little regard to scientific principles or established resistance training programming can result in improved strength adaptations. However, continuing to use this approach without making planned, structured adjustments to the program could result in under- or overtraining, training plateaus where strength development is stagnated, or failure to maximize the window of opportunity for strength gains. For long-term strength development, it is recommended for athletes to work with a coach who implements an evidence-based periodized resistance training program that has demonstrated success in improving maximum strength.

Proper periodization training schemes should implement progressive overload as well as specificity of training. This can be accomplished, in part, with compound bilateral or unilateral multi-joint exercises in multiple planes. A **traditional periodization model** (sometimes incorrectly called a *linear periodization model*), in which the athlete progresses from lower intensity (loads) with more repetitions to higher intensity (loads) with fewer repetitions systematically over time, is a common and effective plan for beginning or novice athletes (13). This model would be appropriate for the high school athlete who has less experience with resistance training by varying the training load and allowing the same number of sets and repetitions across the training days (13). For college and professional athletes, who would generally be considered more trained and experienced, it is recommended that coaches use *nonlinear* periodization models, such as *undulating* periodization. Chapter 4 will provide details about program design and periodization and chapters 9 to 12 will provide resistance training guidelines and sample programs for high school, college, and professional baseball players.

Resistance training to improve strength can have substantial benefits for performance and health, but it is foundational. General, special, and specific strength should be developed to improve power production, which—in combination with excellent mechanics—will optimally improve the skill-related components of throwing, swinging, running, and jumping.

INCREASE POWER

Historically, powerful athletes have been some of the most exciting athletes to watch, and they have often changed the way the game is played. Babe Ruth, Mickey Mantle, Ken Griffey Jr., Ricky Henderson, Nolan Ryan, Pedro Martinez, Bryce Harper, and Mike Trout, to name a few, have amazed and awed spectators across the country with their incredible displays of power in the batter's box, on the pitching mound, on the basepaths, and defensively all over the field.

As explained, power is the term used to describe how much work is accomplished per unit of time (17), or a measurement of the ability to exert force at higher speeds (16). When discussing increased power output, it should be stated that maximal muscular strength may account for as much as 80% of the variance in an athlete's ability to generate force in a rapid manner (called *rate of force development*) (20). Training for increased power output is a very important aspect of training for baseball players. Although all energy systems are involved to some extent over the course of a full game, the primary metabolic demands of baseball-specific skills require the phosphagen system (22, 24). The phosphagen system is the energy pathway that supports explosive and powerful movements such as sprinting, throwing, and swinging (10, 22).

One method of improving strength and power in the same training session is **complex training**, which incorporates a heavy resistance exercise, such as a back squat, followed by a lighter, biomechanically similar exercise, such as a maximal vertical jump (3). It is thought that complex training causes properties of the neuromuscular system to allow an athlete to produce more power while performing the plyometric or lighter exercise, a type of physiological response known as **post-activation potentiation** (PAP). PAP is the phenomenon by which the contractile history of muscles directly affects the rate of force development. Previous authors (3) have provided recommendations on how to best incorporate complex training into the basic strength and strength/power phase (late off-season) and the power phase (preseason).

Otto Greule Jr/Getty Images

An athlete's maximal muscular strength has a dramatic impact on batting power.

INCREASE VELOCITY

Although research demonstrates that increased power relates to developing, enhancing, and maintaining baseball skills, such as throwing, bat swing, and batted-ball exit velocities (21, 23), there is an inverse relationship between the amount of force produced and the velocity of application. Because of this relationship, there is a trade-off between force and velocity. Muscle power decreases with increases in velocity, but only up to a certain point. Therefore, peak or maximum power is produced by optimum force and velocity.

Although there is a lack of power studies conducted on baseball players, the two components of power, strength and velocity, have been studied. Research results have indicated increases in throwing, bat swing, and batted-ball exit velocities from general, special, and specific resistance training (5, 21, 23). Numerous studies have demonstrated that general, special, and specific resistance training in addition to the combination of general and special; general and specific; general, special, and specific; and special and specific resistance training have increased throwing and bat swing velocities (5, 21, 23).

IMPROVE SPEED AND AGILITY

Speed can make an athlete more valuable to his team both offensively and defensively (24). The ability to cover more ground defensively in less time means more opportunities to take hits away from opponents, thus saving their team "average runs against," which is the sum of all runs scored by the team's opponent in all games divided by the number of games played. The lower the number, the better.

Speed on the basepaths also puts pressure on the defense, sometimes causing the defensive player to make a mental or physical error. Depending on offensive strategy, athletes with faster running speeds have more opportunities to take or steal bases, putting them in greater position to score more runs (24).

Speed encompasses the skills and abilities needed to achieve high movement velocities and is most commonly expressed in athletics through sprinting (6). Sprint speed is determined by an athlete's stride length and stride rate. More successful sprinters tend to have longer stride lengths while also demonstrating a more frequent stride rate (6). These findings suggest that the rate of force development and proper biomechanics are two of the primary factors influencing sprint performance (6). Biomechanics research indicates the importance of strength development in the early acceleration phase and the development of reactive strength or leg stiffness for maximum speed running (14).

The foundation of speed development begins in the weight room. Sufficient strength relative to body mass, built with specific power development and velocity-based training methods, will help the athlete apply more force into the ground in a decreased amount of time when sprinting. Understanding the principles of sprinting and proper sprint mechanics during linear and lateral acceleration and deceleration, top speed, curvilinear speed, and change of direction is essential. The basic principles of sprinting include optimal joint and projection angles, force production, and force absorption (6).

It is important for coaches to know that individual differences in relative strength, power, mobility, and coordination will change each athlete's body position while sprinting and also influence speed. Improving strength, power, and mobility in addition to teaching and reinforcing proper running mechanics should be at the forefront of a baseball player's speed development

Ezra Shaw/Getty Images

Speed and agility are critically important factors in the success of an outfielder's ability to be at the right place at the right time.

program. Although not addressed in this book, a progressive, challenging speed training program should be used consistently throughout the training year to enhance running mechanics and ultimately increase an athlete's functional offensive and defensive speed.

From an offensive standpoint, speed training should focus on game-related tasks such as leadoff starts, sprints at various baseball distances (10, 30, and 60 yards [9, 27, and 55 m]), and base running (24). Drills such as flying sprints, wicket runs over 6-inch (15 cm) hurdles, and sprints on a non-motorized curve treadmill will also optimize top speed sprinting capabilities. Additionally, sprinting around curves, such as infield curves (the curved path of grass behind the bases), weaving sprints, and various agility drills should be included to help prepare for the offensive and defensive demands of the game (6, 19, 26).

Acceleration and deceleration speed and agility drills are very important for the majority of game-specific tasks. Although all aspects of a speed and agility development program will be beneficial for all athletes, certain positions have higher demands for these tasks. For example, middle infielders will want to emphasize lateral acceleration and deceleration drills to help increase their range to the left and right on defense, whereas outfielders will emphasize linear acceleration and top speed to prepare them to run down fly balls in the gap. Pitchers, on the other hand, use various types of conditioning, such as jogging, running poles, sprinting, agility drills, and jumping rope to prepare them for the act of pitching and fielding (22). More information about the physical demands and what skills professional baseball personnel are evaluating can be found in chapter 2.

IMPROVE BODY COMPOSITION

Body composition is described as the proportion of lean mass to fat mass within the human body. **Lean mass** refers to muscle, bone, water, tendon, ligament, and organs. **Fat mass** refers to **subcutaneous fat**, which is the visible fat just under the surface of the skin, and **visceral fat**, which refers to the fat that surrounds internal organs.

Testing an athlete's body composition can provide valuable insight to the athlete's health and physical condition. Descriptive data on this topic can be found in chapter 3. Knowing which athletes would benefit from an increase in lean mass or a decrease in fat mass based on position-specific descriptive data can help the strength and conditioning professional build appropriate, individualized programs. When combined with speed and power testing results, body composition data can help indicate optimal weight and body composition to maximize speed and power output.

Improving body composition for an athlete generally means to increase lean mass, decrease fat mass, or both. Nutritional habits should first be examined and improved by a registered dietitian. From a strength and conditioning perspective, anaerobic exercise through resistance training and repeated sprint work exhibits benefits for increasing lean mass while decreasing fat mass (10). Aerobic work such as steady state cardiovascular exercise will also benefit athletes by oxidizing fat for energy (22), contributing to an energy deficit and helping reduce body fat.

PREVENT INJURY

Although baseball is not a contact sport in a traditional sense, injuries are a very real part of baseball. Not only can injuries be devastating at the youth and amateur levels, but they are also serious business for both the organization and the athletes as individuals at the professional level. Injuries can cause athletes a significant loss of development time and, at the major-league level, can result in games lost as well as cost the organization millions of dollars per year for salaries of injured and replacement athletes, plus other injury-related expenditures (4).

An injury review from 2011 to 2016 in Major League and Minor League Baseball shows that muscle-related injuries account for 31% of all injuries in professional baseball and that pitchers were the most common position injured (39.1% of the time) (2). From the same study, the most common injuries of all baseball players were hamstring strains, rotator cuff strain or tear, paralumbar muscle strain, tendinitis of the long head of the biceps, and abdominal oblique muscle strains. Injury to the medial ulnar collateral ligament of the elbow, which, at times, can result in Tommy John surgery, was the sixth most common injury (2).

How to best prevent injury in sports in general, not only in baseball, is something of a constant debate. The best opportunity for strength and conditioning professionals to have a positive impact on injury reduction rates among their athletes is to understand the population and the injuries most common to it, research the mechanisms of those injuries, and then explore and question best practices of how to lower those injury rates.

Strength and conditioning professionals should concern themselves with muscular injuries, modifiable risk factors, and best practices to mitigate those injuries. Further, an awareness of non-modifiable risk factors such as age and previous history of injuries is needed to appropriately design training programs. A solid understanding of this information will allow the strength and conditioning professionals to design performance-based programs that will protect athletes from injury. The goal must be to build resilient and robust athletes who are prepared to play consistently.

A meta-analysis indicated that the resistance training protocols examined reduced sports injuries to less than one-third and reduced overuse injuries by almost half (15). Resistance training may reduce the number of injuries due to increases in the structural strength of ligaments, tendons, tendon to bone junctions, ligament to bone junctions, joint cartilage, and connective tissue sheaths within muscles (9). In conjunction with resistance training, a number of other variables must be included in an athlete's overall program to help reduce injuries, such as enhancing active and passive range of motion, developing anaerobic and aerobic fitness levels, and improving explosive force production through speed training.

With hamstring strains being the most prominent muscular injury in baseball, it is highly recommended that strength and conditioning professionals implement specific exercises to help mitigate the risks of this type of injury. Specifically, it would be advantageous to include eccentrically biased exercises for the hamstrings, flexibility and mobility work for lumbo-pelvic positioning, high-speed sprinting sessions, and sprint mechanics as a part of a comprehensive, performance-based training program. These exercises should strengthen the hamstrings and surrounding musculature as well as help reduce the risk for hamstring injuries (9).

With regards to rotator cuff strains, evaluation and monitoring of shoulder range of motion and scapular function should all be emphasized. Thoracic spine and hip mobility, as well as optimal kinetic sequencing, should also be taken into consideration. A comprehensive rotator cuff and para-scapular strengthening program should be implemented for all athletes to maintain proper glenohumeral position, scapular rotation rhythm, and functional strength during throwing (21).

From a more general and global standpoint for injury prevention, increased levels of relative maximum lower body strength (for example, trap bar deadlift strength that is three times body weight) and the ability to run at maximum aerobic speeds of 4.8 m/s (10.7 mph) and greater have been shown to lower overall injury rates of younger and older athletes (11). Strength and speed, which are part of an athlete's foundation of general fitness and preparation, allow the athlete to handle drastic spikes in workload due to practice and game situations.

CONCLUSION

A major goal for baseball players' training is to enhance muscular strength. This can be achieved by developing general, special, and specific strength. As these types of muscular strength are developed, functional baseball strength and power should be optimized to maintain or improve on-field performance, which includes throwing, bat swing, and batted-ball exit velocities, as well as offensive and defensive speed and agility. Furthermore, a well-designed periodized resistance training program will improve body composition by increasing lean muscle mass and reducing body fat. As a more powerful, physically fit, and mobile athlete is developed, the potential for injury is reduced. If all these goals can be attained, then the training program has achieved its ultimate goal, which is to allow the athlete to perform his best over the course of a long baseball season.

2

ANALYSIS OF THE SPORT AND SPORT POSITIONS

A. EUGENE COLEMAN AND WILLIAM E. AMONETTE

Baseball has always been a game of statistics. Since the first officially recorded game in U.S. history between the New York Nine and the New York Knickerbockers on June 19, 1846, practically every pitch, hit, missed hit, catch, throw, and error has been recorded. Thus, there is an abundance of data and an array of statistics about every aspect of the game in incredible detail. These data allow fans, managers, coaches, and management to evaluate and compare the performances of individual athletes and teams. These data are now used to make decisions related to player personnel and timing of removing pitchers or position players, and to determine tendencies of the athletes or team, among many other uses.

A quick Internet search shows the number of base hits from Babe Ruth in the 1928 World Series, and how Ted Williams performed in the last game of the 1941 season, becoming the only athlete in MLB history to hit .400 or more over an entire season. Publicly available information allows comparisons between Cy Young's performance and that of any Hall of Fame pitcher who followed him. The availability of statistics and other metrics on almost every person who ever played professional baseball has significantly improved the fan experience.

In 2015, all 30 MLB stadiums installed Statcast, a state-of-the-art technology system using TrackMan Doppler radar and high-definition ChyronHego cameras to track the location and movements of the ball and every athlete on the field at any given time. This technology allows managers, coaches, athletic trainers, strength and conditioning professionals, sport scientists, and front office personnel to measure and evaluate performance variables previously not available, or only available using more rudimentary techniques such as stopwatch times, radar gun velocities, or video analysis. Statcast provides instant information about every athlete's speed, distance, and direction on every play. It indirectly measures arm strength by computing ball velocity on all throws; game speed by determining the time it takes a runner to move from one base to another; and conditioning load by measuring how far a fielder or runner travels on each play; along with a plethora of unique pitching and batting analytics never before available to baseball personnel at any level of competition (table 2.1).

Table 2.1   Basic Description of Data Derived From Statcast in All MLB Stadiums

Arm strength	The velocity at which a position player throws every ball
Pitch quality	The velocity of every pitch as well as the spin rate on the ball
Lead distance	The distance a runner is ranging off the bag at the time of a pitcher's first movement or pitch release
Game speed	How long it takes an athlete to run from base to base as well as the speed a position player runs while tracking a ball
Speed endurance	How running velocity changes over the course of a game or a season
Running load	The total distance covered and the velocity of every athlete over the course of a game
Hit quality	The exit velocity and angle of the ball as it leaves the bat
Pop time	How quickly a catcher gets the ball out of his glove and to the base on a stolen base or pickoff attempt

GENERAL PHYSIOLOGICAL ANALYSIS

Baseball requires unique physical and physiologic qualities depending on the playing position. The overall season is a marathon, but the movements required in game situations are often quick and powerful. At the professional level, major-league teams play 162 games in approximately 180 days and minor-league teams play 140 games in about 160 days. College (56 games) and high school teams (20 games) play fewer regularly scheduled games, but the number can increase significantly with the addition of playoffs, fall and summer leagues, and showcase events. Professional teams play almost every day, college teams play three to four games per week, and high school teams play two to three games per week. Depending on the coaching philosophy, position players may compete in nearly every game, and starting pitchers every five days. Relievers' competitive playing time varies significantly depending on their skill set and game situations. Because games can last up to three to four hours with bursts of maximum effort throughout, baseball has high overall metabolic and musculoskeletal demands and athletes must properly train and recover to achieve peak performance and stay healthy for an entire season.

PHYSICAL QUALITIES OF PERFORMANCE

The building blocks of successful athletic performance are strength, power, speed, muscular endurance, flexibility, agility, balance, coordination, and metabolic conditioning. Baseball requires a unique combination of these attributes, and specific requirements may vary depending on position. The following sections will examine the physical and physiological demands of baseball and provide an overview of the requirements for successful, high-level performance.

Strength

Strength, the ability of the musculoskeletal system to exert force on an external object, is the foundation of all physical attributes associated with athletic performance. All other physical qualities arise from strength and can affect each other, but these attributes do not necessarily affect strength. There are strong, stable joints, but there are no weak, stable joints. There are strong, fast athletes, but there are no weak, fast athletes. There are no weak, powerful athletes! Given similar skill-related abilities, the strongest athletes are typically the ones who run faster, throw harder, hit farther, jump higher, and are less prone to injury.

Strength can be divided into three subcategories: absolute (maximum) strength, relative strength, and specific strength (8). **Absolute strength** is the maximum amount of force that can be exerted irrespective of body weight. Larger, heavier athletes usually have more absolute strength because they inherently possess more muscle mass. **Relative strength** is the maximum amount of force that can be exerted in relation to body weight (i.e., force or strength per pound of body weight). Unpublished research on professional baseball players suggests that there are positive relationships between on-field performance variables such as running speed, throwing velocity, and offensive performance and relative strength in the back squat, deadlift, and hand grip. However, there is strong theoretical rationale for each. For example, athletes who are relatively stronger will, in theory, be able to propel their center of mass farther with each step (i.e., run faster) and accelerate and decelerate quicker.

Specific strength, also called *optimal strength*, is the amount of strength needed for maximal peak performance; any additional strength will not necessarily improve performance (20). Although the precise optimal strength level for a baseball player is undetermined, it is known that a baseball player does not need to be as strong as a weightlifter or powerlifter for high performance. A baseball player does not need to bench press 300 pounds or squat 400 pounds to be successful; the ball only weighs 5.5 ounces (156 g) and most bats only weigh 34-36 ounces (~1 kg). **Functional strength**—the ability to swing the bat fast, throw hard, and move efficiently, for example—and **muscle symmetry** (balance) are more important than absolute strength. Balance between the muscles on opposing sides of the body and opposing muscle groups is also important to improve function and reduce the incidence of preventable injuries.

The primary focus of strength and conditioning professionals should be on optimizing relative, sport-specific strength that transfers to baseball (table 2.2), not how much an athlete can lift in the weight room. Most athletes are stronger in their legs than in their upper body. Catchers and corner infielders possess the most upper body strength, while pitchers express the least strength. Pre-, post-, and in-season test results indicate that major-league catchers and corner infielders can usually bench press 1.2 to 1.4 times their body weight, whereas major-league outfielders and middle infielders press between 1.1 and 1.2 times their body weight, and most major-league pitchers press less than their body weight. Because the bench press measures strength from a supine position, it does not necessarily translate to effective hitting and pitching in a standing position. As the saying goes: "The only athletes who play on their backs are bad wrestlers and bad football players."

Lower body strength is similar across most positions. On average, major-league players can squat 1.5 times body weight, press 2.5 to 3 times body weight in the 45-degree leg press, and lift 1.6 to 2 times body weight in the trap bar deadlift.

Baseball authorities agree that grip strength is an important factor in baseball performance (9). Although there are limited scientific data correlating grip strength to hitting or pitching performance among professional baseball players, research on college athletes indicate positive relationships (19). Many experienced scouts state that every modern-era player with 500 or more career home runs had exceptional grip strength and above average hand size. Increased grip strength—the result of forces produced by the muscles of the forearm and hand—should help

Table 2.2   Relative Strength Among Professional Baseball Players by Position

Position	Squat	Deadlift	Bench press	Grip
Pitcher	1.75	2.35	0.70	0.65
Catcher	1.80	2.40	1.25	0.70
Position players	1.85	2.50	1.25	0.80

enhance bat control and grip firmness at impact, reduce bat recoil on contact, and improve the ability to impart force and spin to the ball. In theory, athletes with higher levels of grip strength should be less susceptible to overuse injuries to the wrist, hand, and muscles of the forearms. Position players are equally strong in both hands (2). Pitchers are approximately 5% stronger in the dominant hand. Position players generate 175 to 180 pounds (79-82 kg) of force in a standard grip strength test, pitchers about 5 to 10 (2.3-4.5 kg) pounds less. Grip strength was assessed from a seated position with the arm flexed to 90 degrees at the elbow and the forearm supported by the arm of the chair. Table 2.2 shows relative strength normative values for professional baseball players by position. Grip strength is important, but performance coaches should not neglect total body movements. Baseball-specific programs should emphasize the entire body; strong hands cannot make up for a lack of total body strength. Also, the foundation of grip strength can be established by deadlifting and pulling heavy weights without lifting straps.

Power

Power is the product of both force and velocity. Baseball players must be able to produce a large amount of force, but they must express this force quickly. A 90 mph (145 km/h) fastball, for example, takes approximately 400 ms (0.4 seconds) to reach home plate after it leaves the pitcher's hand. During this time, the hitter has approximately 250 ms—about the time it takes to blink—to decide whether to swing, and about 150 ms to complete his swing with enough bat speed to produce an exit velocity of 90 mph (145 km/h). Because it typically requires 1 to 1.5 seconds to generate peak force, this indicates that peak force is irrelevant for many baseball-specific skills.

The same can be said for pitching, baserunning, and fielding. Research related to pitchers, for example, indicates that the time elapsed between front foot contact and ball release is only 0.145 seconds. During this brief time, the pitcher generates enough force to internally rotate the humerus at 7,500 to 7,700 degrees per second and extend the elbow at 2,500 degrees per second, indicating that power is more important for maximum pitching velocity than absolute strength. Thus, power is critical for both pitchers and hitters. In fact, unpublished data from an MLB organization indicate there is a positive relationship between peak power in the vertical jump and maximum fastball velocity among pitchers.

Baserunning and fielding both require quick reactions and explosive first steps. Unpublished data indicate that elite professional baseball players require less than 0.5 seconds to complete the first step when moving laterally to steal a base or field a ball. Because it takes 0.6 to 0.8 seconds for the muscles of the hips and legs to exert maximum force, elite base runners and fielders will complete their first step before the muscles of the lower body can achieve maximum force production—again suggesting that power is more important for quick, lateral movements than maximum strength.

These rapid and explosive movements needed for successful performance when pitching, hitting, fielding, and running indicate that effective training programs for baseball should emphasize a variety of movements in multiple planes of motion performed with different loads and intentional high velocities.

Local Muscular Endurance

Muscular endurance is the ability to apply submaximal force repeatedly (11). Muscular endurance allows athletes to efficiently perform the number of repetitions of skill movements for high performance in all aspects of the game: hitting, running, fielding, throwing, and pitching. It also helps enhance performance by delaying the onset of fatigue-induced injury. Muscular endurance is important for all athletes, most especially pitchers, who must maintain muscle function over many throws and long seasons.

Body Composition and Lean Body Mass

History indicates that there is a place in baseball for exceptional athletes of all sizes and shapes. Baseball players are not always large, muscular, or strong. Big athletes, like Mike Trout, Cody Bellinger, Christian Yelich, Aaron Judge, Justin Verlander, Clayton Kershaw, and Aroldis Chapman dominate the power-related statistics for baseball, there are many smaller and average-sized players who have been very successful: Greg Maddux, for example, was 6'0" (183 cm) tall and weighed 170 pounds (77 kg), and he won four Cy Young Awards, made the All-Star Team eight times, and earned 18 Gold Gloves in 22 major-league seasons.

The average professional player (table 2.3), from class rookie to the major leagues, is about 25 years of age and 73 inches (185 cm) tall, weighs 212 pounds (96 kg), and has 13% body fat (9). Young athletes are usually lighter and leaner and have less muscle mass than older athletes. Total body weight, lean body mass (LBM), and strength increase with age and maturity, though height remains generally constant after peaking in the young adult years. High school athletes usually gain 30 to 40 pounds (14-18 kg) between the time they sign a professional contract and when they reach maturity; whereas college athletes, because they are older, typically gain only 10 to 20 pounds (4-9 kg) in the same time period.

Pitchers tend to be taller than athletes at other positions—approximately four inches (~10 cm) taller than catchers, second basemen, and shortstops and about 1.5 inches (almost 4 cm) taller than corner infielders and all outfielders (table 2.4). Pitchers, catchers, and those who play the corner infield and outfield positions are heavier than those who play the middle of the field (shortstops, second basemen, and center fielders) (table 2.4). Shortstops, second basemen, and

Table 2.3 Average Anthropometric and Body Composition Comparisons Among Levels of Play in Professional Baseball

Variable	Rookie	A	AA	AAA	MLB	Average
Age (yr)	21.3	22.9	24.9	26.8	28.7	24.9
Height (in.)	72.9	73.0	73.0	73.0	73.5	73.2
Weight (lb)	202.4	202.4	211.2	218.9	222.6	211.5
Body fat (%)	12.0	12.4	12.8	13.7	13.8	12.9
LBM (lb)	177.8	176.9	176.9	188.5	191.6	183.4

Multiply height in inches by 2.54 to yield height in centimeters and divide weight in pounds by 2.2 to yield weight in kilograms.

Table 2.4 Average Anthropometric and Body Composition Comparisons in Professional Baseball by Position

Position	Height (in.)	Weight (lb)	Body fat (%)	LBM (lb)
Pitcher	74.1	210.7	13.5	182.4
Catcher	70.2	211.4	14.4	181.0
Corner INF	72.8	211.9	13.3	183.7
Middle INF	70.7	183.9	10.5	164.6
Corner OF	72.9	211.1	12.2	185.4
Middle OF	72.1	198.8	10.1	178.7

Multiply height in inches by 2.54 to yield height in centimeters and divide weight in pounds by 2.2 to yield weight in kilograms.

center fielders have the least amount of body weight, including muscle mass and relative body fat. On average, pitchers, catchers, and corner infielders have the most body fat.

Professional baseball players, as a group, are not overfat. Being overfat probably would not affect how an athlete throws or swings; however, it would affect range, ability to run the bases, and potential for injury. Fatter athletes are metabolically inefficient and require more energy to overcome more resistance than leaner athletes, which can cause them to fatigue in the latter stages of the game and season. Fat is unproductive weight that that does not contribute to strength and power, slows athletes down, results in fatigue, and places extra stress on joints. From spring training to the last day of the season, pitchers execute nearly 20,000 pitches in game and practice situations and position players complete about 20,000 swings, field almost 20,000 balls, and make over 20,000 throws in games alone; these numbers do not account for the abundance of attempts in practice and the off-season (2). Each of these acts requires strength, power, and energy metabolism. They require calories to fuel movement and strength and power to accelerate, decelerate, change directions, and maintain movement.

Increases in lean body mass have a positive effect on strength and power and are related to improvements in speed, acceleration, deceleration, agility, and on-field variables such as throwing, hitting, fielding, and baserunning. Increases in non-essential body fat provide greater resistance to athletic movement and negative effects on range of motion, endurance, balance, coordination, and the ability to move quickly in multiple directions (10).

The demands of baseball suggest an athlete should maintain a reasonably lean body composition. Although there are some variations by level and position, all athletes should keep their body fat at a reasonable value for peak, injury-free performance (table 2.3). Pitchers, catchers, and those who play the corner positions in the infield and outfield usually have no more than 12% body fat, whereas those who play in the middle of the infield and outfield usually have 8 to 10% body fat. Less fat, however, is not necessarily better. One of the many potential negative effects of very low body fat is that the testes reduce testosterone production, the hormone responsible for muscle growth and repair (13). Without adequate testosterone, athletes lose muscle mass and are more prone to muscle weakness, fatigue, and injury. A minimal level of body fat (no less than 7%) is required to maintain personal health and biological function in adult male athletes (11). Body fat percent values for high school, college, and professional baseball players can be found in chapter 3 (tables 3.20-3.22 on pages 62 and 63).

Athletes at all positions and levels benefit from having reasonably low body fat while maintaining or increasing lean body mass. Although athletes at some positions can tolerate higher levels of body mass and percent body fat, it is generally recommended that athletes participate in resistance training and metabolic conditioning programs designed to reduce body fat and maintain or increase lean body mass, depending on individual needs.

Speed

Running speed, the ability to move quickly between two points, relies heavily on strength and power. Speed is one of the five tools with which baseball scouts, managers, coaches, and executives evaluate talent. It is also the only skill that is used for both offense and defense. Baseball-specific speed involves more than just the ability to move quickly in a straight line. Athletes must move laterally and diagonally to get to baseballs in the hole, over the shoulder, and in the gaps. They also must be able to turn and run to catch balls hit straight over their head and accelerate, decelerate, stop, and change directions quickly.

Because most runs in game situations are under five seconds in duration, quickness and acceleration are more important than pure speed. Sprinter's speed is an asset, but it's not a requisite for success. An athlete can compensate for a lack of speed if he can react quickly, accelerate fast, stop under control, change direction, avoid slowing down, and reduce inefficient steps. Five key components commonly attributed to speed are mechanics, quickness or reaction time, pure acceleration, transitional acceleration, and speed-endurance (2). Mechanics allow an athlete to run efficiently and achieve his speed potential given his relative strength and power. Quickness and acceleration permit an athlete to react quickly, accelerate, quickly track a baseball, or run to a base. Speed-endurance keeps an athlete from slowing down late in the game, at the end of a long sprint, and after sprinting several times with short rest intervals.

Regardless of how much an athlete trains or how strong and powerful he becomes, he will run only as fast as his mechanics permit. Once mechanics break down and become inefficient, progress stops. Therefore, the first step in training for speed should be to optimize running mechanics. Another factor that significantly affects speed is force—the more force an athlete can apply to the ground, the farther he will move with each step. Therefore, two of the initial and most important training recommendations to improve speed are to optimize running mechanics and improve lower body strength and power, especially single-leg strength and power.

Flexibility, Mobility, and Stability

Mobility is often confused with flexibility, but the two are not synonymous. **Flexibility** is the absolute range of motion in a joint or series of joints and the length of muscle that crosses the joint (i.e., the distance the joint can move). Touching the toes from a standing or seated position is an example of a test of flexibility. Flexibility is directly related to range of motion, but not to strength, balance, and coordination. Good flexibility does not always result in optimal mobility.

Mobility is the degree to which an articulation (i.e., joint or point where two bones meet) can move before being restricted by surrounding tissues such as ligaments, tendons, muscles, or fascia. It is how far a joint can move under the body's control without external influence—that is, move freely and easily. Visual analysis of the body-weight squat exercise is an example of a mobility test. An acceptable level of mobility allows an athlete to perform movements without restriction. An athlete who is immobile in one or more of the articulations may visually display compensation patterns such as lifting the heels off the floor, flexing the thoracic spine, or overly flexing at the hips. Such compensation patterns would suggest immobility in a joint, and potentially the need for specific exercises to correct the dysfunctional movement pattern. However, though an adequate level of mobility is good, too much is not better. Hypermobile joints tend to be unstable and at an increased risk of injury. Tension in a joint also increases the elastic recoil of the tissue, improving power production.

Adequate mobility is important for skillful, coordinated movement; **stability**, however, is important for joint control. Efficient movement requires both joint mobility and stability. Joint stability is the ability to maintain postural equilibrium, sense the position of the joint in space, and control joint movement or position. It is achieved by the coordinated actions of surrounding tissues and the central and peripheral nervous systems. Joint stability is influenced by the shape, size, and arrangement of the articular surfaces and cartilage where the bones make contact with each other, the surrounding ligaments, the tone of the muscles that surround the joint, and the athlete's sense of proprioception.

Exercises, movements, warm-up programs, and therapeutic procedures designed to enhance flexibility, mobility, and stability are presented in chapters 5 to 8.

Agility

Agility is the ability to quickly accelerate, decelerate, and change directions under control; additionally, it requires cognitive processing to identify when to initiate each of these phases. It is an important physical attribute in baseball players at all levels for both offensive and defensive movements. For example, a base runner may need to react to a pickoff attempt by quickly changing directions and diving back to the base. If the ball is overthrown, the athlete must quickly get up and run to second base. Likewise, an infielder moving laterally to field a ball must catch the ball, plant the back foot, and throw the ball back the other direction. To complicate fielding, the ball may bounce unpredictably, requiring the fielder to move quickly to get into position. Thus, agility is used in nearly every fielding attempt and often while running the bases.

Agility is improved by teaching athletes to control their center of mass relative to the ground reaction forces exerted by the musculoskeletal system. Newtonian physics demonstrates that when two masses collide, there is an equal and opposite reaction. Therefore, in order to run forward, an athlete must exert a backward ground reaction force; to run backward or to decelerate forward velocity, they must exert a forward ground reaction force. The direction of the ground reaction force vector is manipulated by controlling the angle of the lower leg relative to the ground and the position of the center of mass. Agility can be taught using closed (predictable) drills requiring athletes to change direction and coaching lower leg technique. To optimize transfer of drills to game situations, agility should be progressed from closed to open drills and eventually to baseball-specific scenarios—that is, practice accelerating, decelerating, and changing directions while running the basepath or fielding. Strength and conditioning professionals should coach angles and ground reaction forces on the baseball field, not just in the weight room or conditioning field.

Balance and Coordination

Baseball players use balance and coordination in every movement in the sport. **Balance** is the ability to control one's center of mass, distributing weight in such a way that an athlete is steady and does not fall. Balance is controlled in the central nervous system by the somatosensory (21), visual (7), and vestibular systems (14), and in the peripheral nervous system through reflex reactions. The somatosensory system uses sensory information such as pressure, touch, and vibration to "feel" where the limbs are in physical space. The visual system collects and processes information in the environment as important reference points to balance (7). The otolith organs, located in the inner ear canal, contribute to balance by encoding visual or somatosensory information related to gravitational vectors such as leaning (16). Reflexes also contribute to balance by sensing movements in the peripheral muscular system and quickly correcting position when activated. All sensory information derived from these unique systems is processed within a bundle of cellular tissue in the posterior area of the brain, called the cerebellum. The cerebellum is responsible for balance, muscular coordination, and postural control, among other important motor functions.

Knowing and understanding (without thinking) the positioning of the arms, legs, head, and trunk relative to each other are important in order for an athlete to be able to precisely track a baseball as it crosses the plate, put the bat on a ball traveling over 90 mph (145 km/h), and efficiently move in all planes to avoid injuries. When a joint moves into an irregular position, abnormal stress is placed on the ligaments, cartilage, muscles, and other soft tissues that may result in tissue failure and injury. Thus, it is critically important for athletes to possess postural control to optimize health and improve performance. Coordination and balance can be improved with exercise but most importantly with practice; perfect practice and execution of the skill in multiple environments while challenging the brain in a sport-specific manner will result in the greatest transfer of balance and coordination to the sport.

ENERGY SYSTEM DEMANDS

Before a strength and conditioning professional can determine the most effective strategy to strengthen and metabolically condition athletes to compete at a high level and minimize the risk of injury, they must understand the energy systems that are involved in game situations. Although energy is always metabolized by multiple mechanisms, it is important to understand which system is predominantly used in baseball and in different game situations. This information allows the coach to accurately prescribe metabolic conditioning exercises best suited for improving baseball-specific energy demands.

The ability to run, jump, pitch, swing, field, and throw all require energy in the form of adenosine triphosphate (ATP). There are three energy systems in the human body that provide the ATP needed to fuel training, performance, growth, recovery, and the repair of human tissue: the phosphagen system, glycolytic system, and the oxidative (aerobic) system. These systems work in an integrated continuum and are always active in every aspect of performance. All are available to contribute to energy metabolism at the onset of activity, working simultaneously but at different capacities depending on the rate of energy needed. One system is the primary provider of ATP and the other two are lesser providers, with the predominant energy system dependent on the intensity of effort.

Phosphagen System

The **phosphagen system** is the primary contributor to metabolism when the body needs an immediate, short burst of energy for all-out power or speed. This system is used when an athlete pitches, hits, runs, fields, and throws. This system is also used when lifting heavy loads of 3 to 5 repetitions or fewer. Because ATP and CP (creatine phosphate) are stored within the cytosol of skeletal muscle, they can be metabolized anaerobically (without oxygen). This system provides an immediate source of anaerobic energy for up to 8 to 12 seconds of maximum effort (8). The phosphagen system provides energy at an extremely high rate, is depleted quickly, and replenished during rest intervals between pitches, plays, innings, and games.

Glycolytic System

Similar to the phosphagen system, the **glycolytic system** is used for short-term energy metabolism. It provides energy when activity is too intense and the rate of need is too great for aerobic (with oxygen) metabolism. Glycolytic metabolism is next in line after the phosphagen system is depleted, providing energy for continued maximum and near-maximum intense activity for approximately 25 seconds to 3 minutes (8). Though the phosphagen system generates energy rapidly because it uses the ATP stored in the muscles, glycolysis is a slower process that forms ATP by metabolizing blood glucose, glycogen stored in the muscles, and/or proteins that have been converted to glucose via gluconeogenesis. Glycolysis has two potential end routes of energy metabolism: fast and slow glycolysis. Each is defined by the end result of pyruvate, a salt or ester of pyruvic acid, the end product of the 10 reactions that make up glycolytic metabolism.

Fast glycolysis becomes the primary energy system after maximum power declines around 12 seconds, fueling continued intense activity for up to approximately 30 seconds. When the metabolism of a glucose molecule is completed and two ATP are generated at the end of glycolysis, pyruvate is converted to lactate. Using a system of energy production termed the Cori cycle, lactate is shuttled to the liver and converted back into glucose to provide more substrate for glycolysis (8). The rapid metabolic process is used in baseball to fuel activities such as sprinting to advance extra bases. It also fuels metabolic work in the weight room when athletes perform lower-intensity, higher-volume resistance training to establish a conditioning base and improve local muscular endurance or muscular size (hypertrophy).

Slow glycolysis provides energy for activities approximately 30 to 120 seconds in length (8). The same 10 reactions occur in slow glycolysis as in fast glycolysis, but instead of pyruvate being converted to lactate and entering the Cori cycle, it is converted to acetyl coenzyme A and enters the mitochondria, a small organelle within the cell that plays a large role in ATP production.

Oxidative (Aerobic) System

The Krebs cycle, the beginning of oxidative phosphorylation (i.e., aerobic metabolism), begins when acetyl coenzyme A is shuttled into the mitochondria. Aerobic metabolism yields many more ATP than glycolysis, but also require more reactions and consequently more time. Oxidative metabolism is used when the rate of energy need is low due to lower-intensity efforts. In baseball, a pitcher relies more heavily on these systems because the position requires quick bursts of energy to pitch and lower-intensity efforts during recovery. All positions and movements in baseball recover using aerobic metabolism. A continuum of energy system utilization is shown in figure 2.1.

Important take-home points when discussing the energy systems include the following:

- ATP must be present for muscles to contract and cells to survive.
- ATP can be provided by the phosphagen system, the glycolytic system, or the oxidative system.

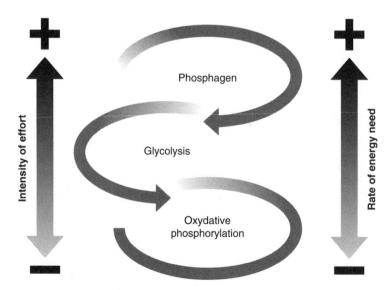

Figure 2.1 Energy system utilization is determined by intensity of effort and rate of need for ATP.

- All three systems work simultaneously, and primary dominance is determined by the intensity of the effort.
- If ATP is depleted, it must be replenished before further muscle contractions can continue.

Baseball is an explosive, powerful game and athletes should condition accordingly. But it is also a sport comprising at least 162 games per major-league season and three to four hours for every game. Successful performance, therefore, requires at least a moderate degree of aerobic fitness to enable recovery from repeated high-intensity efforts. Baseball requires both an adequate anaerobic and aerobic energy base, though position-specific differences suggest that not all athletes should condition the same way. All systems should be conditioned throughout the annual training cycle, but strength and conditioning professionals must prioritize metabolic conditioning efforts. As the old saying goes, "If you chase two rabbits, both will escape."

Use the off-season to develop an aerobic conditioning base, but do not train baseball players like long-distance runners. The aerobic capacity among elite aerobic endurance athletes is 70 to 80 ml/kg/min, whereas the average among MLB players is 50 ml/kg/min (2). Moreover, long-distance efforts place unnecessary stress on joints; research supports the use of interval-based training as more advantageous to improve aerobic capacity with less stress on the joints (22).

Specific training programs to enhance development during each season will be provided in chapters 9 to 12.

POSITION-SPECIFIC ANALYSIS

Baseball players are divided into four general positional groups: pitchers, catchers, infielders, and outfielders. Pitchers are typically categorized as starting pitchers, long relievers, setup men, and closers. Infielders are categorized as corner (first and third base) and middle (second base and shortstop) infielders; outfielders are divided similarly into corner (left and right field) and middle (center field) outfielders. Each position requires different physical attributes, often referred to as "tools," which scouts score from 2 to 8, with 5 being average and 8 being outstanding. Examples of a typical scouting reporting form for position players and pitchers are presented in table 2.5. Scouts evaluate athletes for present capabilities and potential for future development. They also evaluate anthropometrics (size), physical abilities, strengths, weaknesses, and intangibles such as instinct, work ethic, and maturity. Athletes do not have to be outstanding in all categories—if they did, no one would have taken a chance on athletes like Pete Rose and Jose Altuve.

Table 2.5 Scouting Report: Position Players' and Pitchers' Tools

Position players	Present	Future	Pitchers	Present	Future
1. Hitting: Average			1. Fastball velocity		
2. Hitting: Power			2. Movement		
3. Running speed			3. Curve		
4. Baserunning			4. Control		
5. Arm strength			5. Change		
6. Accuracy			6. Slider		
7. Fielding			7. Other		
8. Range			8. Fielding		

The essential tools by position are shown in table 2.6. The first two tools at each position are the dominant or carrying tools; others are considered secondary. The two dominant tools for a shortstop, for example, are fielding and throwing; the other tools are the ability to hit for a high average and power. If an athlete does not rate at least average in the dominant tools for a particular position, it would be difficult to imagine him playing at the major-league level at that position. A catcher, for example, who rates a 4 for both catching and throwing but rates a 7 for batting would fit the profile for first base, but not catcher. Understanding the positional demands and differences between groups is imperative when creating appropriate training programs for athletes at different positions.

Pitchers

Pitchers come in all sizes and shapes, but since 2010, the trend in professional baseball has been to use taller pitchers with more leverage who can throw at high velocities. At the professional level, the days of "finesse" pitchers with average velocity and pinpoint control like Greg Maddux and Tom Glavine have diminished. Current rosters tend to be dominated by starters who throw 95 mph (153 km/h) or more who are run one or two times through the batting order and then replaced by a series of relievers who throw 95 mph (153 km/h) for 1 to 2 innings each. An average MLB fastball will reach 92 to 93 mph (148-150 km/h), an above average fastball will reach 94 to 97 mph (151-156 km/h), and an exceptional fastball will reach 98 to 100+ mph (158-161+ km/h) (table 2.7). As shown in figure 2.2, there is approximately an 8 to 15 mph (13-24 km/h) difference between a four-seam fastball and off-speed pitch velocity.

The practice of recruiting taller pitchers who can throw at high velocities is also seen at the college and high school ranks. Data from online recruiting Web sites indicate that Division I college coaches are searching for right-handed pitchers who can consistently throw 87 to 95 mph (140-153 km/h) or faster (6), with standards decreasing at lower levels of competition. Division II coaches recruit pitchers who consistently throw 85 mph (137 km/h) or faster, and

Table 2.6   Tool Priorities by Position

	Catcher	1B	2B	SS	3B	LF	CF	RF
Baseball-specific tools	**Catch**	**Bat**	**Bat**	**Field**	**Bat**	**Bat**	**Run**	**Bat**
	Throw	**Power**	**Field**	**Throw**	**Power**	**Power**	**Field**	**Power**
	Bat	Field	Run	Run	Field	Run	Bat	Field
	Power	Throw	Power	Bat	Throw	Field	Throw	Throw
	Run	Run	Throw	Power	Run	Throw	Power	Run

The bolded tools are the position's dominant or carrying tools; the others are considered secondary tools.

Table 2.7   Rating Major League Baseball Fastball Velocity

Rating	Velocity (mph)	Velocity (km/h)
8	98-100	158-161
7	94-97	151-156
6	92-93	148-150
5	88-91	142-146
4	85-87	137-140
3	81-84	130-135

Division III and junior college coaches recruit those who consistently throw 82 mph (132 km/h) or faster. The criterion for left-handed pitchers is 2 to 3 mph (3.2-4.8 km/h) slower at all levels. Although there are no published standards for high school pitchers, three online sources indicate that the typical varsity high school pitcher throws with velocities between 75 and 85 mph (121-137 km/h) and better pitchers often reach the upper 80s to low 90s (~140-145 km/h) (5, 6, 12).

Younger high school pitchers exhibit less velocity, with freshmen throwing between 60 and 75 mph (97-121 km/h) and sophomores 77 to 78 mph (124-126 km/h). These findings are consistent with those posted on the Perfect Game USA website (12). Analysis of Perfect Game USA data for the years 2018 to 2020 indicate that the average fastball among over 500 participants in sponsored events was 88 mph (142 km/h); approximately 50% of participants threw 87 to 89 mph (140-143 km/h) and 20% threw 90 mph (145 km/h) or faster (figure 2.3).

It is important to note, however, that gaining more velocity can create problems. Although it is impossible at this time to demonstrate that throwing as hard as physically possible for as many innings as possible is the cause for the increase in elbow and shoulder injuries, data suggest there may be a link (1). In 2017, for example, 80% of MLB pitchers who threw 95

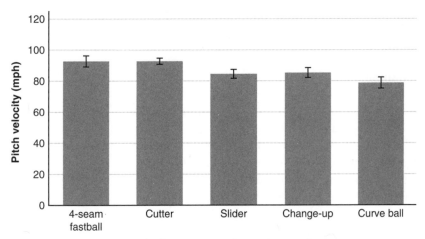

Figure 2.2   Major League Baseball average velocity by pitch type.

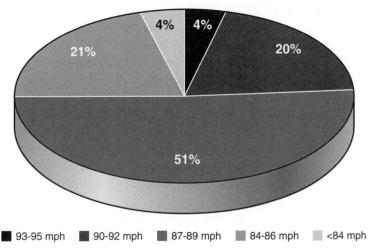

■ 93-95 mph   ■ 90-92 mph   ■ 87-89 mph   ■ 84-86 mph   ▨ <84 mph

Figure 2.3   Perfect Game USA pitcher norms for fastball velocity (2012-2018).

Rich Pilling/MLB via GettyImages

The taller the pitcher, the more leverage he will have to throw at high velocities.

mph (153 km/h) or harder appeared on the injured list (IL) at some point during the season, versus only 29.6% of those who averaged between 93 and 95 mph (150-153 km/h) (10). Data also indicate that MLB pitchers from 2002 to 2014 who threw 96 mph (154 km/h) were over 27% more likely to appear on the IL during the following season (1). The risk almost doubled for those who threw 90 to 93 mph (145-150 km/h). The pitchers throwing with the greatest velocities were also on the IL for longer amounts of time (5).

Preliminary research indicates there is a link between increased pitch velocity and injury, especially ulnar collateral ligament injuries leading to Tommy John surgery (1). In 2010, researchers observed 23 professional pitchers for three seasons. The 14 pitchers who remained injury free were among those with the lowest pitch velocity. The nine pitchers who threw with above average velocity and the three pitchers with the highest maximum velocity all required Tommy John surgery (1). A similar study examining the velocity of every pitch thrown in MLB between 2007 and 2015 found that not only was peak pitch velocity a predictor for a pitcher who would require Tommy John surgery, it was the most significant risk factor (1).

As more young pitchers develop greater pitching velocities, a primary goal of the sports medicine team, including strength and conditioning coaches, is to ensure that every pitcher achieves an adequate muscular and metabolic fitness base. Another important goal is to implement scientifically and medically supported arm care programs to help facilitate recovery and reduce the risk of injury. Finally, pitchers need to be taught to tactically use power and use proper pitching mechanics that place less stress on the elbow and shoulder. Instead of throwing as hard as they can for as long as they can, exceptional power pitchers must learn how to control velocity and locate different pitches. This will help reduce the number of maximum velocity efforts, reduce stress on joints, and allow a power pitcher to successfully throw more innings per game.

Regardless of the level of play, a pitcher will throw only as hard as his mechanics (and perhaps genetics) permit. When mechanical flaws arise, improvements in velocity will decrease and the risk of injury will increase. Nolan Ryan, one of the greatest power pitchers in the history of MLB who was known not only for his velocity but longevity, teaches that pitching with improper mechanics is like running with a rock in your shoe: you cannot run very far or fast (15). Likewise, a pitcher cannot throw over 100 high-velocity pitches per game, 200 innings per season, or multiple seasons of a career with improper mechanics. The body will compensate for errors in the delivery, create stress on joint structures, and increase the risk of injury.

Pitching requires the sequential application of forces from the ground up. As such, it requires strength, stability, endurance, mobility, power, coordination, and balance in each segment of the kinetic chain to effectively produce, transfer, and absorb force. It also requires metabolic conditioning (2). Pitchers must not only be able to produce and reduce force quickly, but must also possess the resilience to repeat these motions many times during a game and over the course of the season. Though the physical requirement for pitching is similar for starting and relief pitchers, the strength and conditioning coach must be creative in the implementation of training for each group during the season. Starting pitchers compete on a predictable schedule, typically a five-day rotation. However, relief pitchers may compete several days in a row and pitch for one or more innings, requiring more flexibility in the training plan. These complexities are discussed in chapters 9 to 12.

Catchers

The position of catcher is the most physically demanding in baseball. Catchers participate in every pitch and therefore have a role in nearly every play. A successful catcher is talented, athletic, durable, and possesses many intangible leadership qualities. He controls the tactics of both the pitching game and running game and must understand the strengths, weaknesses, and needs of every pitcher on the team. In addition, he must know the strengths and weaknesses of each opposing hitter, be able to evaluate his swings, and predict what the batter is thinking to set up the next pitch. While processing this information, he must sometimes perform in extreme heat wearing layers of protective gear. As stated by long-time MLB catcher and former manager Brad Ausmus: "I'm thinking what's the score, what inning are we in, how many outs, what's this hitter's weakness, what's this pitcher's strength, who's on deck, who could pinch hit, who is up after the hitter on deck—and you go through all of these things in an instant. And then you make a decision and put down the next signal."

The two primary tools for catchers are the ability to catch and throw. The ability to hit for average and hit for power are important, but not primary tools. For example, at 87.7 mph (141.1 km/h), average exit velocity among the 65 MLB players who played catcher during the 2019 season was one of the lowest among all positions. Running speed is the least important tool for a catcher. The average MLB catcher runs from home to first base in 4.64 seconds (electronically timed), which would rate a score of 2 on most scouting reports.

When evaluating a catcher, scouts account for the ability to catch different types, speeds, and locations of pitches. They also observe how the catcher receives the ball (e.g., provide a good target, have "soft hands and a quiet glove"). They scout for the ability to frame pitches, move laterally to block balls, and keep blocked balls close to prevent runners from advancing.

When assessing throwing ability, scouts want catchers who keep their footwork short and moving to the plate. Reaching for the ball during the transfer can increase footwork length and slow down **pop time**, which is the elapsed time from the moment the pitch hits the catcher's mitt to the moment the intended fielder receives the throw at the center of the base. Average throwing velocity from home plate to second base for MLB catchers is 81.3 mph (130.8 km/h). Those with outstanding velocity are often clocked at 85 to 88 mph (137-142 km/h). Approximately 80% of MLB catchers throw between 77 and 84 mph (124-135 km/h) (table 2.8). Throwing velocity is important, but pop time is essential. Elite MLB catchers exhibit pop times less than 1.88 seconds, whereas an average pop time is 2.00 seconds. Pop times between 1.88 and 1.93

Table 2.8 Throwing Velocities, Pop Times, and Percentages of Major League Baseball Catchers Who Achieve These Velocities and Times

Velocity (mph)	%	Pop time (sec)	%
85-88	13	1.88-1.93	7
81-84	37	1.94-1.98	25
77-80	42	1.99-2.03	36
<76	8	2.04-2.08	23
		>2.09	9

are above average. Approximately 60% of major-league pop times are between 1.94 and 2.03 seconds, and anything greater than 2.03 seconds is below average.

As expected, throwing velocity is lower and pop times are higher for high school and college athletes. The average Division I catcher throws 80+ mph (129+ km/h) with a pop time of 1.95 seconds. Division II catchers throw 78 mph (126 km/h) with a pop time of 2.0, and Division III and JUCO catchers throw 78 mph (126 km/h) with a pop time of 2.10. Above average high school catchers throw 75 mph+ (121+ km/h) with a pop time of 2.20 to 2.25 seconds. For more detail on this topic and additional data, it is recommended that interested readers go to https://baseballsavant.mlb.com/statcast_search.

When designing a resistance training program for catchers, strength and conditioning coaches must consider the stress placed on catchers both in competition and practice. The typical major-league starting catcher will receive approximately 25,000 pitches per year and approximately 12,000 of these will be with men on base. He will block nearly 800 balls in the dirt. In addition, he will squat and stand 150 times or more per game and throw the ball more than any other athlete on the field. All of this while being hit by foul balls, balls in the dirt, and errant backswings. He must also manage both his pitcher and umpire while keeping base runners from advancing.

Nick Wosika/Icon Sportswire via Getty Images

Catchers have far more duties than simply receiving a pitched ball; they must also strive to minimize pop time as much as possible.

Catchers require muscular endurance, cardiorespiratory endurance, strength, power, balance, and coordination. They also require an aerobic and anaerobic conditioning base, though training must always be implemented in such a way that it minimizes unnecessary stress on the knees and back. Given the increasing number of concussions among catchers and their relationship to neck strength, neck strengthening exercises, especially rotational neck exercises, may need to be implemented year-round to help reduce the incidence of traumatic head injuries (16). Catching is a stressful job that is both physically and mentally demanding. It is imperative that resistance training programs are sufficient to maintain or improve performance but not so intense or frequent to increase fatigue, limit recovery, decrease performance, or increase the risk of injury.

Middle Infielders

Those who play positions in the middle of the field—shortstop, second base, and center field—are often the most athletic players on the team. Top middle infielders are usually evaluated for their defensive skills first and hitting second. Middle infielders are typically the shortest and lightest athletes on the team. Prototypical professional middle infielders are 68 to 74 inches (173-188 cm) tall and weigh between 165 and 190 pounds (75-86 kg). They are fast with quick feet, good hands, and a strong arm. Although pure speed is important, middle infielders must have the ability to start and stop quickly when moving laterally. The shortstop is often the leader of the infield and signals to the other infielders for positioning prior to ball contact. It is not uncommon for some second and third basemen to be drafted as shortstops and later moved to other positions, but it is very rare for a second or third baseman to transition to shortstop.

Shortstops and second basemen differ somewhat in terms of the priority of their dominant tools (table 2.6). The ability to field and throw are dominant tools for shortstops and the ability to hit for average and field are dominant tools for second basemen. The typical MLB shortstop throws the ball across the diamond at a velocity of 85 to 95 mph (137-153 km/h). A second baseman can get away with having a below average arm, provided he can turn a double play, have good range and soft hands, and field his position. Because the ability to hit for average and power are lower priorities for shortstops, those who can consistently contact and drive the ball are highly regarded. Division I middle infielders usually throw with velocities of 85 to 90 mph (137-145 km/h), whereas Division II middle infielders throw 80 to 85 mph (129-137 km/h). Division III, JUCO, and good high school middle infielders throw with velocities of 75 to 80 mph (121-129 km/h) (6).

Although a strong arm has traditionally been a low priority for second basemen because of their proximity to first base, this has changed recently at the professional level. Because tactically shifting positioning on the field often requires second basemen to play on the back edge of the grass on the right side of the infield or in shallow right field, the number of hard throws by second basemen has increased dramatically in the last few years. Research on MLB players indicate that middle infielders throw more often, run farther, and run more sprints than other positions on the team. (This information was obtained from data collected on Texas Rangers players and has not been published.)

Electronic times from home plate to first base are provided in figure 2.4. Major-league middle infielders, as a group, are the second fastest athletes on the field when running from home plate to first base at 4.31 seconds. The fastest athletes, center fielders, run to first base in 4.22 seconds. Shortstops (4.29 seconds) are slightly faster than second basemen (4.32 seconds).

Published and online data describing sprint times from home plate to first base are limited; most information on running speed is based on the time required to run 60 yards (55 m).

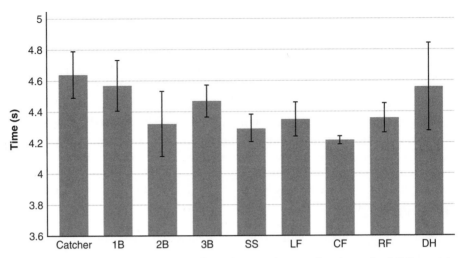

Figure 2.4   Average electronic times from home plate to first base by MLB position in 2019.

Although a standard measurement used by many scouts, the 60-yard sprint has limited application and specificity to baseball. When timed in 10- to 30-yard (9-27 m) intervals, the 60-yard sprint can be used to test pure and transitional acceleration, top speed, and maintenance of top speed. Baseball, however, is a sport of acceleration and deceleration, not top speed, and thus a 60-yard sprint has limited applicability in game situations.

Regardless of its applicability, many coaches and scouts have historically used the 60-yard (55 m) sprint as a rudimentary gauge of athleticism. An average, acceptable handheld stopwatch time in professional baseball is 7.0 seconds or less. Catchers tend to run slower; smaller, more athletic positions tend to run faster. Athletes who run 60 yards in 6.5 to 6.8 seconds are considered to have good speed, whereas 6.3 to 6.5 seconds is exceptional. On average, middle infielders at the Division I level run the 60 yards in 6.8 seconds, Division II in 7.2 seconds, Division III and JUCO in 7.4 seconds, and a typical high school middle infielder runs in 7.2 to 7.4 seconds (14).

Exit velocity is a measure of the power and quality of ball contact in batting; it measures the speed of the baseball as it recoils off the bat. Although bat speed is a more historically used measurement, exit velocity is a stronger descriptive construct because it accounts for the quality of the contact (i.e., center percussion on the bat), not just raw swing speed.

As described earlier in the chapter, MLB uses TrackMan to track the trajectory and spin rate of hit and pitched baseballs. Some professional, college, and high school teams and athletes use portable systems similar to the MLB technology to measure and record exit velocity and other measures of swing performance during practice and training sessions. Amateur programs with limited funds often measure exit velocity by using a radar gun to track the baseball hit off a batting tee.

According to the data available from Statcast, the average exit velocity for all major-league infielders in 2019 was 88 mph (142 km/h); middle infielders were similar at 87 mph (140 km/h) (28). Publicly available data report that the average exit velocity for college infielders is 95 mph (153 km/h) for Division I, 90 mph (145 km/h) for Division II, 80 mph (129 km/h) for Division III and JUCO, and 75 mph (121 km/h) for high school athletes (14). There are several reasons for the apparent difference between MLB middle infielders and collegiate and high school athletes. MLB data are derived from the average of all balls batted into play during actual games: ground balls, fly balls, and line drives. The reported averages were determined from approximately 120,000 batted balls from 475 major-league players. The exit values for college and high school athletes were the result of the best 5 to 10 attempts during batting practice or hitting off a tee in a cage.

When designing resistance training programs for middle infielders, it is important to note that the ability to move quickly and efficiently in multiple directions is a priority in game situations. Increasing strength can be important, but adding needless muscle mass can negatively affect acceleration, first-step quickness, range, and agility. Resistance training programs and movements should be designed to improve lower body, upper body, and core (torso and hip) strength from the ground up without significantly increasing body mass. Such exercises should be implemented to improve joint mobility and stability, agility, balance, and coordination. After developing a base of strength, plyometric exercises and resistance training exercises with appropriate training loads designed to increase the rate of force development for quick, explosive, multi-directional movements will transfer best to baseball-specific skills.

Corner Infielders

Coaches and scouts search for corner infielders with power who can hit for average, with above average defense skills and an ability to drive in runs. Arm strength is more important at third than at first base and first-step quickness in multiple directions is more important than speed or range at both positions. Because first basemen throw less often and throw across the diamond less regularly, arm strength is not extremely important for this position. However, the ability to move gracefully, jump up for errant throws, stretch for short throws, move laterally for wide throws, and dig the ball out of the dirt are essential. Third basemen need first-step quickness, lateral speed, and agility, along with the ability to throw at high velocities with accuracy. Speed is an asset, but not typically a major tool in the corner infielders' game. Corner infielders are larger than middle infielders in height and weight (see table 2.3)—they need to be strong, powerful, and durable. They run less, sprint less, and make fewer throws than middle infielders but must possess more power. Average exit velocity for corner infielders is 89 mph (143 km/h) and average electronic time to first base is 4.52 seconds.

Like strength and power athletes in other sports, corner infielders can benefit from resistance training programs designed to improve maximum strength and power from the ground up. They also need core strength and stability to provide a solid base from which to swing and throw and adequate arm and shoulder strength to make quick, powerful swings and throws from varying angles and positions. Because they are power positions, plyometric exercises designed to increase maximum rate of force development are good additions to the training program after the development of adequate baseball-specific strength.

Center Fielders

As previously stated, center fielders are among the most athletic players on the field. Compared to corner outfielders, they tend to be shorter, lighter, and faster (table 2.4 and figure 2.4). They run more total distance and sprint more than most of the other positions. Speed is essential to cover ground and rundown balls hit in the gaps and over their heads. They also must possess above average or exceptional agility, balance, and coordination to catch the ball and throw it with speed and accuracy to the infield. Arm strength is typically average or above average at 87 to 95 mph (140-153 km/h) and accuracy is essential (6). Because most good base runners can score from second base in 7 seconds or less, all outfielders must be able to react, field the ball, set up, and throw the ball to home in 7 seconds or less.

In terms of hitting, good center fielders tend to bat near the top of the order, have good on-base percentages, and steal bases and score from first base on extra-base hits. Some center fielders may hit with power and therefore bat near the middle of the batting order; this is considered an advantage in the MLB. Intangible leadership traits are also important, because they must be able to communicate with other outfielders and middle infielders. Average electronic time from home plate to first base for MLB center fielders is 4.22 seconds (figure 2.4) and average exit velocity is 87 mph (140 km/h) (20).

Resistance training programs for center fielders are similar to those for middle infielders and are designed to improve acceleration, sprinting, and quick, efficient movement in multiple directions. Increasing strength is important to establish a base of power, but, similar to infielders, it is important not to disrupt agility and acceleration. Resistance training programs should focus on total body movements that increase lower body and core strength and power. Upper body and arm care exercises are also important. Because center fielders run farther than many other positions and need above average speed, their conditioning load may be greater than any other position on the field, except pitchers. However, strength and conditioning coaches should not overemphasize conditioning, which can have a negative impact on power and subsequently speed and agility.

Corner Outfielders

Elite corner outfielders are outstanding hitters; many hit with exceptional average and power (table 2.6). Even those with below average power can hit with a higher batting average and on-base percentage and steal bases. Average exit velocity for MLB corner outfielders is 89 mph (143 km/h) and average electronic time from home plate to first base is 4.36 seconds (17). Defense is slightly more important for left fielders than right fielders, but is not one of the top two tools for either position. Both positions must be able to make routine catches of ground balls, line drives, and fly balls. Although arm strength is not a top priority, it is valued more in right field because of the longer distance to third base. Average throwing velocity for corner infielders is approximately 87 mph (140 km/h). Scouts search for corner outfielders with plus defense and range, but they covet athletes who can also hit with power.

Resistance training programs for corner outfielders are similar to middle outfielders and designed to improve maximum strength before power, all from the ground up. Corner outfielders also need core strength and stability to provide a solid base from which to swing and throw and adequate arm and shoulder strength and stability. Because they are considered power players, plyometric exercises designed to increase maximum rate of force development are strong additions to the training program.

CONCLUSION

Baseball is an athletic sport that requires strength, power, coordination, speed and agility, flexibility, and mobility for success. The relative contribution of each of these physical attributes varies depending on the playing position. Starting pitchers, for example, require the greatest aerobic and muscular endurance because they often throw more than 100 pitches over two or more hours. On the other hand, outfielders are often the fastest athletes and middle infielders the most agile. Corner infielders are typically larger and more powerful and catchers are durable, often possessing intrinsic leadership qualities. Understanding the physiological requirements for each position is important to precisely prescribe exercise for the unique needs of the position.

3

TESTING PROTOCOLS AND ATHLETE ASSESSMENT

DAVID J. SZYMANSKI AND JOSE VAZQUEZ

This chapter will discuss the various testing protocols used to assess baseball players. Some tests are well established, and some may be considered non-traditional for the strength and conditioning professional, but all will evaluate the athlete's physical capabilities and baseball performance. Strength and conditioning professionals do not have to perform all the tests described in this chapter; coaches should select the most appropriate tests for their athletes based on available facilities or equipment. However, with all the information that can potentially be collected, it could be beneficial for coaches to know how to run these tests, interpret the test results, and practically apply the findings to their athletes' development.

This chapter also provides descriptive data tables for high school, college, and professional baseball players. This will allow readers to determine an athlete's percentile ranking or if the athlete is within the average for a specific test. Testing should occur throughout the year, but coaches will have to determine which tests will be performed and when athletes will be tested. Because many of the tests generally require maximum effort, safety to avoid injury is a major concern; therefore, it is important that the appropriate personnel are available for testing. Testing allows coaches to determine objective baseline values for the various testing categories, identify strengths and weaknesses, evaluate the effectiveness of the resistance training program, and identify an athlete's ability to return to practice or play after injury.

GENERAL TESTING GUIDELINES

High school, college, and professional coaches have long debated whether baseball players should be tested. This debate includes which tests to use, which are most important, and when to test the athletes. Before testing, coaches should make sure the athletes have been familiarized with all the tests for at least two weeks (6 sessions) to ensure proper execution and reduce the risk of injury.

An example of strength testing could be the back squat test (see chapter 4 for the protocol). The coach will have to decide if a submaximal test (2- to 10-repetition maximum) or a one repetition maximum (1RM) test should be performed. It is recommended that beginner or intermediate resistance trained athletes with less than 12 months of resistance training experience perform submaximal strength tests (10, 14, 21, 22, 27). Many high school athletes would fit into this type of resistance training classification. On the other hand, it is recommended that advanced resistance trained athletes with 12 months or more of resistance training experience, such as varsity high school (10, 31) and college athletes (15, 17, 20, 23, 25, 26), perform a 1RM test. For safety reasons, make sure that the appropriate number of spotters are available. At the professional level, it will be determined by the strength and conditioning professional as well as the organization whether 1RM or submaximal strength testing will be performed. The athlete's safety will be the main consideration.

To optimally resistance train an athlete using a periodized program that includes percentages of a 1RM or estimated 1RMs, testing should be completed. Without testing, it could be very challenging for a strength and conditioning professional to assign the appropriate amount of weight to lift for a specific percentage. The athlete would need to estimate what weight should be placed on the bar and, unfortunately, athletes tend to underestimate their strength, making the weight lower than the correct percentage of the 1RM if they were actually tested. Therefore, it is important to use *valid* and *reliable* standardized tests to assess an athlete's physical abilities consistently throughout the training year to set and achieve desired goals. **Validity** refers to the degree to which a test measures what it is supposed to measure while **reliability** refers to the consistency of the test (3).

When conducting **anthropometric** (height, body mass, and body composition) and performance tests, it is very important to sequence them correctly; one test should not affect the results of another test. Without proper test sequencing, validity and reliability of results could be jeopardized. In general, if all tests occur on the same day, tests that do not fatigue the athlete, such as body composition measurements, should be performed first. High-skill tests that take a shorter amount of time to recover from (3-5 minutes), such as power, agility, and sprints, should be performed next. Once these tests have been completed, strength tests can be performed. Coaches should follow the appropriate rest times for each test so athletes can perform optimally. If testing can be done over multiple days, coaches should select and sequence tests based on metabolic energy systems (anaerobic or anaerobic), testing categories (agility, speed, strength, power), and environmental factors (temperature, humidity, altitude, indoors or outside).

For the high school and college athlete, testing should occur at or near the beginning of the school year (off-season). In general, high school athletes will be resistance training in late August when the fall term begins. This may be in a physical education class or a team resistance training session if the athlete is not playing a fall sport. In general, college baseball players will begin resistance training sessions after going through routine university medical screening and clearance in late August; however, most college baseball players do not play another sport, which allows them to focus on off-season baseball preparation. At the professional level, testing would not occur until spring training, when all athletes report to their team's facilities.

After completing off-season resistance training, which may be 15 to 16 weeks, testing for the high school and college baseball player could occur. All the tests that were performed in the fall should be reassessed using the same equipment, conditions, protocols, and testing personnel. This would generally occur in early to mid-December before the holiday break.

After the holiday break, high school and college athletes return to their respective schools to begin preseason resistance training. This could be considered "spring training" for these athletes. The beginning of the season will vary depending on where a high school is located, but it generally begins in February or March. The college baseball season will begin in mid-February.

The preseason or spring training for the professional baseball player will begin in early February and finish at the end of March. Testing for the professional baseball player will vary depending on the franchise, but if a team tests, it will occur at or near the beginning of this time.

In general, baseball players at all levels are not tested during the competitive season because of the limitations of the playing and travel schedule and to avoid the risk of injury. However, testing that will likely not cause injury could be conducted to monitor an athlete's anthropometry, body composition, strength, and power in addition to sport-specific skills (20, 25). Example tests for these categories could be height, body mass, percent body fat, lean muscle mass, grip strength, medicine ball overhead throw or side toss, and vertical jump. Additionally, professional and some major Division I college teams record and monitor bat swing velocity, exit velocity, and pitching velocity as well as running times to first base during practices or games using in-stadium technology.

TESTING PROTOCOLS

The testing protocols in this chapter were selected because they are objective, valid, reliable, and have been demonstrated in research to enhance or relate to baseball performance. Furthermore, the multi-joint lower and upper body tests can be used as the primary core exercises in a periodized resistance training program using specific percent ranges of the 1RM for the various training seasons (off-, pre, in-, and postseason) as well as phases (hypertrophy, strength, and power). All tests selected include a purpose, necessary equipment, setup, specific testing protocols, and coaching tips. Make sure the appropriate descriptive data tables are used when comparing athletes, but also review the descriptive data tables from any higher level to create training goals for future aspirations.

Test Finder

STRENGTH TESTS

The strength tests included in this chapter will allow a strength and conditioning professional to evaluate lower and upper body strength. If a coach at any level thinks that the 1RM test is not warranted for safety reasons or lack of experience, the test should not be performed. If a coach thinks that the 1RM test is not warranted but wants to use the exercise as a primary core exercise in their programming using appropriate percentages for a given training phase, 1RM strength can be estimated from a multiple-RM test (e.g., a 2RM-10RM). If strength is tested on a consistent basis during the off- and preseasons, the strength and conditioning professional will know what improvements have occurred over a specific training phase and be able to update the resistance for specific percentages of the 1RM or estimated 1RM from a multiple-RM test.

1RM OR ESTIMATED 1RM BACK SQUAT

Purpose
Measure or estimate maximal multi-joint bilateral lower body strength

Equipment
> Squat rack with safety bars
>
> Barbell
>
> Weight plates
>
> Safety collars or clips

Setup
Position the barbell in the squat rack at the height of the athlete's shoulders to make sure that removing and replacing the barbell is easy. There should be safety bars positioned just below the parallel squat position in case the athlete cannot complete a repetition. The athlete, spotters, or coach should put the appropriate weight onto the barbell. Information about back squat technique and spotting can be found in chapter 6 on page 101. The athlete should perform a proper warm-up before testing (see testing protocol).

Testing Protocol (1)
1. Refer to chapter 6 for the back squat exercise technique.
2. The athlete should warm up with a light resistance, performing 5 to 10 repetitions.
3. After a 1-minute rest, add 30 to 40 pounds (14-18 kg) or 10% to 20% more weight to the barbell and have the athlete perform 3 to 5 repetitions.
4. After a 2-minute rest, add 30 to 40 pounds (14-18 kg) or 10% to 20% more weight to the barbell and have the athlete perform 2 to 3 repetitions.
5. After another 2 to 4 minutes of rest, add 30 to 40 pounds (14-18 kg) or 10% to 20% more weight to the barbell and have the athlete attempt a 1RM.
6. If the athlete completes the 1RM attempt and could lift more weight, repeat step 5. If the athlete does not complete the 1RM attempt, allow 2 to 4 minutes of rest, decrease the weight by 15 to 20 pounds (7-9 kg) or 5% to 10%, and reattempt a 1RM.

7. Keep adjusting the weight until the 1RM is achieved. Ideally, this should occur within three to five testing attempts.

8. If the 1RM back squat is not warranted for the athlete based on experience or safety, estimate 1RM strength from a submaximal multiple-RM test (10).

9. Estimated 1RM can be calculated by dividing the amount of weight lifted for 10 repetitions or less by the decimal 1RM in table 3.1.

Table 3.1 Percent of the 1RM, Decimal 1RM, and Repetitions Allowed (% 1RM–Repetition Relationship)

% 1RM	Decimal 1RM	Number of repetitions allowed
100	1.00	1
95	0.95	2
93	0.93	3
90	0.90	4
87	0.87	5
85	0.85	6
83	0.83	7
80	0.80	8
77	0.77	9
75	0.75	10

Data from J.M. Sheppard, and N.T. Triplett, "Program Design for Resistance Training," in *Essentials of Strength Training and Conditioning*, 4th ed., edited by G.G. Haff and N.T. Triplett, (Champaign, IL: Human Kinetics, 2016), 439-469.

Coaching Tips

• The athlete should have medical clearance before performing the test.

• Make sure the athlete is mentally prepared for the test.

• The athlete may wear a weight belt to provide added stability to the lumbar spine.

• The athlete should use firm footwear with lateral stability.

• Athletes with ankle mobility limitations may use weightlifting shoes with an elevated heel to allow the hips to flex lower while maintaining an upright trunk posture.

• There should be at least two spotters for the test (one spotter on each side of the barbell).

• At the athlete's signal, the spotters assist with lifting and balancing the bar as it is moved off the supports.

• On the downward and upward movement phases, the spotters should keep their hands close to the bar without touching it.

• After the athlete finishes, the spotters should grasp the bar and guide it back into the rack.

• If deemed appropriate by the coach for 1RM testing, use three spotters to increase safety, one on each side of the barbell and one behind the athlete.

Descriptive Data

Tables 3.2 and 3.3 provide descriptive data that can be used to evaluate a high school and NCAA Division I baseball player's 1RM back squat.

Table 3.2 Percentile Values of the 1RM Back Squat and 1RM Barbell Bench Press for High School Baseball Players

	1RM back squat		1RM barbell bench press	
Percentile rank	lb	kg	lb	kg
90-100	365.0-505.0	165.9-229.5	235.0-280.0	106.8-127.3
80-89.9	320.0-360.0	145.5-163.6	220.0-230.0	100-104.5
70-79.9	290.0-315.0	131.8-143.2	205.0-215.0	93.2-97.7
60-69.9	270.0-285.0	122.7-129.5	190.0-200.0	86.4-90.9
50-59.9	255.0-265.0	115.9-120.5	180.0-185.0	81.8-84.1
40-49.9	245.0-250.0	111.4-113.6	170.0-175.0	77.3-79.5
30-39.9	225.0-240.0	102.3-109.1	160.0-165.0	72.7-75.0
20-29.9	205.0-220.0	93.2-100.0	145.0-155.0	65.9-70.5
10-19.9	180.0-200.0	81.8-90.9	130.0-140.0	59.1-63.6
<10	125.0-175.0	56.8-79.5	95.0-125.0	43.2-56.8
Average	241.0	111.1	171.7	76.1
SD	58.0	28.4	37.7	17.4
n	702			

SD = standard deviation, n = sample size.

Data from Szymanski et al. (2008); Szymanski et al. (2007); Szymanski et al. (2006); Szymanski et al. (2011).

Table 3.3 Percentile Values of the 1RM Back Squat and 1RM Barbell Bench Press for NCAA Division I Baseball Players

	1RM back squat		1RM barbell bench press	
Percentile rank	lb	kg	lb	kg
90-100	435.0-535.0	197.7-243.2	290.0-385.0	131.8-175.0
80-89.9	405.0-434.0	184.1-197.6	280.0-289.0	127.3-131.7
70-79.9	390.0-404.0	177.3-184.0	270.0-279.0	122.7-127.2
60-69.9	370.0-389.0	168.2-177.2	265.0-269.0	120.5-122.6
50-59.9	350.0-369.0	159.1-168.1	255.0-264.0	115.9-120.4
40-49.9	340.0-349.0	154.5-159.0	250.0-254.0	113.6-115.8
30-39.9	320.0-339.0	145.5-154.4	240.0-249.0	109.1-113.5
20-29.9	310.0-319.0	140.9-145.4	230.0-239.0	104.5-109.0
10-19.9	280.0-309.0	127.3-140.8	215.0-229.0	97.7-104.4
<10	225.0-279.0	102.3-127.2	185.0-214.0	84.1-97.6
Average	352.1	160.0	251.6	114.4
SD	58.0	26.4	31.9	14.5
n	382		256	

SD = standard deviation, n = sample size.

Data from Szymanski et al. (2011); Szymanski, Beiser et al. (2011); Szymanski et al. (2016); Szymanski et al. (2013); Szymanski et al. (2010); Szymanski et al. (2009).

1RM OR ESTIMATED 1RM BENCH PRESS

Purpose

Measure or estimate maximal multi-joint bilateral upper body pushing strength. Traditionally, the barbell bench press is tested; however, the coach may want to test the dumbbell bench press with a neutral grip to reduce the stress on the anterior shoulders. This test could be used for all pitchers and for those position players who are concerned about their shoulders. Information about dumbbell bench press technique and spotting can be found in chapter 7 on page 147. The barbell bench press test will be described in this section.

Equipment

Barbell

Weight plates

Safety collars or clips

Bench press stand

Bench

Setup

Position the barbell in the center of the rack. Make sure that the area surrounding the bench is clear of other equipment. The athlete, spotter, and/or coach should put the appropriate weight onto the barbell. Make sure the load on the barbell is evenly distributed and collars or clips are used to secure the load. Information about barbell bench press technique and spotting can be found in chapter 7 on page 146. The athlete should perform a proper warm-up before testing (see testing protocol).

Testing Protocol (1)

1. Refer to chapter 7 for the bench press exercise technique.
2. The athlete should warm up with a light resistance, performing 5 to 10 repetitions.
3. After a 1-minute rest, add 10 to 20 pounds (4-9 kg) or 5% to 10% more weight to the barbell and have the athlete perform 3 to 5 repetitions.
4. After a 2-minute rest, add 10 to 20 pounds (4-9 kg) or 5% to 10% more weight to the barbell and have the athlete perform 2 to 3 repetitions.
5. After another 2 to 4 minutes of rest, add 10 to 20 pounds (4-9 kg) or 5% to 10% more weight to the barbell and have the athlete attempt a 1RM.
6. If the athlete completes the 1RM attempt and could lift more weight, repeat step 5. If the athlete does not complete the 1RM attempt, allow 2 to 4 minutes of rest, decrease the weight by 5 to 10 pounds (2-4 kg) or 2.5% to 5%, and reattempt a 1RM.
7. Keep adjusting the weight until the 1RM is achieved. Ideally, this should occur within three to five testing attempts.
8. If the 1RM bench press is not warranted for the athlete based on experience or safety, estimate 1RM strength from a multiple-RM test (10).
9. Estimated 1RM can be calculated by dividing the amount of weight lifted for 10 repetitions or less by the decimal 1RM in table 3.1.

Coaching Tips

- Make sure the athlete uses a five-point body contact position on the bench. The head, upper back, buttocks, and feet should be firmly and evenly placed to promote maximum stability.
- Make sure the athlete is mentally prepared for the test.
- The athlete should use a closed, pronated grip on the barbell with hands evenly spaced.
- The athlete's body position on the bench should allow his eyes to be directly under the barbell. Do not allow a false (open) grip for safety reasons.
- Make sure that the spotter is experienced.
- Make sure there is good communication between the athlete and spotter.

Descriptive Data

Tables 3.2 and 3.3 provide descriptive data that can be used to evaluate high school and NCAA Division I baseball players' 1RM barbell bench press. Table 3.4 provides descriptive data that can be used to evaluate NCAA Division I baseball players' 1RM dumbbell bench press.

Table 3.4 Percentile Values of the 1RM Dumbbell Bench Press and 1RM One-Arm Dumbbell Row for NCAA Division I Baseball Players

	1RM dumbbell bench press		1RM one-arm dumbbell row	
Percentile rank	lb	kg	lb	kg
90-100	120.0-145.0	54.5-65.9	155.0-170.0	70.5-77.3
80-89.9	115.0-119.0	52.3-54.4	145.0-154.0	65.9-70.4
70-79.9	110.0-114.0	50.0-52.2	140.0-144.0	63.6-65.8
60-69.9	105.0-109.0	47.7-49.9	135.0-139.0	61.4-63.5
50-59.9	100.0-104.0	45.5-47.6	130.0-134.0	59.1-61.3
40-49.9	95.0-99.0	43.2-45.4	125.0-129.0	56.8-59.0
30-39.9	90.0-94.0	40.9-43.1	120.0-124.0	54.5-56.7
20-29.9	85.0-89.0	38.6-40.8	115.0-119.0	52.3-54.4
10-19.9	80.0-84.0	36.4-38.5	110.0-114.0	50.0-52.2
<10	60.0-79.0	27.3-36.3	80.0-109.0	36.4-49.9
Average	96.6	43.9	127.4	57.9
SD	15.1	6.9	16.5	7.5
n	126		382	

SD = standard deviation, n = sample size.

Data from Szymanski et al. (2011); Szymanski, Beiser et al. (2011); Szymanski et al. (2016); Szymanski et al. (2013); Szymanski et al. (2010); Szymanski et al. (2009).

1RM OR ESTIMATED 1RM ONE-ARM DUMBBELL ROW

Purpose

Measure or estimate maximal multi-joint unilateral upper body pulling strength. This exercise has not traditionally been used for testing but was chosen here because it has been used in previous research with 382 college baseball players (15, 17, 20, 23, 25, 26) and could be included as one of the multi-joint upper body primary core exercises in a resistance training program. Results from this test would allow a coach to design a well-balanced, periodized resistance training program that specifically includes program intensity (percent of 1RM or estimated 1RM) for a multi-joint upper body pulling exercise, as well as prescribe resistance to use for a specific percentage during various training phases.

If a coach thinks that performing the 1RM one-arm dumbbell row is not warranted for professional baseball players, this test should not be performed. If a coach thinks that performing the 1RM one-arm dumbbell row is not warranted for a player based on experience level, training status, or safety reasons, but wants to use the exercise as a multi-joint upper body primary core exercise in the training program and use appropriate percentages for a given training phase, 1RM strength can be estimated from a multiple-RM test. If a coach does not have dumbbells that go higher than 100-150 pounds (~45-65 kg), submaximal testing can be completed to estimate a 1RM from a multiple submaximal load (e.g., a 2RM-10RM). If a coach does not have dumbbells in the weight room, this specific test cannot be performed.

Equipment

Dumbbell

Bench

Setup

The athlete should place one hand firmly on a flat bench directly under the shoulder so that the torso is slightly above parallel to the floor. The knee (of the same side as the hand on the bench) should be flexed and placed on the flat bench for additional support. (This is a slightly different beginning position than the one described in chapter 7 on page 133.) While keeping the spine neutral, grasp a dumbbell in the other hand with the elbow fully extended.

Testing Protocol (1)

1. Refer to chapter 7 for the one-arm dumbbell row exercise technique.

2. The athlete should complete the bench press test prior to the one-arm dumbbell row; this will serve as a general warm-up.

3. The athlete should perform a specific warm-up with light dumbbell resistance for 5 to 10 repetitions.

4. After a 1-minute rest, select a dumbbell that is 10 to 20 pounds (4-9 kg) or 5% to 10% more weight and have the athlete perform 3 to 5 repetitions.

5. After a 2-minute rest, select a dumbbell that is 10 to 20 pounds (4-9 kg) or 5% to 10% more weight and have the athlete perform 2 to 3 repetitions.

6. After another 2 to 4 minutes of rest, select a dumbbell that is 10 to 20 pounds (4-9 kg) or 5% to 10% more weight and have the athlete attempt a 1RM.

7. If the athlete completes the 1RM attempt and could lift more weight, repeat step 6. If the athlete does not complete the 1RM attempt, allow 2 to 4 minutes of rest, decrease the weight by 5 to 10 pounds (2-4 kg) or 2.5% to 5%, and reattempt a 1RM.

8. Keep adjusting the weight until the 1RM is achieved. Ideally, this should occur within three to five testing attempts.

If the 1RM one-arm dumbbell row is not warranted for the athlete based on experience or safety, estimate 1RM strength from a submaximal multiple-RM test (10).

Estimated 1RM can be calculated by dividing the amount of weight lifted for 10 repetitions or less by the decimal 1RM in table 3.1 on page 35.

Coaching Tips

- Keep the torso in the correct position before beginning the movement; do not round or arch the spine.
- Do not rotate or twist the spine (torso) to pull the dumbbell up.
- Keep the muscles of the torso engaged throughout the entire movement.
- Keep the dumbbell close to the body during the movement.
- No spotter is required for this test.

Descriptive Data

Table 3.4 provides descriptive data that can be used to evaluate the 1RM one-arm dumbbell row for NCAA Division I baseball players.

GRIP STRENGTH

Purpose

Measure isometric, unilateral grip strength. Previous research indicates that grip strength relates to baseball performance, such as doubles (23), home runs (4, 20, 23), total bases (4, 23), runs batted in (23), and slugging percentage (4, 22), in addition to greater bat swing and batted-ball exit velocities (11, 15, 17, 18, 27, 29, 30) and throwing velocity (31).

Equipment

Hydraulic handgrip dynamometer

Chair with no armrests

Setup (7, 27)

The athlete should be seated in a standard chair (46 cm or 18 in.) with back support and no armrests. The shoulder should be adducted and neutrally rotated, elbow flexed at 90 degrees, with the forearm and wrist in neutral position. The athlete can use a wrist position between 0 and 30 degrees extension and between 0 and 15 degrees ulnar deviation. The athlete's head should be in a neutral position (facing straight ahead). The grip size should be adjusted so that the middle finger's (third digit's) mid-portion (second phalanx) is approximately at a right angle. Grip adjustments of 1.3 cm (0.5 in.) on the hand grip dynamometer are made by slipping off the moveable handle and repositioning it into the five manufactured slots. The number one slot is the innermost position for the smallest grip size and the number five slot is the outside position for the largest grip size. The coach should record the grip setting (1 to 5) so this setting can be used for further tests on the same person.

Testing Protocol (7, 27)

1. The athlete should exert maximally and quickly after hearing the coach's following instructions: "Are you ready? Squeeze as hard as you can. Harder! . . . Harder! . . . Relax."
2. The athlete should complete three trials alternately with each hand, resting for at least 30 seconds between trials for the same hand.
3. The coach should record the force in kilograms.
4. The coach should reset the dynamometer's pointer to 0 after each trial.

Coaching Tips

- It is recommended to use a hydraulic handgrip dynamometer to compare data to those in this chapter.
- Make sure the athlete is in the correct setup position (sitting in a standard chair without an armrest), otherwise results will not be comparable to high school (table 3.5) and college (table 3.6) baseball data.
- To compare results to those of professional baseball athletes (table 3.7), the athlete should perform the test while seated in a standard chair with an armrest to support the forearm.
- Positions 2 and 3 are the most common handle positions.
- Make sure the coach holds the dynamometer with one hand at the top of the gauge, palm facing down, and the other hand at the bottom of the dynamometer, palm facing up, to maintain the athlete's wrist position while squeezing the device.
- Do not allow the athlete to jerk the dynamometer out of position while squeezing the device.
- Make sure to identify the athlete's dominant and non-dominant hand.
- Make sure to alternate hands for each trial.
- Make sure to provide enough rest (30 seconds) between attempts to allow ATP to be regenerated.
- It is recommended to use the best trial for both hands for data.

Descriptive Data

Table 3.5 provides descriptive data that can be used to evaluate total grip strength, dominant grip strength, and non-dominant grip strength for high school baseball players. Table 3.6 provides descriptive data that can be used to evaluate total grip strength, dominant grip strength, and non-dominant grip strength for NCAA Division I baseball players. Table 3.7 provides descriptive data that can be used to evaluate professional baseball players' average grip strength changes across age and position. It should be noted that the professional baseball data in table 3.7 was recorded with the tested arm supported on a chair armrest; the data in tables 3.5 and 3.6 did not use a chair with an armrest. Previous research (13) has demonstrated that subject's grip is weaker when the arm is supported on an armrest compared to when the arm is unsupported. For this reason, readers will notice that the average grip strength values for the professional athlete are lower than the average values for college athletes and similar to the average values for high school athletes.

Table 3.5 Percentile Values of Total Grip Strength, Dominant Grip Strength, and Non-Dominant Grip Strength for High School Baseball Players

Percentile rank	Total grip strength		Dominant grip strength		Non-dominant grip strength	
	lb	kg	lb	kg	lb	kg
90-100	286.0-350.0	130.0-159.0	147.4-176.0	67.0-80.0	140.8-167.2	64.0-76.0
80-89.9	266.2-283.8	121.0-129.0	136.4-145.2	62.0-66.0	132.0-136.4	60.0-62.0
70-79.9	257.4-264.0	117.0-120.0	132.0-134.2	60.0-61.0	125.4-129.8	57.0-59.0
60-69.9	246.4-255.2	112.0-116.0	125.4-129.8	57.0-59.0	121.0-123.2	55.0-56.0
50-59.9	239.8-244.2	109.0-111.0	121.0-123.2	55.0-56.0	116.6-118.8	53.0-54.0
40-49.9	231.0-237.6	105.0-108.0	116.6-118.8	53.0-54.0	112.2-114.4	51.0-52.0
30-39.9	220.0-228.8	100.0-104.0	110.0-114.4	50.0-52.0	107.8-110.0	49.0-50.0
20-29.9	209.0-217.8	95.0-99.0	105.6-107.8	48.0-49.0	103.4-105.6	47.0-48.0
10-19.9	198.0-206.8	90.0-94.0	99.0-103.4	45.0-47.0	94.6-101.2	43.0-46.0
<10	123.2-195.8	56.0-89.0	61.6-96.8	28.0-44.0	61.6-92.4	28.0-42.0
Average	238.7	108.5	120.6	54.8	116.2	52.8
SD	39.4	17.9	20.7	9.4	19.6	8.9
n	340					

SD = standard deviation, *n* = sample size.

Data from Szymanski et al. (2008); Szymanski et al. (2013); Szymanski et al. (2006); Szymanski et al. (2004); Szymanski et al. (2008); Szymanski et al. (2011).

Table 3.6 Percentile Values of Total Grip Strength, Dominant Grip Strength, and Non-Dominant Grip Strength for NCAA Division I Baseball Players

Percentile rank	Total grip strength		Dominant grip strength		Non-dominant grip strength	
	lb	kg	lb	kg	lb	kg
90-100	349.8-400.4	159.0-182.0	178.2-200.2	81.0-91.0	173.8-200.2	79.0-91.0
80-89.9	323.4-347.6	147.0-158.0	165.0-176.0	75.0-80.0	160.6-171.6	73.0-78.0
70-79.9	310.2-321.2	141.0-146.0	160.6-162.8	73.0-74.0	156.2-158.4	71.0-72.0
60-69.9	303.6-308.0	138.0-140.0	156.2-158.4	71.0-72.0	151.8-154.0	69.0-70.0
50-59.9	294.8-301.4	134.0-137.0	151.8-154.0	69.0-70.0	147.4-149.6	67.0-68.0
40-49.9	286.0-292.6	130.0-133.0	147.4-149.6	67.0-68.0	140.8-145.2	64.0-66.0
30-39.9	277.2-283.8	126.0-129.0	143.0-145.2	65.0-66.0	136.4-138.6	62.0-63.0
20-29.9	266.2-275.0	121.0-125.0	136.4-140.8	62.0-64.0	132.0-134.2	60.0-61.0
10-19.9	248.6-264.0	113.0-120.0	127.6-134.2	58.0-61.0	125.4-129.8	57.0-59.0
<10	140.8-246.4	64.0-112.0	92.4-125.4	42.0-57.0	88.0-123.2	40.0-56.0
Average	294.4	133.8	149.8	68.1	145.0	65.9
SD	39.2	17.8	20.2	9.2	19.8	9.0
n	420					

SD = standard deviation, *n* = sample size.

Data from Szymanski et al. (2011); Szymanski, Beiser et al. (2011); Szymanski (2016); Szymanski et al. (2013); Szymanski et al. (2020); Szymanski (2010); Szymanski et al. (2009).

Table 3.7 Average Changes in Grip Strength Across Ages and Positions for Professional Baseball Players (mean ± SD)

Age group (yr)		Grip strength	
		lb	kg
All players			
Under 20	AG1	111.3 ± 22.4	50.6 ± 10.2
20-22	AG2	116.4 ± 21.1	52.9 ± 9.6
23-25	AG3	119.9 ± 21.1	54.5 ± 9.6
26-28	AG4	125.0 ± 20.9	56.8 ± 9.5*+
29-31	AG5	128.0 ± 25.7	58.2 ± 11.7*[a]
32-34	AG6	124.3 ± 18.5	56.5 ± 8.4
35+	AG7	125.4 ± 17.2	57.0 ± 7.8*
Position players			
Under 20	AG1	111.3 ± 26.6	50.6 ± 12.1
20-22	AG2	115.7 ± 20.0	52.6 ± 9.1
23-25	AG3	121.7 ± 22.4	55.3 ± 10.2
26-28	AG4	123.4 ± 20.0	56.1 ± 9.1
29-31	AG5	131.3 ± 28.2	59.7 ± 12.8*[a]
32-34	AG6	125.0 ± 20.0	56.8 ± 9.1
35+	AG7	128.0 ± 17.6	58.2 ± 8.0
Pitchers			
Under 20	AG1	111.1 ± 19.4	50.5 ± 8.8
20-22	AG2	116.8 ± 22.2	53.1 ± 10.1
23-25	AG3	118.4 ± 20.0	53.8 ± 9.1
26-28	AG4	125.8 ± 21.6	57.2 ± 9.8*
29-31	AG5	125.8 ± 24.2	57.2 ± 11.0*
32-34	AG6	121.7 ± 15.6	55.3 ± 7.1
35+	AG7	123.6 ± 17.2	56.2 ± 7.8
n	1,157		

*Significantly ($p < 0.05$) different from AG1.

[a]Significantly ($p < 0.05$) different from AG2.

AG = age group, *n* = sample size.

Adapted by permission from G.T. Mangine, J.R. Hoffman, M.S. Fragala, J. Vazquez, M.C. Krause, J. Gillett, and N. Pichardo, "Effect of Age on Anthropometric and Physical Performance Measures in Professional Baseball Players," *Journal of Strength and Conditioning Research* 27, no. 2 (2013): 375-381.

POWER TESTS

Power tests allow the coach to evaluate an athlete's explosive strength. Research has demonstrated that power is related to performance on the baseball field (4, 20, 23, 25) in addition to sport skills (11, 15, 17, 20, 24, 25, 26, 28, 29, 30).

VERTICAL JUMP

Purpose

Measure bilateral lower body vertical jumping height and measure or estimate peak power

Equipment

There are various ways to test vertical jump. One valid and reliable method is to use a Vertec standing scale. Other ways to measure vertical jump height are using a floor-based jump mat or simply having athletes jump and touch as high as they can on a wall, using chalk on the fingers to mark the spot and a measuring tape to record. Finally, peak power can be estimated by using appropriate equations or calculated directly by using force plates.

Setup

When using a Vertec for vertical jump tests, make sure the surrounding area is clear. The athlete should be properly warmed up before testing. It is recommended to measure the athlete's overhead reach to the nearest 0.5 inch (1.3 cm) before testing by raising the Vertec high enough for the athlete's fingers to touch and move the vanes. The athlete should remain flat-footed and use the dominant hand. Record the highest reach.

Testing Protocols

Only the protocols for the Vertec standing scale and force plates will be described below.

Vertec Standing Scale

1. After recording standing reach height, raise the Vertec to an appropriate level based on the athlete's expected jumping ability.

2. The athlete should not stand directly underneath the vanes, but slightly behind them and 10 to 12 inches (25.4-30.5 cm) away from the vertical bar of the Vertec. The outstretched dominant arm should be aligned with the middle of the vanes.

3. When ready, the athlete performs a countermovement and jumps as high as possible, touching the highest vane he can with his dominant hand.

4. The athlete should complete at least three maximal trials or until a vane cannot be touched.

5. Rest time between jumps should be 60 seconds.

6. Record the highest vertical jump to the closest 0.5 inch (1.3 cm).

7. To calculate the maximal jump height, subtract the standing reach height from the maximum vertical jump height achieved.

A Caveat Regarding Peak Power Equations

Descriptive data presented in this section include estimated peak power for all levels of play as well as actual peak power data for college pitchers. The estimated peak power data from professional baseball (4, 6) was reported using the Harman and colleagues (2) equation. In the original 1991 article, the equation, based on a no countermovement squat jump, is listed as

$$\text{Peak power (W)} = (61.9 \times \text{jump height [cm]}) + (36.0 \times \text{body mass [kg]}) + 1{,}822$$

Unfortunately, this equation was not published accurately and was later modified to be

$$\text{Peak power (W)} = (61.9 \times \text{jump height [cm]}) + (36.0 \times \text{body mass [kg]}) - 1{,}822$$

If the former equation is used, it will overestimate actual peak power measured by force plates. This can be verified in the Sayers and colleagues (9) article, where the equation is listed with the "minus 1,822" portion. An additional point of interest to help support the corrected equation is that Harman is the third author of the Sayers and colleagues (9) article. This overestimation of peak power from the original article's equation is important to note because the estimated peak power data provided in table 3.10 for professional baseball players, modified from Mangine and colleagues (6), has values that range between 9,861 and 10,993 W. These values are much higher than what one would calculate if the corrected equation were used. These corrected values, presented in table 3.10 on page 48, are similar to the Sayers and colleagues (9) estimated peak power values. Additionally, the corrected estimated peak power values for professional athletes are very similar to those of college baseball players who jump a similar height (table 3.9) and have a similar body mass (table 3.21 on page 62) to their contemporaries in professional baseball (table 3.22 on page 63). Ultimately, when using the corrected Harman and colleagues (2) equation, it underestimated actual peak power of the 38 college pitchers by 3.4% (24). This would make sense because this equation was based on a squat jump that does not include a lower and upper body countermovement, which would create greater momentum and jump height.

Tables 3.8 and 3.9 include vertical jump data and estimated peak power calculated from Sayers and colleagues (9) and corrected Harman and colleagues (2) equations for high school and college baseball players, even though both equations were not collectively used in the previous research studies. Table 3.10 includes vertical jump data and estimated peak power calculated from the Harman and colleagues (2) equation reported by Mangine and colleagues (6), as well as corrected Harman and colleagues and Sayers and colleagues (9) equations. These tables were created using the various estimation of peak power equations so data could be compared among high school, college, and professional baseball players from different research studies. These tables will help coaches and athletes understand why different values exist in the literature. If a force plate is not available, it is recommended to use the Sayers and colleagues (9) equation.

$$\text{Peak power (W)} = (51.9 \times \text{CMJ [cm]}) + (48.9 \times \text{body mass [kg]}) - 2007$$

This equation is recommended because a countermovement jump (CMJ) was used simultaneously with a force plate and peak power was estimated to be 2.7% higher than actual peak power. The estimation of peak power for the college pitchers (24) using the Sayers and colleagues (9) equation was 2.8% higher than the actual peak power, which was very similar to the difference reported in the Sayers and colleagues article (9).

Force Plate

To determine the actual peak power of an athlete, force plates must be used. There are two ways that force plates can be used: Athletes may jump with their hands on their hips, or the force plates may be used while simultaneously performing the vertical jump test with a Vertec. This will allow the coach to record actual peak power while also measuring vertical jump height. Descriptive data presented in table 3.9 shows actual peak power recorded from two force plates of Division I pitchers while performing the vertical jump test with a Vertec device.

1. Ideally, the athlete stands with one foot on each force plate before jumping. If there is only one force plate, stand in the middle.

2. All jumps are performed using the Vertec standing scale jump protocol. If the athlete uses the hands-on-hips protocol, the peak power values or jump height will be lower than if the hands and arms were used for momentum.

3. A computer with appropriate software connected to the force plate(s) will provide data for jump height, peak power, and rate of force development.

Coaching Tips

- The athlete should position the shoulder by the ear to get the full elevation of their dominant arm when measuring their standing reach. If the athlete retracts the shoulder blade while measuring reach height, their standing reach value will be lower, resulting in a mathematically greater vertical jump height.

- If testing multiple athletes, measure standing reach for all before beginning vertical jump tests and rotate athletes between jump attempts to provide rest time. Both practices will save time.

- Stand far enough behind the athlete to see if contact is made with the dominant hand on the Vertec.

- Note that the colors of the vanes represent different measurements: The blue vanes are whole inches, white vanes are half-inches, and red vanes indicate six-inch intervals.

- The athlete should simply touch the vanes, not swat hard at them, because they could break.

Descriptive Data

Table 3.8 provides descriptive data for a vertical jump test and estimated peak power for high school baseball players. Table 3.9 provides descriptive data for a vertical jump test and estimated peak power for NCAA Division I (DI) baseball players and actual peak power of DI pitchers. Table 3.10 provides descriptive data for a vertical jump test and estimated peak power for professional baseball players.

Table 3.8   Percentile Values of the Vertical Jump and Estimated Peak Power for High School Baseball Players

| Percentile rank | Vertical jump | | Estimated PP (Sayers)* | Corrected estimated PP (Harman)[a] |
	in.	cm	W	W
90-100	27.0-29.0	68.6-73.7	5,344.6-6,056.9	5,119.4-5,649.1
80-89.9	25.0-26.5	63.5-67.3	5,079.7-5,344.5	4,834.8-5,119.3
70-79.9	23.5-24.5	59.7-62.2	4,883.2-5,079.6	4,559.9-4,834.7
60-69.9	22.5-23.0	57.2-58.4	4,664.0-4,883.1	4,408.8-4,559.8
50-59.9	22.0	55.9	4,444.7-4,663.9	4,219.1-4,408.7
40-49.9	21.5	54.6	4,353.4-4,444.6	4,110.7-4,219.0
30-39.9	20.5-21.0	52.1-53.3	4,075.7-4,353.3	3,904.0-4,110.6
20-29.9	19.5-20.0	49.5-50.8	3,910.9-4,075.6	3,743.7-3,903.9
10-19.9	17.5-19.0	44.5-48.3	3,726.5-3,910.8	3,552.5-3,743.6
<10	14.0-17.0	35.6-43.2	2,460.0-3,726.4	2,490.1-3,552.4
Average	21.0	53.5	4,342.3	4,118.7
SD	3.1	8.0	600.8	530.1
n	304			

SD = standard deviation, *n* = sample size.

*Sayers = estimation of peak power from reference 9.

[a]Harman = estimation of peak power from corrected equation from reference 2.

Data from Szymanski et al. (2013); Szymanski et al. (2007); Szymanski et al. (2010); Szymanski et al. (2011).

Table 3.9   Percentile Values of the Vertical Jump and Estimated Peak Power (PP) for NCAA Division I (DI) Baseball Players and Actual Peak Power for DI Pitchers

| Percentile rank | Vertical jump | | Estimated PP (Sayers)* | Corrected estimated PP (Harman)[a] | Actual peak power |
	in.	cm	W	W	W
90-100	31.0-35.5	78.7-90.2	6,522.8-7,280.0	6,272.1-6,970.0	6,875.6-8,500.0
80-89.9	29.5-30.5	74.9-77.5	6,304.3-6,522.7	6,010.6-6,272.0	6,405.2-6,875.5
70-79.9	28.5-29.0	72.4-73.7	6,113.5-6,304.2	5,830.0-6,010.5	6,137.9-6,405.1
60-69.9	27.5-28.0	69.9-71.2	5,947.9-6,113.4	5,696.2-5,829.9	5,888.3-6,137.8
50-59.9	26.5-27.0	67.3-68.6	5,810.9-5,947.8	5,539.1-5,696.1	5,549.8-5,888.2
40-49.9	26.0	66.0	5,668.6-5,810.8	5,368.6-5,539.0	5,311.4-5,549.7
30-39.9	25.0-25.5	63.5-64.8	5,495.0-5,668.5	5,178.3-5,368.5	5,153.9-5,311.3
20-29.9	24.0-24.5	61.0-62.2	5,281.0-5,494.9	5,026.5-5,178.2	4,781.8-5,153.8
10-19.9	22.5-23.5	57.2-59.7	5,114.8-5,280.9	4,805.1-5,026.4	4,369.1-4,781.7
<10	18.5-22.0	47.0-55.9	4,008.3-5,114.7	3,870.2-4,805.0	3,032.0-4,369.0
Average	26.4	67.1	5,818.2	5,527.4	5,628.2
SD	3.2	8.1	567.1	545.2	1,178.8
n	420		420		38

SD = standard deviation, *n* = sample size.

*Sayers = estimation of peak power from reference 9.

[a]Harman = estimation of peak power from corrected equation from reference 2.

Data from Szymanski et al. (2011); Szymanski et al. (2016); Szymanski et al. (2013); Szymanski et al. (2020); Szymanski et al. (2010); Szymanski et al. (2009).

Table 3.10   Average Vertical Jump and Estimated Peak Power Performance Across Age and Position for Professional Baseball Players (mean ± SD)

Age group (yr)		Vertical jump		Estimated peak power (Harman)[f]	Corrected estimated peak power (Harman)[g]	Estimated peak power (Sayers)*
		in.	cm	W	W	W
All players						
Under 20	AG1	26.7 ± 3.1	67.8 ± 7.9	10,371.0 ± 652.0	5,636.4	5,942.2
20-22	AG2	27.7 ± 3.7	70.3 ± 8.6	10,688.0 ± 721.0	5,859.6	6,164.8
23-25	AG3	27.6 ± 3.8	70.0 ± 9.6	10,784.0 ± 814.0	5,963.4	6,315.5
26-28	AG4	27.1 ± 4.5	68.9 ± 11.4	10,781.0 ± 928.0	5,985.3	6,380.7
29-31	AG5	25.9 ± 3.7[b]	65.9 ± 9.5[b]	10,608.0 ± 828.0	5,886.0	6,342.3
32-34	AG6	25.4 ± 4.0[b]	64.6 ± 10.1[b]	10,391.0 ± 759.0[b]	5,675.9	6,098.8
35+	AG7	24.1 ± 3.9[abcd]	61.1 ± 9.9[abcd]	10,199.0 ± 836.0[cd]	5,531.3	6,015.0
Position players						
Under 20	AG1	27.2 ± 3.6	69.0 ± 9.1	10,410.0 ± 676.0	5,667.5	5,945.8
20-22	AG2	27.9 ± 3.4	70.8 ± 8.7	10,669.0 ± 706.0	5,800.5	6,068.5
23-25	AG3	28.0 ± 3.9	71.2 ± 10.0	10,863.0 ± 826.0	5,987.3	6,309.3
26-28	AG4	28.4 ± 4.4	72.1 ± 11.1	10,993.0 ± 902.0	6,133.0	6,478.3
29-31	AG5	26.4 ± 4.1	67.0 ± 10.5	10,583.0 ± 902.0	5,846.1	6,252.7
32-34	AG6	26.2 ± 4.0	66.5 ± 10.1	10,483.0 ± 772.0	5,739.6	6,124.1
35+	AG7	25.5 ± 4.1	64.7 ± 10.3	10,630.0 ± 700.0	5,786.5	6,245.8
Pitchers						
Under 20	AG1	26.3 ± 2.7	66.8 ± 6.8	10,342.0 ± 646.0	5,606.9	5,934.3
20-22	AG2	27.5 ± 3.3	69.8 ± 8.5	10,714.0 ± 740.0	5,915.0	6,256.2
23-25	AG3	27.0 ± 3.6	68.7 ± 9.2	10,717.0 ± 805.0	5,922.5	6,301.8
26-28	AG4	25.9 ± 4.3[b]	65.8 ± 11.0[b]	10,582.0 ± 919.0	5,840.2	6,283.4
29-31	AG5	25.6 ± 3.3	65.0 ± 8.5	10,628.0 ± 773.0	5,920.3	6,417.9
32-34	AG6	24.6 ± 4.0[b]	62.4 ± 10.1[b]	10,304.0 ± 755.0	5,619.0	6,092.2
35+	AG7	23.0 ± 3.5[bc]	58.3 ± 9.0[bc]	9,861.0 ± 797.0[bcde]	5,322.0	5,820.8
n	1,157					

[a]Significantly (*p* <0.05) different from AG1.

[b]Significantly (*p* <0.05) different from AG2.

[c]Significantly (*p* <0.05) different from AG3.

[d]Significantly (*p* <0.05) different from AG4.

[e]Significantly (*p* <0.05) different from AG5.

[f] = Harman et al. (2) estimated peak power equation from 1991 article.

[g] = estimated peak power values were corrected using the Harman et al. (2) equation subtracting 1,822 at the end of the regression equation instead of adding 1,822 as listed in the original 1991 article.

* = Sayers et al. (9) estimated peak power equation.

AG = age group, *n* = sample size.

Data from Mangine et al. (2013)

LATERAL TO MEDIAL JUMP

Purpose

Measure unilateral lower body horizontal plane jumping distance, which is similar to the movement of throwing or pitching a baseball. Previous research has reported that community college and NAIA pitchers and position players with greater horizontal power threw with greater velocity (5). However, other research did not find these relationships with NCAA Division I pitchers (24).

Equipment

Tape

Tape measure

Meter stick

Setup

The athlete should stand parallel to the starting line with the inside edge (medial side) of their testing foot closest to the starting line. Allow athletes to practice lateral jumping before testing.

Testing Protocol

1. To begin, the athlete will perform a countermovement by flexing the tested leg at the knee and hip while sliding the front leg behind the tested leg, simultaneously swinging the arms in a pendulum motion away from the jump, before jumping as far as possible to their left or right in the frontal plane, swinging the arms and landing on both feet simultaneously parallel to the starting line.
2. Distance will be recorded from the outside of the back tested foot to the starting line.
3. Alternate between jumping legs to allow rest.
4. Three attempts will be given with 30 seconds of rest between jumps to regenerate ATP.

Coaching Tips

- Make sure that the athlete lands on both feet simultaneously. Do not let the athlete land on one foot and then bring the trailing foot to the landing position.
- If the athlete falls or moves his feet, the jump attempt does not count.
- The athlete can place his hands on the floor in front or to either side of the body to maintain position.
- The athlete cannot place his hands behind the body because this generally results in the athlete falling or moving his feet.

Descriptive Data

Table 3.11 provides descriptive data for a lateral to medial jump for NCAA Division I pitchers.

Table 3.11 Percentile Values of the Lateral to Medial Jump for NCAA Division I Pitchers

Percentile rank	Lateral to medial jump (right)		Lateral to medial jump (left)	
	in.	cm	in.	cm
90-100	89.5-93.0	227.0-236.0	90.0-94.5	228.0-240.0
80-89.9	85.5-89.4	217.0-226.9	86.5-89.9	219.0-227.9
70-79.9	82.5-85.4	209.0-216.9	84.5-86.4	214.0-218.9
60-69.9	81.0-82.4	205.0-208.9	83.0-84.4	210.0-213.9
50-59.9	79.5-80.9	201.0-204.9	80.5-82.9	204.0-209.9
40-49.9	77.5-79.4	196.0-200.9	80.0-80.4	203.0-203.9
30-39.9	76.5-77.4	194.0-195.9	77.0-79.9	195.5-202.9
20-29.9	75.5-76.4	191.0-193.9	76.5-76.9	194.0-195.4
10-19.9	73.0-75.4	185.0-190.9	75.5-76.4	191.0-193.9
<10	67.0-72.9	170.0-184.9	70.0-75.4	177.5-190.9
Average	79.5	202.0	81.1	206.0
SD	6.3	16.0	5.5	14.0
n	38			

SD = standard deviation, *n* = sample size.

Data from Szymanski et al. (2020).

MEDICINE BALL OVERHEAD THROW

Purpose
Measure bilateral upper body throwing power (velocity) in the sagittal plane. Previous research has reported that there were moderate positive correlations between this test and the mean and the best fastball velocity from the wind-up and from the stretch with a slide step in NCAA Division I pitchers (24).

Equipment
4 lb (1.8 kg) medicine ball

Radar gun

Solid wall

Tape

Tape measure

Setup
Using athletic tape, clearly mark a throwing line 20 feet (6.1 m) from a solid (e.g., brick) wall. Tape a 3- × 3-foot (0.9 × 0.9 m) box on the wall 3 feet (0.9 m) above the floor directly in front of the throwing line. Stand behind the athlete with the radar gun recording velocity in mph to the second decimal place.

Testing Protocol
1. The athlete stands facing the solid wall with feet side-by-side and hip-width apart behind the throwing line.
2. The athlete holds the medicine ball with both hands on the side of the ball and slightly behind the center.

3. The medicine ball is brought back behind the head, then thrown vigorously forward into the target taped to the wall. This throwing action is similar to that used for a soccer sideline throw-in.

4. The athlete is permitted to step forward over the line as they throw (right-handed pitcher should step forward with the left foot; left-handed pitcher should step forward with the right foot).

5. Record the best of three trials.

Coaching Tips

- Make sure that the athlete practices the two-hand overhead throwing technique before testing.

- Throws that do not enter the target do not count and are not recorded.

- Other variations of this test include throwing the ball for distance, but throw technique can affect the distance the ball is thrown; thus why it is recommended to standardize the test with a fixed target on the wall.

Descriptive Data

Table 3.12 provides descriptive data for the medicine ball overhead throw for NCAA Division I pitchers.

Table 3.12 Percentile Values of the Overhead Medicine Ball Throw for NCAA Division I Pitchers

Percentile rank	mph	m/s
90-100	33.0-33.5	14.8-15.0
80-89.9	32.1-32.9	14.3-14.7
70-79.9	31.0-32.0	13.9-14.2
60-69.9	30.5-30.9	13.6-13.8
50-59.9	29.8-30.4	13.3-13.5
40-49.9	29.5-29.7	13.1-13.2
30-39.9	28.5-29.4	12.7-13.0
20-29.9	27.8-28.4	12.4-12.6
10-19.9	27.3-27.7	12.2-12.3
<10	26.0-27.4	11.6-12.2
Average	30.0	13.4
SD	2.2	1.0
n	38	

SD = standard deviation, *n* = sample size.

Data from Szymanski et al. (2020).

MEDICINE BALL SIDE TOSS

Purpose

Measure bilateral rotational tossing power (velocity) in the transverse plane. Positive correlations were reported between rotational power using this test to the mean and best bat swing velocity of high school and college hitters (11, 12, 17, 20, 25, 26, 30, 31).

Equipment

6 lb (2.7 kg) medicine ball

Radar gun

Solid wall

Tape

Tape measure

Setup

Using athletic tape, clearly mark a tossing line on the floor 15 feet (4.6 m) from a solid (e.g., brick) wall. Tape a 3- × by 3-foot box (0.9 × 0.9 m) on the wall 3 feet above the floor directly in front of the tossing line. Stand behind the athlete with the radar gun recording velocity in mph to the second decimal place.

Testing Protocol (12)

1. The athlete should assume an athletic stance with a wide, stable base, similar to hitting stance. The feet should be wider than shoulder-width apart with the torso facing perpendicular to the wall. The athlete holds the medicine ball approximately chest high with the front hand supporting the ball from underneath and the back hand placed at the rear of the ball, palms at a right angle. The forearms should be extended from the body with the upper arms supported by the torso.

2. From the preparatory stance, the athlete rotates the torso away from the wall (approximately 90 degrees), shifting the weight to the rear leg.

3. At the completion of the backswing, the athlete explosively rotates toward the wall and tosses the medicine ball into the target. The lower body motion is very similar to hitting the ball on a line drive back to the pitcher. To generate maximum angular velocity, the athlete must toss the ball parallel to the floor (not upward) and rotate the hips around a rigid front leg.

4. The best of three trials is recorded for both the dominant and non-dominant tossing sides.

Coaching Tips

- Although alternate medicine ball weights can be substituted, the descriptive data presented in this chapter are specific to a 6-pound (2.7 kg) medicine ball. Testing with medicine balls of different weights will require the use of descriptive data that are specific to those weights.

- For appropriate statistical discrimination, the radar gun should have the capability to measure velocity in mph to two decimal places.

- While using the radar gun, the coach should stand behind the athlete, opposite the target, and away from the intended flight path, keeping the target, the athlete, and the coach in a straight line.

- If testing time is limited, test only the athlete's dominant tossing (hitting) side.

- If a radar gun is not available, it is possible to measure the distance the medicine ball is tossed as a substitute for ball velocity; however, tossing technique will affect distance.

- Encourage the athlete to use the legs, back, and arms to maximize tossing velocity.

Descriptive Data

Table 3.13 provides descriptive data for the medicine ball side toss (rotational power) for high school and NCAA Division I baseball players.

Table 3.13 Percentile Values of the Medicine Ball Side Toss for High School (HS) and NCAA Division I (DI) Baseball Players

	HS medicine ball side toss		DI medicine ball side toss	
Percentile rank	mph	m/s	mph	m/s
90-100	23.1-24.0	10.33-10.73	27.7-30.5	12.4-13.6
80-89.9	22.3-23.0	9.97-10.32	26.6-27.6	11.9-12.3
70-79.9	22.0-22.2	9.83-9.96	25.9-26.5	11.6-11.8
60-69.9	21.6-21.9	9.66-9.82	25.2-25.8	11.3-11.5
50-59.9	21.2-21.5	9.48-9.65	24.9-25.1	11.1-11.2
40-49.9	20.8-21.0	9.30-9.47	24.4-24.8	10.9-11.0
30-39.9	20.5-20.7	9.16-9.29	23.8-24.3	10.6-10.8
20-29.9	20.2-20.4	9.03-9.15	23.4-23.7	10.4-10.5
10-19.9	20.0-20.1	8.94-9.02	22.9-23.3	10.2-10.3
<10	18.5-19.9	8.27-8.93	21.3-22.8	9.5-10.1
Average	21.3	9.5	25.0	11.2
SD	1.3	0.6	1.9	0.8
n	84		286	

SD = standard deviation, *n* = sample size.

Data from Szymanski et al. (2011); Szymanski et al. (2016); Szymanski et al. (2010); Szymanski et al. (2009); Szymanski et al. (2008); Szymanski et al. (2011).

1RM OR ESTIMATED 1RM POWER CLEAN

Purpose

Measure or estimate total body power. This test is used in high school and some college baseball resistance training programs; however, it is not used in professional and some college programs due to the potential risk of injuries to the wrist, elbow, or shoulder joints. In general, there is not enough time to teach and perfect the technical skills to safely perform this exercise at the professional level.

If a coach thinks that performing the 1RM power clean is not warranted for professional baseball players, this test should not be performed. If a coach thinks that performing the 1RM power clean is not warranted for a player based on experience level, training status, or safety reasons, but they want to use this exercise as a total body primary core exercise in the training program, the 1RM can be estimated from a multiple-RM test.

Equipment

Olympic bar

Bumper plates

Safety clips

Setup

The coach loads the appropriate weight onto the bar. The athlete should perform a proper warm-up before testing (see testing protocol).

Testing Protocol (1)

1. Refer to chapter 5 for the power clean exercise technique.
2. The athlete should warm up with a light resistance, performing 5 repetitions.
3. After a 1-minute rest, add 30 to 40 pounds (14-18 kg) or 10% to 20% more weight to the bar and have the athlete perform 3 to 5 repetitions.
4. After a 2-minute rest, add 30 to 40 pounds (14-18 kg) or 10% to 20% more weight to the bar and have the athlete perform 2 to 3 repetitions.
5. After another 2- to 4-minute rest, add 30 to 40 pounds (14-18 kg) or 10% to 20% more weight to the bar and have the athlete attempt a 1RM.
6. If the athlete completes the 1RM attempt and could lift more weight, repeat step 5. If the athlete fails, allow a 2- to 4-minute rest, decrease the load by 15 to 20 pounds (7-9 kg) or 5% to 10%, and reattempt a 1RM.
7. Keep adjusting the load until the 1RM is determined; ideally within three to five attempts.
8. If the 1RM power clean is not warranted for the athlete based on experience or safety, estimate the 1RM from a multiple-RM test (10).
9. Estimated 1RM can be calculated by dividing the amount of weight lifted for 10 repetitions or less by the decimal 1RM in table 3.1 on page 35.

Coaching Tips

- Other variations of the power clean include the power clean from power position (barbell starts midthigh), hang power clean, and full clean (athlete catches the bar in the bottom position of a squat).
- The power clean should not be spotted (see chapter 5 for more details).

Descriptive Data

Table 3.14 provides descriptive data that can be used to determine the percentile values for a NCAA Division I baseball player's 1RM power clean.

Table 3.14   Percentile Values of the 1RM Power Clean for a NCAA Division I Baseball Player

Percentile rank	lb	kg
90	265.0	120.0
80	239.0	109.0
70	225.0	102.0
60	216.0	98.0
50	206.0	94.0
40	200.0	91.0
30	190.0	86.0
20	182.0	83.0
10	162.0	74.0
Average	210.0	95.0
SD	36.0	16.0
n	149	

SD = standard deviation, *n* = sample size.

Adapted by permission from J. Hoffman, *Norms for Fitness, Performance, and Health* (Champaign, IL: Human Kinetics, 2006), 38.

SPEED AND AGILITY TESTS

Speed and agility are very important in baseball, especially for the position player. Chapter 2 describes how these physical capabilities relate to playing the game both offensively and defensively.

10-30-60-YARD (9.1-27.4-54.9 M) SPRINT

Purpose

Measure linear starting, acceleration, and maximal speed. This test allows the strength and conditioning professional to capture all times for the various distances that relate to stealing or running bases (4, 6, 15, 25, 26). Some teams use the 10-yard (9.1 m) sprint to measure speed, but this test only provides information about a baseball player's start and acceleration. Because the risk of hamstring injury tends to increase with sprints of longer distance, most strength and conditioning professionals rarely test professional athletes over distances greater than 10 yards (9.1 m). The 60-yard (54.9 m) sprint is commonly used for testing high school and college athletes. Some major-league scouts use the 60-yard sprint when evaluating talent; however, most teams do not use it when testing professional athletes. Historically, major-league scouts look for 60-yard times under 7 seconds when evaluating prospects at the high school and collegiate levels. For a 60-yard sprint—comparable to running from first to third base or second base to home plate—a time of 6.7 to 6.9 seconds is generally considered average in professional baseball.

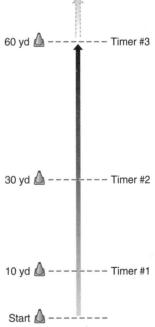

Equipment

Cones

Stopwatch or timing system

Measuring tape

Setup

Place four cones at 0, 10, 30, and 60 yard (0, 9.1, 27.4, 54.9 m) locations. This will allow times to be recorded for the various distances. A minimum of three coaches must be used to time the athlete at the three distances. If two athletes are running simultaneously, then six coaches will be necessary.

Testing Protocol

1. The athlete starts from a base-stealing stance at the starting line.

2. The stopwatch or timer starts on the athlete's first movement.

3. The stopwatch or timer stops when the athlete's chest crosses the various distances or finish line.

4. After sprinting 60 yards (54.9 m), the athlete decelerates in a safe, controlled manner.

5. The athlete runs two trials to the right, simulating the direction of running on the baseball field, with 3 to 5 minutes of rest between trials to recover and regenerate ATP.

6. The time for each trial is recorded and the best of the two trials is used for evaluation.

Coaching Tip

Make sure the athlete changes sprinting lanes if running against another athlete so other coaches record their sprint time(s).

Descriptive Data

Tables 3.15 and 3.16 provide descriptive data of the 10-30-60-yard (9.1-27.4-54.9 m) sprint for NCAA Division I position players and pitchers. Table 3.17 provides descriptive data of 10-yard (9.1 m) sprint times across age and position in professional baseball players.

Table 3.15 Percentile Values of 10-30-60-Yard (9.1-27.4-54.9 m) Sprint Times for NCAA Division I Position Players (in Seconds)

Percentile rank	10-yd sprint	30-yd sprint	60-yd sprint
90-100	1.53-1.36	3.68-3.29	6.67-6.29
80-89.9	1.59-1.54	3.72-3.67	6.81-6.68
70-79.9	1.61-1.60	3.79-3.73	6.92-6.80
60-69.9	1.63-1.62	3.84-3.80	7.00-6.93
50-59.9	1.65-1.64	3.91-3.85	7.10-7.01
40-49.9	1.67-1.66	3.98-3.92	7.16-7.11
30-39.9	1.70-1.68	4.04-3.99	7.32-7.17
20-29.9	1.73-1.71	4.10-4.05	7.44-7.33
10-19.9	1.78-1.74	4.16-4.11	7.57-7.45
<10	1.97-1.79	4.74-4.17	8.36-7.58
Average	1.66	3.92	7.13
SD	0.10	0.21	0.36
n	184		

SD = standard deviation, *n* = sample size.

Data from Szymanski et al. (2011); Szymanski et al. (2010); Szymanski et al. (2009).

Table 3.16 Percentile Values of 10-30-60-Yard (9.1-27.4-54.9 m) Sprint Times for NCAA Division I Pitchers (in Seconds)

Percentile rank	10-yd sprint	30-yd sprint	60-yd sprint
90-100	1.58-1.31	3.83-3.50	7.04-6.66
80-89.9	1.61-1.59	3.91-3.84	7.14-7.05
70-79.9	1.65-1.62	3.97-3.92	7.22-7.15
60-69.9	1.67-1.66	4.01-3.98	7.29-7.23
50-59.9	1.71-1.68	4.04-4.02	7.34-7.30
40-49.9	1.74-1.72	4.09-4.05	7.40-7.35
30-39.9	1.76-1.75	4.13-4.10	7.49-7.41
20-29.9	1.80-1.77	4.18-4.14	7.55-7.50
10-19.9	1.83-1.81	4.27-4.19	7.71-7.56
<10	1.95-1.84	4.47-4.28	8.16-7.72
Average	1.71	4.05	7.36
SD	0.11	0.18	0.29
n	120		

SD = standard deviation, *n* = sample size.

Data from Szymanski et al. (2011); Szymanski et al. (2010); Szymanski et al. (2009).

Table 3.17 Average Changes in Sprint (10-Yard) Time Across Ages and Positions for Professional Baseball Players (mean ± SD)

Age group (yr)		10-yd sprint
All players		
Under 20	AG1	1.65 ± 0.09
20-22	AG2	1.64 ± 0.10
23-25	AG3	1.63 ± 0.09
26-28	AG4	1.62 ± 0.14
29-31	AG5	1.66 ± 0.15
32-34	AG6	1.66 ± 0.14
35+	AG7	1.72 ± 0.13
Position players		
Under 20	AG1	1.65 ± 0.09
20-22	AG2	1.63 ± 0.10
23-25	AG3	1.63 ± 0.09
26-28	AG4	1.60 ± 0.12
29-31	AG5	1.63 ± 0.13
32-34	AG6	1.63 ± 0.12
35+	AG7	1.71 ± 0.16
n	1,157	

AG = age group, *n* = sample size.

Data from Mangine et al. (2013).

5-10-5 AGILITY TEST (ALSO CALLED THE PRO AGILITY DRILL)

Purpose

Measure lateral speed and change of direction speed. This test relates to stolen bases (4, 15, 20, 23, 25, 26) and is important for identifying those who can quickly move defensively.

Equipment

Cones

Stopwatch or timing system

Measuring tape

Turf running surface or infield dirt

Setup

Place three cones in a straight line on a turf surface marked with three parallel lines 5 yards (4.6 m) apart. If there are no lines on the turf, use a tape measure to place

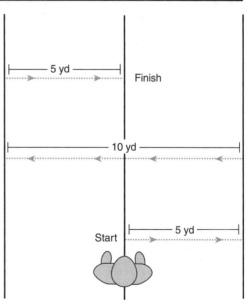

Reprinted by permission from M.P. Reiman and R.C. Manske, *Functional Testing in Human Performance* (Champaign, IL; Human Kinetics, 2009), 193.

the cones to ensure reliability and validity. If turf is not available, use the infield dirt and measure for accurate cone placement.

Testing Protocol

For this test to be valid and reliable, a standardized test should be used. Traditionally, it has been performed from a three-point stance. This beginning position can be selected if a coach wants to compare results to published normative data (3) or to the descriptive data in table 3.18. However, if the coach would like this test to be more baseball-like and compare to descriptive data in table 3.19, then the athlete should be in a leadoff/baserunning stance.

1. The athlete starts facing forward behind the middle cone in a three-point stance with his hand touching the ground in line with the middle cone. If using the leadoff/baserunning stance, the athlete should be standing with the middle cone lined up with the midline of his body.
2. The stopwatch or timer starts when the athlete lifts his hand from the three-point stance or makes the first movement from the leadoff/baserunning stance.
3. When running to the right, the athlete should turn with a left crossover step, sprint for 5 yards (4.6 m), and touch the line with his right hand.
4. After touching the line with his right hand, the athlete will turn to his left with a right crossover step and sprint for 10 yards (9.1 m), where he will touch the line with his left hand.
5. After touching the line with his left hand, the athlete will turn back to his right with a left crossover step and sprint 5 yards (4.6 m) past the starting (middle) cone to complete the test.
6. The stopwatch or timer will stop as soon the athlete's chest crosses the finish line at the middle cone.
7. On the second trial, the athlete will go in the opposite direction (to his left) to begin the test.
8. The athlete runs two trials in each direction with 3 to 5 minutes of rest between trials to recover and regenerate ATP.
9. The best of two trials in each direction is used to evaluate the athlete's performance.

Coaching Tips

- Make sure the athlete completes a warm-up before performing the test.
- Do not perform this test on the outfield grass. The grass may be too long, resulting in slower times, or too wet, which could be unsafe. It will also be bad for the field because the athlete's spikes will rip up the grass.

Descriptive Data

Table 3.18 provides descriptive data of the 5-10-5 for NCAA Division I position players and pitchers. Table 3.19 provide descriptive data of the 5-10-5 changes across age and position in professional baseball players.

Table 3.18 Percentile Values of the 5-10-5 Agility Test for NCAA Division I Position Players and Pitchers (in Seconds)

Percentile rank	Position players	Pitchers
90-100	4.21-4.04	4.37-4.17
80-89.9	4.29-4.22	4.45-4.38
70-79.9	4.34-4.30	4.52-4.46
60-69.9	4.41-4.35	4.56-4.53
50-59.9	4.45-4.42	4.62-4.57
40-49.9	4.51-4.46	4.69-4.63
30-39.9	4.57-4.52	4.74-4.70
20-29.9	4.63-4.58	4.78-4.75
10-19.9	4.79-4.64	4.89-4.79
<10	5.09-4.80	5.50-4.90
Average	4.48	4.64
SD	0.21	0.24
n	278	158

SD = standard deviation, *n* = sample size.

Data from Szymanski et al. (2011); Szymanski et al. (2016); Szymanski et al. (2013); Szymanski et al. (2020); Szymanski et al. (2010); Szymanski et al. (2009).

Table 3.19 Average Changes in Agility (5-10-5) Across Ages and Positions for Professional Baseball Players (mean ± SD)

Age group (yr)		5-10-5
All players		
Under 20	AG1	4.56 ± 0.27
20-22	AG2	4.45 ± 0.33
23-25	AG3	4.46 ± 0.26
26-28	AG4	4.47 ± 0.22
29-31	AG5	4.57 ± 0.22
32-34	AG6	4.62 ± 0.31
35+	AG7	4.68 ± 0.20
Position players		
Under 20	AG1	4.45 ± 0.29
20-22	AG2	4.40 ± 0.37
23-25	AG3	4.40 ± 0.27
26-28	AG4	4.40 ± 0.20
29-31	AG5	4.48 ± 0.22
32-34	AG6	4.54 ± 0.32
35+	AG7	4.57 ± 0.04

(continued)

Table 3.19 Average Changes in Agility (5-10-5) Across Ages and Positions for Professional Baseball Players (mean ± SD) *(continued)*

Age group (yr)		5-10-5
Pitchers		
Under 20	AG1	4.68 ± 0.19
20-22	AG2	4.57 ± 0.19
23-25	AG3	4.53 ± 0.22
26-28	AG4	4.59 ± 0.20
29-31	AG5	4.67 ± 0.18
32-34	AG6	4.80 ± 0.20
35+	AG7	4.80 ± 0.25
n	1,157	

AG = age group, *n* = sample size.

Data from Mangine et al. (2013).

BODY COMPOSITION AND ANTHROPOMETRY

Body composition tests allow the strength and conditioning professional to measure the percentage of the athlete's body that is adipose (fat) tissue and fat-free (lean) tissue. In general, for those athletes who want to maximize performance, increasing lean body mass and decreasing body fat can contribute to optimal performance. The device recommended to analyze body composition sends a low-level electrical current through the body and the impedance is determined by bioelectrical impedance analysis (BIA). If a BIA device is not available (it can be expensive), a skinfold caliper can be used to measure skinfold thickness. This technique is commonly used and relatively inexpensive, but it does take more time and calculations and requires skill to be valid and reliable. The protocol for skinfold measurements is displayed and described by McGuigan (8). Only the BIA protocol will be described in this chapter.

Anthropometry is the measurement of the human body and includes such variables as height, weight, and body girths (8). For this chapter, it is recommended that height and weight are measured because these variables differ from high school to professional athletes and, in general, have an impact on baseball performance. Weight or body mass can also be used to calculate the relative strength or power of an athlete and to compare athletes to one another. For example, an athlete who is 6'5" (196 cm) and 265 pounds (120 kg) and back squats 385 pounds (175 kg) has a relative back squat strength of 1.45, whereas an athlete who is 6'0" (183 cm) and 200 pounds (91 kg) and back squats 385 pounds (175 kg) has a relative back squat strength of 1.93. Pound for pound, the 6'0" athlete is much stronger than the 6'5" athlete. These relative strength values can then be correlated to various sport skills and performance variables such as throwing velocity, bat swing velocity, exit velocity, home runs, total bases, and slugging percentage. Previous research (4, 15, 20, 23, 26, 28, 29, 30) has reported such findings.

BIOELECTRICAL IMPEDANCE ANALYSIS

Purpose

Measure body mass, percent body fat, fat mass, and lean body mass. It has been demonstrated in research that body composition relates to baseball performance and sport skills (4, 6, 15, 17, 20, 23, 26, 28, 29, 30).

Equipment

Multi-frequency bioelectrical impedance analysis (MF-BIA) device

Setup

When using the MF-BIA method, the athlete should wear shorts and T-shirt. The athlete should remove his shoes and socks before stepping onto the MF-BIA device. Once the athlete steps on the MF-BIA device in his bare feet, body mass will be calculated. Then the athlete will enter his personal information (a coded ID that represents each athlete for future assessments, height, age, and sex) into the display area.

Testing Protocol

1. Once all appropriate personal data is entered while the athlete is standing with his heels on the rear sole electrodes, he will grasp the handles in both hands, keeping elbows straight, thighs apart, and holding arms away from the body.

2. The athlete should hold the hand electrodes so that the four fingers wrap the surface of the bottom hand electrode and the thumb is on the oval electrode.

3. The test will take 60 to 90 seconds, depending on which MF-BIA device is used.

4. Once the test is completed, the results will be shown on the screen and printed.

Coaching Tips

- The athlete should be properly hydrated before testing. MF-BIA is very sensitive to changes in body water. Dehydration can cause estimations of body composition to be less accurate.

- The athlete should not eat at least two hours before testing. This is because food mass is included in the athlete's weight and may result in measurement errors.

- The athlete should use the bathroom before testing. Waste is not included in the body's compositional elements, but the volume of urine and excrement is included in the weight measurement and may affect the accuracy of the test results.

- The athlete should not exercise for six hours before testing. Strenuous exercise can cause temporary changes in hydration status and fluid distribution. Even light exercise can change a person's fluid status and fluid composition temporarily.

- The athlete should not consume alcohol for 48 hours before testing.

- The athlete should not take diuretic medications before testing.

- Note that taking the test immediately after lying in bed or sitting for a long period of time might result in a slight change in the test results. This is because body water tends to move to the lower body as soon as the person stands or gets up.

- Administer the test in the morning, if possible. Body water tends to gravitate towards the lower body throughout the day, affecting accuracy of the test results.

- Avoid physical contact with the athlete during testing. Contact may lead to interference that could affect test results.

Descriptive Data

Tables 3.20 and 3.21 provide descriptive data for body mass, percent body fat, fat mass, and lean body mass for high school and NCAA Division I baseball players. Table 3.22 provides descriptive data for body mass, lean body mass, and percent body fat across age and position for professional baseball players. Skinfold calipers were used to measure skinfold thickness of the professional baseball players.

Table 3.20 Percentile Values of Body Mass, Percent Body Fat, Fat Mass, and Lean Body Mass for High School Baseball Players

Percentile rank	Body mass		Percent body fat	Fat mass		Lean body mass	
	lb	kg	%	lb	kg	lb	kg
90-100	205.0-250.0	93.0-113.6	6.1-3.0	8.6-4.8	3.9-2.2	159.0-180.5	72.5-82.0
80-89.9	186.0-204.9	84.0-92.9	7.3-6.2	10.3-8.7	4.7-4.0	151.0-158.9	68.7-72.4
70-79.9	174.0-185.9	79.0-83.9	8.5-7.4	12.1-10.4	5.5-4.8	147.5-150.9	67.1-68.6
60-69.9	166.5-173.9	75.6-78.9	9.8-8.6	14.5-12.2	6.6-5.6	143.0-147.4	65.0-67.0
50-59.9	158.0-166.4	71.6-75.5	11.7-9.9	17.2-14.6	7.8-6.7	138.5-142.9	63.0-64.9
40-49.9	149.0-157.9	68.0-71.5	13.3-11.8	21.6-17.3	9.8-7.9	134.1-138.4	61.0-62.9
30-39.9	144.0-148.9	65.5-67.9	16.0-13.4	24.9-21.7	11.3-9.9	129.5-134.0	59.0-60.9
20-29.9	135.0-143.9	61.5-65.4	19.7-16.1	34.5-25.0	15.7-11.4	121.5-129.4	55.0-58.9
10-19.9	128.5-134.9	58.5-61.4	23.5-19.8	53.7-34.6	22.4-15.8	117.0-121.4	53.3-54.9
<10	100.0-128.4	45.5-58.4	23.6-39.4	84.9-53.8	38.6-22.5	91.0-116.9	41.4-53.2
Average	160.5	73.0	14.1	24.4	11.1	136.1	61.9
SD	30.7	14.0	7.5	18.0	8.2	17.0	7.7
n	585						

SD = standard deviation, *n* = sample size.

Data from Szymanski et al. (2008); Szymanski et al. (2013): Szymanski et al. (2007); Szymanski et al. (2006); Szymanski et al. (2004); Szymanski et al. (2008); Szymanski et al. (2010); Szymanski et al. (2008); Szymanski et al. (2011).

Table 3.21 Percentile Values of Body Mass, Percent Body Fat, Fat Mass, and Lean Body Mass for NCAA Division I Baseball Players

Percentile rank	Body mass		Percent body fat	Fat mass		Lean body mass	
	lb	kg	%	lb	kg	lb	kg
90-100	226.0-265.0	102.5-120.5	8.0-4.0	14.2-6.0	6.4-2.7	190.2-231.6	86.5-105.3
80-89.9	216.4-225.9	98.4-102.4	9.4-8.1	16.7-14.3	7.5-6.5	181.7-190.1	82.6-86.4
70-79.9	207.5-216.3	94.3-98.3	10.2-9.5	18.9-16.8	8.5-7.6	176.7-181.6	80.3-82.5
60-69.9	201.0-207.4	91.0-94.2	11.4-10.3	21.2-19.0	9.6-8.6	172.6-176.6	78.4-80.2
50-59.9	194.6-200.9	88.5- 90.9	12.7-11.5	24.6-21.3	11.2-9.7	168.6-172.5	76.6-78.3
40-49.9	189.1-194.5	86.0-88.4	13.7-12.8	27.8-24.7	12.6-11.3	165.5-168.5	75.2-76.5
30-39.9	183.0-189.0	83.0-85.9	15.1-13.8	30.6-27.9	13.9-12.7	162.0-165.4	73.6-75.1
20-29.9	176.1-182.9	80.1-82.9	16.3-15.2	35.0-30.7	15.9-14.0	156.3-161.9	71.0-73.5
10-19.9	168.1-176.0	76.4-80.0	18.6-16.4	40.2-35.1	18.2-16.0	149.8-156.2	68.1-70.9
<10	130.0-168.0	59.0-76.3	26.9-18.9	68.4-40.3	31.1-18.3	122.5-149.7	55.5-68.0
Average	195.9	89.0	13.0	26.0	11.8	169.8	77.2
SD	23.1	10.5	4.1	10.5	4.8	16.0	7.3
n	442						

SD = standard deviation, *n* = sample size.

Data from Szymanski et al. (2011); Szymanski, Beiser et al. (2011); Szymanski, Beiser, Bassett, Till, and Szymansk (2011); Szymanski et al. (2016); Szymanski et al. (2013); Szymanski et al. (2020); Szymanski et al. (2010); Szymanski et al. (2009).

Table 3.22   Average Anthropometric Measures Across Age and Position for Professional Baseball Players (mean ± SD)

Age group (yr)		Body mass		Lean body mass		Percent body fat
		lb	kg	lb	kg	%
All players						
Under 20	AG1	199.3 ± 22.9	90.6 ± 10.4	176.2 ± 15.2	80.1 ± 6.9	11.3 ± 4.4
20-22	AG2	203.5 ± 22.7	92.5 ± 10.3	178.2 ± 15.4	81.0 ± 7.0	12.1 ± 4.0
23-25	AG3	211.0 ± 22.2[ab]	95.9 ± 10.1[ab]	183.3 ± 15.4[ab]	83.3 ± 7.0[ab]	12.9 ± 4.0
26-28	AG4	216.5 ± 20.0[ab]	98.4 ± 9.1[ab]	186.8 ± 15.2[ab]	84.9 ± 6.9[ab]	13.6 ± 3.6[ab]
29-31	AG5	221.8 ± 21.8[abc]	100.8 ± 9.9[abc]	188.5 ± 14.7[abc]	85.7 ± 6.7[abc]	14.8 ± 4.1[abc]
32-34	AG6	213.8 ± 24.2[ab]	97.2 ± 11.0[ab]	183.7 ± 16.1	83.5 ± 7.3	13.8 ± 3.7[a]
35+	AG7	218.2 ± 23.5[ab]	99.2 ± 10.7[ab]	184.4 ± 15.0	83.7 ± 6.8	14.9 ± 4.4[abc]
Position players						
Under 20	AG1	196.7 ± 27.1	89.4 ± 12.3	174.5 ± 16.1	79.3 ± 7.3	10.8 ± 5.1
20-22	AG2	198.0 ± 20.7	90.0 ± 9.4	175.8 ± 15.2	79.9 ± 6.9	11.0 ± 3.6
23-25	AG3	207.9 ± 21.6[b]	94.5 ± 9.8[b]	182.6 ± 15.4[b]	83.0 ± 7.0[b]	12.1 ± 4.0
26-28	AG4	213.4 ± 18.5[ab]	97.0 ± 8.4[ab]	186.1 ± 15.0[ab]	84.6 ± 6.8[ab]	12.7 ± 3.3[b]
29-31	AG5	215.2 ± 20.7[ab]	97.8 ± 9.4[ab]	186.8 ± 15.8[ab]	84.9 ± 7.2[ab]	13.2 ± 3.4[b]
32-34	AG6	210.5 ± 23.1[b]	95.7 ± 10.5[b]	181.3 ± 15.2	82.4 ± 6.9	13.6 ± 4.1[b]
35+	AG7	220.2 ± 21.3[ab]	100.1 ± 9.7[ab]	186.8 ± 12.3[b]	84.9 ± 5.6[b]	14.2 ± 3.9[ab]
Pitchers						
Under 20	AG1	201.3 ± 19.1	91.5 ± 8.7	177.3 ± 14.5	80.6 ± 6.6	11.7 ± 3.8
20-22	AG2	208.8 ± 23.3	94.9 ± 10.6	180.6 ± 15.2	82.1 ± 6.9	13.2 ± 4.0
23-25	AG3	213.4 ± 22.7[a]	97.0 ± 10.3[a]	183.9 ± 15.6	83.6 ± 7.1	13.6 ± 3.8
26-28	AG4	219.3 ± 21.1[ab]	99.7 ± 9.6[ab]	187.4 ± 15.6[ab]	85.2 ± 7.1[ab]	14.4 ± 3.8[a]
29-31	AG5	227.3 ± 21.1[abc]	103.3 ± 9.6[abc]	190.1 ± 13.6[ab]	86.4 ± 6.2[ab]	16.1 ± 4.2[abc]
32-34	AG6	218.7 ± 25.7[a]	99.4 ± 11.7[a]	187.4 ± 17.2	85.2 ± 7.8	14.0 ± 3.3
35+	AG7	216.0 ± 26.0	98.2 ± 11.8	181.5 ± 17.2	82.5 ± 7.8	15.6 ± 4.8[a]
n	1,157					

[a]Significantly (*p* <0.05) different from AG1.

[b]Significantly (*p* <0.05) different from AG2.

[c]Significantly (*p* <0.05) different from AG3.

AG = age group, *n* = sample size.

Data from Mangine et al. (2013).

HEIGHT AND BODY MASS

The protocols to measure height and body mass will not be described here in detail because they are common lab measurements. It is recommended that a stadiometer be used to measure height to the nearest half-inch (or 0.5 cm if measured in metric) while the athlete's shoes are off. If a stadiometer is not available, a tape measure and a flat wall can be used. If a MF-BIA device is not available to measure body mass, use a certified calibrated scale or a calibrated electronic scale (8). Athletes should wear shorts, T-shirts, and no shoes. Ideally, height and body mass should be measured in the morning and then at the same time of day for future comparison measurements.

CONCLUSION

Testing high school, college, or professional baseball players takes time, organization, planning, and skilled coaches. Testing should be safe and provide valid and reliable data that is useful to the athlete, baseball coach, and strength and conditioning professional. With the limited time that athletes are available due to high school or NCAA regulations and during MLB spring training, it is very important that the strength and conditioning professionals know what they want to test and why. The tests described in this chapter emphasize some of the major physiological categories that may be evaluated, but coaches might select others based on their own experiences or preferences.

Although various physical attributes or characteristics may be correlated with baseball performance at all levels, research has not consistently found which tests are most important. The physical and emotional maturation status, the level of play, and the sport-specific skills developed are all different from the high school to the professional athlete. Just because an athlete is physically superior at performing many of the tests listed in this chapter does not mean that this athlete will necessarily be a great baseball player—however, if an athlete has excellent baseball skills and performs well in some or all these tests, these could be the ingredients for professional success. Testing provides baseline data, which can be used later for comparison to see if the athlete has made improvements over the course of a year or years with the team. Testing allows an individual athletes' physical strengths and weaknesses to be identified, which can help determine an athlete's resistance training program. Finally, test data can also be used to assist in an athlete's injury rehabilitation.

If a strength and conditioning professional wants to conduct the most common tests for baseball players at all levels, the following would be recommended: lower and upper body strength, lower body power, speed, and agility. These tests will provide a foundation from which to build a resistance training program and allow the coach to objectively evaluate their athletes. From a practical standpoint, however, coaches and strength and conditioning professionals should use tests that are meaningful to them and to the athletes and should be relatively easy to conduct. Finally, it is important to remember that testing can provide valuable information to help identify an athlete's physical abilities, but they should not be used solely to make player selections—test results may not predict success on the baseball field.

SPORT-SPECIFIC PROGRAM DESIGN GUIDELINES

SEAN MAROHN AND ZACH GJESTVANG

Baseball requires numerous qualities of athleticism, including strength, speed, power, agility, balance, coordination, muscular endurance, and cardiorespiratory fitness. For strength and conditioning programs to be successful, it is important that the physical, physiological, and movement requirements of the sport, strengths and weaknesses of the participants, and goals and objectives of the program are understood. Training programs need to be individualized and based on the requirements of the sport, position, phase of the training year, and season. The primary goals should be to prepare athletes to meet the physical demands and mental stresses of the game and season; reduce the risk of acute, chronic, and overuse injury; and enhance performance on the field.

The training program must be general enough to improve athleticism and specific enough to reduce the risk of injury and maximize performance in practice and game situations. Exercises that do not address at least one of these goals should not be included in a strength and conditioning program for baseball. Baseball players are not football players, bodybuilders, Olympic lifters, gymnasts, distance runners, or Special Forces personnel. Baseball is a non-contact sport; athletes do not need the mass and strength of football players to block and tackle. Baseball players do not stand on a stage and flex one muscle group at a time like bodybuilders. The snatch and clean and jerk used in weightlifting do not represent the movements found on the field. Baseball players need to be flexible, but they do not have to contort their bodies like gymnasts. Nor do they have to possess the aerobic capacity to run a marathon or the fitness needed to swim to a beach, jump from an aircraft, infiltrate a hostile facility, or engage in hand-to-hand combat.

Baseball is a skill sport that does not require brute strength. Athletes must be able to start, stop, run, throw, catch, field, hit, pitch, jump, slide, and react to the actions of opposing players. Training programs should help athletes apply and use these skills during game and practice situations. Although strength is important for both performance and injury prevention, hitting, pitching, throwing, and running are power activities. Strength is important for maximum performance, but power is essential. Athletes need a total development program that produces an optimal level of strength, speed, agility, power, and conditioning to enhance individual and team skill training.

Training programs must also address the needs of specific positions. The needs of a starting pitcher, for example, are different from those of a relief pitcher, and a catcher has different needs than a middle infielder. Athlete needs will also vary depending on the time of year (off-season, preseason, in-season, or postseason).

To prepare effective individualized programs, the strength and conditioning professional needs to understand the specific goals of each athlete to appropriately manipulate the specific training principles and variables to address those goals. This chapter explains the training principles and variables of a resistance training program and the importance of manipulating them in an orderly and progressive manner to help players achieve specific results.

PRINCIPLES OF TRAINING: SPECIFICITY, OVERLOAD, AND PROGRESSION

Effective resistance training programs include specific training variables that can be manipulated from month to month, week to week, and workout to workout to achieve desired results. These variables include choice of exercise, order of exercise, frequency of exercise, volume of exercise, intensity of exercise, and length of rest periods between sets and between workouts. An overview of these variables is presented in the next section to design effective exercise programs and set realistic, attainable training goals.

Specificity Principle

The **specificity** principle dictates that you get what you train for. In resistance training program design, this means selecting specific exercises to elicit specific results. In exercise science texts, the specificity principle is represented by the acronym **SAID**—specific adaptations to imposed demands—and most indicate that adaptations to resistance training are specific to the muscles trained, intensity of exercise performed, and joint angles trained (10). The SAID principle involves more than just doing work, however—for maximum results, the work has to have a specific purpose that relates to the movements and demands of the sport (i.e., it must have carryover value) (9).

Although baseball is a highly skilled sport and most of the movements performed on the field cannot be duplicated in the weight room, there are a variety of exercises that can be used to match specific movement patterns, either whole or in part. Training the body in movement patterns (or parts of movement patterns) similar to those involved in game and practice situations at similar velocities and through similar ranges of motion can help improve strength, speed, power, stability, and durability and help athletes transfer the gains made in the weight room to the baseball diamond.

Overload Principle

For training adaptations to occur, the muscles must experience **overload** (i.e., an exercise stimulus at a level above that to which they are normally accustomed) (10). If, for example, an athlete whose goal is to increase strength can perform 6 to 8 repetitions of the back or front squat with a given amount of weight, the strength and conditioning professional should prescribe a resistance that the athlete can lift at least 6 times and no more than 8 times. If the athlete is prescribed a resistance he can lift 10 to 12 times, the resistance may be too light to provide an effective stimulus for adaptation, and the athlete will not achieve his goal. To achieve adaptation and growth, the athlete's musculoskeletal system must be trained at an intensity that will stimulate the needed physiological adjustments. Overload can be achieved by manipulating the variables of intensity, volume, and frequency of training. It is important to note that, although overload is the foundation of the training process, a strength and conditioning professional should not increase more than one of these variables at a time. A well-designed resistance training program will help ensure that progressive adaptations in strength and power are achieved throughout the training phase and year.

Progression Principle

The principle of **progression** asserts that athletes must progressively or gradually increase the workload for improvement to continue. If the goal is to improve local muscular endurance, the athlete must progressively increase the number of repetitions (volume) for a given workload. If the goal is to increase strength or power, the athlete must progressively increase the resistance (intensity) or movement velocity for a given number of repetitions. For a training program to produce consistently higher levels of strength and power, the intensity of the training program must be progressively increased. If an athlete fails to progressively overload the musculoskeletal system, the body will cease to perceive an overload and strength and power gains will plateau. To see good training results from phase to phase and season to season, the principle of progressive overload must be a primary principle in program design.

TRAINING PROGRAM VARIABLES

In addition to specificity, progression, and overload, strength and conditioning professionals must consider exercise selection, training frequency, exercise order, volume, intensity, and rest periods. If the training program addresses all these variables and is well designed for the athlete based on the training phase, the training level, and the position, the athlete should become stronger and more powerful.

Exercise Selection

Exercise selection is based on the specific movements and muscle actions that need to be trained and developed. It is also influenced by the training age of the athlete, available equipment and space, training objectives, and amount of training time available. To maximize the transfer from the weight room to the baseball diamond, strength and conditioning professionals should select exercises that improve general athleticism; incorporate the muscles, movements, and ranges of motion similar to those used in the sport; and improve strength and endurance of the muscles and joints that are frequently injured in baseball.

The NSCA divides exercises into three classifications: core, assistance (auxiliary), and special exercises (13). Classification is based on the amount of muscle mass involved in the exercise movement and how much the exercise contributes to the movements involved in each sport. Although the term "core" is often associated with the trunk, **core exercises** in the NSCA classification system are not trunk exercises; they are the primary or most important exercises in the training program (13). Core exercises involve larger muscle groups, two or more joints changing angles as the exercise is performed, and have direct application to the sport. The squat, bench press, and deadlift are examples of core exercises; that is, they involve large muscle groups, movement across multiple joints, and simulate some of the major movements used in many sports.

Core exercises can be subdivided into two types: structural and power exercises. **Structural exercises** load the spine directly or indirectly and stabilize posture during multi-joint movements in the weight room and on the field. The squat is a structural exercise that loads the spine directly and stabilizes the posture, and the deadlift is an example of a structural exercise that loads the spine indirectly and stabilizes the posture. **Power exercises** are structural exercises that are performed explosively, such as the Olympic lifts (i.e., the snatch and the clean and jerk) and their related movements (e.g., push press, hang clean, power clean, trap bar jump); see chapter 5 for descriptions of these exercises.

Assistance exercises, sometimes called *auxiliary exercises*, involve fewer muscle groups and less muscle mass. Single-joint exercises such as the leg extension, biceps curl, and triceps extension are examples of assistance exercises. Assistance exercises are less important for improving sports performance.

Special exercises are designed to increase strength and muscular endurance in smaller muscle groups that isolate and stabilize joints and reduce the risk of injury. Thrower's 10 and Y, T, I, and W exercises for the rotator cuff, scapula stabilization exercises, T-spine rotations, and wrist and forearm exercises are examples of special exercises; other examples can be found in chapter 7.

Baseball is a game of acceleration, speed, power, and muscular endurance. Programs should consist primarily of multi-joint, core, power, and plyometric exercises designed to maximize strength and power with a blend of single-joint assistance exercises to assist the movements in the core exercises and improve muscular endurance. A select number of special exercises designed to improve joint stabilization, improve muscular coordination, and reduce the risk of injury should also be included.

Training Frequency

Training frequency refers to the number of training sessions per week. Frequency will vary depending on the training goals, training background of the athlete, sport season, training load, type of training, and any other types of training that the athlete is engaged in (13). The first phase of the training year for baseball is usually the off-season (other sports may consider the postseason as the first training phase), which is designed to establish a sound training base. This is usually achieved through total body workouts with higher volume and lower intensities. Because low-intensity training is easier to recover from, the training frequency can be higher—up to three to four times per week when training the same muscle groups.

As athletes move into the later stages of the off-season training phase, the goal shifts from building a solid training base to increasing maximum or near-maximum strength. Increases in maximum strength are achieved with higher-intensity, lower-volume work, which requires more recovery. Because of the need for additional recovery between workouts, the schedule will shift to either a four-day split in which athletes train the upper and lower body separately two times per week, or a four-day push-pull split.

The goal of the preseason shifts from maximum strength to maximum power; the training frequency will be reduced to two to three times per week to allow adequate recovery between training sessions that are very high in intensity and very low in volume. During the competitive season, the goal for most athletes is to maintain the strength, endurance, and power developed in the previous training phases while allowing enough time to adequately recover from the stresses of competition, travel, and training. Training frequency will decrease to two to three days per week during the in-season, depending on the athlete's training background, needs, and goals; volume and intensity of the workouts; travel schedule; and availability of training equipment, facilities, and time.

Training programs must be individualized during all phases, especially the competitive season. Younger athletes with less training and game experience may not be able to recover adequately if in-season training sessions are too frequent. Likewise, older athletes, especially those with a history of injury or who play daily, might also need to train less frequently during the competitive season.

Finally, stress is cumulative. Athletes who perform other forms of exercise—aerobic training, anaerobic training, speed, agility, plyometrics, and sport skills—will experience more total body stress and therefore the frequency of training may need to be reduced.

Exercise Order

The **order** or *sequence* in which exercises are performed is important (12, 13). The performance of one exercise can have a significant effect on the quality of the exercises that follow. Performing the triceps extension before the bench press, for example, can create fatigue in the triceps, and a fatigued muscle cannot produce as much force as a rested muscle. Because increases in strength and power are related to exercise intensity, pre-exhausting the triceps can result in less force production and less than optimal strength or power adaptation.

A strength and conditioning professional should use the concept of **priority training** when determining exercise order (13). In priority training, the athlete performs power exercises first, non-power core exercises second, assistance exercises third, and special exercises last. Power exercises are performed first because they require the highest level of speed, skill, coordination, technique, and concentration and are the most affected by fatigue, which can reduce speed, impair technique, and increase the risk of injury. Workouts should be organized so that power exercises are first to ensure that athletes are metabolically fresh and have enough energy to complete them with good form and give maximum effort.

If a workout does not include power exercises, the exercise order should be core (multi-joint) first, assistance (single-joint) second, and special exercises last. The athlete can also alternate upper and lower body or pushing and pulling exercises when they are performed in the same workout to ensure full recovery between exercises. When athletes alternate exercises, one muscle group rests while the other works, which increases workout **density** (i.e., the amount of work performed in a given time) and saves time.

Volume

Training **volume** can be expressed as either *repetition volume* (total number of repetitions performed) or *load volume* (sets × repetitions × load). Training volume is affected by training history and primary resistance training goals. Beginners (i.e., those who are not resistance-trained) usually cannot tolerate high volumes of work and should start with lower volume and gradually increase over time. Athletes with a longer history of resistance training can tolerate higher volumes of work.

Volume is affected by training goals and inversely related to intensity (13). As intensity increases, volume decreases and vice versa. High-volume, low-intensity workouts increase local muscular endurance. Low-volume, high-intensity workouts increase strength and power. During off-season workouts, when the goal is to increase local muscular endurance and build a solid fitness base, the volume is relatively high and the intensity is relatively low. As the athlete moves into the latter phases of the off-season and preseason, the focus shifts to improving maximum strength and power, workouts use heavier loads for fewer repetitions, and volume decreases.

High-volume work, regardless of whether it is performed in the weight room or on the field, creates fatigue; therefore coaches should monitor the volume of total work. Higher volumes of resistance training are, in general, prescribed in the early off-season to establish a sound base when skill work is minimal. During the preseason, volume is reduced to accommodate the increased emphasis on skill work and higher-intensity resistance training. During spring training and in-season training, the primary focus is on skill work and volume is just high enough to maintain the improvements made in previous training phases.

Intensity

Training **intensity** generally indicates the quality of the work performed (i.e., how hard an athlete is working). In the weight room, it refers to the weight, or **load**, lifted and is typically expressed as a percentage of the **one repetition maximum** (or **1RM**; the most weight an athlete can lift in a certain exercise for one repetition) or as a **repetition maximum** (or **RM**; the maximum number of repetitions that can be performed in a particular exercise with a given amount of weight). A **repetition** is the number of times an exercise is performed before the **set** ends and the subsequent rest period begins. If, for example, an athlete can squat 225 pounds (102 kg) 5 times with perfect form and is unable to perform another repetition, his 5RM is 225 pounds (102 kg). Although either the percent of the 1RM method or the repetition maximum method can be used to assign specific training intensities for a given exercise, professional (and some collegiate) baseball coaches may not want to accept the risk–reward ratio associated with 1RM testing. Fortunately, there are resources coaches and athletes can consult to accurately estimate training loads up to a 10RM (5, 13). Also, refer to the 1RM and multiple-RM testing protocols beginning on page 34 in chapter 3.

Repetitions and load have an inverse relationship, as do force and velocity. As load (i.e., the force needed to move the load) increases, the number of repetitions that an athlete can perform decreases, as does the velocity of movement; the load simply becomes too heavy to be able to move it quickly. Stated another way, maximum force production (peak force) occurs at very slow speeds. Alternatively, lighter loads can be lifted for a relatively high number of repetitions and, because they are lighter, they allow the athlete to perform the exercise with greater velocity. When the goal is peak power, the interdependence of force and velocity requires a compromise in maximal force and velocity (6) to yield an optimal load. See figure 4.1 for a visual repre-

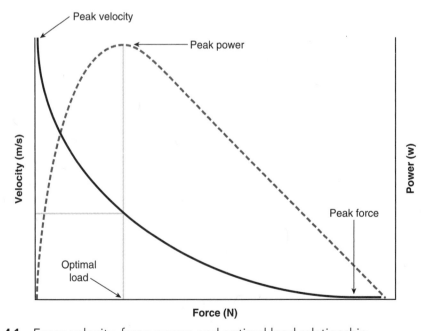

Figure 4.1 Force-velocity, force-power, and optimal load relationship.

Reprinted by permission from G.G. Haff and S. Nimphius, "Training Principles for Power," *Strength and Conditioning Journal* 34, no 6 (2012): 2-12.

sentation of these relationships. Ultimately, the end goal for those who train baseball players is to increase power.

The RM and the percent of 1RM are related to training goals. If the goal is to increase local muscular endurance, the RM prescribed is relatively high—12 or more repetitions with up to 67% of the 1RM; if the goal is hypertrophy (increased muscular size), a wide range can be used (i.e., 6-12RM; 67%-85% of the 1RM); and when training for strength, the RM is typically 6 or fewer using 85% of the 1RM or greater (13). The key to achieving maximum results is to determine and use the right load for the desired result. Ultimately, the baseball player's training should focus on developing power during the preseason and maintaining it during the in-season.

To achieve the desired force generation, strength and conditioning professionals can use various percent of 1RM ranges to elicit the appropriate response. Figure 4.2 displays percent 1RM ranges for five specific training zones (15). For example, to train an athlete for peak power, an intensity range of 30% to 80% of the 1RM should be assigned.

Rest Period

The rest period between exercises, sets, and training sessions determines the extent of recovery. The stimulus for muscle groups occurs during workouts, but adaptation occurs during recovery. Therefore, work and rest are both important, and neither is beneficial without the other. Work without adequate rest can lead to chronic fatigue and an increased risk of an overuse injury. Adequate rest without adequate work will not provide the consistent and progressive stress needed to stimulate muscle growth.

The amount of rest needed during workouts is related to the training goals of the workout (13). When the goal is to improve local muscular endurance and the loads are light and the volume is relatively high, most athletes can recover in 30 seconds or less. As the intensity of exercise increases and the training goal becomes hypertrophy, strength, or power, the length of the recovery period increases. Athletes need 30 to 90 seconds of recovery when training for hypertrophy and 2 to 5 minutes when training for strength and power. Table 4.1 displays the various rest periods for the respective training goals (13).

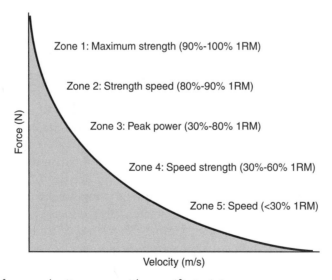

Figure 4.2 A force-velocity curve with specific training zones.

Adapted from Unholz. www.trainwithpush.com/blog/want-to-get-the-most-out-of-your-training-get-ahead-of-the-curve-the-force-velocity-curve-that-is.

Table 4.1 Rest Period Length Assignments Based on the Training Goal

Training goal	Rest period length
Strength	2-5 min

Power
  Single-effort event
  Multiple-effort event
	2-5 min

Hypertrophy	30 sec to 1.5 min
Muscular endurance	<30 sec

Reprinted by permission from J.M. Sheppard and N.T. Triplett, "Program Design for Resistance Training," in *Essentials of Strength Training and Conditioning,* 4th ed., edited by G.G. Haff and N.T. Triplett (Champaign, IL: Human Kinetics, 2016), 439-470.

Most athletes need approximately 48 hours of rest between workouts of the same muscle groups. Workouts that emphasize multi-joint exercises performed with high intensity tend to require longer rest periods similar to those seen in split workouts.

SPORT-SPECIFIC GOALS OF A RESISTANCE TRAINING PROGRAM

As discussed in chapter 2, baseball has two components: the actual game-play situations, which are a sprint, and the games, which are a marathon. Most plays are over in three to five seconds, but games can last three to five hours and the season is anywhere from 25 to 162 (or more) games, depending on the level of play. The key to effective, injury-free performance is to first develop a sound fitness base and then prepare the athlete to generate the speed and power needed in game situations on a daily or near-daily basis.

Training athletes is a year-round process that addresses all aspects of performance, but not all at once. There is no need to train for acceleration, speed, and power in October when it will not be needed until March or April. These are advanced movement qualities that are best developed after athletes have developed a solid fitness base. Likewise, there is no need to perform base training during the season when the game requires quick acceleration, fast speed, and explosive power.

The key is to develop the physical and physiological aspects required for optimal performance when they are needed and when the athlete is prepared to handle the training loads and volumes required to elicit the desired results. Most coaches use some form of **periodization training**, sometimes called *planned performance training*, to achieve these objectives (8). The goal is to get what you need for optimal, safe performance when you need it.

One application of the periodization model divides the baseball training year into five separate, interactive training phases (not to be confused with or replace the four sport seasons). The phases are progressive—each is more difficult and sport-specific than the previous phase and each includes specific training and performance objectives. The first phase is "active rest." It starts after the last game of the season and involves three to four weeks of rest to give the body and mind time to relax, repair, and recover from the daily stresses of practice, training, and competition. There are no formal workouts during this phase, but athletes are encouraged to remain active enough to avoid losing the gains attained during the previous training year and season. The second phase, called the "train to train" phase, is the first part of the off-season, during which the athlete establishes general fitness and local muscular endurance. Resistance work consists of high-volume, low-intensity general fitness training for the entire body. The third phase, "train to compete," occurs in the second half of the off-season and includes more sport-specific movements with higher loads and less volume to increase strength. The fourth phase occurs in February and March, which is spring training for professional athletes and preseason for high school and college athletes (7). This is the "train to play" phase. The volume of resistance training work decreases and the focus turns to the skill work needed for optimal performance in game situations. Intensity is increased to maintain maximum strength and optimize power development. The last phase, the in-season or "train to win" phase, is the longest phase of the training year. Intensity is high, volume is low, and frequency is reduced. The goal is to maintain the strength and power developed in the previous phases without increasing the risk of chronic fatigue, overtraining, or injury.

As mentioned in chapter 1, there are different types of periodization models that have been successfully used to achieve peak performance in the weight room. The traditional model uses a program that prescribes the same number of sets and repetitions across successive training sessions within a microcycle, with gradual and progressive mesocycle increases in intensity over time (5). The undulating model is a more varied model that uses variations in intensity and training focus within a microcycle (5). Coaches should use the scheduling information they have available to determine when and how long periodization phases can be structured for individual athletes.

POSITION-SPECIFIC EXERCISE SELECTION

Before a strength and conditioning professional can design a program, it is important to perform a needs assessment of both the athlete and the sport. When assessing the athlete, start by examining the athlete's medical records, including any history of injuries, and then evaluate the athlete's training background and exercise history to better understand his technical ability in the weight room and capacity for training. Finally, the appropriate anthropometric and performance tests should be administered to determine the athlete's strengths and weaknesses and identify needs and training goals (see chapter 3).

When evaluating the sport, the strength and conditioning professional should identify the primary movements, physiological demands, energy system requirements, and types and fre-

Courtesy of The Cincinnati Reds.

Resistance training exercises should be selected based on the primary movements of the sport and the specific demands of a player's position.

quency of injury associated with the sport. Identifying common injuries associated with the sport will help determine which exercises should produce positive adaptations as well as those that are contraindicated for an individual athlete or for athletes participating in the sport as a whole.

Although resistance training can provide numerous benefits to baseball players, not all exercises are appropriate. There are members of the medical staff and strength and conditioning professionals in professional and collegiate baseball, for example, do not support the general incorporation of Olympic lifts (i.e., the snatch and the clean and jerk), power cleans, and overhead exercises in baseball (3, 4, 14).

The opposition to Olympic lifts is attributable to their technical nature and the plane of movement through which they are performed (5). These exercises are highly technical and require excellent instruction and a thorough training background to safely perform them, which are not available to most baseball players. The time needed to learn how to perform Olympic lifts with perfect technique could be better spent developing skills needed to improve performance in game situations. Olympic lifts are also performed in only one plane (sagittal); whereas successful baseball players must be explosive in multiple planes of motion.

Similar concerns are often expressed for the power clean, another single-plane exercise (14). Although triple extension is important for power production, the technical nature and lack of previous training among many athletes can lead to faulty technique that can increase the stress and risk of injury to the back, shoulder, and wrist. The stress on the wrists of baseball players is particularly high, especially at the highest levels. Athletes take thousands of swings and make thousands of throws during the season, and are constantly at risk of catching a hand on the ground during a slide or jamming a wrist into the bag. The catch phase of Olympic and power clean exercises can add more stress to an essential part of the body that is already under constant stress due to the nature of the game. The potential for error in these exercises, especially among inexperienced athletes, is high and other safer exercises can be performed explosively to achieve the same outcomes. Triple extension and explosive power, for example, can be safely developed with plyometric jumps, medicine ball throws, sprints, and sled pushes.

Some have advocated substituting high pulls, jump shrugs, and midthigh pulls as substitutes for the power clean as a means of protecting the wrists, elbow, and shoulder joints (14). These alternatives, however, do not entirely eliminate the aforementioned concerns and can produce problems of their own. Overhead athletes need good upper rotation of the scapula on the thoracic spine/rib cage to allow the glenohumeral shoulder joint to function properly and achieve good humeral head–glenoid alignment to allow the rotator cuff muscles to center the humeral head for repeated throws (2). If one of the muscles of the posterior shoulder is overactive, it can inhibit the surrounding muscles and alter scapular kinematics. The recommended substitute exercises can lead to the overdevelopment and shortening of the upper trapezius muscle, which in turn can limit scapular upward rotation and create compensatory scapular elevation, altering shoulder kinematics and increasing the risk of injury.

Another area of concern among medical personnel and strength and conditioning professionals is the use of overhead exercises. Research indicates that many baseball athletes are predisposed to poor range of motion and stability in the shoulder, and loading an overhead position can put an athlete in a vulnerable position (3). As a result, overhead exercises can be considered as high risk, low reward movements.

When prescribing exercises, strength and conditioning professionals must understand the main goals of resistance training in baseball. The ability to snatch or overhead press a large amount of weight is not the goal. Improving stability, strength, power, and durability is paramount. Coaches need to be aware of the minimal time dedicated to resistance training during the competitive season, the time required for training adaptations to occur, and the risk–reward ratio of certain exercises and positions.

Every resistance training program will have its core exercises, and each position will need specific exercises to help maximize individual training outcomes. Exercises should be selected based on the needs of the athlete, movement patterns of the sport and position, and potential for injuries within the sport and for specific positions. There are no *required* exercises in any sport, including baseball. Strength and conditioning professionals need to select exercises that provide the most bang for the buck—that is, those that help produce optimal performance on the field day after day and minimize the risk of injury. The recommended core exercises and their variations include the following:

Total body

- Trap bar jump
- Landmine row to rotational press
- Landmine lunge to press
- Two-arm kettlebell swing
- Various medicine ball throws
- Battle rope slam
- Turkish get-up
- Bear crawl

Lower body

- Barbell back and front squat. These core exercises may include the following variations:

  - Back squat with bands or chains
  - Goblet squat (dumbbell or kettlebell)
  - Body weight squat (weight vest can be added)
  - Safety bar squat

Courtesy of The Cincinnati Reds.

Pitchers move through multiple planes of motion so they benefit from exercises that are also multi-planar.

- Deadlift. The conventional straight bar deadlift is the most common variation of the deadlift, but it can include the following variations:
  - Trap bar deadlift
  - Kettlebell deadlift
  - Band deadlift

- Romanian deadlift (RDL). The RDL is an excellent exercise to engage the hamstrings, gluteus maximus, and erector spinae (low back) muscles. Though traditionally performed with a barbell, this exercise may include the following variations:
  - Dumbbell RDL
  - Single-leg RDL with a dumbbell or kettlebell

- Nordic hamstring curl. This movement is a knee dominant and eccentrically dominant exercise for the hamstrings. Including this exercise in a resistance training program has been shown to decrease hamstring injury risk (11). Variations to the Nordic hamstring exercise to include more concentric force production can include the following:
  - Glute-hamstring raise
  - Barbell hip thrust

- Stability ball leg curl
- Leg curl
- Double-leg and single-leg bridge

Upper Body

- Pulls. These exercises focus on the posterior musculature of the upper body. When prescribing these exercises, it is important to include training in both a vertical and horizontal plane.
  - Vertical plane variations include the following exercises:
    - Chin-up or pull-up
    - Lat pulldown
    - Half-kneeling cable high row
  - Horizontal plane variations include the following exercises:
    - One-arm dumbbell or kettlebell row
    - Bent-over row
    - Pendlay row
    - Seated row
    - Inverted row
    - Face pull
    - Cable or band row
- Presses. These exercises focus primarily on the anterior musculature of the upper body. Although these exercises can be performed with variation in the position of the upper arm, provocative positions should be avoided in athletes that lack sufficient range of motion, particularly in ranges that approach overhead, as previously discussed. Variations to the pressing movements include the following exercises:
  - Dumbbell and barbell bench press (flat or incline)
  - Push-up
  - Floor press
  - Landmine press variations
  - Band or cable press
- Grip. A high level of grip strength has been shown to be related to several performance variables, including throwing velocity and bat speed (1). Variations of grip strength exercises include the following:
  - Wrist flexion and extension
  - Wrist ulnar and radial deviation
  - Forearm pronation and supination
  - Rice bucket exercises
  - Wrist rollers
  - Farmer's walk

Although all athletes need a sound, effective, and comprehensive resistance training program, the approach can differ between athletes at different positions and between those at similar positions who have different needs and goals. As previously stated, the core exercises and their variations should be based on a needs analysis of the athlete, sport, and specific position on the

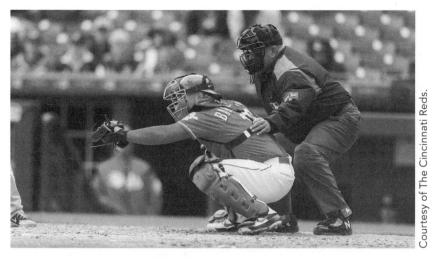

Courtesy of The Cincinnati Reds.

The deep squatting position that catchers have to handle for long durations require an exceptional level of ankle and hip mobility.

field. A discussion of the specific needs of each position is presented below. Sample workouts for each training phase of the season are presented in chapters 9 through 12.

Pitchers (Starter, Middle Relief, Setup, and Closer)

The movements involved in pitching occur primarily in the frontal and transverse planes. In addition to the core resistance training exercises outlined for all athletes, there are variations that are specific to the pitching delivery. Single-leg balance, strength, and stability in a lunge pattern are essential for providing a base from which to transfer power from the ground up through the trunk, shoulder, arm, wrist, and fingers. Resistance training exercises that help pitchers improve the ability to transfer force and power from the ground throughout the kinetic chain include the step-up, single-leg squat, single-leg RDL, lateral and forward lunge variations, balance training on the drive and landing leg, rotational medicine ball throw, and thoracic spine mobility to help increase hip and shoulder separation. The ability to stabilize and protect the elbow and shoulder during repeated throwing is also essential. Variations of exercises designed to stabilize the scapula and strengthen the muscles of the rotator cuff are also essential in a comprehensive resistance training program for a pitcher.

Catchers

Catchers have a unique set of requirements because most of their time on the field is spent in an isometric squatting position. A major requirement for their success is the ability to produce sufficient ankle and hip mobility to position the body into catching-specific positions. Resistance training exercises that are unique to the position of catcher are the seated and standing calf raise, back squat with wide foot position, and lateral squat. Other exercises, not presented in this book, are the groin squeeze at various angles and hip abduction (monster walks, clamshells).

Infielders

Each infield position requires a different skill set. The corner infielders (first and third base) are closer to home plate, which makes reactionary explosiveness an important trait. Having the ability to reach and quickly move laterally to a batted ball will improve their success on

Tom Pennington/Getty Images

Explosive lateral and diagonal movements, coupled with short reaction times, are a hallmark of infielders.

the field. Corner infielders are also generally expected to hit for power and are often placed in the middle of the batting order, where run production is vital.

The middle infielders (second base and shortstop) must also be able to react quickly and explosively move in lateral and diagonal patterns on the field. Middle infielders, in general, need to be more athletic than corner infielders because they have more ground to cover. They must be able to field the ball, start, stop, set their feet, and position the body to make quick, accurate throws to first base.

All infielders need exercises that improve agility, lateral lower body strength, and power. Resistance training exercises that can help them achieve these needs are lateral lunges, crossover step-ups, and lateral step-ups. Other exercises, not presented in this book, are the band-resisted lateral monster walk, cable-resisted lateral shuffle, and skater jump.

Outfielders

Outfielders, in general, need speed on both offense and defense. The ability to react quickly, accelerate, and achieve maximum or near-maximum speed quickly are essential needs for outfielders. Reactive lower body power exercises are essential for outfielders. In addition to the core exercises, the outfield positions require more ballistic and explosive movement patterns to improve rate of force development. Specific resistance training exercises for outfielders are the forward lunge, step-up, step-up with leg lift, and single-leg squat. Other exercises, not presented in this book, are the hill sprint, standing long jump, lateral bound, resisted sprint, and sled pull.

CONCLUSION

When designing strength programs for baseball players, a strength and conditioning professional must consider the many factors that can influence performance. It is important to have a thorough understanding of the principles of resistance training and the personal and positional needs of each athlete and the sport. The information provided in this chapter can be used to design resistance training programs that will help improve strength, speed, and power in the weight room that will ultimately improve performance and reduce the risk of injury on the field.

PART II

EXERCISE TECHNIQUE

5

TOTAL BODY EXERCISE TECHNIQUE

JAY DAWES

Whether swinging a bat, throwing a ball, stealing a base, or jumping to catch a line drive, the ability to coordinate the upper and lower body to produce explosive movements is essential to most skills in baseball (1, 3-5). For these reasons, developing both power and coordinative abilities is critical to optimize on-field performance (1, 6). Total body resistance exercises can be used to help develop these specific attributes (1-6). Similar to most baseball skills, these exercises require a sequencing of movements that transfer forces from the ground through each joint segment (i.e., legs, trunk, and upper extremities) to produce efficient and effective movements (6). Indeed, strength and conditioning professionals should consider using total body conditioning exercises in their programming to create synergistic linkages between joint segments, develop explosive power, and effectively transfer training in the weight room to success on the diamond (1, 2, 4). The purpose of this chapter is to discuss a variety of total body exercises aimed at improving these attributes and provide detailed instructions on how to perform these exercises.

Most of the total body exercises in this chapter emphasize triple extension and triple flexion of the ankles, knees, and hips to both produce and absorb force (5). These types of exercises have a high level of correspondence to many activities required by baseball athletes (i.e., sprinting, jumping, sliding, diving) (1, 5). In many athletic conditioning programs, Olympic lifts are emphasized for total body conditioning and power (1, 2, 5). However, these exercises are often considered controversial for overhead throwing athletes because they may increase injury risk due to greater levels of stress placed on the shoulders and wrists (5). For these reasons, weightlifting derivatives and ballistic exercises may be a more appropriate substitute for the full Olympic lifts in this population (2, 5). These exercises were selected based on their ability to preferentially recruit larger motor units, produce high motor unit firing frequencies, and improve muscular coordination (4, 7).

Furthermore, several exercises in this chapter, such as the Turkish get-up and crawling variations, are not considered "explosive" in nature but have been included to help develop general coordinative abilities and fundamental movement patterns. These exercises focus on developing trunk stability during dynamic movement patterns, as well as good body awareness and orientation. These attributes may not only be important for improving performance, but also reducing an athlete's injury potential.

Exercise Finder

POWER CLEAN

Primary Muscles Trained

Gluteus maximus, biceps femoris, semitendinosus, semimembranosus, vastus lateralis, vastus intermedius, vastus medialis, rectus femoris, soleus, gastrocnemius, deltoids, trapezius

Beginning Position

- Begin with the feet approximately hip-width apart and turned slightly outward.
- Flex the ankles, knees, and hips and grasp the barbell using a pronated (i.e., overhand) grip, simultaneously bracing the trunk, elevating the chest, and pulling the shoulder blades down and together.
- Evenly distribute the majority of the body weight between the big toe, little toe, and heel.

Movement Phases

1. Keeping the back flat, arms straight, and bar close to the body (a), lift the barbell to midthigh level by extending the hips and knees. The shoulders and hips should rise at the same speed (b).

2. While keeping the arms straight (c), rapidly extend the ankles, knees, and hips (i.e., triple extension) and explosively shrug the shoulders (d).

3. Keeping the bar close to the torso, pull the barbell to approximately sternum height.

4. When the bar reaches sternum height, flex the ankles, knees, and hips and drop to a quarter-squat position.

5. While keeping the torso upright and braced, rotate the wrists under the bar and drive the elbows upward in front of the body until the upper arms are parallel to the floor.

Figure 5.1 Power clean: (a) beginning position; (b) lift barbell off the floor; (c) lift barbell above the knees; (d) extend the ankles, knees, and hips and shrug the shoulders; (e) catch; (f) end position.

6. Receive or "catch" the barbell across the front of the shoulders by allowing the fists to open and the barbell to roll into the fingertips (e).

7. Stand up straight (f) and return the barbell to the beginning position.

Breathing Guidelines

Inhale just prior to lifting the barbell from the floor and hold the breath during the exercise. Exhale once the barbell has been caught across the deltoids.

Exercise Modifications and Variations

One-Arm Dumbbell Clean

Begin by assuming a hip-width stance with a dumbbell or kettlebell positioned between the feet. Using a pronated grip, grasp the dumbbell or kettlebell with one hand. In one smooth motion, clean the dumbbell or kettlebell from the floor and catch it on the working side shoulder in a neutral grip position.

Hang Clean

This exercise is performed in the same manner as the power clean, except the exercise will begin with the barbell positioned just above or just below the knees.

Jump Shrug

To perform this exercise, forcefully extend the hips and knees until the bar reaches the midthigh, then explosively shrug the shoulders and extend the ankles. Jump as high as possible and land in an athletic stance with the feet approximately hip- to shoulder-width apart.

Note that after triple extension has been achieved, the athlete may choose to drop the bar to reduce stress on the shoulders and elbows.

Midthigh Clean Pull

Begin with the barbell across the midthighs. Explosively shrug the shoulders and extend the ankles. On the descent, flex the ankles, knees, and hips, and return the barbell to the beginning position.

Note that after triple extension has been achieved, the athlete may choose to drop the bar to reduce stress on the shoulders and elbows.

Coaching Tips

- Pop the hips and violently shrug the shoulders.
- Pull the body under the bar.
- Drive the elbows toward the sky.
- Be explosive.

PUSH PRESS

Primary Muscles Trained

Gluteus maximus, biceps femoris, semitendinosus, semimembranosus, vastus lateralis, vastus intermedius, vastus medialis, rectus femoris, soleus, gastrocnemius, deltoids, trapezius

Beginning Position

- Begin by holding a barbell at shoulder height in the rack position (a) (i.e., barbell resting on the anterior deltoids, bar in the fingertips, and upper arms parallel to the floor).

Movement Phases

1. While keeping the bar across the anterior deltoids, perform a rapid quarter squat (the controlled dip) by flexing the hips, knees, and ankles (b).

Figure 5.2 Push press: (a) beginning position; (b) controlled dip; (c) upward drive; (d) press overhead.

2. Once this position is achieved, quickly extend the hips, knees, and ankles to generate enough force so that the barbell leaves the anterior deltoids (the drive) *(c)*.

3. Because the drive is not forceful enough to move the bar to its final overhead position, finish the upward movement phase by pressing the bar up until the elbows are fully extended *(d)*.

4. Lower the barbell back to the beginning position in a controlled manner. Allow the arms to flex and perform a quarter squat to help cushion the receipt of the bar.

Breathing Guidelines

Inhale just prior to performing the quarter squat and exhale after the barbell is overhead. Inhale prior to the weight being lowered and exhale once the bar is racked in the beginning position across the anterior deltoids.

Exercise Modifications and Variations

Dumbbell Push Press

Begin by holding a dumbbell on each deltoid using a neutral grip. Perform the push press exercise as previously discussed. At the end of this movement, the dumbbells should be directly over each shoulder with the wrists in either a neutral or pronated position.

Coaching Tips

- Dip the hips and drive the barbell overhead (i.e., "dip and drive").
- Focus on "punching" the weight upward.
- Maintain a neutral spinal position and brace the trunk.
- When returning the weight to the deltoids, absorb the force to cushion the impact (similar to catching a ball).
- Be explosive.

PUSH JERK

Primary Muscles Trained

Gluteus maximus, biceps femoris, semitendinosus, semimembranosus, vastus lateralis, vastus intermedius, vastus medialis, rectus femoris, soleus, gastrocnemius, deltoids, trapezius

Beginning Position

- Begin by holding a barbell at shoulder height in the rack position *(a)* (i.e., barbell resting on the anterior deltoids, bar in the fingertips, and upper arms parallel to the floor).

Movement Phases

1. While keeping the bar across the anterior deltoids, perform a rapid quarter squat (the controlled dip) by flexing the hips, knees, and ankles *(b)*.

2. As rapidly as possible, extend the hips, knees, and ankles to generate enough force so that the barbell leaves the anterior deltoids (the drive; not seen in the figure 5.3).

3. As the barbell travels upward, drop back to a quarter-squat position and catch the bar overhead with the elbows fully extended *(c)*. The goal is to catch the bar at the same moment as it reaches its maximal height.

4. Fully stand up; in this position, the barbell should be directly overhead *(d)*.

5. Once this has been achieved, lower the barbell back to the beginning position in a controlled manner by allowing the arms to flex and performing a quarter squat to help cushion the receipt of the bar.

Figure 5.3   Push jerk: *(a)* beginning position; *(b)* controlled dip; drive (not shown); *(c)* catch; *(d)* end position.

Breathing Guidelines

Inhale just prior to performing the quarter squat, and exhale after the barbell is overhead.

Exercise Modifications and Variations

Dumbbell Push Jerk

This exercise should be performed in the same manner as the barbell push jerk, except the dumbbells will be positioned on each deltoid while using a neutral grip. At the end of this movement the dumbbells should be directly over each shoulder with the wrists in either a neutral or pronated position.

Coaching Tips

- Dip the hips and drive the weight overhead during the upward phase (i.e., "dip and drive").
- "Punch" the weight upward while simultaneously pushing the body under the barbell (or dumbbells).
- Be explosive.

TRAP BAR JUMP

Primary Muscles Trained

Gluteus maximus, biceps femoris, semitendinosus, semimembranosus, vastus lateralis, vastus intermedius, vastus medialis, rectus femoris, soleus, gastrocnemius, trapezius

Beginning Position

- Begin by standing in the center of a trap bar with the feet approximately hip-width apart and turned slightly outward.
- Flex the ankles, knees, and hips and grasp the trap bar handles using a neutral grip; simultaneously brace the trunk, elevate the chest, and pull the shoulder blades down and together (a).
- Evenly distribute the majority of the body weight between the big toe, little toe, and heel.

Movement Phases

1. Forcefully extend the hips and knees until the bar reaches the midthigh, then explosively shrug the shoulders and extend the ankles (b).

Figure 5.4 Trap bar jump: (a) beginning position; (b) explosive jump and shrug.

2. While maintaining good balance and body control, flex the ankles, knees, and hips and drop to a quarter-squat position.

3. Return the trap bar to the beginning position.

Breathing Guidelines

Inhale just prior to lifting the barbell to midthigh level and exhale once the barbell has been caught and is in the rack position.

Coaching Tips

- Pop the hips and violently shrug the shoulders.
- Be explosive.

MEDICINE BALL BLOB (BETWEEN LEGS OVER BACK) THROW

Primary Muscles Trained

Gluteus maximus, biceps femoris, semitendinosus, semimembranosus, vastus lateralis, vastus intermedius, vastus medialis, rectus femoris, soleus, gastrocnemius, posterior deltoid, anterior deltoid, erector spinae

Figure 5.5 Medicine ball BLOB (Between Legs Over Back) throw: *(a)* lift the medicine ball overhead; *(b)* lower medicine ball and squat; *(c)* jump and throw medicine ball backward.

Beginning Position

- While holding a medicine ball on the hips, stand with the arms straight and feet approximately shoulder-width apart.

Movement Phases

1. While keeping the arms straight, lift the medicine ball overhead (a).
2. Swing the medicine ball downward and between the legs to create a rapid counter-movement arm swing (b).
3. Continuing to keep the arms straight, perform a countermovement jump while explosively throwing the medicine ball overhead and backward as far as possible (c).

Breathing Guidelines

Inhale just before the downward phase of this movement and exhale upon release of the ball.

Exercise Modifications and Variations

Medicine Ball BLSU (Between Legs Straight Up) Throw

This exercise is performed in a similar manner to the BLOB throw except the medicine ball should be thrown straight up overhead as high as possible. Upon release of the ball, the athlete should step out of the way.

Coaching Tips

- Keep the arms straight throughout the duration of the exercise.
- Minimize the transition time between the downward phase of this action and the upward phase.

MEDICINE BALL SQUAT-TO-PRESS THROW

Primary Muscles Trained

Gluteus maximus, biceps femoris, semitendinosus, semimembranosus, vastus lateralis, vastus intermedius, vastus medialis, rectus femoris, soleus, gastrocnemius, anterior deltoid, pectoralis major, pectoralis minor, triceps brachii, erector spinae

Beginning Position

- Stand in an athletic position while holding a medicine ball at chest level (not seen in figure 5.6).

Movement Phases

1. While keeping the medicine ball at chest height, flex the hips, knees, and ankles into a squat (a).
2. When the thighs are parallel to the floor, simultaneously extend the hips, knees, and ankles and rapidly push the medicine ball out and upward at a 45-degree angle, releasing the ball (b).

Breathing Guidelines

Inhale just before the downward phase of this movement and exhale upon release of the ball.

Figure 5.6 Medicine ball squat-to-press throw: *(a)* squat; *(b)* throw.

Exercise Variations and Modifications

Medicine Ball Squat-to-Push Overhead

This exercise will be performed in the same manner as the medicine ball squat-to-press throw except the medicine ball will be released directly overhead. Once the ball is released the athlete should step out of the way.

Coaching Tips

- Minimize the transition time between the downward phase of this action and the upward phase.
- Release the ball quickly.

TWO-ARM KETTLEBELL SWING

Primary Muscles Trained

Gluteus maximus, biceps femoris, semitendinosus, semimembranosus, vastus lateralis, vastus intermedius, vastus medialis, rectus femoris

Beginning Position

- Assume a shoulder-width stance while holding the kettlebell in both hands *(a)*.

Figure 5.7   Two-arm kettlebell swing: (a) beginning position; (b) swing kettlebell backward; (c) swing kettlebell forward.

Movement Phases

1. While maintaining a slight flex in the knees and keeping the chest up and shoulder blades back and together, begin to flex and extend the hips using small amplitudes of movement.
2. Allow the kettlebell to swing back and forth.
3. Progressively increase the amplitude of movement until the kettlebell is between the legs in the down position (b) (similar to a Romanian deadlift) and at approximately shoulder height in the top position (c) (similar to a front raise).

Breathing Guidelines

Inhale on the downward portion of the movement, and exhale when the kettlebell reaches the highest position in the upward phase of the movement.

Coaching Tips

- Reach back and touch the buttocks with the kettlebell during the downward swing.
- Quickly transition between the lowest position of the swing and hip extension.
- Explosively extend the hips (i.e., pop the hips) to drive the kettlebell upward.
- Maintain a neutral spine throughout the movement.

LANDMINE ROW TO ROTATIONAL PRESS

Primary Muscles Trained

Gluteus maximus, biceps femoris, semitendinosus, semimembranosus, vastus lateralis, vastus intermedius, vastus medialis, rectus femoris, soleus, gastrocnemius, trapezius

Beginning Position

- Begin by standing perpendicular to a landmine.

- Flex the hips, knees, and ankles and grasp the end of the landmine in the hand closest to the anchor point (a).

Movement Phases

1. Extend the hips, knees, and ankles and lift the end of the landmine to approximately waist height (b). The hips and shoulders should raise simultaneously and at the same speed.

2. Once this position has been achieved, transition the landmine into the opposite hand and pivot on the back foot (c and d) while rotating the hips and fully extending the working arm at a 45-degree angle (e).

3. Once this has been accomplished, lower the weight back to the shoulder, switch hands, and return the weight to the beginning position.

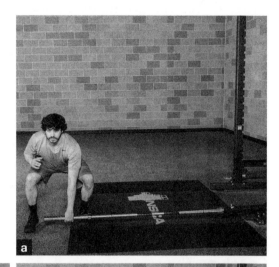

Figure 5.8   Landmine row to rotational press: (a) beginning squat position; (b) lift; (c) switch hands; (d) finish pivot; (e) finish extension.

Breathing Guidelines

Inhale prior to lifting the weight off the floor and exhale once the arm is fully extended after the pressing portion of the exercise.

Exercise Modifications and Variations

Landmine Reverse Lunge to Press

Assuming a hip-width stance, grasp the landmine in one hand using a neutral grip and place it on the right shoulder. Lunge backward on the right leg, return to the beginning position, and press the landmine away from the body at a 45-degree angle. Perform the desired number of repetitions and then switch sides.

Half-Kneeling Landmine Press

Assume a half-kneeling position with the right knee on the floor under the right hip and the left foot on the floor in front of the body, knee and hip flexed. Grasp the landmine with the right hand using a neutral grip and place it on the right shoulder. The left hand can be placed on the left hip or can be hanging to the side. Press the landmine away from the body at a 45-degree angle and then return it to the beginning position.

Coaching Tips

- "Squash the bug" on the back foot to rotate the hips.
- When lowering the weight to the shoulder, "absorb" the load (similar to catching a ball).

BATTLE ROPE SLAM

Primary Muscles Trained

Gluteus maximus, biceps femoris, semitendinosus, semimembranosus, vastus lateralis, vastus intermedius, vastus medialis, rectus femoris, soleus, gastrocnemius, posterior deltoid, anterior deltoid, erector spinae, rectus abdominus

Beginning Position

- Wrap the battle rope around a stationary object (e.g., squat rack, support pole).
- Grasp the handles of the rope with a neutral grip and face the attached end of the rope.
- Step forward and position each hand next to the outside of the hips.
- Place the feet hip- to shoulder-width apart, maintain a neutral spine position, and assume a quarter-squat position (not seen in figure 5.9).

Movement Phases

1. Extend the hips, knees, and ankles while simultaneously lifting the ropes overhead (a).
2. Forcefully slam the ropes downward, then return to the beginning position (b).

Breathing Guidelines

Inhale as the rope is lifted upward and exhale as it is slammed downward.

Exercise Modifications and Variations

Rather than rising to the balls of the feet, perform a vertical jump prior to slamming the rope downward.

Rotational Battle Rope Slam

As the rope is slammed downward, rotate the hips and pivot on the back foot (i.e., "squash the bug"), then slam the rope down to either the right or left side of the body.

Coaching Tip

Slam the ropes downward as hard as possible.

Figure 5.9 Battle rope slam: *(a)* lift the ropes; *(b)* slam the ropes downward.

TURKISH GET-UP

Primary Muscles Trained

Gluteus maximus, biceps femoris, semitendinosus, semimembranosus, vastus lateralis, vastus intermedius, vastus medialis, rectus femoris, soleus, gastrocnemius, posterior deltoid, anterior deltoid, erector spinae, rectus abdominus, internal and external obliques

Beginning Position

- Begin lying supine on the floor with a kettlebell next to the left shoulder.
- Using a pronated grip, grasp the kettlebell in the left hand.
- Flex the left hip and place the left foot flat on the floor.
- Lift the kettlebell to a position over the face with the left arm (elbow) extended.
- Place the right arm flat on the floor *(a)*.

Movement Phases

1. Begin this movement by pushing off the floor with the left foot while rotating the hips and torso so that the body is balanced on the right forearm and hip *(b)*.
2. Extend the right arm and put the right palm flat on the floor *(c)*.

3. Push off the left leg until the left knee is at a 90-degree flexed position, then lift the hips off the floor while balancing body weight between the right hand and left leg (d).

4. Continue holding the kettlebell overhead with the left hand and elbow extended, keeping the eyes focused on the kettlebell throughout the duration of the exercise.

Figure 5.10   Turkish get-up: (a) beginning position; (b) support on forearm; (c) support on hand; (d) extend hips; (e) move right leg back and kneel; (f) assume an erect single kneeling stance; (g) end position.

5. While keeping the left leg in the same position, sweep the right leg underneath and behind the body to place the right knee and foot on the floor (e).

6. Extend the right hip and lift the right hand off the floor while simultaneously bringing the torso to an upright neutral posture with the lower body in a lunge position (f).

7. Step forward with the right foot and stand, keeping the kettlebell directly over the left shoulder (g).

8. Maintain this position for a moment to demonstrate balance and control, then return to the beginning position using each step in this process in reverse chronological order.

Exercise Modifications and Variations

This exercise can be modified so that each stage of this movement may be considered an exercise. For example, an athlete can perform only step 1 of this movement with a hip lift (Turkish get-up to forearm with hip lift), steps 1 through 3 (Turkish get-up to hand with hip lift), or steps 1 through 5 (Turkish get-up to leg sweep). These variations can be performed for continuous repetitions or for timed holds. A dumbbell or handled medicine ball may also be used instead of a kettlebell.

Breathing Guidelines

Exhale during each active movement and inhale during each pause between movements. If this exercise is performed without pausing between movements, maintain a normal breathing rhythm throughout the exercise.

Coaching Tips

- When learning to perform this exercise, it is recommended that the athlete move through each stage of this movement, pausing between each stage as needed.

- Make certain the full foot is in contact with the floor between each movement to help ensure proper balance.

BEAR CRAWL

Primary Muscles Trained

Gluteus maximus, biceps femoris, semitendinosus, semimembranosus, vastus lateralis, vastus intermedius, vastus medialis, rectus femoris, soleus, gastrocnemius, posterior deltoid, anterior deltoid, erector spinae, rectus abdominus

Beginning Position

- Begin in a quadruped position on the floor with the hands placed directly under the shoulders, elbows extended, knees flexed at 90-degree angles and directly under the hips, and the spine neutral (a).

Movement Phases

1. Raise up the hips and lift the knees off the floor, maintaining a neutral spine while both hands and feet are in contact with the floor. The knees should be at a 90-degree angle (b).

2. Reach forward with the right hand while simultaneously stepping forward with the left foot simulating a crawling motion (c).

3. Once this has been accomplished, reach forward with the left hand while simultaneously stepping forward with the right foot (d).

4. Continue crawling forward for the desired number of repetitions or distance.

Breathing Guidelines

Exhale during each active movement and inhale during each pause between movements. If this exercise is performed without pausing between movements, maintain a normal breathing rhythm throughout the exercise.

Exercise Modifications and Variations

This exercise can also be performed moving laterally, backpedaling, or in a diagonal fashion.

Coaching Tips

- The arms and legs should always move in opposition (i.e., left hand/right foot, right hand/left foot).
- Brace the trunk throughout the duration of the exercise.
- Keep proper body position with short crawling movements while maintaining stability.

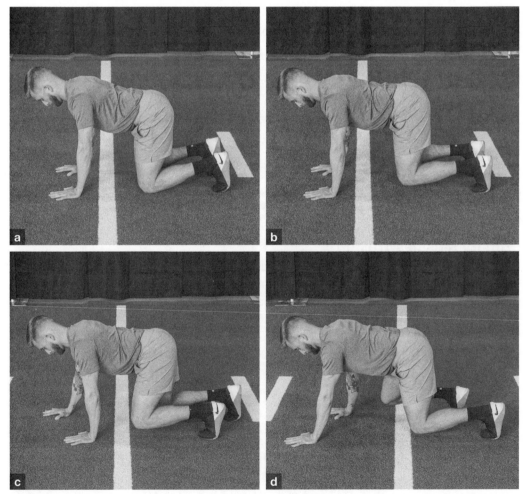

Figure 5.11 Bear crawl; (a) beginning position; (b) lift knees off the floor; (c) move right arm and left leg forward; (d) move left arm and right leg forward.

6

LOWER BODY EXERCISE TECHNIQUE

MATTHEW KRAUSE AND RIGO FEBLES

Baseball is a power sport. Increasing strength in the lower body will improve the ability to apply force through the muscles of the hip, thigh, and lower leg muscles. As the legs get stronger, the potential to improve the speed and power needed for optimal skill performance is enhanced.

Baseball requires more acquired skill than most other team sports. Hitting a baseball is among the most difficult skills in sports, giving athletes less than 0.4 second to decide to swing. Throwing a baseball as hard as possible between the letters and knees across a 17-inch (43 cm) home plate is not an easy task—and the faster the pitch, the harder the ball comes off the bat. The explosive reaction and change of direction required to field a baseball at 100 mph (161 km/h) or more requires an equally strong athletic foundation. Therefore, it is extremely important to resistance train the lower body when preparing to play baseball at any level. Strength is the base upon which all explosive movements and effective training protocols are built.

When resistance training the lower body, a baseball player should have two goals in mind: to improve on-field performance when running, throwing, swinging, and fielding, and to reduce the risk of volume overload injuries associated with all-out throws, powerful swings, and high-speed sprints that occur every day in all levels of baseball. Stronger athletes reduce the risk of developing overuse injuries that occur due to frequent game-play.

Athletes need to get stronger in three primary lower body exercises (back squat, front squat, and deadlift) in order reach their full athletic potential. The stronger the muscles, the more force that an athlete can apply into the ground to accelerate, decelerate, and change directions when pitching, hitting, fielding, and running the bases. The primary and secondary exercises described in this chapter will help athletes reach their full muscular potential and develop the movement efficiency and quality needed for skill acquisition.

Sometimes when strength development for baseball is addressed, the focus is primarily on upper body movements designed to improve pitching and hitting, especially in the shoulders and elbows. However, lower body strength is essential for improving the rotational movements involved in pitching and hitting. These forces are initiated in the lower body and then transferred through the anatomical core to the shoulders, arms, and hands, where they are applied to the bat and ball. The hamstrings and glutes, for example, are responsible for hip extension, a primary source of athletic power. The glutes are also essential to the lateral movements involved in daily game performance. These muscles are therefore extremely important for successful, injury-free performance. Training the muscles in the lower body will help maximize the ability to throw hard, hit for power, and run fast.

BREATHING GUIDELINES

Proper breathing while performing lower body exercises is important. When the diaphragm and the deep muscles of the anatomical core contract, pressure is generated within the abdominal cavity (3). This pressure creates a "fluid ball" that helps support the vertebral column during resistance training (1). This allows the body to maintain good posture and may significantly reduce both the forces required by the erector spinae muscles to perform an exercise and the associated compressive forces on the discs (1). The abdominal pressure created by proper breathing also aids in the transfer of force up and down the kinetic chain. As a rule of thumb, the athlete should inhale prior to or during the less strenuous portion of the movement (typically eccentric muscle action) and exhale during the most strenuous portion of the movement (typically the concentric muscle action). The transition from the eccentric portion to the concentric portion of the movement is when the athlete should begin to exhale. For example, during a lateral lunge, the athlete should inhale prior to or during the lowering of the body and begin to exhale while beginning the upward phase of the movement.

It is important to note that the Valsalva maneuver is not necessary for generation of intra-abdominal pressure (3). In the **Valsalva maneuver**, the glottis is closed, thus keeping air from leaving the lungs, and the muscles of the abdomen and rib cage contract, creating rigid compartments of liquid in the lower torso and air in the upper torso (3). An advantage of the Valsalva maneuver is that it increases the firmness of the entire torso, making it easier to support a heavy load, similar to what might occur when squatting (2). However, pressure in the chest associated with the Valsalva maneuver can put compressive force on the heart. This can make it more challenging for blood to return to the heart and also raise blood pressure—both undesirable side effects (2, 3). Therefore, it is recommended that athletes increase intra-abdominal pressure without using the Valsalva maneuver. This will keep the airway open while contracting the diaphragm and abdominal muscles.

Exercise Finder

BACK SQUAT

Primary Muscles Trained

Gluteus maximus, semimembranosus, semitendinosus, biceps femoris, vastus lateralis, vastus intermedius, vastus medialis, rectus femoris

Beginning Position

- Set the bar at shoulder height on a squat rack.
- Grip the bar at a comfortable width (slightly wider than shoulder width) and vertically align the body under the bar. The bar is positioned at the base of the posterior neck and top of the trapezius (a).
- Pack the chin (make a "double chin") to maintain the integrity of the cervical spine.
- Pull the bar down into the body to activate the latissimus dorsi and scapular stabilizers and maintain the integrity of the thoracic and lumbar spine.
- Push both feet through the floor to lift the bar off the rack (b) and take a step forward to position the body to execute the back squat (c). (Note: Ideally, the athlete steps back a step to get into position and then steps forward to re-rack the bar.)

- Position feet at a comfortable width (slightly wider than shoulder width), rotated out slightly.
- Begin all repetitions from this position.

Movement Phases

1. Brace the anatomical core and push hard into the floor.
2. Allow the hips, knees, and ankles to flex while the weight is being lowered. Heels remain in contact with the floor throughout the entire movement. The knees track in line with the angle of the feet. The torso and shin maintain a consistent angle throughout the entire movement.
3. Allow the weight to descend until the hips and knees are parallel to the floor (d).
4. Forcefully drive both feet into the floor while extending the hips, knees, and ankles to return to the beginning position (e).

Breathing Guidelines

Inhale prior to the downward portion of the movement. Exhale as the upward portion of the movement is initiated.

Spotting Guidelines

- Stand behind the athlete with feet shoulder-width apart and arms extended under the arms of the athlete.
- Squat down in rhythm with the athlete while maintaining arms close to the athlete's upper body.
- Support or push the athlete's upper body vertically to return to the beginning position if needed.

Exercise Modifications and Variations

Back Squat With Bands

This exercise can be modified to use bands as a form of variable resistance. Attach resistance bands to each side of the bar from fixed anchors (on the rack or dumbbells on the floor). Make sure to use the same band for each side of the bar. The pull of the bands should be in a vertical line from where the movement is being executed, not where the bar is set up. If the rack does not have an attachment site, place dumbbells on the floor on both sides of the bar. Make sure that the dumbbells are in line with where the squat would be performed. Anchor the band around the dumbbell and wrap the other end around the barbell. Do the same for the other side. The beginning position, movement guidelines, and breathing guidelines are the same. This is a modification to use with more trained athletes to challenge acceleration of the bar and proprioception.

Back Squat With Chains

This exercise can also be modified to use chains as a form of variable resistance. Load the bar with the prescribed weight. Attach the chains after the bar has been loaded. The beginning position, movement guidelines, and breathing guidelines are the same. This is a modification to use with more trained athletes to challenge acceleration of the bar and proprioception.

Safety Bar, Body Weight, Kettlebell, or Dumbbell Squat

The squat exercise can be performed with a safety bar, no resistance, or while using a kettlebell or dumbbell in a side hang, goblet, rack, or overhead position with one or two arms.

Coaching Tips

- Placement of the hands on the bar will depend on the athlete's shoulder mobility and comfort level. Adjust grip width as needed.
- Foot placement will also depend on the athlete's hip and ankle mobility. Place feet at a comfortable width that allows for proper form and execution.

Figure 6.1 Back squat: *(a)* position the body under the bar; *(b)* lift the bar from the rack; *(c)* step away from the rack; *(d)* bottom position; *(e)* top/end position.

FRONT SQUAT

Primary Muscles Trained

Gluteus maximus, semimembranosus, semitendinosus, biceps femoris, vastus lateralis, vastus intermedius, vastus medialis, rectus femoris

Beginning Position

- Set the bar at shoulder height on a squat rack.
- Step under the bar so that it rests across the front of the shoulders and clavicle, just below the neck.
- Position feet at a comfortable width (slightly wider than shoulder width), rotated out slightly.
- Grab the bar in a crossed-arm position. Flex the elbows and cross the arms in front of the chest. The fingers will hold the bar in place with the elbows positioned parallel to the floor.
- Pack the chin (make a "double chin") to maintain the integrity of the cervical spine and brace the core.
- Push both feet through the floor to lift the bar off the rack and take a step forward to position the body to execute the front squat. (Note: Ideally, the athlete steps back a step to get into position and then steps forward to re-rack the bar.)
- Begin all repetitions from this position (a).

Movement Phases

1. Allow the hips, knees, and ankles to flex while the weight is being lowered. Heels remain in contact with the floor throughout the entire movement. The knees track in line with the angle of the feet. The torso will have a consistent upright angle throughout the entire movement.
2. Allow the weight to descend until the hips and knees are parallel to the floor (b).
3. Forcefully drive both feet into the floor while extending the hips, knees, and ankles to return to the beginning position.

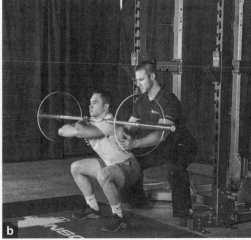

Figure 6.2 Front squat: (a) beginning position; (b) bottom position.

Breathing Guidelines

Inhale prior to the downward portion of the movement. Exhale as the upward portion of the movement is initiated.

Spotting Guidelines

- Stand behind the athlete with feet shoulder-width apart and arms extended under the arms of the athlete.
- Squat down in rhythm with the athlete while keeping arms close to the athlete's upper body.
- The spotter can support or push the athlete's upper body vertically to return to the beginning position if needed.

DEADLIFT

Primary Muscles Trained

Gluteus maximus, semimembranosus, semitendinosus, biceps femoris, vastus lateralis, vastus intermedius, vastus medialis, rectus femoris

Beginning Position

- Stand next to the bar with the feet at a comfortable width (between hip and shoulder width), rotated out slightly. The bar should be positioned close to the shins.
- Flex the hips and allow the torso to tilt forward to grab the bar. Grip the bar slightly wider than the knees in an overhand position or alternated grip.
- From the lateral view, the shoulders are positioned higher than the hips, the hips are positioned higher than the knees, the shin angle is vertical (slightly more than what is seen in figure 6.3), and the spine is in a neutral position. The arms are completely extended and perpendicular to the floor.
- Pack the chin (make a "double chin") to maintain the integrity of the cervical spine (more than what is seen in figure 6.3). The line of sight should be a couple of feet in front of the bar.

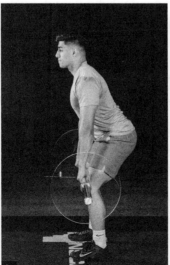

Figure 6.3 Deadlift: *(a)* beginning position; *(b)* extend the knees; *(c)* end position.

- Create tension by pulling up on the bar and wedging the hips down and back. The hips will lower slightly. Depress the scapulae to activate the latissimus dorsi and scapular stabilizers. Brace the anatomical core. Grip the bar with maximal effort.
- Begin all repetitions from this position (a).

Movement Phases

1. Push the middle of the feet hard into the floor while extending the knees and driving the hips forward (b).
2. Keep the bar close to the body until the knees and hips are fully extended and the torso is upright (c).
3. To return to the beginning position, continue to push the middle of the feet into the floor while maintaining tension in the upper back and bracing the anatomical core.
4. Push the hips back, allowing the hips and knees to flex. Maintain a neutral spine and keep the bar aligned with the midfoot until the weight reaches the floor. Do not allow the torso to flex forward and the bar to travel away from the body. The torso angle during the descent is created by the flexion of the hips.

Breathing Guidelines

Inhale prior to lifting the weight off the floor. Exhale once the weight is returned to the floor.

Exercise Modifications and Variations

Trap Bar, Kettlebell, or Band Deadlift

This exercise can be modified by using a trap bar, kettlebell, or band. This will allow the athlete to have more degrees of freedom around the ankle joint. The location of the grip on the bar is moved to the athlete's sides. The movement guidelines remain consistent.

Coaching Tips

- Always maintain a braced anatomical core.
- It is critical to maintain a neutral spine throughout the movement.
- Do not allow the spine to extend during the upward portion of the movement or flex during the downward portion of the movement.
- Starting from an elevated surface or blocks is recommended for athletes who have long limbs or demonstrate movement flaws when starting from the floor.

FORWARD STEP LUNGE

Primary Muscles Trained

Gluteus maximus, semimembranosus, semitendinosus, biceps femoris, vastus lateralis, vastus intermedius, vastus medialis, rectus femoris, iliopsoas

Beginning Position

- Set the bar at shoulder height on a squat rack (not shown in figure 6.4).
- Grip the bar at a comfortable width (slightly wider than shoulder width) and vertically align the body under the bar. The bar is positioned at the base of the posterior neck and top of the trapezius.

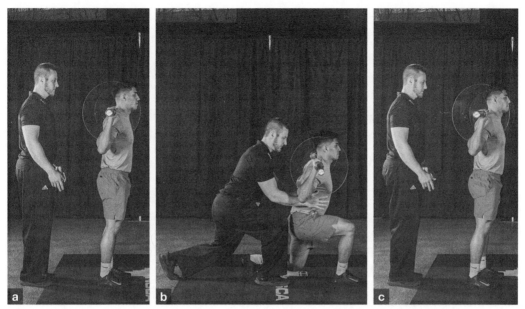

Figure 6.4   Forward step lunge: *(a)* beginning position; *(b)* bottom lunged position; *(c)* return to beginning position.

- Pack the chin (make a "double chin") to maintain the integrity of the cervical spine and brace the core.
- Pull the bar down into the body to activate the latissimus dorsi and scapular stabilizers and maintain the integrity of the thoracic and lumbar spine.
- Position the feet directly under the hips.
- Push both feet through the floor to lift the bar off the rack and take a few steps back to position the body to execute the forward step lunge.
- Begin all repetitions from this position *(a)*.

Movement Phases

1. Take a large step forward with either leg while maintaining an upright posture with the upper body.
2. Allow the hip and knee of the lead leg to flex in a controlled manner while the weight is being lowered. The entire foot of the lead leg will be in contact with the floor, absorbing the weight, while the ball of the foot on the back leg will stabilize the body. The lead knee will track in line with the angle of the foot. The back knee will track down toward the floor. The torso will have a consistent upright angle throughout the entire movement.
3. Allow the weight to descend until the thigh of the lead leg is parallel to the floor *(b)*.
4. Forcefully drive the foot of the lead leg into the floor while extending the hips, knee, and ankle to return to the beginning position *(c)*.

Breathing Guidelines

Inhale prior to the downward portion of the movement. Exhale as the upward portion of the movement is initiated.

Spotting Guidelines

- Stand about a foot (~30 cm) behind the athlete with the hands close to the athlete's waist, hips, or upper body.
- Take a step forward with the same lead leg that the athlete does while maintaining contact with their torso.
- Mimic the athlete's movement and provide assistance when returning to the beginning position, stabilizing the body with the hands when needed.

Exercise Modifications and Variations

Walking Lunge

The walking lunge can be performed with a barbell, dumbbells, kettlebells, or body weight. The positioning of the load can be on the athlete's back (like a back squat) or side hang (holding dumbbells or kettlebells by the athlete's side) or front rack position (like a front squat or goblet squat, with one or two kettlebells). The athlete will take a large step forward while maintaining an upright posture with the upper body. The lead leg's knee should not go further than the toes of the lead foot. The body will be balanced on the ball of the foot of the rear leg. Allow the hips to lower until the thigh is parallel to the floor. Drive the lead foot into the floor to stand up. This will allow the rear leg to step forward to return to the standing position. Pause and repeat with the opposite leg.

Reverse Lunge

The reverse lunge can be performed with a barbell, dumbbells, kettlebells, or body weight. The positioning of the load can be on the athlete's back, sides, or front. The athlete will take a large step backward while maintaining an upright posture with the upper body. The rear leg will be in contact with the floor through the ball of the foot. Allow the hips to lower until the thigh is parallel to the floor. Drive the lead foot into the floor, allowing the rear leg to step forward to stand up.

Dumbbell Forward Step Lunge and Reach

The dumbbell forward step lunge and reach is initiated by holding a dumbbell at chest height. Take a large step forward while maintaining an upright posture with the upper body. Allow the hips to lower until the thigh is parallel to the floor. Press the dumbbell forward in line with the chest and shoulders while maintaining a braced core. Return the dumbbell to the chest while not allowing the angle of the arms to drop. Drive the lead foot into the floor to stand up. This will allow the lead leg to step backward to return to the standing position.

Forward and Backward Mini-Band Walk

The athlete should stand with shoulders, hips, knees, and feet pointing forward. Place a band around the ankles or above the knees. Feet should be hip- to shoulder-width apart depending on the mini-band resistance. The band should be taut, but not stretched. Flex knees slightly and move into a half-squat position. Maintaining this position, take a medium to large step forward to exaggerate the movement. Lift up from the hip flexor and extend the leg outward when moving forward. The arms and legs should move in opposition while walking. Make sure that the elbows are flexed and arms swing from the shoulders, similar to sprinting-arm mechanics. Complete the same movement in reverse to walk backward.

Coaching Tips

- Maintain a braced anatomical core and upright upper body position throughout the entire movement.
- Do not allow excessive forward or backward leaning during any portion of the movement.
- Be aware of the length of each step to ensure for proper form.
- Do not allow the knee of the lead leg to travel further than the toes and ensure that the pelvis stays in a neutral position.

STEP-UP

Primary Muscles Trained

Gluteus maximus, semimembranosus, semitendinosus, biceps femoris, vastus lateralis, vastus intermedius, vastus medialis, rectus femoris

Beginning Position

- Set the bar at shoulder height on a squat rack (not shown in figure 6.5).
- Grip the bar at a comfortable width (slightly wider than shoulder width) and vertically align the body under the bar. The bar is positioned at the base of the posterior neck and top of the trapezius.
- Pack the chin (make a "double chin") to maintain the integrity of the cervical spine and brace the anatomical core.
- Pull the bar down into the body to activate the latissimus dorsi and scapular stabilizers and maintain the integrity of the thoracic and lumbar spine.
- Position the feet directly under the hips.

Figure 6.5   Step-up: (a) beginning position; (b) step and press foot into bench to lift body; (c) stand on top of bench.

- Push both feet through the floor to lift the bar off the rack and execute the step-up.
- Begin all repetitions from this position (a).

Movement Phases

1. Lift one leg and step onto a box or bench while maintaining an upright posture with the upper body (b). (Note: Ideally, the width of the bench would be wider than the length of the athlete's shoes; i.e., the bench in figure 6.5 is too narrow.)

2. Firmly plant the lead foot on the box or bench and drive the foot down to extend the hip and knee. Transfer the weight onto the lead leg, forcing the rear leg to come off the floor. Continue to extend the hip and knee of the lead leg and bring the rear leg up to stand on the box or bench (c).

3. Pause at the top and begin the downward portion of the movement with the same leg.

4. Maintain a braced anatomical core and upright posture as the rear leg dismounts from the box or bench, leaving the body supported by the lead leg. Slowly flex the hip and knee while the weight is being lowered. Once the rear foot is planted on the floor, transfer the weight onto the rear leg and step off the box or bench.

Breathing Guidelines

Inhale prior to stepping onto the box or bench. Exhale during the downward portion of the movement.

Exercise Modifications and Variations

Lateral Step-Up

The lateral step-up can be performed with a barbell, dumbbells, kettlebells, or body weight. Standing next to the box in a tall position, take a lateral step onto the box with the closer leg. Drive the foot down into the box and transfer the weight onto the lead leg. Extend the hip and knee of the lead leg, allowing the rear leg to come off the floor. Continue to extend the hip and knee and bring the rear leg up to stand on top of the box. Step off the box using the rear leg to initiate the movement. Brace the anatomical core and slowly flex the hip and knee of the lead leg until the rear leg is in full contact with the floor. Transfer the weight onto the rear leg and return the lead leg to the floor.

Crossover Step-Up

Standing next to the box in a tall position, lift the leg that is opposite the box and take a crossover step onto the box. Drive the foot down into the box and transfer the weight onto the lead leg. Extend the hip and knee, allowing the rear leg to come off the floor. Continue to extend the hip and knee and bring the rear leg up to stand on top of the box. Step off the box using the same leg to initiate the movement. Brace the anatomical core and slowly flex the hip and knee of the leg on the box until the rear leg is in full contact with the floor. Transfer the weight onto the rear leg and return the lead leg to the floor.

Crossover Step-Up With Reach

The athlete performs the crossover step-up as previously described, but as the hip and knee are extended to perform the concentric phase of the exercise, the athlete simultaneously extends the elbows to push or press the resistance away from the body. As the athlete returns to the beginning position, the resistance is pulled to the goblet/chest position.

Step-Up With Leg Lift (Hip Flexion)

Stand in front of the box in a tall position, lift one leg and take a step onto the box. Drive the foot down and transfer the weight onto the lead leg. Extend the hip and knee of the lead leg, allowing the rear leg to come off the floor. Continue to extend the hip and knee of the lead leg on the box while forcefully flexing the hip and knee of the rear leg in a marching fashion. Stand on the box with the lead leg fully extended and rear leg in the air. The hip and knee are flexed and the foot is dorsiflexed. Begin to lower the weight by returning the non-weight-bearing leg to the floor. Brace the anatomical core and slowly flex the hip and knee of the lead leg until the rear leg is in full contact with the floor. Transfer the weight onto the rear leg and return the lead leg to the floor.

Coaching Tips

- Ensure that the box or surface supporting the athlete is stable.
- Maintain a braced anatomical core and upright upper body throughout the entire movement.
- Do not allow excessive forward or backward leaning during any portion of the movement.
- Do not allow the knee of the lead leg to travel further than the toes.
- Ensure that the pelvis stays in a neutral position.

SPLIT SQUAT

Primary Muscles Trained

Gluteus maximus, semimembranosus, semitendinosus, biceps femoris, vastus lateralis, vastus intermedius, vastus medialis, rectus femoris, iliopsoas

Beginning Position

- Set the bar at shoulder height on a squat rack (not shown in figure 6.6).
- Grip the bar at a comfortable width (slightly wider than shoulder width) and vertically align the body under the bar. The bar is positioned at the base of the posterior neck and top of the trapezius.
- Pack the chin (make a "double chin") to maintain the integrity of the cervical spine and brace the core.
- Pull the bar down into the body to activate the latissimus dorsi and scapular stabilizers and maintain the integrity of the thoracic and lumbar spine.
- Position the feet directly under the hips.
- Push both feet through the floor to lift the bar off the rack and take a few steps back to position the body to execute the split squat.

Movement Phases

1. Take a large step backward with either leg while maintaining an upright posture with the upper body (like a reverse lunge). All repetitions begin from this split-stance position (a).
2. Allow the hip and knee of the lead leg to flex in a controlled manner while the weight is being lowered. The entire foot of the lead leg will be in contact with the floor, absorbing the weight, while the ball of the back foot will stabilize the body. The front knee will track in line with the angle of the foot. The back knee will track down toward the floor. The torso will have a consistent upright angle throughout the entire movement.
3. Allow the weight to descend until the back knee is close to touching the floor (b).
4. Forcefully drive the foot of the lead leg into the floor while extending the hips, knees, and ankles to return to the beginning position, maintaining both feet in a fixed split stance position.

Breathing Guidelines

Inhale prior to the downward portion of the movement. Exhale as the upward portion of the movement is initiated.

Spotting Guidelines

- Stand about a foot (~30 cm) behind the athlete with the hands close to the athlete's waist, hips, or upper body.
- Take a small step backward with the same leg that the athlete does while maintaining contact with their torso.
- Mimic the athlete's movement and provide assistance when returning to the beginning position, stabilizing the body with the hands when needed.

Exercise Modifications and Variations

The split squat can be modified to use kettlebells, dumbbells, a weight vest, or body weight. The alignment of the load can vary from a front rack position or side hang position as well.

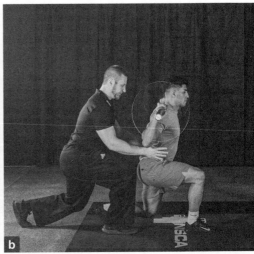

Figure 6.6 Split squat: (a) beginning position; (b) squat down (not lunge forward).

Coaching Tips

- Maintain a braced anatomical core and upright upper body throughout the entire movement.
- Do not allow excessive forward or backward leaning during any portion of the movement.
- Do not allow the knee of the lead leg to cave in during the movement.
- Be aware of the length of the stance to ensure proper form.
- Do not allow the knee of the lead leg to travel further than the toes.
- Ensure that the pelvis stays in a neutral position.

SINGLE-LEG SQUAT (BULGARIAN SQUAT)

Primary Muscles Trained

Gluteus maximus, semimembranosus, semitendinosus, biceps femoris, vastus lateralis, vastus intermedius, vastus medialis, rectus femoris, iliopsoas

Beginning Position

- Stand facing away from a bench, box, or roller pad that is approximately knee height.
- Set the bar at shoulder height on a squat rack.
- Grip the bar at a comfortable width (slightly wider than shoulder width) and vertically align the body under the bar. The bar is positioned at the base of the posterior neck and top of the trapezius.
- Pack the chin (make a "double chin") to maintain the integrity of the cervical spine and brace the anatomical core.
- Pull the bar down into the body to activate the latissimus dorsi and scapular stabilizers and maintain the integrity of the thoracic and lumbar spine.
- Push both feet through the floor to lift the bar off the rack. Take a few steps back and rest the rear foot on top of the bench, box, or roller pad to initiate the movement.
- Begin all repetitions from this position (a).

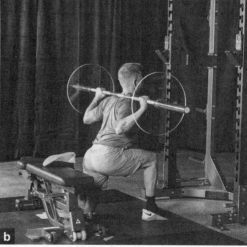

Figure 6.7 Single-leg squat: (a) beginning position; (b) squat down (not lunge forward).

Movement Phases

1. Allow the hip and knee of the lead leg to flex in a controlled manner while the weight is being lowered. Maintain an upright angle with the torso throughout the entire movement.
2. Allow the weight to descend until the back knee is close to touching the floor (b).
3. Forcefully drive the foot of the lead leg into the floor while extending the hips, knees, and ankles to return to the beginning position.

Breathing Guidelines

Inhale prior to the downward portion of the movement. Exhale as the upward portion of the movement is initiated.

Exercise Modifications and Variations

The single-leg squat can be modified to use kettlebells, dumbbells, a weight vest, or body weight. The alignment of the load can vary from a front rack position or side hang position as well.

Coaching Tips

- Maintain a braced anatomical core and upright upper body throughout the entire movement.
- Do not allow excessive forward or backward leaning during any portion of the movement.
- Do not allow the knee of the lead leg to cave in during the movement.
- Be aware of the length of the stance to ensure proper form.

LATERAL SQUAT

Primary Muscles Trained

Gluteus maximus, semimembranosus, semitendinosus, biceps femoris, vastus lateralis, vastus intermedius, vastus medialis, rectus femoris, adductors

Beginning Position

- Grip the bar at a comfortable width (slightly wider than shoulder width) and vertically align the body under the bar. The bar is positioned at the base of the posterior neck and top of the trapezius.
- Pack the chin (make a "double chin") to maintain the integrity of the cervical spine and brace the anatomical core.
- Pull the bar down into the body to activate the latissimus dorsi and scapular stabilizers and maintain the integrity of the thoracic and lumbar spine.
- Push both feet through the floor to lift the bar from the rack. Take a step to the side with either leg, as though to perform a lateral lunge, and brace the core.
- Begin all repetitions from this position (a).

Figure 6.8 Lateral squat: *(a)* beginning position; *(b)* side lunge.

Movement Phases

1. Sit back into the hips over the side leg. Maintain an upright angle with the torso throughout the entire movement.

2. Allow the weight to descend until the thigh of the side leg is parallel to the floor or just above it *(b)*.

3. Forcefully drive the foot of the lead leg into the floor while extending the hips, knee, and ankle of the side leg to return to the beginning position.

Breathing Guidelines

Inhale prior to the downward portion of the movement. Exhale as the upward portion of the movement is initiated.

Exercise Modifications and Variations

The lateral squat can be modified to use kettlebells or dumbbells.

Lateral Lunge

The lateral lunge can be performed with a barbell, dumbbells, kettlebells, a plate, or body weight. The positioning of the load can be on the athlete's back (like a back squat), front rack (like a front squat, goblet squat, or front rack with one or two kettlebells), or side hang (using dumbbells or kettlebells). The athlete will take a large step to one side while maintaining an upright posture with the upper body. Once the foot is flat on the floor, drive the hips back and flex at the hip and knee, maintaining the body's weight over the midfoot of the lead leg. The torso and shin should maintain a consistent angle throughout the movement. Drive through the floor with the lead leg, allowing the foot to lift off and retrace the step it completed during the downward portion of the movement.

Lateral Lunge With Plate Press

The lateral lunge to press can be performed while holding a plate, kettlebell, or dumbbell in the goblet position. While executing the eccentric phase of flexing the hip and knee to lower the body, simultaneously extend the elbows so the resistance is pressed or pushed away from the chest. While executing the concentric phase of extending the hip and knee to return to the beginning position, pull the resistance back to the chest or goblet position.

Lateral Mini-Band Walk

The athlete should stand with shoulders, hips, knees, and feet pointing forward, feet shoulder-width apart. Place bands around ankles or above the knees. The band should be taut, but not stretched. Flex knees slightly and move into a half-squat position. Maintaining this position, shift body weight over the left leg and take a step laterally with the right leg. Then move the left foot toward the right foot so both feet are under each shoulder. Continue to move laterally in this manner for the desired number of repetitions. Once complete, switch directions.

Coaching Tips

- Maintain a braced anatomical core and upright upper body throughout the entire movement.
- Do not allow excessive leaning (forward, backward, or laterally) during any portion of the movement.
- Do not allow the knee of the lead leg to cave in during the movement.
- Be aware of the length of the stance to ensure proper form.

LEG EXTENSION

Primary Muscles Trained

Rectus femoris, vastus medialis, vastus lateralis, vastus intermedius

Beginning Position

- Sit on the machine.
- Adjust and line up the roller pads with the front of the ankle (i.e., just above the instep of the foot).

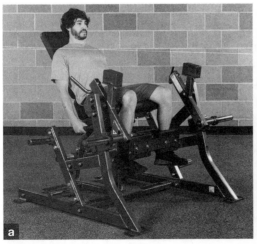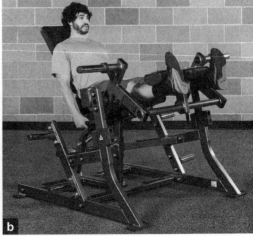

Figure 6.9 Leg extension: *(a)* beginning position; *(b)* extend the knees.

- Adjust the back pad so that the knee joint is even with the axis of the machine.
- Grab the handles on either side of the machine to stay in place during the exercise (a).

Movement Phases

1. Raise the feet until legs are straight and parallel with the floor.
2. Pause at the top position, contracting the quad muscles (b).
3. Lower feet back to the flexed knee beginning position.

Breathing Guidelines

Exhale as the upward portion of the movement is initiated. Inhale prior to the downward portion of the movement.

Exercise Modifications and Variations

This exercise can be executed in a variety of ways. The athlete can sit on end of a table and do manuals against a hand, using a band or cuff weight.

STANDING CALF RAISE

Primary Muscles Trained

Gastrocnemius (emphasis), soleus

Beginning Position

- Stand with the back straight and shoulders under the pads of the machine. (Note: figure 6.10 shows a simpler version using a step instead of a machine; the movement phases are the same.)
- Place the toes and balls of the feet on the foot plate and raise up on the machine with heels off the foot plate.
- Lower the heels into ankle dorsiflexion (a).

Movement Phases

1. Rise up as high as possible on toes (ankle plantar flexion) while keeping the knees extended and torso erect.
2. Pause at the top position (b).
3. Lower heels back into dorsiflexion and the straight-legged beginning position.
4. Keep the movement around the ankle joint.

Figure 6.10   Standing calf raise: (a) beginning position; (b) rise onto the toes.

Breathing Guidelines

Exhale as the upward portion of the movement is initiated. Inhale prior to the downward portion of the movement.

Exercise Modifications and Variations

This exercise can be modified in a variety of ways. Standing on the foot plate with toes turned out will stress the gastrocnemius medial head. By turning the feet inward, the lateral head of the gastrocnemius can be stressed.

The standing calf raise can also be executed with a barbell on the shoulders or using a Smith machine with blocks of plates under the feet. Performing the standing calf raise off the floor will limit range of motion.

SEATED CALF RAISE

Primary Muscles Trained

Soleus (emphasis), gastrocnemius

Beginning Position

- Sit on the machine and place the restraint pad tightly across the thighs. (Note: figure 6.11 shows a simpler version using a step, bar, and thigh pad instead of a machine; the movement phases are the same.)
- Place toes on the foot bar with heels off the foot plate.
- Lower heels into ankle dorsiflexion *(a)*.

Movement Phases

1. Rise up as high as possible on the toes into ankle plantar flexion.
2. Pause at the top position *(b)*.
3. Lower heels back into ankle dorsiflexion.
4. Keep the movement around the ankle joint.

Breathing Guidelines

Exhale as the upward portion of the movement is initiated. Inhale prior to the downward portion of the movement.

Exercise Modifications and Variations

This exercise can be modified by using a barbell across the thighs and by placing toes on a plate or a block (as seen in figure 6.11).

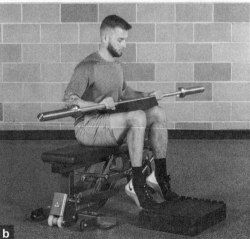

Figure 6.11　Seated calf raise: *(a)* beginning position; *(b)* rise onto the toes.

ROMANIAN DEADLIFT (RDL)

Primary Muscles Trained

Gluteus maximus, biceps femoris, semimembranosus, semitendinosus, erector spinae

Beginning Position

- Stand with feet about hip-width apart, holding the barbell at mid-thigh height in an overhand or alternated grip.
- Keep the knees slightly flexed throughout the entire movement.
- Pack the chin (make a "double chin") to maintain the integrity of the cervical spine. The line of sight should be a couple of feet in front of the bar.
- Create tension by depressing the scapulae to activate the latissimus dorsi and scapular stabilizers. Brace the core and grip the bar with maximal effort (a).

Movement Phases

1. Slowly lower the weight toward the floor while pushing the hips backward, hinging at the hips.
2. Lower the bar until a slight stretch in the hamstrings is achieved or until the torso is parallel to the floor. Keep the bar in contact with the legs when lowering (b).
3. Push hard into the floor with the feet while driving the hips forward to return to the beginning position. It is important to maintain a neutral spine throughout the movement.

Figure 6.12 Romanian deadlift (RDL): (a) beginning position; (b) end position.

Breathing Guidelines

Inhale prior to the downward phase of movement. Exhale through the upward phase of movement.

Exercise Modifications and Variations

This exercise can be modified by using a dumbbell, kettlebell, medicine ball, or cable. Athletes may execute this exercise on one leg to facilitate proprioception or stand on a block to increase range of motion.

Single-Leg Dumbbell or Kettlebell RDL

Stand with weight balancing on the right leg and hold a dumbbell in the left hand in front of the thigh. The right knee should have a slight flex or soft straight. Sit hips back into an athletic stance, shoulders back. At the same time, start to lower the dumbbell toward the shin while raising the left leg directly behind the body to hip height. Keep the back flat and shoulders back. Pause when there is a stretch sensation in the right hamstring, then drive the right heel into the floor and push the hips forward to return to the beginning position. Over time the hamstring will become more flexible and the pause position will lower. Athletes with good hip mobility and hamstring flexibility can perform this exercise on a box to increase range of motion.

Single-Leg RDL With a Barbell

Stand with feet hip-width apart and weight balancing on the right leg. Grab the bar with hands shoulder-width apart. Lower the bar in a straight line as the left leg is raised to hip height. Pause when a stretching sensation is felt in the right hamstring. Drive the right heel into the floor and push hips forward to return to the beginning position.

Coaching Tips

- Do not arch the back at standing position.
- Keep a good tempo with speed of movement.
- Use an alternating grip if the overhand grip is uncomfortable.
- Focus eyes on a fixed object out in front.
- Set the neck in the "double chin" position.
- Squeeze the dumbbell.
- Flex the glute and core to maintain balance.
- Keep the back flat and shoulders back as the bar is lowered toward the shins.
- Lower the dumbbell in a straight line.
- With barbell RDL, grip the bar with overhand grip. As weight gets heavier, use an alternating grip.

GLUTE-HAMSTRING RAISE

Primary Muscles Trained

Gluteus maximus, vastus lateralis, vastus medialis, biceps femoris long head, rectus femoris

Beginning Position

- Put the ankles in the roller pads of the glute-ham bench. The feet should be flat against the vertical foot plate and the thighs should press against the pads just above the knees.
- Flex knees to 90 degrees to position the upper body perpendicular to the floor. The upper body should be aligned with the head.
- Cross the arms in front of the body (a).

Movement Phases

1. Allow the knees to extend until the whole body is parallel to the floor (b).
2. Continue the downward movement until the upper body is once again perpendicular to the floor (c).
3. While maintaining crossed arms and straight hips, contract the glutes and hamstrings to return to the starting position.

Breathing Guidelines

Inhale prior to the downward phase of the movement. Exhale as the upward portion of the movement is initiated.

Figure 6.13 Glute-hamstring raise: *(a)* beginning position; *(b)* midway through downward phase; *(c)* bottom position.

Exercise Modifications and Variations

This exercise can be modified by doing it on the floor, off a BOSU, or with a band, vest, dumbbell, or plate to add resistance.

NORDIC HAMSTRING CURL

Primary Muscles Trained

Biceps femoris long head, biceps femoris short head, semimembranosus, semitendinosus, gastrocnemius, glute maximus, erector spinae

Beginning Position

- Kneel on a pad and hook feet under the roller pads.
- Position the body in a straight line from knees to head.
- Place hands in front of chest with palms facing out *(a)*.

Movement Phases

1. Using the hamstrings, eccentrically lower the body down to the floor in a slow tempo (b). Contract the glutes and erector spinae to keep the body in a straight line while lowering. Do not flex the hips or round the back.

2. Use hands to catch the torso as the body lands in a straight line (c).

3. To return to the beginning position, use the arms to push back up into the tall kneeling position.

Breathing Guidelines

Inhale at the beginning position prior to the upward phase of the movement. Exhale prior to or during the downward phase of the movement.

Exercise Modifications and Variations

This exercise can be executed in a variety of ways. The athlete can kneel on an Airex pad with a spotter holding the heels. This can also be done as a test on the Nord Board to record the athlete's score as he performs the exercise.

Figure 6.14 Nordic hamstring curl: (a) beginning position; (b) midway through the downward phase; (c) end position.

BARBELL HIP THRUST

Primary Muscles Trained

Gluteus maximus, vastus lateralis, vastus medialis, biceps femoris long head, rectus femoris

Beginning Position

- Place a loaded barbell parallel to a bench.
- Slide legs under the barbell and sit on the floor with back against the side of the bench. Roll the barbell over the hips.
- Grasp the barbell at each side.
- Flex the knees and place feet flat on the floor, shoulder-width apart (a).

Movement Phases

1. Keeping the torso flexed, raise the barbell on the hips until they are fully extended. If the barbell feels uncomfortable on the hips, add padding (b).
2. Squeeze and hold the glutes for 2 seconds.
3. Slowly lower the weight on the hips down to the beginning position, but do not touch the floor.

Breathing Guidelines

Inhale prior to the downward phase of the movement. Exhale as the upward portion of the movement is initiated.

Exercise Modifications and Variations

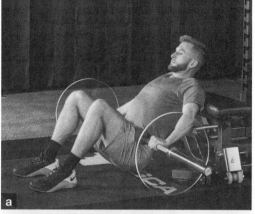

Figure 6.15   Barbell hip thrust: (a) beginning position; (b) full thrust.

This exercise can be modified by using dumbbells, plates, or bands. Hip thrusters in a kneeling position with a band or cable is another variation.

Single-leg hip thrusts from the floor or off the bench may also be considered for more trained athletes.

STABILITY BALL LEG CURL

Primary Muscles Trained

Biceps femoris long head, biceps femoris short head, semimembranosus, semitendinosus, gastrocnemius, glute maximus, erector spinae, obliques

Beginning Position

- Lie supine with arms at sides and heels on top of an exercise ball.
- Keep the legs straight and toes pointing up. The body should be in a straight line with shoulders touching the floor and heels on the ball (a).

Movement Phases

1. Press heels into the ball and contract the glutes to lift the hips up off the floor (b).
2. Contract the hamstrings to flex the knees and bring the heels toward the buttocks while keeping the hips elevated (c).
3. Pause for a one count. Feet should be on the ball and knees flexed to 90 degrees.

Figure 6.16   Stability ball leg curl: (a) beginning position; (b) lift hips and lower back off floor; (c) flex knees to 90 degrees.

4. Slowly and in a controlled manner, extend the knees back to the fully straight body position but with the hips still lifted off the floor.

Breathing Guidelines

Exhale at the beginning position until the knees get to 90 degrees. Inhale while slowly returning to the beginning position.

Spotting Guidelines

- Stand behind the exercise ball.
- As the athlete pulls the feet toward the buttocks, gently guide the ball in a straight line. It will take a few repetitions for the athlete to get comfortable with the stability of the exercise ball; do not let him slide off the side.
- Release hands as the athlete returns to beginning position.

Exercise Modifications and Variations

This exercise can be modified in a variety of ways, including one leg at a time on a physioball or using a slide board, Val-slide, glute-ham roller with the strength and conditioning professional spotting from the same position.

DOUBLE-LEG BRIDGE

Primary Muscles Trained

Glute maximus, biceps femoris long head, biceps femoris short head, gastrocnemius

Beginning Position

- Lie on the floor with the spine in contact with the floor.
- Place hands on the floor next to the hips.
- Place feet flat on the floor and flex knees to approximately 90 degrees *(a)*.

Movement Phases

1. Push the feet into the floor to raise the hips and buttocks *(b)*.
2. Hold the hips as high as possible for 2 seconds.
3. Lower hips back to the floor.

Breathing Guidelines

Exhale as the movement is initiated and hips are raised. Inhale as hips are lowered and returned to beginning position.

Exercise Modifications and Variations

Once the basic floor movement of bridging is mastered, adding a BOSU or

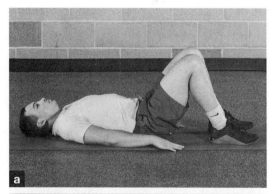

Figure 6.17   Double-leg bridge: *(a)* beginning position; *(b)* end position.

stability ball as well as performing the exercise with the feet elevated on a bench or box can increase the intensity and facilitate proprioception.

SINGLE-LEG BRIDGE

Primary Muscles Trained

Glute maximus, biceps femoris long head, biceps femoris short head, gastrocnemius

Beginning Position

- Lie on the floor with spine in contact with the floor.
- Place hands on the floor next to hips.
- Place the right foot flat on the floor and flex the right knee to 90 degrees (a).
- Hold the left leg straight up, even with the hip (not seen in figure 6.18a).

Movement Phases

1. Raise the right hip and buttock off the floor by pushing the right foot into the floor and driving through the heel. Keep the left leg even with the right thigh (b).
2. Do not use arms for assistance.
3. Hold hips as high as possible for 2 seconds.
4. Lower hips back to floor.

Figure 6.18 Single-leg bridge: (a) beginning position; (b) end position.

Breathing Guidelines

Exhale as the movement is initiated and hips are raised. Inhale as hips are lowered and returned to beginning position.

Exercise Modifications and Variations

Once the basic floor movement of single-leg bridging is mastered, adding a BOSU or stability ball can increase the intensity and facilitate proprioception.

Single-Leg Bridge With Extended Knee

Lie on the floor with the spine in contact with the floor and hands next to the hips. Place heels on an elevated surface such as a bench, BOSU, or stability ball to keep the legs straight. Drive the right heel into the elevated surface. Bring the left knee toward the chest while raising the hips off the floor. Lower the left leg down to elevated position and return the body back to beginning position. Do not use arms for assistance. This exercise can also be performed with one foot elevated on a bench or box.

LEG CURL

Primary Muscles Trained

Biceps femoris, semimembranosus, semitendinosus

Beginning Position

- Kneel on the machine with one leg, grab the handles, straighten the working knee, and hook one foot under the roller pad.
- Keep hips and thighs in contact with the surface pad (a).

Movement Phases

1. Raise the heel toward the buttock until the knee is as fully flexed as range of motion allows (try to touch the buttock with the heel) (b).
2. Lower the heel back to the fully straight-legged position.

Breathing Guidelines

Exhale as the movement is initiated and the knee is flexed. Inhale as the knee is extended and returned to the beginning position.

Exercise Modifications and Variations

This exercise can be modified in a variety of ways. A lying (prone) leg curl machine or a seated leg curl machine can be used instead the standing version seen in figure 6.19. This exercise may also be performed on a physioball, on a slide board, or with the strength and conditioning professional providing manual resistance. Another option is to place a dumbbell or medicine ball between the athlete's feet while performing this exercise lying prone on the floor.

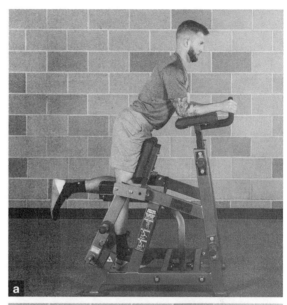

Figure 6.19 Leg curl: (a) beginning position; (b) end position.

7

UPPER BODY EXERCISE TECHNIQUE

PAUL FOURNIER

Resistance training for the baseball player is a necessity. Although it has historically been viewed as controversial, athletes and coaches are now better informed about the merits of resistance training and better able to interpret the research and apply it practically. Consistent, year-round resistance training has led to baseball players being physically larger, stronger, and quicker than their predecessors. These improved physical characteristics have enhanced baseball performance with increased batted-ball exit velocities, pitch velocities, and spin rates, as well as running acceleration and speed, just to name a few. In a game of inches, the ability to generate force as quickly as possible is a game changer.

With increased rapid force generation, baseball players need to have an appropriate braking system. Upper body resistance training also allows the athlete to slow down or stop the force with less potential for injury. Through the body's adaptation to exercise and the strength and conditioning professional's manipulation of training variables, performance will improve, along with the athlete's durability and ability to recover.

Normal scapula (shoulder blade) function is essential for optimal shoulder function, especially for the baseball player. If the shoulder does not function properly or has a loss of control during normal motion (called *scapula dyskinesis*), there is a potential increased risk of injury (3). The **Thrower's 10 (T10)** is a series of fundamental exercises for any throwing athlete, regardless of position, that was designed to help strengthen the muscles of the rotator cuff while allowing for proper scapula kinematics (3). The following are included in the T10 exercises and all could be performed with different types of resistance equipment such as elastic tubes, weight plates, dumbbells, cuff weights, or manual resistance (1, 2). The following are the movements that comprise the T10 exercises.

    1a and 1b. Diagonal pattern (D2) extension and flexion

    2a and 2b. External and internal rotation at 0 degrees of shoulder abduction (elbow at waist)

    2c and 2d. External and internal rotation at 90 degrees of shoulder abduction (elbow at shoulder level)

        3. Shoulder abduction to 90 degrees (e.g., dumbbell lateral shoulder raise)

        4. Scaption with external rotation or full can

        5. Sidelying external rotation

6a. Prone horizontal abduction (e.g., dumbbell bent-over lateral shoulder raise)

6b. Prone horizontal abduction at 100 degrees (e.g., full shoulder external rotation with thumb up)

6c. Prone rowing (e.g., one-arm dumbbell row)

6d. Prone rowing into external rotation

7. Press-up

8. Push-up (i.e., push-up plus)

9a and 9b. Elbow flexion and extension (e.g., dumbbell biceps curl and one-arm overhead dumbbell triceps extension)

10a and 10b. Wrist flexion and extension

10c and 10d. Forearm pronation and supination

All upper body exercises need to be performed with proper technique and within the joint's full range of motion (ROM). The scapula must also be allowed to move and function in all planes of movement (i.e., protraction, retraction, elevation, depression, upward rotation, and downward rotation) when performing these exercises. While progressing through the T10 exercises and advancing to the other upper body primary exercises, the athlete needs to be aware of joint positioning, appropriate intra-abdominal bracing, foot placement, posture, and appropriate breathing. Athletes should focus on diaphragmatic breathing by exhaling through the sticking point of the concentric portion of the exercise and inhaling during the eccentric portion. This will help to engage the anatomical core to form a stable base for resistance training, while allowing for oxygen-rich blood to flow to working muscles. Athletes should strive to make a habit of including diaphragmatic breathing on a mental checklist when training.

An athlete's training age or experience with an exercise will help dictate the initial load of a movement; however, once a movement is learned and properly performed, the athlete can progress the intensity or volume. Form degradation and the inability to maintain full ROM should signal to the coach and athlete that the intensity or volume (or both) is too great and needs to be adjusted.

Exercise Finder

(continued)

BENT-OVER ROW

Primary Muscles Trained
Latissimus dorsi, teres major, middle trapezius, rhomboids, posterior deltoids

Beginning Position
- Stand next to the bar with the feet between shoulder- and hip-width apart, pointed forward, with the bar over the forefoot.
- Hinge at the hips with a neutral spine, keeping the eyes down to maintain a neutral cervical spine.
- Brace the anatomical core.
- Grip the bar with a closed, pronated (overhand) grip outside the slightly flexed knees, with the shoulders directly over or slightly in front of the bar (a).

Movement Phases
1. Pull the weight to the abdomen. The bar should follow up the thigh, close to the body.
2. Pull the elbows in past the torso's midline (b).
3. Return the bar to the knees while remaining braced and hinged.
4. Return the bar to the floor when set is complete.

Breathing Guidelines
Exhale through the sticking point of the concentric portion of the exercise and inhale during the eccentric portion. As the movement starts (the concentric phase of the row), exhale through the mouth, maintaining the braced anatomical core. Inhale through the nose while lowering the weight to the beginning position (the eccentric phase of the row).

Exercise Modifications and Variations

Chest Supported Row

The athlete may elect to do a chest supported row with dumbbells or a barbell. This will allow for more isolation of the primary muscles trained. The athlete may use the incline bench, straddling the bench seat facing the padded surface. While in this position, brace the anatomical core to maintain a neutral pelvis with the chest in contact with the padded surface. The cervical spine should remain neutral as well.

Pendlay Row

Begin with the barbell on the floor. Feet should be shoulder-width apart. Flex the knees slightly and hinge at the hips so that the torso is parallel to the floor. Grab the barbell with a wide, pronated grip. Exhale through the sticking point of the concentric portion of the exercise as the barbell is pulled toward the chest and inhale during the eccentric portion as the barbell is lowered back to the beginning position. Make sure the weight has contacted the floor and pause before beginning the next repetition.

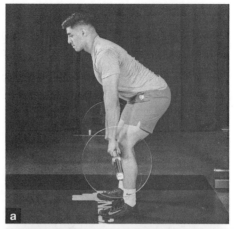

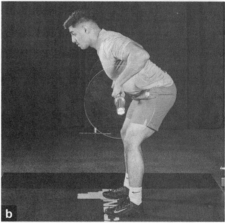

Figure 7.1 Bent-over row: (a) beginning position; (b) pull bar toward torso.

Coaching Tips

- Drive the elbows back and pinch the scapula.
- Brace the anatomical core.
- Keep the eyes down.
- Keep the hips back.

ONE-ARM DUMBBELL ROW (T10)

Primary Muscles Trained

Latissimus dorsi, teres major, middle trapezius, rhomboids, posterior deltoids

Beginning Position

- Stand at the bench with the feet between shoulder- and hip-width apart, pointed forward and slightly staggered.
- Hinge at the hips, keeping the eyes down to maintain a neutral cervical spine.
- Brace the anatomical core.
- Place one hand (the same side as the slightly forward foot) on the bench for support and grip the dumbbell with the opposite hand with a closed neutral grip (a).

Movement Phases

1. Pull the dumbbell toward the lower abdomen while keeping the elbow close to the body.
2. Pull the elbow back past the torso's midline while maintaining a braced anatomical core and neutral spine *(b)*.
3. Lower the dumbbell until the elbow is fully extended.
4. Return the dumbbell to the floor when the desired repetitions for each arm are completed.

Breathing Guidelines

Exhale through the sticking point of the concentric portion of the exercise and inhale during the eccentric portion of the exercise.

Exercise Modifications and Variations

One-Arm Landmine Row

Place one end of a barbell into a landmine device or into the corner of a squat or power rack. Add weight to the opposite end of the barbell. There should also be a portable bench or box located by the opposite end of the barbell that will be used for additional support. It is recommended to use plates that are no larger in diameter than a 25-pound (11 kg) iron plate so the athlete can use a full range of motion with the pulling arm. The athlete should position themselves with the barbell between the legs and the feet between shoulder- and hip-width apart, pointed forward and slightly staggered. Hinge at the hips with a neutral spine, keeping eyes down to maintain a neutral cervical spine. Place one hand (the same side as the slightly forward foot) on the bench or box for support and grasp the barbell shaft directly behind the large sleeve end with the opposite hand using a closed neutral grip. Make sure to brace the anatomical core. Pull the weight toward the lower abdomen while keeping the elbow close to the body. The elbow should be pulled back past the torso's midline while maintaining a braced anatomical core and neutral spine. Return weight to the point of an extended elbow. Return weight to the floor when the desired repetitions for each arm are completed.

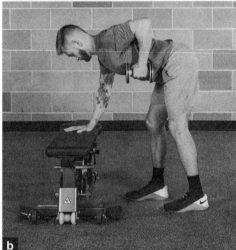

Figure 7.2 One-arm dumbbell row: *(a)* beginning position; *(b)* pull dumbbell toward torso.

Coaching Tips

- Drive the elbow back.
- Do not rotate the torso.
- Swing an arm path similar to sawing wood.

LAT PULLDOWN

Primary Muscles Trained

Latissimus dorsi, teres major, middle trapezius, rhomboids, posterior deltoids

Beginning Position

- Grab the bar with a closed, pronated (overhand) grip wider than shoulder-width apart and elbows extended.
- Sit down on the seat with the knees flexed at 90 degrees under the pads (a).

Movement Phases

1. With a slight torso lean backward and a braced abdomen, pull the bar down to the upper chest by driving the elbows down and back (b).
2. Return the bar to the beginning position by allowing the elbows to extend.
3. Maintain torso position throughout the movement.

Breathing Guidelines

Exhale through the sticking point of the concentric portion of the exercise and inhale during the eccentric portion of the exercise.

Exercise Modifications and Variations

Two-Arm Cable Pulldown

The athlete may elect to do a cable or lat pulldown in a half-kneeling (one knee on the floor) or tall kneeling (both knees on the floor) position. This will allow for greater anatomical core engagement. Good posture and abdominal bracing

Figure 7.3 Lat pulldown: (a) beginning position; (b) pull down to upper chest.

are necessary to maintain a neutral pelvis. If independent cables are available, this exercise may be performed alternating or one-sided.

Neutral Grip Lat Pulldown

Grip the V-bar attachment or an individual handle attachment in each hand with a closed, overhand grip in a neutral position. The movement phases will remain the same as the lat pulldown, but also may be done in succession, alternating, or one-sided. The athlete may elect to do a pulldown in a half-kneeling or tall kneeling position.

Supinated Grip Lat Pulldown

Grip the straight bar attachment or two individual handle attachments with a closed, supinated (underhand) grip. The movement phases will remain the same as the lat pulldown, but also may be done in succession, alternating, or one-sided. The athlete may elect to do a pulldown in a half-kneeling or tall kneeling position.

Wide Grip Lat Pulldown

Grip the lat pulldown bar attachment with hands slightly wider than shoulder width in a closed, pronated (overhand) grip. The movement phases will remain the same as the lat pulldown. The athlete may elect to do a pulldown in a half-kneeling or tall kneeling position.

Coaching Tips

- Drive the elbows down and back and pinch the scapula.
- Maintain a braced anatomical core with no thoracic extension or arched back.
- Maintain a neutral cervical spine with the eyes forward and slightly elevated.

LOW-PULLEY SEATED ROW

Primary Muscles Trained

Latissimus dorsi, teres major, middle trapezius, rhomboids, posterior deltoids

Beginning Position

- Sit at on the floor pad (or on the floor) with the feet on the foot supports and knees slightly flexed.
- Grab the handle with a closed neutral or overhand grip with elbows extended.
- Brace the anatomical core in a neutral position with the torso vertical (a).

Movement Phases

1. With a braced anatomical core, pull the handle to the lower abdomen.
2. Drive the elbows back past the torso midline.
3. Maintain a neutral torso throughout the pull (b).
4. Return the handle to the beginning position by extending the elbows.
5. Maintain torso position throughout the movement.

Figure 7.4 Low-pulley seated row: (a) beginning position; (b) pull handles back.

Breathing Guidelines

Exhale through the sticking point of the concentric portion of the exercise and inhale during the eccentric portion of the exercise.

Coaching Tips

- Drive the feet into the supports.
- Drive the elbows back and pinch the scapula.
- Maintain a braced torso with no thoracic extension.
- Keep the eyes forward.

FACE PULL

Primary Muscles Trained

Latissimus dorsi, teres major, middle trapezius, rhomboids, posterior deltoids

Beginning Position

- Stand in a slightly staggered stance (to prevent excessive torso extension) facing the cable machine with the pulley at chin height.
- Grasp the rope with a closed overhand grip.
- With the cable loaded, start with the elbows extended and shoulders internally rotated.
- Keep the eyes forward and the torso braced in a neutral position (a).

Movement Phases

1. Pull the rope toward the face while driving the elbows back on the same plane as the beginning position.
2. As the point of attachment of the rope gets closer, slightly externally rotate the shoulders and pinch the scapula. The point of attachment should finish close to the forehead (b).

Figure 7.5 Face pull: (a) beginning position; (b) pull toward face.

Breathing Guidelines

Exhale through the sticking point of the concentric portion of the exercise and inhale during the eccentric portion of the exercise.

Exercise Modifications and Variations

This exercise can also be performed with one arm using a handle, or alternating using an independent cable machine with handles.

Coaching Tips

- Brace the anatomical core to minimize thoracic extension.
- Drive the elbows back and pinch the scapula.
- Do a complete pull; do not separate the horizontal pull and shoulder external rotation.

CABLE ROW

Primary Muscles Trained

Latissimus dorsi, teres major, middle trapezius, rhomboids, posterior deltoids

Beginning Position

- Sit in the machine facing the handles with feet flat on floor supports.
- Brace the anatomical core with the chest against the support pad and the torso neutral.
- With the elbows fully extended, grip the handles with a closed grip in neutral or overhand position.

Movement Phases

1. While maintaining chest contact with the support pad, pull the handles toward the torso.
2. Drive the elbows back past the midline of the torso.
3. Return the handles by extending the elbows back to the beginning position.

Breathing Guidelines

Exhale through the sticking point of the concentric portion of the exercise and inhale during the eccentric portion of the exercise.

Exercise Modifications and Variations

Cable Variations for the Cable Row

The athlete may elect to perform a one-arm cable row in a standing staggered stance, half-kneeling (one knee on the floor), or tall kneeling (both knees on the floor) position. This variation allows for more torso engagement when performing the movement. When the athlete is in staggered stance, the opposite side leg of the rowing arm is in front with the foot flat on the floor, and the rear leg is extended at the hip with slight knee flexion. When the athlete is in half-kneeling position, the same side knee of the rowing arm is resting on the floor and the opposite leg is at 90 degrees of hip flexion and 90 degrees of knee flexion. Tall kneeling requires the athlete to have both knees on the floor at 90 degrees of flexion and 0 degrees of hip flexion. When performing these movements, posture and abdominal bracing is necessary to minimize excessive anterior pelvic tilt.

Coaching Tips

- Brace the anatomical core to minimize thoracic extension.
- Drive the elbows back and pinch the scapula.
- Maintain chest contact with the support pad.

CHIN-UP

Primary Muscles Trained

Latissimus dorsi, teres major, middle trapezius, rhomboids, posterior deltoids, biceps brachii

Beginning Position

- Grab the bar with the hands shoulder-width apart in a closed underhand (supinated) grip.
- With the arms extended and in a hang position, brace the anatomical core to minimize thoracic and lumbar extension (a).

Movement Phases

1. Pull the body upward while driving the elbows down.
2. Keep the elbows close to the torso and pull until the chin is above the bar (b).
3. Return to the beginning hang position by extending the elbows.

Breathing Guidelines

Exhale through the sticking point of the concentric portion of the exercise and inhale during the eccentric portion of the exercise.

Figure 7.6 Chin-up: (a) beginning position; (b) pull chin above bar.

Exercise Modifications and Variations

Neutral Grip Pull-Up

Rather than using a standard pull-up bar, use adjustable handles or the neutral handles attached to the pull-up bar. Grip the bars or handles with a closed overhand grip in a neutral position. The movement phases will remain the same as the chin-up.

Pull-Up

Grip the pull-up bar with a closed pronated (overhand) grip slightly wider than shoulder-width apart. The elbows will be pulled down and back with the chin above the bar position.

Weighted or Band-Assisted Chin-Up or Pull-Up

The athlete may wear weights to increase the intensity of the exercise. Intensity may be decreased by using a band attached to the pull-up bar to assist the athlete in the execution of the pull. The movement phases will remain the same as the standard chin-up or pull-up.

Towel Chin-Up or Pull-Up

To increase the challenge, the athlete may use two towels draped over the pull-up bar. The athlete will grip the towels with a closed overhand grip. The movement phases will remain the same as the standard chin-up and pull-up.

Coaching Tips

- Drive the elbows down.
- Fully extend the elbows at the bottom of the exercise.
- Maintain a braced anatomical core.
- Pull the chin over the bar or hands (if using towels or handles).
- Do not kip.

INVERTED ROW

Primary Muscles Trained

Latissimus dorsi, teres major, middle trapezius, rhomboids, posterior deltoids

Beginning Position

- Place bar on safety rack bars or on J-hooks.
- Lay underneath the bar and place hands slightly wider than shoulder-width apart with a closed pronated grip or, as seen in figure 7.7, shoulder-width apart with a closed underhand (supinated) grip.
- With the elbows extended, the torso should be off the floor.
- Brace the torso so that the ankles, hips, and shoulders are in a line (a).

Movement Phases

1. With the heels on the floor, pull the chest to the bar (farther than what is seen in figure 7.7b).
2. Drive the elbows past the midline of the torso (b).
3. Return by extending the elbows.

Figure 7.7 Inverted row: *(a)* beginning position; *(b)* pull body up.

Breathing Guidelines

Exhale through the sticking point of the concentric portion of the exercise and inhale during the eccentric portion of the exercise.

Exercise Modifications and Variations

Suspension Trainer

Using a suspension trainer instead of a bar will allow for more freedom of the grip. The movement phases and coaching tips remain the same as the inverted row.

Coaching Tips

- Body position should look like an inverted plank.
- Drive the elbows back, pinching the scapula.
- Maintain a braced anatomical core to avoid lumbar or thoracic extension.
- Adjust the height of the bar to increase or decrease exercise intensity.

SHOULDER SHRUG

Primary Muscle Trained

Trapezius

Beginning Position

- Stand at the bar with feet hip-width apart and pointed forward in an athletic position.
- Grab the bar with a closed overhand (pronated) grip.
- Brace the anatomical core *(a)*.

Movement Phases

1. With the eyes forward, raise the shoulders up and slightly back.
2. Keep the torso as tall as possible (b).
3. Allow the shoulders to return to the beginning position.

Breathing Guidelines

Exhale through the sticking point of the concentric portion of the exercise and inhale during the eccentric portion of the exercise.

Exercise Modifications and Variations

Dumbbell Shrug

Instead of using a barbell, the athlete may elect to use two dumbbells instead. The dumbbells are gripped with a closed overhand grip and are in a neutral position to the side of the body. The movement phase is the same as the standard shoulder shrug with barbell.

Power Shrug

A power shrug using a barbell or dumbbells could be substituted when using heavier loads during a power phase. The athlete will extend the ankles, knees, and hips to perform the exercise. A dip and drive movement is used to gain momentum to elevate the shoulders as high as possible while keeping the elbows extended. The exercise now becomes a total body explosive movement rather than an isolated strengthening movement.

Figure 7.8   Shoulder shrug: (a) beginning position; (b) shrug.

Coaching Tips

- Do not jerk the bar to elevate the load.
- Move in a straight line and slightly back; no shoulder circles.
- Maintain a neutral cervical spine.

DUMBBELL PULLOVER

Primary Muscles Trained

Latissimus dorsi, pectoralis major

Beginning Position

- Place the shoulders and upper back on a bench that is perpendicular to the body with the head off the bench and in neutral position.
- Place the feet flat on the floor with 90 degrees of knee flexion and the hips extended, with abdomen and glutes braced.

- Grasp one end of the dumbbell with both hands and hold the dumbbell above the chest with slightly flexed elbows and shoulders at 90 degrees of flexion *(a)*.

Movement Phases

1. While bracing the anatomical core and keeping the elbows slightly flexed, allow the dumbbell to lower (i.e., allow the shoulders to flex) until the dumbbell is behind and in line with the top of the head *(b)*.
2. Return to the dumbbell the beginning position (i.e., above the chest with slightly flexed elbows).

Breathing Guidelines

Exhale through the sticking point of the concentric portion of the exercise and inhale during the eccentric portion of the exercise.

Spotting Guidelines *(not shown in figure 7.9)*

- Stand at the athlete's head, allowing room for the dumbbell to lower.
- Place the hands as close to the dumbbell as possible to assist in the movement or to intervene if the athlete drops the weight.

Exercise Modifications and Variations

EZ Bar Pullover

An EZ curl bar can be used to create a wider grip if mobility disallows full range of movement without thoracic and lumbar extension.

Coaching Tips

- Brace the anatomical core.
- Keep the hips extended (i.e., 0 degrees of flexion) and the knees flexed at 90 degrees.
- Minimize lumbar and thoracic extension.
- Keep the eyes focused on the ceiling with a neutral cervical spine.
- If the athlete cannot go to full shoulder flexion without excessive torso extension, limit the shoulder ROM.

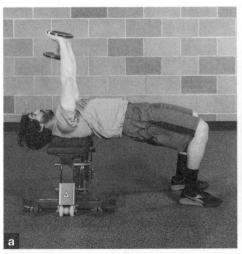 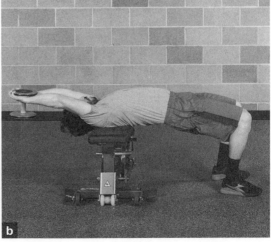

Figure 7.9   Dumbbell pullover: *(a)* beginning position; *(b)* end position.

DUMBBELL BICEPS CURL (T10)

Primary Muscles Trained

Biceps brachii, brachialis, brachioradialis

Beginning Position

- Stand in an athletic position with feet about hip-width apart.
- Hold the dumbbells in a closed neutral grip with the arms at the sides.
- Brace the anatomical core with shoulders down and back *(a)*.

Movement Phases

1. While maintaining body posture, flex the elbows.
2. As the elbows flex, rotate (supinate) the wrists so the palms face upward *(b)*.

Figure 7.10 Dumbbell biceps curl: *(a)* beginning position; *(b)* curl.

3. Return the dumbbells to beginning position in the opposite fashion. As the elbows extend, rotate (pronate) the wrists back to neutral.
4. The exercise can be done with both arms simultaneously or by alternating them.

Breathing Guidelines

Exhale through the sticking point of the concentric portion of the exercise and inhale during the eccentric portion of the exercise.

Exercise Modifications and Variations

Dumbbell Biceps Hammer Curl

Instead of supinating the forearm, a hammer curl is performed by maintaining a neutral grip position throughout the ROM.

Barbell Biceps Curl

The athlete may elect to use a straight bar or barbell to perform the curl. This will restrict motion by only allowing an underhand (supinated) grip throughout the entire ROM.

EZ Bar Biceps Curl

An athlete may find that the EZ curl bar is better for the wrists due to the angle of the bar allowing for a more comfortable grip.

Cable Curl

A cable attachment and pulley may be used instead of dumbbells or free weights.

Dumbbell Rollover Curl

A dumbbell rollover curl can be performed by initiating the movement like the dumbbell biceps curl, but when the elbows are fully flexed (i.e., the dumbbell is at the top of the movement), the athlete pronates the forearms before lowering the dumbbells with the elbows extended.

Coaching Tips

- Maintain proper posture with a braced abdomen.
- Maintain a neutral cervical spine.
- Do not use the torso to cheat the weight up (i.e., lean back or rock with the load).
- Make sure the elbows return to full extension prior to beginning a new repetition.

REVERSE GRIP BARBELL CURL

Primary Muscles Trained

Brachioradialis, biceps brachii, brachialis

Beginning Position

- Stand at the bar in an athletic position with feet hip-width apart.
- Grab the bar with both hands with a closed pronated (overhand) grip, hands at a natural width and elbows fully extended (a).

Movement Phases

1. While maintaining body posture, flex the elbows (b).
2. Once elbows are fully flexed, return the weight to the beginning position by extending the elbows.

Breathing Guidelines

Exhale through the sticking point of the concentric portion of the exercise and inhale during the eccentric portion of the exercise.

Coaching Tips

- Maintain proper posture with a braced abdomen.
- Maintain a neutral cervical spine.
- Do not use the torso to cheat the weight up (i.e., lean back or rock with the load).
- Make sure the elbows return to full extension prior to beginning a new repetition.

Figure 7.11   Reverse grip barbell curl: (a) beginning position; (b) curl.

BENCH PRESS

Primary Muscles Trained

Pectoralis major, anterior deltoids, triceps brachii

Beginning Position

- Lay on the bench face up so the forehead is centered directly underneath the racked bar.
- Place the feet flat on the floor.
- Place the hands slightly wider than shoulder-width apart in a closed pronated (overhand) grip.
- Brace the abdomen and hips.
- Lift the bar off the supports with stiff wrists and move it directly over the chest with the elbows extended (a).

Movement Phases

1. Lower the bar to the chest by flexing the elbows.
2. Allow the bar to touch the chest with elbows at approximately 45 degrees of shoulder abduction.
3. Maintain a braced anatomical core to minimize lumbar and thoracic extension (b).
4. Drive the bar up and slightly back by extending the elbows to full extension.
5. Re-rack the bar once the set is over.

Breathing Guidelines

Exhale through the sticking point of the concentric portion of the exercise and inhale during the eccentric portion of the exercise.

Figure 7.12 Bench press: (a) beginning position; (b) lower the bar.

Spotting Guidelines

- Stand at the athlete's head for safety. An athletic stance and alternate grip are preferred.
- Help with the lift-off to start the movement and to assist with the concentric movement if the athlete lacks the ability to return the weight to the beginning position.
- Assist with racking of the bar when the set is complete, if necessary.

Exercise Modifications and Variations

Dumbbell and Kettlebell Variations for the Bench Press

Dumbbells and kettlebells may be used instead of the barbell to add instability to the exercise as well as focus on each arm independently. The exercise may be performed bilaterally, alternating, or unilaterally. The spotter should be stationed at the head of the athlete in an athletic stance, with the hands ready to support the wrists (not the elbows). The spotter follows the path of the wrists, ready to brace the wrists at any point and take the weight away when appropriate. Two spotters can be used if the athlete is using heavy dumbbells.

Incline Bench Press

The incline bench press may be used to promote a more overhead movement. Dumbbells may be used in the same manner as the regular bench press, either bilaterally, alternating or unilaterally.

Close-Grip Bench Press

The grip width may also be adjusted to a narrow grip to change focus of the exercise. Dumbbells may also be used.

Cable Variations for the Bench Press

The athlete may elect to perform a one-arm cable press in a standing staggered stance, half-kneeling (one knee on the floor), or tall kneeling (both knees on the floor) position. This variation allows for more torso engagement when performing the movement. When the athlete is in a staggered stance, the opposite side leg of the pressing arm is in front with the foot flat on the floor, and the rear leg is extended at the hip with slight knee flexion. When the athlete is in half-kneeling position, the same side knee of the pressing arm is resting on the floor, and the opposite leg is at 90 degrees of hip flexion and 90 degrees of knee flexion. Tall kneeling requires the athlete to have both knees on the floor at 90 degrees of flexion and 0 degrees of hip flexion. When performing these movements, posture and abdominal bracing is necessary to minimize excessive anterior pelvic tilt.

Floor Press

The athlete may elect to lay supine on the floor while pressing to add more isolation or to restrict ROM. In this position, hips and knees could be extended or flexed. A spotter may assist in getting the bar into the beginning position as well as to aid in the safety of the exercise.

Towel or Planks of Wood

The athlete may use rolled towels or planks of wood to restrict ROM. Place the wood or towel on the athlete's chest prior to un-racking the barbell. The movement phases are the same as the standard bench press.

Coaching Tips

- Maintain torso and head contact on the bench.
- Drive the body away from the bar in the concentric phase.
- Keep the feet on the floor.
- Do not bounce the bar off the chest.

PUSH-UP (T10)

Primary Muscles Trained

Pectoralis major, anterior deltoids, triceps brachii

Beginning Position

- Lay face down on the floor.
- Place feet slightly apart and hands flat on the floor with thumbs in line with the nipples.
- Brace the abdomen and hips.
- Keep the cervical spine neutral with eyes facing the floor (a).

Movement Phases

1. Press up by fully extending the elbows and flexing the shoulders.
2. Elevate the hips and torso at the same rate (b).
3. Return to the beginning position.
4. Lower the hips and torso at same rate.

Breathing Guidelines

Exhale through the sticking point of the concentric portion of the exercise and inhale during the eccentric portion of the exercise.

Exercise Modifications and Variations

Suspension Trainer Chest Press

To add instability to the push-up, the athlete may elect to use a suspension trainer instead of the floor. The more parallel the athlete becomes in relation to the floor, the more difficult the movement becomes. The movement phases and coaching tips remain the same as the push-up.

Push-Up Variations

An athlete can also do a *push-up plus*, which is a complete push-up followed by retraction and protraction of the shoulder blades. Another option is a *yoga push-up*, which is

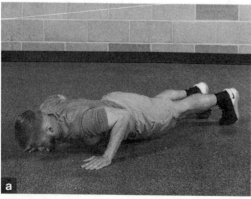

Figure 7.13 Push-up: (a) beginning position; (b) end position.

a complete push-up followed by raising the buttocks to a pike or downward facing dog position. If the athlete walks their hands back toward their feet, this will allow the heels to end up flat on the floor.

A medicine ball can also be incorporated into the push-up in numerous ways. In the *one-sided medicine ball push-up*, the athlete places one hand on a medicine ball and the other hand on the floor while completing all push-up repetitions, then switches hands. The *alternating medicine ball push-up* is similar, but the athlete will alternate from one side of the medicine ball to the other for each repetition. Another variation is the *push-up shoulder tap*. The athlete completes a push-up, then takes one hand from the floor and taps the opposite shoulder while stabilizing the body with the hand that is on the floor. The athlete switches hands with each repetition.

The push-up can also be performed with resistance bands. Make sure the band is held securely in both hands while wrapped around the athlete's upper back. Finally, push-ups can be modified with a variety of foot positions. An athlete can have one foot in contact with the floor while the top of the other foot is resting on the back of the ankle, or one foot can be held in the air while the leg is straight. Feet can also be elevated on a bench or box to perform an incline push-up. All previous variations apply to the elevated foot position.

Medicine Ball Chest Pass

To push more explosively, an athlete can perform a medicine ball chest pass into a solid wall or into the floor. Use a medicine ball that bounces so it rebounds to the beginning position. This exercise can be performed while standing on two feet or one foot, half-kneeling, or tall kneeling.

Coaching Tips

- Drive and twist the palms outwardly into the floor.
- Push the floor away.
- Maintain abdomen bracing and gluteal musculature engagement.

STANDING BARBELL SHOULDER PRESS

Primary Muscles Trained
Anterior deltoid, medial deltoid, triceps brachii

Beginning Position

- In an athletic position with the feet slightly wider than the hips, stand in front of the bar that is position on safety bars or J-hooks at shoulder height (not shown in figure 7.14).
- Grab the bar with a closed pronated (overhand) grip with the elbows directly below or slightly in front of the barbell, slightly wider than shoulder width.
- Brace the abdomen and hips while maintaining a neutral spine.
- Unload the barbell from the J-hooks or safety bars and hold it in a secured racked position at the front of the shoulders with the elbows slightly forward of the hands.
- Resume standing in an athletic position with the feet slightly wider than the hips *(a)*.

Figure 7.14 Standing barbell shoulder press: (a) beginning position; (b) press overhead.

Movement Phases

1. With no leg involvement and keeping wrists neutral, press the bar above the head by extending the elbows.
2. After the initial press, slightly extend the neck so the bar can pass safely in front of the face as it is raised.
3. Once the bar passes the face, return the neck to a neutral position with eyes forward for the remainder of the press.
4. At full extension, the upper arms should cover the ears (b).
5. Lower the bar by allowing the elbows to flex; slightly extend the neck until the bar passes the chin and then immediately return the neck back to a neutral position.
6. Continue lowering the bar to the beginning position.

Breathing Guidelines

Exhale through the sticking point of the concentric portion of the exercise and inhale during the eccentric portion of the exercise.

Spotting Guidelines

- Spotting the standing barbell shoulder press is difficult. The athlete should be instructed on how to "dump" the weight forward (while taking a step back) prior to execution of the exercise.
- Stand behind the athlete with hands placed at the wrists to assist in all phases of the movement if needed.

- If the spotter needs assistance, the athlete may perform the exercise seated. When seated, use a staggered stance and alternated grip with hand placement at the bar rather than the wrists.

Coaching Tips

- The exercise is changed if the legs assist the upward movement (i.e., it becomes the push press).
- Maintain a braced anatomical core to avoid lumbar and thoracic extension.
- "Punch the sky" with a neutral wrist.
- "Hide the ears" with the upper arms at full extension.
- Maintain a neutral head placement.

STANDING DUMBBELL PRESS

Primary Muscles Trained

Anterior deltoid, medial deltoid, triceps brachii

Beginning Position

- Hold the dumbbells at the sides in a neutral position (not shown in figure 7.15).
- Stand in an athletic position with the feet slightly wider than the hips.
- Move the dumbbells up to shoulder height and hold them in a pronated position with the elbows directly below or slightly forward of the hands (a).

Figure 7.15   Standing dumbbell press: (a) beginning position; (b) press overhead.

Movement Phases

1. While maintaining a neutral spine, brace the abdomen and press the dumbbells up with no leg involvement.
2. Maintain a neutral cervical spine with eyes forward.
3. At full extension of the elbows, the upper arms should block the ears and the palms should face forward (b).
4. Lower the dumbbells to the beginning position.

Breathing Guidelines

Exhale through the sticking point of the concentric portion of the exercise and inhale during the eccentric portion of the exercise.

Spotting Guidelines

- Stand behind the athlete in an athletic or staggered stance with hands at the wrists to assist in all phases of the movement, if needed.
- If the spotter needs assistance, the athlete could perform the exercise seated.

Exercise Modifications and Variations

Seated Barbell or Dumbbell Shoulder Press

The exercise may also be performed seated with either dumbbells or a barbell. The adjustable bench is put in a vertical position so that the head and back have points of contact. The movement phases are the same as the standard standing dumbbell press.

Dumbbell Front Shoulder Raise

If the athlete needs to avoid an overhead movement, the dumbbell front raise may be used. Instead of pressing the dumbbells overhead, the dumbbells are held with a closed overhand grip in front of the thighs and are raised in front of the body up to shoulder height. Throughout the movement, the elbows remain in a slightly flexed position (i.e., the elbows do not flex or extend during the exercise).

Coaching Tips

- The exercise is changed if the legs assist the upward movement of the dumbbells (i.e., it becomes the dumbbell push press).
- Brace the anatomical core to avoid excessive lumbar and thoracic extension.
- "Punch the sky" with rotation.
- "Hide the ears" with the upper arms at full extension.
- Maintain a neutral head position.

DUMBBELL LATERAL SHOULDER RAISE (T10)

Primary Muscle Trained

Medial deltoid

Beginning Position

- With an overhand grip, hold the dumbbells at the sides of the body in a neutral position.
- Stand in an athletic position with the feet slightly wider than the hips (a).

Movement Phases

1. Maintaining a braced anatomical core, raise the dumbbells to the sides with slightly flexed elbows. At the end of the upward movement, the palms should be facing the floor.

Figure 7.16   Dumbbell lateral shoulder raise: (a) beginning position; (b) raise.

2. Raise the dumbbells to shoulder height (b).
3. Return the dumbbells back to beginning position.

Breathing Guidelines

Exhale through the sticking point of the concentric portion of the exercise and inhale during the eccentric portion of the exercise.

Coaching Tips

- Keep the elbows in the same slightly flexed position throughout the exercise (slightly more than what is shown in figure 7.16).
- Do not move the legs.
- Maintain a braced anatomical core to limit lumbar and thoracic extension.
- Maintain a neutral cervical spine with eyes forward.

DUMBBELL BENT-OVER LATERAL SHOULDER RAISE (T10)

Primary Muscle Trained

Posterior deltoid

Beginning Position

- Hold the dumbbells with a neutral grip and feet between hip- and shoulder-width apart.
- Hinge at the hips so the back is parallel to the floor.
- Brace the abdomen to maintain a neutral cervical spine.
- Keep the eyes focused on the floor (a).

Movement Phases

1. With slightly flexed elbows, lift the dumbbells to the sides to shoulder height. At the end of the upward movement, the palms should be facing the floor.
2. Maintain a neutral spine and the eyes focused on the floor (b).
3. Return the dumbbells to the beginning position.

Breathing Guidelines

Exhale through the sticking point of the concentric portion of the exercise and inhale during the eccentric portion of the exercise.

Coaching Tips

- Keep the elbows in the same slightly flexed position throughout the exercise (slightly more than what is shown in figure 7.17).
- Do not swing the weight up.
- Maintain a braced abdomen.
- Drive the hips back.
- Keep the eyes locked on the floor.

Figure 7.17 Dumbbell bent-over lateral shoulder raise: (a) beginning position; (b) raise.

LYING TRICEPS EXTENSION

Primary Muscle Trained

Triceps brachii

Beginning Position

- Lay face up on a bench with the head in contact with the bench, both feet flat on the floor, and the knees flexed to 90 degrees.
- Reach the arms toward the ceiling with a closed overhand grip on the bar.
- Brace the abdomen and hips (a).

Movement Phases

1. While maintaining 90 degrees of flexion in the shoulders, lower the bar by flexing the elbows so the bar passes just beyond the forehead (past the top of the head).
2. Maintain a neutral spine and contact with the bench (b).
3. Return the bar to the beginning position by extending the elbows.

Breathing Guidelines

Exhale through the sticking point of the concentric portion of the exercise and inhale during the eccentric portion of the exercise.

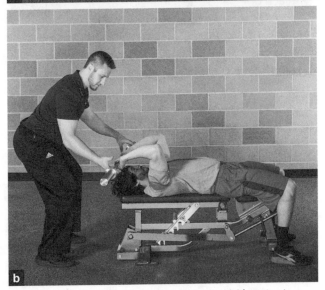

Figure 7.18 Lying triceps extension: (a) beginning position; (b) lower bar toward head.

Spotting Guidelines

- Stand behind the athlete's head in an athletic position to protect the athlete when the bar is directly overhead.
- If a spot is needed, grasp the bar using an alternated grip outside the athlete's hands.
- Assist in any of the movement phases, if needed.

Exercise Modifications and Variations

The exercise can be made more difficult by using dumbbells instead of the bar. The movement could be done simultaneously or by alternating sides. The dumbbells should be held in a neutral position rather than a pronated position as with the bar.

Coaching Tips

- Screw the feet into the floor.
- Keep the head, spine, and hips in contact with the bench.
- Allow minimal shoulder movement throughout the exercise.

DUMBBELL TRICEPS KICKBACK

Primary Muscle Trained

Triceps brachii

Beginning Position

- Stand next to the bench with feet between shoulder- and hip-width apart, pointed forward and slightly staggered.
- Hinge at the hips, keeping eyes down to maintain a neutral cervical spine.
- Brace the abdomen.
- Place one hand (the same side as the slightly forward foot) on the bench for support and grip the dumbbell with the opposite hand with a closed neutral grip.

Movement Phases

1. Pull the dumbbell toward the lower abdomen, keeping the elbow close to the body.
2. With the shoulder completely adducted, flex the elbow to 90 degrees (a).
3. Lift dumbbell by extending the elbow while maintaining upper arm contact with the torso (b).
4. Lower the dumbbell until the elbow is flexed back to 90 degrees.
5. Return the dumbbell to the floor when the set is complete.

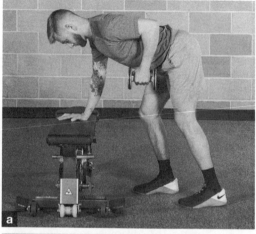

Figure 7.19 Dumbbell triceps kickback: (a) flex elbow to 90 degrees; (b) extend elbow.

Breathing Guidelines

Exhale through the sticking point of the concentric portion of the exercise and inhale during the eccentric portion of the exercise.

Coaching Tips

- Do not rock the weight up.
- Maintain a braced abdomen.

- Keep the eyes focused on the floor.
- All movement should occur at the elbow joint; there should be minimal upper arm movement.

TRICEPS PUSHDOWN

Primary Muscle Trained

Triceps brachii

Beginning Position

- Stand at the cable machine in an athletic position, eyes forward and feet hip-width apart, with the straight bar attachment between shoulder and head height.
- Brace the abdomen.
- Grip the bar with a closed overhand grip.
- Extend the shoulders to move the upper arms next to the sides of the torso (a).

Movement Phases

1. Extend the elbows to push the bar down (b).
2. Return the bar to the beginning position by allowing the elbows to flex.

Breathing Guidelines

Exhale through the sticking point of the concentric portion of the exercise and inhale during the eccentric portion of the exercise.

Exercise Modifications and Variations

Rope Triceps Pushdown

A rope attachment may be used to allow for greater radial deviation of the wrists at the end of the pushdown.

Band Triceps Pushdown

If a cable machine is not available, a band could be used for resistance. The band will also allow for greater radial deviation of the wrists at the end of the pushdown.

V-Bar Triceps Pushdown

The V-bar can be used to change the grip from the standard bar attachment. However, it will not allow for active radial deviation.

Figure 7.20 Triceps pushdown: (a) beginning position; (b) extend elbows.

Reverse Grip Triceps Extension

The athlete can also use a closed underhand grip on the bar to do the reverse triceps extension exercise.

Coaching Tips

- Maintain a braced anatomical core to avoid excessive lumbar (low back) extension.
- Keep the elbows in line with the midline of the torso.
- All movement should occur at the elbow joint; there should be minimal upper arm movement.

ONE-ARM OVERHEAD DUMBBELL TRICEPS EXTENSION (T10)

Primary Muscle Trained

Triceps brachii

Beginning Position

- Stand in an athletic position with feet slightly wider than hip width, or sit on a bench with hips and knees at 90 degrees of flexion.
- Brace the abdomen.
- Hold the dumbbell in a neutral position.
- Flex the shoulder to 180 degrees and elbow to 90 degrees while minimizing thoracic extension.
- Keep the eyes forward (a).

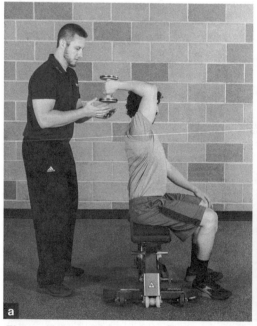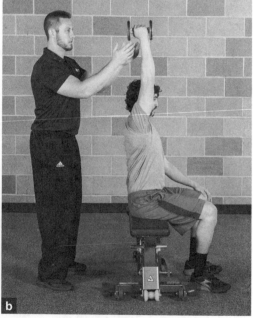

Figure 7.21 One-arm overhead dumbbell triceps extension: (a) lower dumbbell behind head; (b) extend elbow.

Movement Phases

1. Lift the dumbbell overhead by extending the elbow *(b)*.
2. To lower the dumbbell, allow the elbow to flex.

Breathing Guidelines

Exhale through the sticking point of the concentric portion of the exercise and inhale during the eccentric portion of the exercise.

Spotting Guidelines

- Stand behind the athlete in an athletic stance with hands positioned at the dumbbell.
- Assist with all phases of the movement, if needed.

Coaching Tips

- The only movement should be from the elbows.
- Maintain a braced torso to avoid excessive thoracic extension.
- Keep the eyes forward.

WRIST FLEXION AND EXTENSION (T10)

Primary Muscles Trained

Extensor carpi ulnaris, extensor carpi radialis brevis and longus, flexor carpi ulnaris, flexor carpi radialis, palmaris longus

Beginning Position

- Sit on a bench with the hips and knees at 90 degrees of flexion.
- Grip the barbell or dumbbell with a closed underhand (supinated) grip (for wrist flexion) *(a)* or a closed overhand (pronated) grip (for wrist extension) *(c)*.
- Brace the abdomen and place the forearms on the thighs with the wrists slightly in front of the knees.

Movement Phases

1. Raise the barbell or dumbbell by flexing *(b)* or extending *(d)* the wrists (based on the specific exercise).
2. Return the barbell or dumbbell to beginning position.

Breathing Guidelines

Exhale through the sticking point of the concentric portion of the exercise and inhale during the eccentric portion of the exercise.

Coaching Tips

- Maintain forearm contact with the thighs.
- Maintain a braced anatomical core to maintain appropriate posture.
- The only movement should be from the wrists.

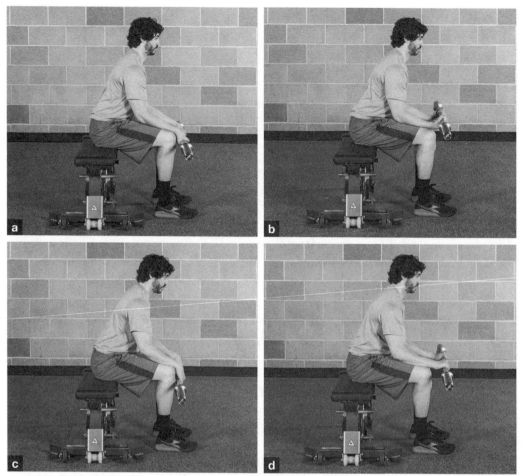

Figure 7.22 Wrist flexion and extension: *(a)* beginning position for wrist flexion; *(b)* flex the wrist; *(c)* beginning position for wrist extension; *(d)* extend the wrist.

WRIST ULNAR DEVIATION AND RADIAL DEVIATION

Primary Muscles Trained

Flexor carpi radialis, flexor carpi ulnaris, extensor carpi radialis, extensor carpi ulnaris

Beginning Position

- Sit on a bench with the hips and knees at 90 degrees of flexion.
- Brace abdomen and keep the eyes forward to sit tall.
- Grip the dumbbell with a closed overhand grip in a neutral position.
- Hold the arm adducted to the torso and elbow fully extended.

Movement Phases

1. Raise the dumbbell by flexing the wrist to thumb side for ulnar deviation or to pinky side for radial deviation.
2. Return to neutral position.

Breathing Guidelines

Inhale for 2 to 3 repetitions and exhale for 2 to 3 repetitions.

Coaching Tips

- Maintain a braced anatomical core to sit tall.
- Movement should be very small and only at the wrists.
- If the elbow starts to flex and extend, the load is too great.

FOREARM PRONATION AND SUPINATION (T10)

Primary Muscles Trained

Pronator teres, biceps brachii, supinator

Beginning Position

- Sit on a bench with the hips and knees at 90 degrees of flexion.
- Grip the offset (e.g., a dumbbell-length bar with a weight only on one end) implement with a closed underhand grip in a neutral position so the load is above the thumb (not shown in figure 7.23).
- Brace the abdomen and place the forearm on the thigh with the wrist slightly in front of the knee.

Movement Phases

1. Stabilize the forearm on the thigh with the uninvolved hand.
2. Turn the wrist and forearm fully so the hand is palm down (pronated) (a).
3. Return by turning the wrist and forearm fully so the hand is palm up (supinated) (b).
4. Return to neutral when set is complete.

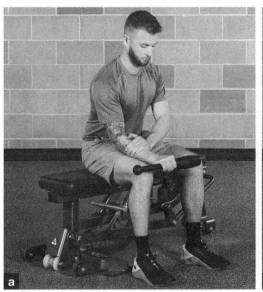 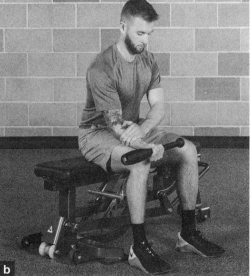

Figure 7.23   Forearm pronation and supination: (a) forearm pronation; (b) forearm supination.

Breathing Guidelines

Inhale for 2 to 3 repetitions and exhale for 2 to 3 repetitions.

Coaching Tips

- Maintain a braced anatomical core.
- Maintain forearm contact with the thigh.
- The only movement should be from the wrists.

RICE BUCKET EXERCISES

Primary Muscles Trained

Extensor carpi ulnaris, extensor carpi radialis brevis and longus, flexor carpi ulnaris, flexor carpi radialis, palmaris longus, pronator teres, biceps brachii, supinator, extensor digitorum, extensor pollicis brevis and longus, flexor digitorum superficialis and profundus

Beginning Position

- Sit on a bench with a plastic bucket between the feet on the floor that has uncooked rice inside it. The bucket should be filled deep enough so that the hand and the majority of the forearm are covered.
- Brace the abdomen.

Movement Phases

1. Insert the hand (with the palm facing the body) into the rice so the rice reaches the wrist or the distal end of the forearm.
2. Open and close the hand; make a fist, then extend the fingers to evenly disperse the rice.
3. Supinate the forearm by rotating the forearm as far as possible until the palm is facing away from the body and then return to the beginning position.
4. Extend the wrist as far as possible and then return to the beginning position.
5. Flex the wrist as far as possible and then return to the beginning position.
6. Without permitting wrist flexion or extension, flex the wrist toward the thumb (radial deviation) as far as possible and then return to the beginning position.
7. Without permitting wrist flexion or extension, flex the wrist toward the pinky side of the hand (ulnar deviation) as far as possible and then return to the beginning position.
8. Supinate the forearm so the palm faces away from the body; this is the new beginning position. Repeat steps 3 through 7 (note that step 3 in the new position involves pronation first, then supination back to the beginning position).

Breathing Guidelines

Inhale for 2 to 3 repetitions and exhale for 2 to 3 repetitions.

Coaching Tips

- The deeper the hand is in the rice, the more difficult the exercise becomes.
- Minimize torso movement; all movement comes from the wrist and forearm.

WRIST ROLLER

Primary Muscles Trained

Extensor carpi ulnaris, extensor carpi radialis brevis and longus, flexor carpi ulnaris, flexor carpi radialis, palmaris longus, flexor digitorum superficialis and profundus

Beginning Position

- Stand in an athletic position with the feet between hip- and shoulder-width apart.
- Grab the roller with a closed pronated grip. The load is attached to a rope that is fully extended (hanging down).
- With slightly flexed elbows that are held in this position throughout the exercise, flex the shoulders to slightly under 90 degrees.
- Keep the scapula down and pinched (figure 7.24).

Figure 7.24 Wrist roller

Movement Phases

1. To initiate rolling, alternate left to right wrist extension and flexion until the load on the end of the rope reaches the rollers (top position with rope rolled up).
2. Return the load back to the hanging position by reversing the movement.

Coaching Tips

- Maintain a braced anatomical core to avoid excessive lumbar and thoracic extension.
- Keep the eyes forward.
- Adjust the distance of the load from the midline of the torso by flexing or extending the elbows to add or decrease the strain on the deltoids.

Breathing Guidelines

Inhale for 2 to 3 repetitions and exhale for 2 to 3 repetitions.

Y, T, I, AND W

Primary Muscles Trained

Infraspinatus, supraspinatus, teres minor and major, subscapularis, rhomboids, deltoids

Beginning Position

- Lie face down on a table or an adjustable bench at an angle less than 45 degrees with the forehead on a rolled towel. (If there is not a table or the coach wants to have all athletes in a training session perform these exercises at one time, get into the beginning position for the dumbbell bent-over lateral shoulder raise.)

- Maintain a neutral cervical spine and braced abdomen.
- With the arms extended down to the floor, grip the dumbbells with a closed overhand grip (a and c).

Movement Phases

1. Lift the dumbbells by flexing the shoulders to 180 degrees at a 45-degree angle with the thumbs up (Y) (b).
2. Once the set is complete, return to the beginning position and lift the dumbbells directly out to the sides perpendicular to the torso with the thumbs up (T) (not shown in figure 7.25).
3. Once the set is complete, return to the beginning position and lift the dumbbells to 180 degrees of shoulder flexion with the thumbs up (I) (d).
4. Once the set is complete, return to the beginning position and lift the dumbbells so the upper arms are at a 45-degree angle to the torso then externally rotate the arms at the shoulders with the palms down (W) (not shown in figure 7.25).

Breathing Guidelines

Exhale while raising the weight to initiate the Y, T, I, or W (the concentric phases of the movements). Inhale while lowering the weight to the beginning position (the eccentric phases of the movements).

Coaching Tips

- Maintain a braced anatomical core to avoid excessive thoracic extension.
- Maintain head contact with the table.
- Keep the scapula down and pinched.
- Keep the elbows extended.

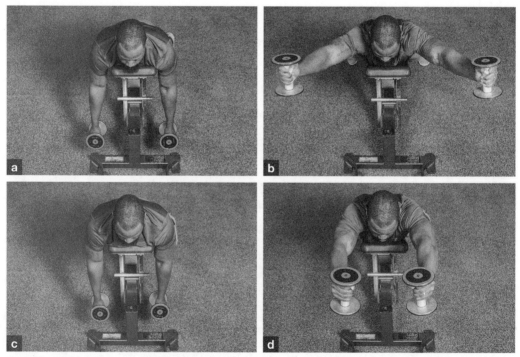

Figure 7.25 Y, T, I, and W: (a) beginning position; (b) Y position; (c) beginning position; (d) I position. (Photos for the T and W positions are not shown.)

8

ANATOMICAL CORE EXERCISE TECHNIQUE

NATE SHAW AND DEREK SOMERVILLE

The anatomical core consists of multiple muscles originating from the spine and rib cage working together to drive the human body in both breathing and performance. These muscles work together to drive function as well as create and transfer forces from the lower extremities to the upper extremities during sport. The main muscles used to help drive core function consist of the erector spinae, gluteus maximus, gluteus medius, gluteus minimus, internal oblique, external oblique, transverse abdominis, and rectus abdominis.

The anatomical core has two main purposes to make sport movements possible: core function and force production. **Core function** provides the groundwork for optimizing performance and force production; exercises focus on breathing mechanics and specific muscle activation to emphasize proper rib and pelvis positioning. Breathing and muscle activation exercises are considered to be foundational and should be the primary emphasis of an athlete's anatomical core training. This will ensure that athletes are not loading the spine without knowing how to create proper core stability (4).

The second purpose of the anatomical core is **force production**; it is a driver of an anatomical core training program. After the athlete learns how to execute proper function and positioning, programming can then be added to help with performance. This can be done by implementing sport-specific exercises performed in the sagittal, frontal, transverse, and diagonal planes with a goal of transferring energy from the lower half to the upper half of the body (7-10). Many of these exercises require coordinated, sequential movements that involve the hips, thoracic spine, and arms. The anatomical core should be trained from a standpoint of proper total body function and performance. Proper function must be obtained before adding force production to ensure proper patterns are being loaded (1). Just as a strength and conditioning professional would never load a bad squat pattern, they should not load an anatomical core that is not functioning properly.

In this chapter, athletes learn how to incorporate specific breathing patterns while they perform core function exercises in addition to force production exercises. These exercises were selected based on the authors' experience and various philosophies and disciplines (5, 7-10). Developmental strategies, efficient movement patterns, dynamic neuromuscular stabilization, practical solutions, and research from the NSCA and the Postural Restoration Institute have helped determine the exercise choices in this chapter (2, 3, 6-10). Any anatomical core exercise can be performed once the correct breathing and movement patterns are taught and then further enhanced with an appropriate progression. It is recommended that athletes learn how to perform core function exercises properly before progressing to the force production exercises.

EXERCISE TYPE

In this chapter, each anatomical core exercise will be described by its exercise type. There are two general categories: movement and exercise. Each category has various definitions that will be used to describe each anatomical core exercise.

Movement Category

Anti-flexion exercises train the athlete to resist flexion through the lumbar spine in the sagittal plane. *Anti-rotation* exercises increase stability and strength to prevent rotation in the transverse plane. *Rotational* exercises produce rotation in the transverse pane. *Anti-extension* exercises resist extension in the lumbar spine in the sagittal plane. *Extension* exercises produce extension in the hips and lumbar spine in the sagittal plane. Finally, *anti-lateral flexion* exercises train the athlete to resist side flexion of the lumbar spine in the horizontal plane.

Exercise Category

Exercises for the anatomical core are categorized as follows:

- Educational re-patterning: Efficient anatomical core movements with breathing awareness that allow the athlete's body to be in its most effective position from a length–tension relationship
- Core strengthening: Exercises that train the abdominal musculature to function with both strength and capacity through a full range of motion
- Repositioning: Exercises and feedback aimed at regaining ideal length–tension relationships to ensure optimal anatomical core function
- Traditional: Exercises that involve flexion or extension of spine in the sagittal plane
- Isometric: Exercises that maintain a rigid spine and are statically held so that there is no movement in any plane
- Medicine ball: Exercises that use added resistance while flexing, extending, twisting, or maintaining a rigid lumbar spine
- Throwing: Exercises that release the medicine ball with a throwing or tossing motion
- Functional: Exercises that maintain a rigid spine while doing an activity

Some of the exercises in this chapter will be listed in more than one category. Many of the exercise modifications and variations of the main exercises in this chapter can be in different categories as well. It is recommended that athletes perform the exercises in this chapter as described so the anatomical core musculature can become functionally strong. This will allow the athlete to perform other multi-joint compound exercises more effectively and, ultimately, play the game more explosively.

Exercise Finder

(continued)

WEIGHTED BREATHING

Exercise Type
Educational re-patterning

Primary Muscles Trained
Diaphragm, internal oblique, external oblique

Beginning Position

- Lie supine (face up) with knees flexed and feet flat on the floor.

Figure 8.1 Weighted breathing

- Hold a small weight plate on the abdomen with both hands with the elbows flexed and the upper arm at approximately a 45-degree angle to the trunk (figure 8.1).

Movement Phases

1. Begin **4-4-4 breathing** (exhale for 4 seconds, hold breath for 4 seconds, and inhale for 4 seconds) for 4 minutes.
2. Try to elevate and depress the abdomen with each breath while reducing reciprocal rib cage movement.
3. Increase air pressure awareness in the pelvic floor, oblique areas, and posterior lumbar areas.
4. Gradually build awareness into the ability to maintain pressure in these areas.

Exercise Modifications and Variations
Hold a plate or weight on the abdomen and focus on raising the weight while breathing.

Coaching Tip
Developing an awareness of the breathing pattern is the first priority (2).

CHILD'S POSE BREATHING

Exercise Type
Core strengthening, repositioning

Primary Muscles Trained
Diaphragm, serratus anterior, internal oblique, external oblique

Beginning Position
- Begin in a quadruped position, then flex the hips and sit the buttocks back into the heels.
- Lower the chest to the knees in a prone position.
- Place elbows, forearms, and palms comfortably on the floor below (if flexibility levels permit it) and slightly in front of shoulders.
- Keep the eyes trained on the floor (figure 8.2).

Figure 8.2   Child's pose breathing

Movement Phases
1. Move the sternum away from the floor by pushing elbows down and into the floor.
2. Elongate the spine, as if trying to pull the ears away from the toes.
3. Maintain hip and knee flexion.

Breathing Guidelines
Exhale while pushing elbows into the floor and try to maintain that position. Use 4-4-4 breathing. While inhaling, imagine trying to fill the entire abdominal region, including the low back area, with air. Try to feel the pressure of the expanding abdominal wall on the thighs while inhaling.

Exercise Modifications and Variations
As competency is achieved, athletes will increase their ability to expand the posterior abdominal wall and lumbar area.

Coaching Tip
Maintain cervical neck extension by looking at the floor directly below the eyes (2).

90-90 HIP LIFT

Exercise Type
Core strengthening, repositioning

Primary Muscles Trained
Biceps femoris, semimembranosus, semitendinosus, serratus anterior

Beginning Position

- Lie supine (face up) with both feet on the wall at 90 degrees of hip and knee flexion. Flex both shoulders to a 90-degree angle with the elbows extended and the arms held directly above the shoulders.

- Reach the hands toward the ceiling, thereby activating the serratus anterior and causing rib depression (a).

Movement Phases

1. Press both heels into the wall and use them as an anchor point.

2. Activate the hamstrings by lifting the tailbone 1 to 2 inches (2.5-5 cm) off the floor thereby lifting the knees toward the ceiling.

3. Keep the heel pressure on the wall constant and stationary.

4. When executed properly, the pelvis will rotate posteriorly (b).

Breathing Guidelines

Use 4-4-4 breathing. Reach with arms while exhaling.

Figure 8.3 90-90 hip lift: (a) beginning position; (b) lift hips while pushing heels into the wall.

Exercise Modifications and Variations

In the presence of too much quadriceps activity, the athlete can shorten the distance between the tailbone and the wall. If hamstring activation is still minimal, the athlete can then take steps up the wall.

Coaching Tips

- Be sure the athlete feels the exercise in the hamstrings.

- Make sure the knees are directly above the hips and feet are at the level of the knees.

This technique has been modified and used with permission from the Postural Restoration Institute (4).

90-90 HEEL TAP

Exercise Type

Core strengthening, repositioning

Primary Muscles Trained

Diaphragm, internal oblique, external oblique

Beginning Position

- Lie supine (face up) with 90 degrees of hip and knee flexion with feet 1 to 2 inches (2.5-5 cm) away from the wall with the ankles dorsiflexed.
- The hands should be resting on the sides of the trunk (obliques) with the elbows flexed at 90 degrees and the upper arms each at a 45-degree angle to the trunk (a).

Movement Phases

1. Begin 4-4-4 breathing.
2. Maintain an exhaled position with the rib cage and create an isometric contraction of the internal and external obliques.
3. Extend one hip to move the heel of the foot toward the wall; softly tap the heel on the wall and return it to the beginning position. The other leg remains stationary (b).
4. Alternate for the desired number of repetitions while maintaining the intense outward pressure during the 4-4-4 breathing.

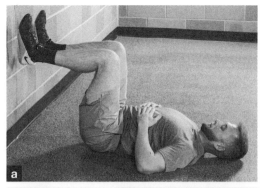

Figure 8.4   90-90 heel tap: (a) beginning position; (b) end position.

Breathing Guidelines

Use 4-4-4 breathing. Take small inhales during the breathing cycle and maintain outward pressure in all directions (anterior, lateral, and posterior).

DBACK'S BASEBALL PLANK

Exercise Type

Core strengthening, repositioning, isometric

Primary Muscles Trained

Gluteus medius, minimus, anterior fibers of the maximus, internal oblique, external oblique, rhomboid, serratus anterior, trapezius

Beginning Position

- Assume a side-lying running position (bottom hip extended with knee flexed to 90 degrees, top hip and knee both flexed to 90 degrees).
- Hold the top arm straight with the elbow comfortably extended and hand on hip.
- Position the bottom elbow directly underneath the shoulder on the floor, flexed to 90 degrees, with forearm in a neutral position and hand held in a fist (a).

Figure 8.5 Dback's baseball plank: *(a)* beginning position; *(b)* lift hips and top of lower leg off the floor.

Movement Phases

1. Slightly lift torso off the floor using the bottom knee and shoulder.
2. Isometrically hold a rigid position for 30 seconds *(b)*.
3. Switch sides and repeat.

Breathing Guidelines

Use 4-4-4 breathing.

Exercise Modifications and Variations

Progress time and repetition as earned.

Coaching Tips

- Only lift the torso off the floor enough to slide a piece of paper underneath.
- Maintain a neutral spine through the duration of the exercise.

HIP LIFT SIDE CRUNCH

Exercise Type

Anti-rotation, anti-extension, functional

Primary Muscles Trained

Transverse abdominis, rectus abdominis, internal oblique, external oblique, gluteal group

Beginning Position

- Lie on the floor on the left side with hips and knees flexed to 90 degrees.
- Position the left elbow on the floor directly under the shoulder with the forearm perpendicular to the body.
- Flex the right shoulder and elbow to 90 degrees with the palm of the hand cupping the right ear *(a)*.

Movement Phases

1. Begin by lifting up hips off the floor and fully exhaling to get the left abdominal wall engaged (b).
2. With the left abdominal wall engaged, inhale and flex the right hip to bring the right knee to meet the right elbow in a side crunch contracting the right oblique (c).
3. Exhale and return to the beginning position and repeat.

Breathing Guidelines

Do not hold the breath while performing the exercise; exhale during the crunch and inhale to return to the beginning position.

Coaching Tip

Be sure not to move into lumbar extension at any time.

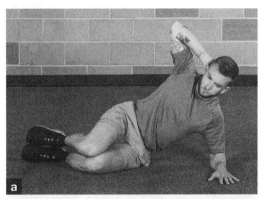

Figure 8.6 Hip lift side crunch (a) beginning position; (b) lift hips off the floor; (c) bring the right knee to the right elbow.

ALL-FOUR BELLY CROSS CONNECTS

Exercise Type

Core strengthening, repositioning

Primary Muscles Trained

Transverse abdominis, rectus abdominis, internal oblique, external oblique, gluteals, serratus anterior, rhomboids, rotator cuff muscles

Beginning Position

- Get into bear position. To achieve this position, start in a quadruped position with the elbows extended. The hands are in contact with the floor directly under the shoulders and the knees are flexed at 90 degrees directly under the hips. The ankles are dorsiflexed and the toes are in contact with the floor. Then, raise the knees off the floor so only the hands and toes are in contact with the floor (a).

Figure 8.7   All-four belly cross connects: *(a)* beginning position; *(b)* bring the left elbow to the right knee; *(c)* bring the right elbow to the left knee.

Movement Phases

1. Raise the ribs and hips.
2. Bring the right knee to meet the left elbow under the belly button *(b)*.
3. Return to the beginning position while keeping the abdominals engaged and ribs up.
4. Bring the left knee to meet the right elbow under the belly button and return to the beginning position *(c)*.
5. Repeat exercise for the desired number of repetitions.

Breathing Guidelines

Use 4-4-4 breathing; exhale while performing the movement (i.e., bringing the knee to the elbow) and inhale when engaging the abdominals between the leg–arm movements.

ALL-FOUR BELLY DISCONNECTS

Exercise Type

Core strengthening, repositioning

Primary Muscles Trained

Transverse abdominis, rectus abdominis, internal oblique, external oblique, serratus anterior, rhomboids

Figure 8.8 All-four belly disconnects: *(a)* beginning position; *(b)* move and flex the left knee upward; *(c)* bring the right knee next to the left knee.

Beginning Position

- Assume a prone push-up position (hands on the floor directly under the shoulders with the elbows extended and the toes on the floor in line with the hips and knees extended).
- Insert a yoga block under the left hand *(a)*.

Movement Phases

1. Inhale and then exhale while raising the ribs in the prone position.
2. Move the left foot up toward the outside of the left hand, flexing the left knee *(b)*.
3. Move the right foot up toward the inside of the left foot, flexing the right knee.
4. Touch the right knee to the left elbow and hold the position for three or four breaths *(c)*.
5. Return the feet to the push-up position. Step back with the right foot, then the left foot.
6. Repeat in the other direction (with the yoga block under the right hand).

Breathing Guidelines

Follow the guidelines in the Movement Phases section. Exhale as feet get close to the line created by the hands.

Exercise Modifications and Variations

Progression can be measured by walking the feet closer to the line created by the hands.

MEDICINE BALL WOOD CHOP

Exercise Type
Anti-rotation, medicine ball, functional

Primary Muscles Trained
Transverse abdominis, rectus abdominis, internal oblique, external oblique, gluteals

Beginning Position
- Stand with feet shoulder-width apart.
- Hold medicine ball above the head with shoulders flexed and elbows extended.

Movement Phases
1. Initiate movement by flexing the lumbar spine (trunk) while keeping elbows and knees extended. The feet remain flat on the floor.
2. Stop movement when the medicine ball reaches the ankles or feet.
3. Return to the beginning position by extending the lumbar spine while keeping the elbows and knees extended.

Breathing Guidelines
Exhale during trunk flexion. Inhale during trunk extension.

Exercise Modifications and Variations

Medicine Ball Wood Chop Throw

Perform this exercise the same way as the medicine ball wood chop, but throw the ball explosively into the floor in front of the head. Let the medicine ball rebound before attempting to catch it. Make sure to keep the head down on follow-through.

Medicine Ball Twisting Wood Chop Throw

Begin with feet shoulder-width apart and trunk flexed. Hold the medicine ball in both hands at the ankles. Initiate the movement by extending and rotating the trunk with the medicine ball over the right shoulder. Once in this position, rotate the medicine ball over the head and explosively throw the ball into the floor in front of the head. Repeat in the other direction.

Medicine Ball Diagonal Wood Chop (figure 8.9)

Begin by standing with feet shoulder-width apart. Hold the medicine ball above the head and over the left shoulder with shoulders flexed and elbows extended (a). Diagonally flex the lumbar spine (trunk) down and to the right, keeping the elbows extended, until the medicine ball is over the left ankle or foot (b). Extend and untwist the lumbar spine to return to the beginning position with the ball over the left shoulder and the elbows still extended. When finished with the desired number of repetitions, repeat in the other direction.

Medicine Ball Diagonal Wood Chop Throw

Perform this exercise the same way as the medicine ball diagonal wood chop, but explosively throw the ball down and across the body into the floor.

Figure 8.9 Medicine ball diagonal wood chop: *(a)* beginning position; *(b)* end position.

Medicine Ball Overhead Throw

Begin by standing with feet hip-width apart facing a solid wall. The medicine ball is held with both hands on one side of the ball and slightly underneath. The medicine ball is brought back behind the head, then thrown vigorously into the wall (similar to the action used for a soccer sideline throw-in). The athlete is permitted to aggressively step forward as they throw.

Seated Partner Medicine Ball Overhead Toss

Begin seated with the heels touching the floor, knees flexed, and arms extended overhead while facing a partner who is holding a medicine ball at his chest. Engage the abdominal muscles by leaning back. To initiate the exercise, the partner passes the medicine ball, aiming between the forehead and hands raised over the athlete's head. Maintain an engaged core while catching the medicine ball. The shoulders will flex and the trunk will extend, causing a stretch reflex. Once the shoulder blades touch the floor, perform explosive trunk flexion to accelerate the upper body off the floor and toss the medicine ball back to the partner.

Coaching Tips

- Do not flex elbows during exercise.
- Maintain good posture throughout the exercise.

SEATED TWIST

Exercise Type

Rotational, medicine ball

Primary Muscles Trained

Transverse abdominis, rectus abdominis, internal oblique, external oblique

Beginning Position

- Begin in a seated position with legs and feet in front of body and torso in an upright position.
- Hold the medicine ball in front of the belly button with elbows flexed (a).

Movement Phases

1. Rotate to the right and place the medicine ball down on the floor directly behind the back (b).
2. Rotate to the left until medicine ball can be picked up.
3. Once the medicine ball is picked up, rotate torso with the medicine ball back to the right.
4. Once repetitions are completed, repeat on the other side.

Breathing Guidelines

Inhale while loading the ball backward. Exhale while moving the ball forward.

Exercise Modifications and Variations

Standing Half Twist

Have two athletes stand back-to-back. One athlete will hold the medicine ball at the belly button with elbows flexed. When the exercise begins, the athlete with the medicine ball

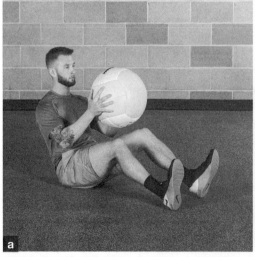 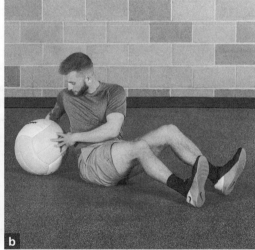

Figure 8.10   Seated twist: (a) beginning position; (b) rotate the torso.

will rotate to the right while the other athlete rotates to the left, where they exchange the medicine ball at the hip. The athletes will then rotate in the opposite direction to exchange the medicine ball by the other hip.

Standing Full Twist

Have the athletes stand with their backs to each other 2 feet (61 cm) apart so the medicine ball can be exchanged behind them while both athletes rotate to their right. This will require greater range of motion than the standing half twist. Once repetitions are completed, athletes will switch direction.

Seated Trunk Rotation Toss

Begin in a seated position with an upright torso and legs and feet in front of body. Rotate lumbar spine to the right with extended arms and open hands. The coach will be standing 4 to 5 feet (1.2-1.5 m) behind the athlete to chest pass a medicine ball to the athlete. The athlete will catch the medicine ball, rotate quickly in the opposite direction, and toss the medicine ball explosively back to the coach. Once the desired number of repetitions are completed, the athlete will perform the exercise in the other direction.

Standing Trunk Rotation Toss

This exercise follows the same format as the seated trunk rotation toss, but from a standing position.

Coaching Tips

- Make sure to turn the lumbar spine and shoulders simultaneously.
- Maintain good posture throughout the exercise rotation.
- Do not let the medicine ball roll on the floor.
- Rotate as fast as possible while maintaining control.
- Make sure to go both directions.

MEDICINE BALL SIDE TOSS

Exercise Type
Rotational, medicine ball, throwing

Primary Muscles Trained
Transverse abdominis, rectus abdominis, internal oblique, external oblique, glutes

Beginning Position

- Assume an athletic stance perpendicular to a solid wall with a wide stable base, similar to a hitting stance, with feet wider than shoulder width.
- Hold a medicine ball approximately chest high with the palms positioned at a right angle (the front hand supporting the ball from underneath and the back hand placed at the rear of the ball). The arms should be extended from the body with the upper arms supported by the torso (a).

Figure 8.11   Medicine ball side toss: *(a)* beginning position; *(b)* rotate away from wall; *(c)* rotate toward the wall and throw the ball.

Movement Phases

1. From the beginning position, rotate the torso away from the wall (approximately 90 degrees) with arms fully extended, shifting the weight to the rear leg *(b)*.
2. After completing the backswing, explosively rotate toward the wall and toss the medicine ball in the transverse plane at the wall *(c)*.
3. Once appropriate repetitions are completed, repeat in the other direction.

Breathing Guidelines

Inhale as the torso and medicine ball are rotated away from the wall. Exhale as the torso and medicine ball are rotated and tossed toward the wall.

Exercise Modifications and Variations

Front-Facing Medicine Ball Toss

A medicine ball can also be tossed while facing a wall. This will require the athlete to perform a countermovement rotation to the right while internally rotating the left foot and hip before explosively rotating to the left to toss the medicine ball into the wall. After the medicine ball rebounds off the wall, the athlete must catch and decelerate the medicine ball before tossing it again. Once repetitions are completed, switch sides.

Front-Facing Medicine Ball Toss Across

The medicine ball can also be tossed across the body so the athlete has to catch the ball on the opposite side of the body. This will incorporate more hip rotation in both directions. Make sure to toss the medicine ball far enough across the body against the wall so that it can be caught with arms extended and hands open on the opposite side of the body before performing the countermovement rotation of the next repetition.

Lateral Rotation Medicine Ball Shot Put

Assume the same beginning position as the medicine ball side toss with the ball at chest level. The left hand supports the ball from the front while the right hand acts as a pushing hand. To perform the movement, shift the weight back to the right foot as a countermovement, then explosively rotate the torso while pushing the medicine ball with the right hand toward the wall. When repetitions are completed, switch directions.

Coaching Tips

- Toss the medicine ball parallel to the floor, not upward.
- Rotate the hips around a rigid front leg.
- Use the legs, torso, and arms to help maximize tossing velocity.
- Maintain a good position while rotating.

FRONT PLANK

Exercise Type
Anti-extension, anti-flexion, isometric

Primary Muscles Trained
Transverse abdominis, rectus abdominis, multifidus, internal oblique, external oblique, erector spinae, glutes

Beginning Position

- Lie prone (face down) on the floor with the knees and hips fully extended, feet hip-width apart, and ankles dorsiflexed so toes are in contact with the floor.
- Flex the elbows to 90 degrees and position them directly underneath the shoulders so the forearms

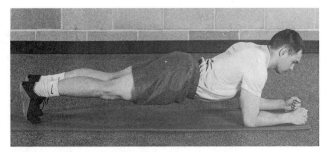

Figure 8.12 Front plank

are in contact with the floor with palms down or forearms supinated in a neutral position with hands in fists.

Movement Phases

1. Begin by pushing the toes into the floor and engaging the muscles of the legs.
2. Keeping the legs engaged, push the elbows into the floor and lift the hips off the floor to the neutral spine position (figure 8.12).
3. Hold the plank position for a predetermined time determined by coach.

Breathing Guidelines

Breathe normally throughout the exercise.

Exercise Modifications and Variations

This exercise can be made more advanced by bracing the hands on the floor with elbows extended. The athlete could also have both elbows and one foot in contact with the floor, with the free foot either resting on the back of the other ankle or with the free leg extended and lifted in the air with the toe pointed down (i.e., the ankle dorsiflexed). The athlete could also have both feet and one elbow in contact with the floor with the free arm outstretched, or the opposite elbow and foot in contact with the floor with both the free arm and leg extended and lifted in the air. Resistance could also be added to the athlete's body with a weighted vest or by placing a weight plate on the upper back. Finally, a stability ball could be used for foot placement while the athlete performs this exercise.

Side Plank

Lie on one side with the feet and knees together. The lower arm should have the elbow placed directly under the shoulder and flexed at 90 degrees with the palm resting on the floor. The elbow of the upper arm should be extended with the arm resting on the side of the torso and the palm resting on the side of the hip or upper thigh. Begin the exercise by pushing the lower elbow and outside edge of the lower foot into the floor to raise the hips off the floor until a neutral spine position is achieved. Hold the side plank position for a determined time. To make this exercise more advanced, the athlete can balance on the hand of the lower arm with the elbow extended. Resistance could be held by the upper hand on the hip, or a weighted vest could be worn. Different positions of the upper leg or arm can also be performed.

Coaching Tips

- Keep head, shoulders, hips, knees, and feet in a straight line.
- Contract glutes and push the hips forward to maintain correct posture in the side plank.

DEAD BUG

Exercise Type

Anti-rotation, anti-extension, anti-lateral flexion, functional

Primary Muscles Trained

Transverse abdominis, rectus abdominis, internal oblique, external oblique

Beginning Position

- Lie supine (face up) on the floor with the knees and hips flexed at 90 degrees.

- Place the arms straight out in front of the body and hold a stability ball in place with the hands (or forearms) and knees *(a)*.

Movement Phases

1. While keeping the entire back in contact with the floor, apply light pressure with the knees and hands against the stability ball to engage the abdominal muscles.

2. Extend contralateral limbs (i.e., limbs on opposite sides such as the right arm and the left leg, or the left arm and the right leg) simultaneously and in a controlled manner until both the leg and arm reach full extension a few inches (~5 cm) off the floor. The non-moving hand and knee should actively press into the ball to provide isometric anatomical core stability *(b and c)*.

3. Hold the end position for a moment and return the contralateral hand and knee back to the ball in the beginning position.

4. Repeat the movement with the other contralateral limbs and continue to alternate for the recommended repetitions.

Figure 8.13   Dead bug: *(a)* beginning position; *(b and c)* contralateral movements.

Breathing Guidelines

Begin with a full exhalation and apply pressure into the ball with the hands and knees. Inhale during the extension of the contralateral limbs. Exhale as the contralateral limbs return to the beginning position.

Exercise Modifications and Variations

If the athlete cannot maintain lower back contact with the floor during contralateral limb movement, then regress and have the athlete hold the beginning position for a designated time. This exercise can also be performed without a stability ball with arms and legs straight and moving in an alternate fashion.

Coaching Tips

- Check to see if the lumbar spine is in contact with the floor during the initial positioning.
- If there is a gap, slide a hand under the low back and cue the athlete to tilt the hips anteriorly to get the lumbar spine in contact with the floor.

SINGLE-LEG ABDOMINAL CURL-UP

Exercise Type

Anti-extension, traditional

Primary Muscles Trained

Rectus abdominis

Beginning Position

- Lie in a supine (face up) position with one foot flat on the floor, knee flexed, and the other leg fully extended with the toes pointed up.
- Place both hands palm down with fingers pointed and touching each other under the lumbar spine (curve of the low back) with elbows pointed away from the body (a).

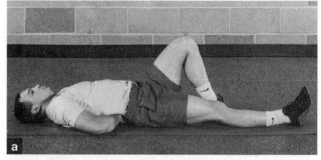

Figure 8.14 Single-leg abdominal curl-up: (a) beginning position; (b) curl the torso.

Movement Phases

1. Maintain neck in neutral position, aligned with the spine.
2. Curl the torso up to raise the upper back and shoulder blades off the floor (b).
3. Hold for 2 to 3 seconds.
4. Uncurl the torso back to the beginning position.

Breathing Guidelines

Use a smooth, controlled exhale during the concentric phase. Inhale during the eccentric phase.

Exercise Modifications and Variations

The athlete can raise the extended leg and elbows off the floor to make the exercise more challenging.

Abdominal Curl-Up

The exercise is performed with both feet on the floor, knees flexed, and arms fully extended at the sides of the body with palms down. Initiate the curl by raising the upper back and shoulder blades off the floor while sliding the hands forward. When the concentric phase is completed, uncurl the torso to the beginning position.

Coaching Tip

Maintain a rib-down position during the entire exercise.

ABDOMINAL CRUNCH

Exercise Type

Anti-extension, traditional

Primary Muscles Trained

Transverse abdominis, rectus abdominis, external oblique

Beginning Position

- Lie in a supine (face up) position on the floor with hips and knees flexed at 90 degrees and arms folded across the chest.
- Place heels on a bench with toes pointed up (a).

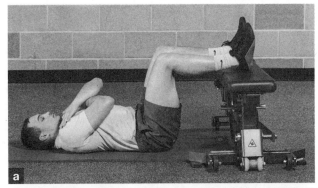

Movement Phases

1. Flex the neck to move the chin toward the chest.
2. Keeping the feet, buttocks, lower back, and arms in the same position, curl torso toward the thighs until the

Figure 8.15   Abdominal crunch: (a) beginning position; (b) curl the torso.

upper back and shoulder blades are off the floor (b).

3. When the concentric phase is completed, uncurl the torso back to beginning position.

Breathing Guidelines

Exhale during the concentric phase. Inhale throughout the entire eccentric phase.

Exercise Modifications and Variations

Crossover Crunch

Place the hands behind the head with elbows pointed away from the body. During the concentric phase of the exercise, rotate the right elbow toward the left knee. On the next repetition, rotate the left elbow toward the right knee.

Suitcase Crunch

Place hands on the head for a landmark only. Do not pull the head forward with the arms. The head and heels begin on the floor; elbows and knees meet simultaneously in the middle for a split second and return to the beginning position.

Side Crunch

Begin in a side-lying position with legs slightly flexed and hands on the head. Laterally flex the trunk, contracting the abdominals and oblique muscles. Lower the trunk to the beginning position.

Reverse Abdominal Crunch

Lie with head, shoulders, and buttocks in contact with the surface of a stable bench or floor. Grab the bench behind the head for stability, keeping forearms against the sides of head. (If on the floor, place extended arms palms down to the sides of the body or positioned under the lumbar spine for additional support.) Flex hips and knees at 90-degree angles. Thighs should be perpendicular to the floor. Slowly lift pelvis (buttocks) off the bench or floor until feet point to the ceiling. Bring knees slowly toward chest, lifting hips and glutes off the bench or floor. Use abdominal muscles, rather than the momentum of the legs. Maintain the flexion in the knees throughout the movement. Pause briefly at the top of the motion. Contract abdominal muscles hard and lower legs slowly to the beginning position.

Stability Ball Crunch Variations

Most of the previous exercises can be performed on a stability ball, such as the abdominal crunch and crossover crunch.

Coaching Tip

Maintain a rib-down position during the entire exercise.

SUPERMAN

Exercise Type

Anti-rotation, extension, functional

Primary Muscles Trained

Transverse abdominis, rectus abdominis, internal oblique, external oblique, glutes, quadratus lumborum

Figure 8.16   Superman: *(a)* beginning position; *(b)* raise arms and legs simultaneously.

Beginning Position

- Begin in prone (face down) position on the floor with arms and legs fully extended *(a)*.

Movement Phases

1. Activate the core to raise arms and legs simultaneously, keeping them fully extended.
2. Hold extended position *(b)*.
3. Relax core and return to beginning position.

Breathing Guidelines

Breathe normally throughout the exercise.

Exercise Modifications and Variations

This exercise can be performed while raising the opposite arm and leg simultaneously. Resistance can be added by holding a weight plate on the back of the head with elbows out to the side or by attaching weights around the wrists and ankles.

Coaching Tip

Focus on activating the glutes, core, and back extensors to lift the arms and legs.

SUPINE GLUTE BRIDGE

Exercise Type

Extension, functional

Primary Muscles Trained

Erector spinae, gluteus maximus, hamstrings (semimembranosus, semitendinosus, biceps femoris)

Beginning Position

- Lie supine (face up) with knees flexed, heels on the floor, and lumbar spine pressed into the floor (a).

Movement Phases

1. Press feet into floor to raise hips toward the ceiling.
2. Maintain a straight-line position from shoulders to knees.
3. Contract the glutes, keeping hamstrings loose (b).
4. Eccentrically lower hips slowly back to the floor while maintaining core position.

Breathing Guidelines

Inhale in the beginning position. Use a smooth, controlled exhale during the concentric and eccentric phases while maintaining the core position.

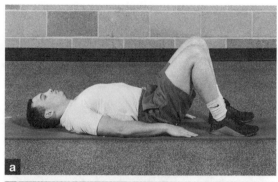

Figure 8.17 Supine glute bridge: (a) beginning position; (b) lift hips.

Exercise Modifications and Variations

Single-Leg Glute Bridge

Lift one knee into the chest while the opposite foot is flat on the floor. Press the foot into the floor and extend hips until alignment between shoulders and knees is straight.

Coaching Tip

Maintain rib-down position and core pressure throughout the entire exercise.

FARMER'S WALK

Exercise Type

Anti-lateral flexion, functional

Primary Muscles Trained

Transverse abdominis, internal oblique, external oblique, rectus abdominis, erector spinae, iliopsoas, gluteal, forearm muscles

Beginning Position

- Stand erect and hold one dumbbell or kettlebell in each hand with arms hanging down and slightly away from the sides of the body.
- Maintain a neutral hand position.

Movement Phases

1. Begin walking forward with control for the prescribed distance or time.
2. Keep shoulders square and level throughout the movement while maintaining a normal walking gait.
3. While moving, maintain complete control of the dumbbells or kettlebells; do not allow momentum to cause them to swing.
4. Engage the abdominals and maintain trunk stiffness throughout the movement (figure 8.18).

Breathing Guidelines

Use smooth, controlled breaths, maintaining intra-abdominal pressure throughout the movement.

Figure 8.18 Farmer's walk

Exercise Modifications and Variations

The farmer's walk exercise can be performed with barbells rather than dumbbells or kettlebells. It could also be performed while holding a barbell, dumbbell, kettlebell, or free weight plate in one hand hanging at the side. The athlete could hold one or two dumbbells or kettlebells in a rack position by the shoulder or over the head with the arm extended like a waiter in a restaurant. The athlete could hold one dumbbell or kettlebell in the rack position and the other in the side hanging position. Finally, the farmer's walk and its variations could be performed while walking backward.

Coaching Tips

- Keep the trunk stiff and ribs down.
- Do not lean to one side.
- Maintain a normal walking pattern.

KNEELING PALLOF PRESS

Exercise Type

Anti-rotation, functional

Primary Muscles Trained

Transverse abdominis, rectus abdominis, internal oblique, external oblique, erector spinae, glutes

Beginning Position

- Start in a tall kneeling position (both knees on the floor while body is upright) slightly behind the resistance cable machine with the ribs stacked on the pelvis and pushing down, activating the glutes.

- Use the outside hand to support the handle attached to the resistance cable machine at the sternum (a).

Movement Phases

1. Maintain the rib position while pushing arms out (extending the elbows), using the core to prevent torso rotation (b).
2. Bring the arms back to the sternum and reset.

Breathing Guidelines

Inhale during the eccentric phase and exhale during the concentric phase, focusing on maintaining core pressure throughout the entire movement.

Exercise Modifications and Variations

This exercise can be performed while standing with feet shoulder-width apart, toes pointed forward, and knees slightly flexed. The glutes should be contracted, and the athlete should be applying pressure into the floor with the feet. This exercise can be performed from a half-kneeling, kneeling, or staggered position while pressing the resistance cable overhead.

Landmine Rainbow

Stand facing a landmine with the end of the bar at shoulder height while holding the bar in the palms of both hands and elbows flexed. Maintain an athletic body position, with the toes, knees, hips, and shoulders pointed forward, feet shoulder-width apart, and knees slightly flexed. Get into the beginning position by extending the elbows so the bar is pressed up in front of the face. Rotate the bar from side-to-side in an arching motion with elbows extended while not allowing the torso to rotate (i.e., maintain a neutral spine while engaging the anatomical core musculature).

Figure 8.19   Kneeling pallof press: (a) beginning position; (b) press.

Coaching Tips

- Maintain anatomical core pressure throughout the entire exercise.
- Focus on keeping the ribs down and in a stacked position with the abdominals throughout the entire movement.
- When elbows are extended, the bar should be at a 90-degree angle to the hands.

KNEELING STICK CHOP

Exercise Type
Anti-rotation, anti-lateral flexion, functional

Primary Muscles Trained
Transverse abdominis, rectus abdominis, internal oblique, external oblique, erector spinae, glutes

Beginning Position
- Start in a tall kneeling position with the cable overhead, activating glutes and keeping ribs down and stacked over the pelvis.
- Grab the bar with an overhand, pronated grip.
- Extend the elbow of the inside arm (closest to the machine) and flex the elbow of the outside arm *(a)*.

Movement Phases
1. While maintaining a neutral spine position, extend the elbow of the outside arm so the stick is in front of the body, diagonal to the machine *(b)*.
2. Adduct the shoulder of the inside arm and press the bar across the chest into a locked-out position, keeping the elbow of the outside arm extended *(c)*.
3. Return the inside arm to the chest by flexing the elbow *(d)*.
4. Return the outside arm to a flexed-elbow position while extending the elbow of the inside arm *(e)*.

Breathing Guidelines
Inhale at the beginning position. Use a smooth, controlled exhale during the concentric and eccentric phases (as the stick moves).

Exercise Modifications and Variations
This exercise can be performed while standing in an athletic body position with the toes, knees, hips, and shoulders pointed forward, feet shoulder-width apart, and knees slightly flexed. The movement of the bar will be the same as from the kneeling position. The athlete can also use a half-kneeling or staggered stance while performing the exercise.

Coaching Tips
- Maintain anatomical core pressure throughout the entire exercise.
- Focus on keeping the ribs down and in a stacked position throughout the entire movement.
- Focus on breathing normally throughout the movement and obtaining full range of motion.
- Do not allow the body to rotate.

Figure 8.20   Kneeling stick chop: *(a)* beginning position; *(b)* extend outside arm; *(c)* press inside arm away from chest; *(d)* return inside arm to chest; *(e)* flex outside arm.

KNEELING STICK LIFT

Exercise Type

Anti-rotation, anti-extension, functional

Primary Muscles Trained

Transverse abdominis, rectus abdominis, internal oblique, external oblique, erector spinae, glutes

Beginning Position

- Start in a tall kneeling position, activating glutes and keeping ribs down and stacked over the pelvis.
- Grab the bar with an overhand, pronated grip.
- Flex the outside elbow (furthest from the machine) and extend the inside elbow (a).
- The location of the cable, attached to the bar, is below the athlete's hip.

Movement Phases

1. Extend the elbow of outside arm so the stick is in front of the chest diagonal to the machine while maintaining a neutral spine position (b).
2. Keeping the elbow of the outside arm extended, adduct the inside shoulder, pressing the bar up and diagonally away from the chest and cable machine so the outside hand is at the level of the head or higher (not shown in figure 8.21).
3. Return the inside arm by abducting the shoulder while keeping the elbow in the locked-out position.
4. Return the outside arm by flexing the elbow to the beginning position.

Figure 8.21   Kneeling stick lift: (a) beginning position; (b) extend outside arm (final position is not shown).

Breathing Guidelines

Inhale at the beginning position. Use a smooth, controlled exhale during the concentric and eccentric phases (as the stick moves).

Exercise Modifications and Variations

This exercise can be performed while standing in an athletic body position with the toes, knees, hips, and shoulders pointed forward, feet shoulder-width apart, knees slightly flexed while holding the bar. The movement of the bar will be the same as from the kneeling position. The athlete can also use a half-kneeling or staggered stance while performing the exercise.

Coaching Tips

- Maintain anatomical core pressure throughout the entire exercise.
- Focus on keeping the ribs down and in a stacked position throughout the entire movement.
- Focus on breathing normally throughout the movement and obtaining full range of motion.
- Do not allow the body to rotate.

STABILITY BALL CABLE ROTATION

Exercise Type

Rotational, functional

Primary Muscles Trained

Transverse abdominis, rectus abdominis, internal oblique, external oblique, erector spinae, glutes

Beginning Position

- Stand in an athletic position perpendicular to the cable machine with the left side of the body facing the column. Make sure to stand 2 to 3 feet (61-91 cm) away from the machine so the cable is already outstretched, and the weight is pulled up off the rest of the stack. This will allow room for a countermovement toward the cable machine to lower the weight and eccentrically load the muscles.
- Hug a stability ball with both arms while holding the handle with the outside (right) hand (a).

Movement Phases

1. Rotate to the left toward the cable machine, lowering the weight to eccentrically load the muscles (b).
2. When the weight touches the stack, rotate to the right to concentrically load the muscles (c).
3. When repetitions are completed, perform exercise in the opposite direction.

Breathing Guidelines

Inhale while rotating toward the machine column (eccentric movement). Exhale while rotating away from the machine column (concentric movement).

Figure 8.22 Stability ball cable rotation: *(a)* beginning position; *(b)* rotate toward the cable machine; *(c)* rotate away from the cable machine.

Exercise Modifications and Variations

This exercise can also be performed while sitting on a stability ball, holding the cable handle with both hands at chest level with the elbows of both arms fully extended. Make sure to maintain body posture with the head looking forward while pulling the cable across the body. Once the repetitions are completed, switch directions.

Coaching Tips

- Maintain anatomical core pressure throughout the entire exercise.
- Focus on keeping the ribs down and in a stacked position throughout the entire movement.
- Focus on breathing normally throughout the movement and obtaining full range of motion.
- Focus on loading the hips while maintaining anatomical core pressure.
- Maintain body posture throughout the entire exercise.

STABILITY BALL
REVERSE BACK EXTENSION

Exercise Type

Extension, traditional

Primary Muscles Trained

Erector spinae

Beginning Position

- Kneel on the floor in front of the stability ball.
- Roll forward onto the ball so that the abdomen rests on the top of the ball in a prone position.
- Place the hands on the floor directly underneath the shoulders with the elbows extended.
- Squeeze the legs together with knees extended and toes in contact with the floor.
- Isometrically contract the muscles of the torso to create a rigid trunk (a).

Figure 8.23 Stability ball reverse back extension: (a) beginning position; (b) end position.

Movement Phases

1. Keep the lower body in a rigid position and raise the legs by extending the hips until they are at the level of the torso (b).
2. Lower the legs back to the beginning position.

Breathing Guidelines

Inhale at the beginning position. Use a smooth, controlled exhale during the concentric and eccentric phases of the repetition.

Exercise Modifications and Variations

Stability Ball Back Extension

Follow the same beginning position guidelines, but once balance is achieved, push the feet into the floor and place hands behind the head with elbows pointed away from the head. Raise the upper body off the stability ball by performing a back extension until it is in line with the hips and thighs.

Coaching Tips

- Do not rotate the legs, pelvis, or upper body during the exercise.
- Do not swing the legs up; focus on concentrically contracting the muscles of the low back.

PART III

PROGRAM DESIGN GUIDELINES AND SAMPLE PROGRAMS

9

OFF-SEASON PROGRAMMING

PATRICK MCHENRY (HIGH SCHOOL), CHRIS JOYNER (COLLEGE), JOE KESSLER (PROFESSIONAL)

The off-season is the beginning of a new annual training cycle; therefore, it is presented first in this section. The off-season is considered the preparatory period (5). Because the duration of in-season play and yearly scheduling is unique for each level of play, the length of time each athlete trains in the off-season is different. However, it generally lasts from the end of the postseason to the beginning of the preseason (5).

The off-season resistance training program provided in this chapter is designed for the baseball athlete. It includes goals and objectives; length, structure, and organization of the off-season; recommended exercises; positional exercise considerations; intensity; volume; and exercise order for high school, college, and professional athletes.

GOALS AND OBJECTIVES

In general, the off-season comprises three or four phases, made up of four or five microcycles, depending on how the coach designs the resistance training program for their level of play. At the beginning of the off-season, athletes' strengths and weaknesses are evaluated (testing protocols are covered in chapter 3). After testing is completed, the athletes begin a hypertrophy/ strength endurance phase, which is often called the "train to train" phase. Then the training program will transition to incorporate a basic strength phase, followed by a maximum strength phase. Finally, the athletes will begin a power or speed strength phase that generally leads into preseason training. The maximum strength and power phases, which occur during the second half of the off-season, are often called the "train to compete" phase. In this section, each level of play's goals and objectives will be discussed.

High School

Off-season resistance training for the high school baseball player usually runs from mid- to late August to mid- to late December, when students begin the holiday break. Some high school athletes will play with a club baseball team in the fall or participate in a fall sport; however, this chapter will only address those athletes who are training at their high school beginning in August. This allows the coach approximately four months to work with the athletes. Coaches should keep in mind that athletes will have limited time to resistance train during finals week, as well as over the holiday break, when they may not have access to a weight room.

The objectives for the high school off-season training program are to assess the athlete's health status, make sure there are no chronic injuries that need to be addressed, look for imbalances in the muscular system, work on rehab areas, and develop proper lifting technique. The goal of the off-season is to develop basic and maximum strength as well as get the athlete ready for the preseason. The athlete should have a solid base of strength established to allow for power training by the beginning of the preseason.

College

The off-season is a great time for the coach to begin to implement and design individualized year-round training programs with three goals in mind: maximizing sports performance by improving athletic ability, decreasing the risk of injury, and improving lifestyle characteristics that promote career longevity. This training season is typically the only time athletes can dedicate themselves to heavy training without playing games simultaneously.

Because baseball is a sport that requires complex and repetitive movement patterns, there is a high impact on an athlete's body. Therefore, it is essential for the coach to evaluate how their athletes move prior to designing and prescribing resistance training programs that will optimize athletic development and minimize injury risk. A great way to look at the progression of human movement is to use Gray Cook's Functional Performance Pyramid, where movement is the foundation, performance is in the middle, and skill is at the top (3). Within each of these blocks the components are further described as follows: movement requires proprioception, flexibility, mobility, and stability; performance includes strength, power, speed, agility, and anatomical core stability; and sports skill is athlete- and position-specific. There should also be individualized corrective exercise strategies prescribed based on any movement assessment screens that have been performed on the athlete prior to the start of resistance training. Targeted mobility areas include, but are not limited, to thoracic spine (T-spine), hips, hamstrings, and ankles. See "Warm-Ups: Mobility, Corrective, Active Dynamic, and In-Place Flow Stretch Exercises" on page 211. Mobility and corrective exercises are available online (see https://functionalmovement.com/exercises).

Professional

Baseball is played with skills that require reaction and acceleration, demanding strength, power, and superior mobility from the athlete. To maximize physical development, a linear progression works best for off-season planning. Because baseball is a rotational, shoulder, and hip dominant sport, the emphasis during this time is on maximizing the athlete's strength and power while maintaining mobility within the thoracic spine as well as the shoulder, hip, and ankle joints. A thoughtful approach to exercise positioning, external load volume, mobility, and stability provides opportunities for athletes to develop physically while retaining the skill-related attributes of swinging, fielding, and throwing.

The baseball athlete must be able to move efficiently within all three planes of motion—sagittal, frontal, and transverse. To accomplish this, they must first develop movement efficiency within the sagittal plane, which accounts for dissociation of the anatomical core and hip musculature. Once movement competency and strength have been developed in the sagittal plane, the athlete can progress to frontal plane movements, and then transverse, sport-specific movements for rotation. A general approach to the athlete's strength and power needs should also be prescribed with a template protocol for overall physical development throughout the off-season phase.

The transition through the seasons should also continue to address the specific needs associated with the athlete's individualized skill fundamentals and physical development goals. To maximize the athlete's potential, individualized training programs should be developed to meet these needs. Training should be prescribed to complement the athlete's skill-related ability while working to correct deficiencies such as body composition, movement capacity, strength, power, and speed.

The exercise prescription assists in meeting the athlete's needs and goals prior to the start of the next preseason. Because there is less skill-related practice and game-play during the off-season, these goals are best addressed through an off-season program. Although the duration of an off-season program may vary from athlete to athlete given their developmental goals and postseason playing opportunities, there should be adequate time devoted to addressing the athlete's individual needs and goals during this period.

LENGTH, STRUCTURE, AND ORGANIZATION

The length, structure, and organization of the off-season program is determined by the level of play (high school, college, or professional), facilities, and geographic location. Each level of play will be addressed in this section. In general, the structure for all levels of training includes a warm-up before resistance training begins. Page 211 shows various warm-up options that include mobility, corrective, active dynamic, and in-place flow stretch exercises that are recommended for athletes at the beginning of every resistance training session. Coaches should pick the most appropriate option for the specific training day. Some of these exercises are incorporated into the sample off-season programs for college and professional athletes.

High School

The first two weeks of the high school off-season can be used to assess the athletes (see chapter 3 for testing protocols). Test results will help a coach determine each athlete's strengths and weaknesses, which can be used to personalize the athlete's resistance training program. Because the first two weeks of the off-season are used for testing, the resistance training programs provided in tables 9.1 and 9.2 begin with week 3. The off-season will be divided into three general phases: basic strength, maximum strength, and power. Each phase consists of four days a week of resistance training, with the lower body trained on Mondays and Thursdays and the upper body trained on Tuesdays and Fridays. Wednesday is an off day. The off-season program is not position specific and can be divided into groups based on training age, which allows the coach to focus on the athletes' needs and development. After completing the initial testing, athletes will begin training with a four-week basic strength phase in September (see tables 9.1 and 9.2). The resistance training program will then transition to a three-week maximum strength phase in October (see tables 9.3 and 9.4). (Note that many high schools have a fall break or finals week at the end of October to conclude the first nine weeks of classes.) After this phase, there will be a power phase that is divided into two microcycles. Microcycle 3 will be a three-week power phase that goes until the Thanksgiving break at the end of November (see table 9.5). Microcycle 4 will be a three-week power phase, which leads to finals week and winter break at the end of December (see table 9.6). When the athletes return to school in January, the preseason phase will begin.

College

The off-season length and start time will most likely vary among college programs, so it is important to keep in mind that the training program must adapt to the individual situation and off-season calendar structure. The example programs outlined in this mesocycle are based on a 20-week off-season beginning in August following the active rest period and postseason phase, and ending in December around the NCAA discretionary period and academic finals (see tables 9.7-9.10). It will be linear in nature with changes in volume and intensity throughout. Exercise selection will be based on upper body push and pull exercises, lower body hinge and squat exercises, and anatomical core stability exercises that include loaded carries and proximal stability exercise variations. Exercises are basic in nature to allow the athlete to develop proficiency in the movements and patterns that matter the most, which will ultimately transfer into the demands of the sport.

The resistance training program will initially be a four-days-per-week split routine, with the lower body trained on Monday and Thursday and the upper body on Tuesday and Friday. Wednesday is an off day, with a focus on recovery. The program focus will be on hypertrophy/strength endurance (see table 9.7). Each resistance training session typically lasts 50 to 60 minutes.

Summer school for incoming freshman and returning athletes as well as summer baseball also occur during this time. Coaches may design and conduct resistance training programs provided such workouts are voluntary and conducted at the request of the athlete per NCAA rules and regulations. This is a great opportunity for the coach to perform a movement screen assessment for new athletes to direct individualized programming, educate them on exercise selection and technique, and inform them about the overall training expectations. For returning athletes, this time in the summer gives them and the coach a chance to address issues and deficiencies from the previous season, such as lack of mobility and stability in certain areas, anatomical core strength, and any injuries that occurred during the in-season.

When the fall semester or quarter begins, the athletes will transition to a basic strength phase, comprising two four-week microcycles (see table 9.8). Unique to the college off-season, where typically no competition or practices take place, most athletes will have a 45-day fall practice window in which the team can practice, have intrasquad games, and compete in two preseason games. Each college team designates when this period will begin, but it is generally the first of October through early November. During this time, there is a delicate balance of training, practice, and competition. Strength and conditioning professionals can continue training athletes as planned by transitioning to a four-week maximum strength phase (see table 9.9), or they can simulate the in-season training phase for position players and relief pitchers or starting pitchers where intrasquad games occur up to four days a week (Tuesday, Friday, Saturday, and Sunday). Ultimately, this can add up to 16 games over the four weeks.

Scheduling a well-balanced resistance training program can be challenging, but one way for position players and relief pitchers to continue to train and compete simultaneously is to have two total body resistance training days and one mobility/recovery session per week. This can be accomplished by combining the four-day upper/lower body split routine into two total body routines for position players and relief pitchers (see table 11.4 on page 271). Collectively, pitchers will be on a different routine based on their throwing program and innings thrown in the intrasquad games. A starting pitcher, for example, will most likely perform two to three resistance training days and one to two mobility/recovery sessions (see tables 11.3 and 11.5 on pages 270 and 272). Relief pitchers tend to throw more frequently in intrasquad games and typically have at least two total body resistance training days and one to two mobility/recovery sessions per week, similar to position players (see tables 11.3 and 11.4 on pages 271 and 272).

Once fall practice is over, athletes resume the four-days-per-week split routine that focuses on sport-specific power (see table 9.10).

The coach must also consider several holidays that occur during the off-season, such as Thanksgiving, Christmas, and the New Year. Programming may need to be adjusted to accommodate athletes traveling off-campus at this time. One solution is to provide a "pick list" for athletes to choose from a list of exercises based on equipment availability and their individual situation. This may be a great opportunity to use this time as an unloading period.

Finally, many college baseball programs include a "Road to Omaha" challenge. Over the course of the off-season and fall practice period, athletes are divided into several small teams and captains draft teammates to engage in various competition formats and challenges. Not knowing what competitions or events lie ahead, a team must be constructed of athletes with multiple physical strengths and abilities. In the end, the team with the most points will be declared the "Road to Omaha" fall champions. The event is a fun way to compete and build team unity for the upcoming season.

Professional

The typical length of an off-season program for a professional baseball player is 16 weeks. It is broken into four mesocycles each comprised of three weeks of progressive training and one week of decreased load and intensity (see tables 9.11-9.14). This period does not include postseason recovery or general physical preparation.

To address individual physical development goals, an athlete may be prescribed different training structures during their initial strength phase. Athletes that require greater amounts of strength or muscular development may be prescribed a traditional four-day split routine that maximizes volume training of the lower and upper body, spaced out for maximal recovery. Conversely, athletes who need minimal volume training would be placed on a three-day total body training routine. The three-day program allows for more potential versatility, as it contains two additional days that may be used for alternate training stimuli such as yoga, Pilates, conditioning, speed, or agility work. Three-day programs can also be structured as a circuit-type routine, designed to maximize caloric expenditure for those with a goal of improving their body composition.

The program prescribed should address the athlete's individual needs while progressing through each phase of the off-season. A progressive overload is applied to continuously provide training stimuli for adaptive recovery throughout each mesocycle. When applying a four-day upper/lower split, the training days will focus on movements related to either the upper or lower body. This provides three days of alternate training or recovery. A three-day total body training split will alternately emphasize the upper or lower body on days 1 and 2, with a total body workout on day 3.

For each exercise split, the workout is superset-structured, pairing two or more exercises. For example, in a four-day split, upper body pushing and pulling movements may be paired, whereas lower body movements and anatomical core or corrective exercises may be paired on lower body day. In a three-day split, upper and lower body movements are coupled, with the addition of anatomical core or corrective exercises. The supersetting of exercises is beneficial for improving anaerobic workload and conserving time.

Determination of training structure is based on the athlete's physical development and skill-related needs. As the athlete progresses through the off-season, training structure adjustments may be made to better serve the athlete's individual goals and objectives, as necessary, or to include swinging, throwing, and fielding work as spring training approaches. As the athlete progresses from the initial hypertrophy phase (table 9.11), into a strength phase (table 9.12), then to a power phase (table 9.13), and finally to a speed strength phase (table 9.14), exercise selection will also slightly alter.

RECOMMENDED EXERCISES

Exercise selection for the off-season training program involves choosing exercises that provide a foundation from which to develop strength and power. To make an informed decision, coaches need to understand what equipment is available, the nature of various types of resistance training exercises, the athlete's experience, the amount of training time available, and the movement and muscular requirements of the sport (8).

High School and College

Specific attention should be given to ankle mobility, hip mobility, and upper cross syndrome, which is characterized by protracted shoulders and a forward tilted head (6). This occurs when there is an imbalance between anterior and posterior muscles of the upper torso, such as a tight chest, upper trapezius, and neck while having a weak lower trapezius, serratus anterior, and rotator cuff (7). The high school and college student-athlete may sit at a desk up to five hours a day in class, which may have a negative impact on ankle and hip mobility. Furthermore, poor posture because of sitting in a classroom, library, or study hall for extended periods of time, looking down at a cell phone, and performing too many anterior upper body lifts can cause upper cross syndrome (2).

To address these areas of concern, a total body warm-up should be incorporated at the beginning of each training session. Example warm-up options can be found on page 211. The coach should select an appropriate warm-up that focuses on the T-spine, hip, and ankle range of motion while also including posterior back and shoulder stretching. Different warm-up options could be selected for each training day to emphasis the various areas of concern. One possible exercise that could be included in the warm-up before beginning a resistance training session is the forward wall squat. When performing this exercise, the athlete faces a wall with his feet shoulder-width apart and toes about 6 inches (15 cm) from the wall. The athlete places his hands on the wall shoulder-width apart over his head with arms extended, then squats down to parallel or lower. This will help the athlete sit back into his hips to maintain an upright torso position, so as to avoid leaning forward and touching the wall with his head or face.

Following the total body warm-up, athletes should perform a well-balanced resistance training program three or four days per week with anterior and posterior multi-joint and single-joint exercises as well as anatomical core exercises. To specifically address the issue of offsetting weak posterior musculature, the coach should make sure that baseball players perform the Thrower's 10 and Y, T, I, and W exercises and upper body pulling exercises (10). These exercises will help strengthen the rotator cuff and other posterior muscles, maintain balance between anterior and posterior muscles of the upper body, and improve posture.

Professional

Exercise selection during off-season training should continue to complement the athlete's needs based on assessment data collected before the off-season, and should use movements performed during in-season training. For example, an athlete assessed as a poor squatter should not be programmed to squat under increased loads throughout the off-season. Primary exercises where the load will increase significantly, particularly lower body exercises, should remain relatively consistent throughout the off-season. However, secondary or assistance exercises become more progressive or interchangeable as the off-season progresses due to their decreased joint angles or unilateral patterns. For instance, a program may use a progression of split squat, to single-leg squat, to reverse lunge, to walking lunge. This is a manageable progression due to the uniformity of unilateral movement within the sagittal plane. An athlete who is proficient in a movement pattern should be allowed to progress within that pattern through load and implementation. For example, athletes assessed with good squatting ability should be programmed to squat using various modes, such as barbells, safety squat bars, kettlebells, dumbbells, and front squats as they progress throughout the off-season.

Total Body Exercises

An excellent resistance training exercise for developing total body strength, explosiveness, and mobility is the power clean. Teaching the athlete to pull from the floor, midshin, and above the knee will improve hip drive and develop posterior upper back muscles. However, as previously stated in chapter 4, this exercise is not implemented in some college and most professional baseball teams due to the high risk of injury through improper technique. Therefore, it is up to the coach and athlete to decide whether to use this exercise and its derivatives—the coach should have the time to properly teach and coach it, and the athlete should have the interest and no physical or positional limitations. Chapter 5 describes additional total body primary exercises that may have a similar training effect and lower risk–reward ratio than Olympic-style lifts.

High school athletes with at least one to two years of resistance training experience can divide power clean derivatives into "pull" days and "catch" days. On pull days, they learn to pull from midshin, as well as below and above the knee, ending in a shrug with a weight that allows for proper form in the beginning position. On the "catch" day, they use a light weight such as a PVC bar. As technique is improved, athletes progress to a 35-pound (16 kg) bar and then a 45-pound (20 kg) bar so the athlete can perform an upright row while keeping the bar close to the sternum and finish the movement with the shoulder rotation, allowing the bar to rest across the anterior deltoids and collarbone. Once the athlete has become proficient at the upright row to catch, he can complete the hang clean. Other total body exercise selections to develop strength, power, and range of motion include the medicine ball squat-to-press throw, medicine ball squat-to-push overhead, battle rope slam, Turkish get-up, and bear crawl.

The high school athlete with three or more years of resistance training experience can perform the power clean and its derivatives in addition to the kettlebell swing, landmine row to rotational press, one-arm dumbbell clean, midthigh clean pull, and trap bar jump, which can also help develop explosiveness and provide a good training stimulus.

Lower Body Exercises

Baseball is a ground-based sport that requires the athlete to be able to flex, extend, abduct, adduct, internally and externally rotate their hips and legs to run, field and catch, throw, and hit. A back or front squat to or below 90 degrees; deadlift; forward step, reverse, and lateral lunges; split or single-leg squats; and step-up allow for lower body strength development, mobility, and balance. The Romanian deadlift, glute-hamstring raise, Nordic hamstring curl, double- and single-leg bridge, leg curl, and other variations of lower body pulling exercises will allow for full leg development.

Upper Body Exercises

As mentioned in the Recommended Exercises section, shoulder muscle imbalance or upper cross syndrome is a common problem for baseball players because of the weak posterior muscles that result, in part, from the chronic overuse action of throwing a baseball. Another cause of upper cross syndrome is that many high school and college athletes perform too many bench press exercises and focus more on their anterior muscles than posterior muscles (i.e., pectoralis major, anterior deltoids, and triceps versus latissimus dorsi, posterior deltoids, trapezius, rhomboids, and rotator cuff). A potential solution to this imbalance is for a coach to make adjustments to the training program—for example, having the athlete perform two posterior multi-joint exercises for every one anterior multi-joint exercise. Specifically, when developing the training program for the upper body, have one posterior multi-joint pulling exercise, such as one-arm dumbbell row, followed by an anterior multi-joint pushing exercise, such as dumbbell bench press, and end with another posterior multi-joint pulling exercise, such as a seated or half-kneeling lat pulldown. Furthermore, it is important to train the small muscles of the rotator cuff with the Thrower's 10 and Y, T, I, and W exercises for a warm-up before training.

The multi-joint primary exercises used for posterior upper body development should include the bent-over row, one-arm dumbbell row, lat pulldown, cable row, inverted row, chin-up, pull-up, and dumbbell pullover. The multi-joint primary exercise used for anterior upper body development should include the bench press and its variations, as well as the push-up and its variations.

Anatomical Core Exercises

As described in chapter 8, all the muscles of the anatomical core are needed to allow the athlete's torso to flex, extend, and rotate. Exercises that strengthen and stabilize the anatomical core can be performed before, during, and at the end of resistance training sessions.

Anatomical core development can be achieved by using the various types of exercises described in chapter 8. They are listed in "movement" and "exercise" categories. For example, two types of movement category exercises are anti-rotation and rotational. Both movements are needed to play baseball. When the athlete throws or hits, he will need explosive rotational strength. However, when he is running the bases, he will use anti-rotational strength to keep his torso in the appropriate postural position, provide a stable base from which the limbs can move, and enhance running efficiency. The anatomical core program will need to incorporate exercises that develop the muscles for both movements.

Exercises that focus on core stabilization while the athlete is moving should be included in the off-season resistance training program. Exercises such as the kneeling Pallof press, landmine rainbow, kneeling stick chop, kneeling stick lift, front plank, and side plank allow the athlete to develop anti-rotational muscle strength in a controlled environment. Rotational strength is an important aspect of throwing and hitting; therefore, it also needs to be addressed by incorporating various medicine ball lifts, chops, and throws in multiple planes, as well as seated and standing medicine ball trunk twists and throws that are performed from various body positions.

POSITIONAL ADJUSTMENTS

During the off-season phase, positional adjustments can be made for high school, college, and professional athletes based on specific needs, training age, and lifting ability. Any performance testing data that was recorded before training began should be used to help determine an athlete's needs with regard to mobility, stability, strength, power, and adequate movement competency within fundamental movement patterns. All of these programming considerations should support the movement efficiency of the athlete's position and ability. Coaches should attempt to individualize the training program as best they can so not to create further dysfunction in the athlete's throwing, pitching, hitting, or fielding skills.

High School

During the off-season, the general workout template will be the same for all the positions at the high school level; however, exercises can differ depending on the needs, limitations, or position requirements of the athlete. For example, a high school pitcher may also be a starting position player. Based on this information, the coach may want to only allow this athlete to use dumbbells for upper body exercises where arm and hand position is more easily changed to put less stress on the athlete's throwing shoulder. Additionally, assessment and training age will determine which exercises are most appropriate. In general, however, all the athletes in the off-season training program will perform exercises that require similar movement patterns and recruit similar major muscle groups. The main focus of the off-season training program is to develop a solid foundation of strength to allow the athletes to transition well to the preseason, where developing power will be the main focus.

College and Professional

The off-season program is designed to address the athlete's physical, functional, injury-prevention, and skill-related needs. The primary goal of creating a more efficient, stronger, more powerful athlete is not position specific, but achieving this requires an individualized approach for each athlete. For example, one pitcher may need to add strength and power while decreasing body fat, whereas another pitcher may need more movement-based mobility and stability through body control and segmentation. Although both pitchers would perform similar skill-related activities, they require different training stimuli to achieve their specific goals prior to the preseason or spring training.

Although each program should primarily focus on specific considerations for each athlete's physical and fundamental goals, some general considerations should be considered when designing programs for pitchers and position players. For pitchers and hitters to create rotational power when performing their respective skills, they must be able to effectively load the back leg by performing a hinging-type movement while internally rotating the hip. These movements can be addressed by adding simple, hinging-type exercises to an athlete's program, such as the deadlift, Romanian deadlift (RDL), single-leg RDL, and double- and single-leg bridge. To achieve internal rotation, exercises should be added that include lower leg adduction while rotating toward the adducted leg, such as the crossover step-up and crossover step-up with a reach.

Other considerations should include the addition of lateral resistance exercises, such as lunge and step-up variations, for infielders and pitchers. Although all athletes should have adequate strength levels in the three planes of movement, infielders and pitchers should complete progressions of these movements due to the lateral acceleration and deceleration demands of their respective positions. The necessary progression for all exercises during the off-season should be determined by the intensity of each phase.

INTENSITY

Training intensity is based on the load or weight lifted. During the off-season, intensity can be based on specific percent ranges from an athlete's one repetition maximum (1RM). This can be accomplished by testing various multi-joint core exercises, such as (but not limited to) the back squat, barbell or dumbbell bench press, and one-arm dumbbell row. However, some coaches do not test their athletes, whether for lack of time or the inherent risk that comes along with maximum testing. If coaches are concerned about 1RM testing, they can consider sub-maximal testing (e.g., a 10RM), which will allow for an estimation of 1RM from how many repetitions an athlete can complete before fatiguing. For example, if an athlete can only perform 5 repetitions with a respective load of 300 pounds (136 kg) for back squat, this is indicative of 87% of the 1RM (see table 3.1 on page 35). If the coach divides 300 pounds by 0.87, the estimated 1RM for the back squat would be 345 pounds (156 kg).

High School

During the off-season, the intensity for total body exercises, such as Olympic-style lifts, needs to be in the range of 40% to 60% of the 1RM so the athlete can focus on technique (1). Although the repetitions are in the strength range of 6 repetitions or less, that does not mean the load or weight should be in that strength range (≥85% 1RM) at this time. This is part of the preparatory period where basic strength and neurologic development are being emphasized. The nervous system is crucial to strength development because the "training process should be principally aimed at an increase of the body's work output in a given motor routine" so that the athlete can have continuous motor potential development (9). The intensity for the multi-joint lower body and upper body primary and assistance exercises will be between 60% and 85% of the 1RM to focus on technique, hypertrophy, and strength development (8). When performing the Thrower's 10; Y, T, I, W; and other rotator cuff exercises, it is recommended to use 5 pounds (2.3 kg) or less (10).

College

The intensity for the college baseball player's off-season training will vary based on the training phase. For the first four weeks, the athlete will be in a hypertrophy/strength endurance phase that will have low to moderate intensity of 50% to 75% of the 1RM (1, 8). After completing this phase, the athlete should be in an eight-week basic strength phase that will have higher intensities ranging from 80% to 95% of the 1RM (1, 8). The athlete will then transition into a four-week maximum strength phase that will have very high intensities ranging from 87% to 95% of the 1RM. Once this phase has been completed, the athlete will start a four-week sport-specific power phase that will have low to high intensities ranging from 30% to 85% of the 1RM (1, 8).

Professional

The initial training phase of the off-season begins by focusing on hypertrophy through foundational exercises and progresses through each phase of the program. The intensity for this phase should match a resistance training–specific rating of perceived exertion (RPE) of 6 to 8 (moderate intensity) for all movements, or 73.5% to 77% of the estimated 1RM for lower body primary exercises (8, 11). Table 9.15 (page 232) displays the resistance training–specific RPE described by Zourdos and colleagues (11). A resistance training–specific RPE of 6 to 8 means that an athlete could perform 2 to 4 additional repetitions beyond the number of repetitions that were actually completed. As this program progresses, lower body primary exercises should increase by 5 pounds (2.3 kg) each week, or 1 to 2 points on the resistance training–specific RPE scale. The second phase, or strength phase, should see a resistance training–specific RPE range of 7 to 9 (moderate to moderately high intensity), or 80% to 86.5% of the estimated 1RM for lower body primary exercises (8, 11). As before, this should increase by 5 pounds (2.3 kg), or 1 to 2 resistance training–specific RPE points, each week. The third and fourth phases of the off-season program will continue to focus on strength with the addition of power and speed strength. These phases should produce a resistance training–specific RPE range of 8 to

10 (moderately high to high intensity), or 86.5% to 92% of the 1RM for strength movements and 40% to 60% of the estimated 1RM for velocity-based, total body movements (1, 8, 11). As with earlier phases, lower body primary exercise should increase by 5 pounds (2.3 kg), or 1 to 2 points on the resistance training–specific RPE scale, each week. Upper body assistance exercises should remain in the resistance training–specific RPE range of 7 to 9 for all three phases.

VOLUME

Volume relates to the total amount of weight lifted in a training session (8), and a set is a group of repetitions sequentially performed before the athlete stops to rest (4). **Repetition volume** is the total number of repetitions performed during a workout session (4), and **volume load** is the total number of sets multiplied by the number of repetitions per set, then multiplied by the weight lifted per repetition (8). Volume for high school, college, and professional players will be discussed in this section.

High School

The basic strength phase of the off-season program is four weeks long, with all the sets and repetitions remaining the same. The total body exercises will be 3 to 4 sets of 6 to 8 repetitions with a focus on technique. The athlete will perform 3 to 4 sets of 8 to 10 repetitions of multi-joint lower body and upper body primary as well as single-joint assistance exercises (see tables 9.1 and 9.2).

The maximum strength phase of the off-season program is three weeks long, with all the sets and repetitions remaining the same. The total body exercises will be 3 to 4 sets of 4 to 10 repetitions. Some exercises, such as the trap bar jump, battle rope slam, kettlebell swing, and medicine ball throw are performed with more repetitions; however, the power clean and its variations are performed with 4 to 8 repetitions depending on the experience of the athlete. The athlete will perform 3 to 4 sets of 4 to 8 repetitions of multi-joint lower body and upper body primary as well as single-joint assistance exercises (see tables 9.3 and 9.4).

The power phase of the off-season program is two three-week microcycles, with all the sets and repetitions remaining the same. The total body exercises will be 3 to 5 sets of 5 to 10 repetitions. Some exercises, such as the trap bar jump and battle rope slam, are performed with more repetitions; however, the power clean and its variations, medicine ball throw, and kettlebell swing are performed with 5 repetitions. The athlete will perform 5 sets of 5 repetitions of multi-joint lower body and upper body primary as well as single-joint assistance exercises (see tables 9.5 and 9.6).

College

The volume for the college baseball player's off-season will vary based on the training phase. For the first four weeks of the off-season program, the athlete will be in a hypertrophy/strength endurance phase that has a high volume with 8 to 12 repetitions for 3 to 4 sets (8). During the basic strength phase, there will be moderate to high volume with 6 to 8 repetitions for 3 to 4 sets. During the maximum strength phase, there will be low to moderately high volume with 4 to 8 repetitions for 3 to 4 sets (8). During the sport-specific power phase, there will be low to moderate volume with 3 to 6 repetitions for 3 to 4 sets. Each phase shares similar volume titration throughout the weeks, with week 1 being high volume, week 2 moderately high volume, week 3 very high volume, and week 4 moderate volume, respectively.

Professional

The first phase of the off-season program consists of hypertrophy training, which includes 2 sets of 10 repetitions for the first week, progressing to 3 sets of 8 repetitions for the next two weeks, before unloading during the fourth week (8). The goal is to complete all working sets of lower and upper body primary and anatomical core exercises within the appropriate RPE range. The focus on hypertrophy work for the first phase applies mainly to lower body primary exercises. Most assistance exercises will remain at 8 repetitions for 2 to 4 sets. During the next phase, the strength phase, repetitions range from 4 to 6 for 3 to 4 sets (8). The third and fourth phases, the power and speed strength phases, will progress from 5 repetitions to 2 repetitions, for 3 to 5 sets. The assistance exercises in this phase remain similar to what was performed during the strength phase. The velocity-based total body exercises in the power and speed strength phases have repetition ranges of 2 to 5 for working sets of 2 to 5 (8).

EXERCISE ORDER

Exercise order is a sequence of resistance exercises performed during a single training session. When determining the exercise order, strength coaches need to consider how one exercise will affect the quality of effort or the technique of another exercise (8). Typically, exercises are organized with the most physically demanding multi-joint exercises performed first so that an athlete's maximal force capabilities are available to perform with proper technique (8).

High School

Before the high school athlete begins doing primary exercises, he should perform rotator cuff and scapula stabilization exercises. When those are completed, the exercise order is total body explosive lifts followed by multi-joint lower body and upper body exercises. When those are completed, the anatomical core exercises are performed.

College

For the college athlete, the exercise order during the off-season is consistent for all four phases (hypertrophy, basic strength, maximum strength, and sport-specific power) for position players, relief pitchers, and starting pitchers. Monday will be a lower body day with an emphasis on hinge-related movements. Tuesday will be an upper body day with an emphasis on pushing exercises. Thursday will be a lower body day with an emphasis on squat-related exercises, and Friday will be an upper body day with an emphasis on pulling exercises. In general, the exercise order for each training session will be a multi-joint lower or upper body primary exercise or primary exercise variation combined with an anatomical core stability, mobility, or corrective exercise.

Professional

For professional athletes, the exercise order is designed to maximize training efficiency by pairing assistance exercises. This includes pairing exercises for antagonist muscle groups with anatomical core strengthening or mobility exercises, allowing for a greater volume of work to be done in a shorter period of time. For training sessions that focus on strength, the multi-joint primary exercises should be performed first, followed by single-joint assistance exercises, and finishing with anatomical core strengthening and mobility exercises.

The sample workouts in this chapter, as well as subsequent chapters, exhibit this sequencing by focusing first on primary exercises, then supporting exercises. Antagonistic muscle groups are paired to maximize training time and efficiency while optimizing the rest time for the primary exercise. This is accomplished by pairing opposite muscle groups or muscle groups from upper and lower body regions. For example, a lower body primary pushing exercise may be placed in a tri-set with an upper body pulling exercise and an anatomical core strengthening or mobility exercise. This works several muscle groups in a short period of time and gives the lower body primary muscle group a chance to recover between sets.

CONCLUSION

The off-season training program is designed to provide the foundation for exercise technique in addition to developing basic and maximum strength that transitions to power development for preseason training. The off-season resistance training program must meet the specific needs of the athlete based on each athlete's individual assessment. This means that the coach and athlete must select the appropriate training frequency, exercises, intensity, volume, and exercise order to achieve the desired goals. Because of these considerations, the sample programs in this chapter provide sound guidelines for the high school, college, and professional baseball player; however, they can and should be modified for each athlete and training facility as needed.

Warm-Ups: Mobility, Corrective, Active Dynamic, and In-Place Flow Stretch Exercises

Choose the most appropriate warm-up option based on the specific training day.

OPTION 1

Foam roll, activation, and movement-based warm-up

- T-spine rotation with reach (3 × 10 each) or trunk stability rotation with knees flexed (3 × 10)
- Starter rolling upper body (3 × 5 each side) or rolling upper body (3 × 5 each)
- Standing scapular wall slide with back on wall (3 × 10)
- Half-kneeling hip flexor stretch (3 × 10 each leg)
- Toe touch progression (3 × 5 each)
- Single-leg stance with core engagement with cable system or Cook band (3 × 5 each leg)
- Tall kneeling hold anterior load (3 × 10 breaths) or tall kneeling hold anterior load with optional head turn or head and shoulder turn (3 × 5 each side)

OPTION 2

Foam roll, activation, and movement-based warm-up

- Quadruped T-spine rotation or quadruped T-spine rotation lumbar locked (3 × 10 each)
- Rolling lower body (3 × 5 each leg)
- Standing forearm wall slide (3 × 10)

(continued)

(continued)

- Half-kneeling rotation with dowel (3 × 5 each side)
- Assisted single-leg lowering (3 × 10 each leg)
- Tall or half-kneeling kettlebell halo (3 × 5 each direction)
- 90-90 breathing position (3 × 5)

OPTION 3

Foam roll, activation, and movement-based warm-up

- Brettzel (3 × 5 breaths each side) or Brettzel 2.0 variation (3 × 5 each side)
- Core control rolling with knee touch (3 × 5 each side)
- Seated scapular wall slide with back on wall (3 × 10)
- Open half-kneeling ankle mobility with KB (3 × 10 each leg)
- Active leg lowering to bolster (3 × 10 each leg)
- Deep squat assisted with Functional Movement Trainer (FMT) (3 × 10)
- Tall kneeling hold posterior load (3 × 10 breaths) or tall kneeling hold posterior load with optional head turn or head and shoulder turn (3 × 5 each side)

OPTION 4

Activation and dynamic warm-up

Activation

- Lateral mini-band walk (1 × 12 each leg)
- Forward and backward mini-band walk (1 × 12 each leg)
- Double-leg bridge (1 × 15)
- Supine single-leg lowering with full exhale (1 × 8 each leg)
- Quadruped opposite arm and leg reach with full exhale (1 × 8 each leg)
- Yoga push-up with full exhale (1 × 5)
- Bear crawl forward and backward (1 × 10 yards or meters each)

Dynamic warm-up (1 × 10 yards or meters for each movement)

- Walking knee hug
- Walking quad stretch with overhead reach
- Walking leg cradle
- Walking toe touch
- Walking RDL with reach
- World's greatest stretch
- Forward lunge with rotation
- Lateral shuffle lunge and reach
- Lateral shuffle
- Carioca high knee
- Butt kick
- A-skip

- Lateral A-skip
- Backward run with reach
- Lateral shuffle to sprint acceleration

OPTION 5

In-place flow stretch (each movement flows into the next)

Cluster 1

- Squat to stand
- World's greatest stretch (alternate legs × 3 each leg)

Cluster 2

- Inchworm
- Yoga push-up
- Half-kneeling hip flexor stretch (alternate legs × 3 each leg)

Activate (done independently)

- Butterfly bridge (1 × 15)
- Lateral plank on knees with abduction (1 × 30 seconds each side)
- Turkish get-up (1 × 3 each side)

Note: The mobility and corrective exercises can be found at https://functionalmovement.com/exercises.

Interpreting the Sample Program Tables

BB = Barbell

BW = Body weight

DB = Dumbbell

MB = Medicine ball

KB = Kettlebell

RDL = Romanian deadlift

Side hang = Holding BB, DB, or KB with the arms hanging down, palms facing legs, and elbows extended

Rack position = Holding BB, DB, or KB in the catch or rack position on the anterior shoulder

Goblet = Holding DB or KB with both hands below the chin and elbows pointed out to the side in the midline of the body

Order = Performing one set of each exercise (1a, 1b, 1c) in the group one after the other. After the first set is completed, go back to the first exercise in the group and do the second set of each exercise. If certain exercises call for fewer sets than others in the group, perform those sets on the back end of the grouping. For example, if exercise 1a calls for 4 sets and exercise 1b calls for 3 sets, perform exercise 1b during sets 2 through 4 of exercises 1a.

Each = Each side (arm or leg), direction, or exercise.

Table 9.1   High School: Off-Season Microcycle 1, Basic Strength (Training Age: 1-2 years), Weeks 3-6*

Monday: Lower Body

Order	Exercise	Sets × reps Week 3	Sets × reps Week 4	Sets × reps Week 5	Sets × reps Week 6
1a	Overhead squat (use PVC bar)	3 × 10	3 × 10	3 × 10	3 × 10
1b	Wall squat (hands on wall)	3 × 10	3 × 10	3 × 10	3 × 10
1c	Prone Y, T, I, W	3 × 10 each	3 × 10 each	3 × 10 each	3 × 10 each
2	Power clean (from shins)	4 × 8	4 × 8	4 × 8	4 × 8
3	Body weight squat	4 × 10	4 × 10	4 × 10	4 × 10
4	Leg curl	4 × 10	4 × 10	4 × 10	4 × 10
5	Forward step lunge	4 × 10 each	4 × 10 each	4 × 10 each	4 × 10 each
6	RDL	4 × 10	4 × 10	4 × 10	4 × 10
7a	Front plank	3 × 30 sec	3 × 30 sec	3 × 30 sec	3 × 30 sec
7b	Half-kneeling stick chop	3 × 10 each	3 × 10 each	3 × 10 each	3 × 10 each
7c	Side plank with hip flexion	3 × 30 sec each	3 × 30 sec each	3 × 30 sec each	3 × 30 sec each

Tuesday: Upper Body

Order	Exercise	Sets × reps Week 3	Sets × reps Week 4	Sets × reps Week 5	Sets × reps Week 6
1a	Thrower's 10	3 × 10 each	3 × 10 each	3 × 10 each	3 × 10 each
1b	Wrist ulnar and radial deviation	3 × 10 each	3 × 10 each	3 × 10 each	3 × 10 each
2	Bench press	4 × 8	4 × 8	4 × 8	4 × 8
3	Lat pulldown	4 × 8	4 × 8	4 × 8	4 × 8
4	Standing BB shoulder press	4 × 10	4 × 10	4 × 10	4 × 10
5	Inverted row	4 × 10	4 × 10	4 × 10	4 × 10
6	Prone Y, T (use elastic band)	4 × 10 each	4 × 10 each	4 × 10 each	4 × 10 each
7a	Seated row	4 × 10	4 × 10	4 × 10	4 × 10
7b	Wall hold	20 sec	20 sec	20 sec	20 sec
8a	Superman	3 × 10	3 × 10	3 × 10	3 × 10
8b	MB diagonal wood chops	3 × 10 each	3 × 10 each	3 × 10 each	3 × 10 each
8c	Side crunch	3 × 10 each	3 × 10 each	3 × 10 each	3 × 10 each

Thursday: Lower Body

Order	Exercise	Sets × reps Week 3	Sets × reps Week 4	Sets × reps Week 5	Sets × reps Week 6
1a	Trap bar jump (no weight on bar)	3 × 10	3 × 10	3 × 10	3 × 10
1b	Battle rope slam	3 × 10	3 × 10	3 × 10	3 × 10
1c	Hurdle step over	3 × 10 each	3 × 10 each	3 × 10 each	3 × 10 each
2	Split squat	4 × 10 each	4 × 8 each	4 × 8 each	4 × 8 each
3	Stability ball leg curl	4 × 10	4 × 8	4 × 8	4 × 8
4	Two-arm KB swing	4 × 10	4 × 10	4 × 10	4 × 10
5	RDL	4 × 10	4 × 10	4 × 10	4 × 10
6	MB squat to press overhead	4 × 10	4 × 10	4 × 10	4 × 10
7a	MB seated twist	3 × 10 each	3 × 10 each	3 × 10 each	3 × 10 each
7b	Front plank	3 × 30 sec	3 × 30 sec	3 × 30 sec	3 × 30 sec
7c	Side plank	3 × 30 sec each	3 × 30 sec each	3 × 30 sec each	3 × 30 sec each

Friday: Upper Body

Order	Exercise	Sets × reps Week 3	Sets × reps Week 4	Sets × reps Week 5	Sets × reps Week 6
1a	Prone Y, T, I, W	3 × 10 each	3 × 10 each	3 × 10 each	3 × 10 each
1b	Wrist ulnar and radial deviation	3 × 10 each	3 × 10 each	3 × 10 each	3 × 10 each
2	Push-up	4 × 8	4 × 8	4 × 8	4 × 8
3	Low pulley seated row	4 × 8	4 × 8	4 × 8	4 × 8
4	DB front shoulder raise	4 × 10	4 × 10	4 × 10	4 × 10
5	Plate pullover	4 × 10	4 × 10	4 × 10	4 × 10
6	MB chest pass	4 × 10	4 × 10	4 × 10	4 × 10
7a	Face pull	4 × 10	4 × 10	4 × 10	4 × 10
7b	Wall hold	20 sec	20 sec	20 sec	20 sec
8a	Superman	3 × 10	3 × 10	3 × 10	3 × 10
8b	MB diagonal wood chop	3 × 5 each	3 × 5 each	3 × 5 each	3 × 5 each
8c	Side crunch	3 × 10 each	3 × 10 each	3 × 10 each	3 × 10 each

*Testing occurs in weeks 1-2.

Table 9.2 High School: Off-Season Microcycle 1, Basic Strength (Training Age: 3+ Years), Weeks 3-6*

Monday: Lower Body

Order	Exercise	Sets × reps Week 3	Sets × reps Week 4	Sets × reps Week 5	Sets × reps Week 6
1a	Overhead squat (use PVC bar)	3 × 10	3 × 10	3 × 10	3 × 10
1b	Wall squat (hands on wall)	3 × 10	3 × 10	3 × 10	3 × 10
1c	Prone Y, T, I, W	3 × 10 each	3 × 10 each	3 × 10 each	3 × 10 each
2	Power clean	4 × 6-8	4 × 6-8	4 × 6-8	4 × 6-8
3	Back squat	4 × 6-8	4 × 6-8	4 × 6-8	4 × 6-8
4	Glute-hamstring raise	4 × 8-10	4 × 8-10	4 × 8-10	4 × 8-10
5	Single-leg squat	4 × 8-10 each	4 × 8-10 each	4 × 8-10 each	4 × 8-10 each
6	RDL	4 × 8-10	4 × 8-10	4 × 8-10	4 × 8-10
7a	Front plank	3 × 30 sec	3 × 30 sec	3 × 30 sec	3 × 30 sec
7b	Half-kneeling stick chop	3 × 10 each	3 × 10 each	3 × 10 each	3 × 10 each
7c	Side plank with hip flexion	3 × 30 sec each	3 × 30 sec each	3 × 30 sec each	3 × 30 sec each

Tuesday: Upper Body

Order	Exercise	Sets × reps Week 3	Sets × reps Week 4	Sets × reps Week 5	Sets × reps Week 6
1a	Thrower's 10	3 × 10 each	3 × 10 each	3 × 10 each	3 × 10 each
1b	Wrist ulnar and radial deviation	3 × 10 each	3 × 10 each	3 × 10 each	3 × 10 each
2	Bench press	4 × 6-8	4 × 6-8	4 × 6-8	4 × 6-8
3	Lat pulldown	4 × 6-8	4 × 6-8	4 × 6-8	4 × 6-8
4	Standing DB shoulder press	4 × 8-10	4 × 8-10	4 × 8-10	4 × 8-10
5	Inverted row	4 × 8-10	4 × 8-10	4 × 8-10	4 × 8-10
6	Prone Y, T (use elastic band)	4 × 8-10 each	4 × 8-10 each	4 × 8-10 each	4 × 8-10 each

(continued)

Table 9.2 High School: Off-Season Microcycle 1, Basic Strength (Training Age: 3+ Years), Weeks 3-6* *(continued)*

Tuesday: Upper Body *(continued)*

Order	Exercise	Sets × reps Week 3	Sets × reps Week 4	Sets × reps Week 5	Sets × reps Week 6
7a	Seated row	4 × 8-10	4 × 8-10	4 × 8-10	4 × 8-10
7b	Wall hold	20 sec	20 sec	20 sec	20 sec
8a	Superman	3 × 10	3 × 10	3 × 10	3 × 10
8b	MB diagonal wood chop	3 × 5 each	3 × 5 each	3 × 5 each	3 × 5 each
8c	Side crunch	3 × 10 each	3 × 10 each	3 × 10 each	3 × 10 each

Thursday: Lower Body

Order	Exercise	Sets × reps Week 3	Sets × reps Week 4	Sets × reps Week 5	Sets × reps Week 6
1a	Trap bar jump (no weight on bar)	3 × 10	3 × 10	3 × 10	3 × 10
1b	Battle rope slam	3 × 10	3 × 10	3 × 10	3 × 10
1c	Hurdle step over	3 × 10 each	3 × 10 each	3 × 10 each	3 × 10 each
2	Split squat	4 × 8 each	4 × 8 each	4 × 8 each	4 × 8 each
3	Stability ball leg curl	4 × 8-10	4 × 8-10	4 × 8-10	4 × 8-10
4	Two-arm KB swing	4 × 8-10	4 × 8-10	4 × 8-10	4 × 8-10
5	Single-leg bridge	4 × 8-10 each	4 × 8-10 each	4 × 8-10 each	4 × 8-10 each
6	MB squat-to-press overhead	4 × 8-10	4 × 8-10	4 × 8-10	4 × 8-10
7a	MB seated twist	3 × 10 each	3 × 10 each	3 × 10 each	3 × 10 each
7b	Front plank	3 × 30 sec	3 × 30 sec	3 × 30 sec	3 × 30 sec
7c	Side plank	3 × 30 sec each	3 × 30 sec each	3 × 30 sec each	3 × 30 sec each

Friday: Upper Body

Order	Exercise	Sets × reps Week 3	Sets × reps Week 4	Sets × reps Week 5	Sets × reps Week 6
1a	Prone Y, T, I, W	3 × 10 each	3 × 10 each	3 × 10 each	3 × 10 each
1b	Wrist ulnar and radial deviation	3 × 10 each	3 × 10 each	3 × 10 each	3 × 10 each
2	DB bench press	4 × 6-8	4 × 6-8	4 × 6-8	4 × 6-8
3	Low pulley seated row	4 × 6-8	4 × 6-8	4 × 6-8	4 × 6-8
4	DB front shoulder raise	4 × 8-10	4 × 8-10	4 × 8-10	4 × 8-10
5	DB pullover	4 × 8-10	4 × 8-10	4 × 8-10	4 × 8-10
6	MB chest pass	4 × 8-10	4 × 8-10	4 × 8-10	4 × 8-10
7a	Face pull	4 × 8-10	4 × 8-10	4 × 8-10	4 × 8-10
7b	Wall hold	20 sec	20 sec	20 sec	20 sec
8a	Superman	3 × 10	3 × 10	3 × 10	3 × 10
8b	MB diagonal wood chop	3 × 5 each	3 × 5 each	3 × 5 each	3 × 5 each
8c	Side crunch	3 × 10 each	3 × 10 each	3 × 10 each	3 × 10 each

*Testing occurs in weeks 1-2.

Table 9.3   High School: Off-Season Microcycle 2, Maximum Strength (Training Age: 1-2 Years), Weeks 7-9

Monday: Lower Body

Order	Exercise	Sets × reps Week 7	Sets × reps Week 8	Sets × reps Week 9
1a	Overhead squat (use PVC bar)	3 × 10	3 × 10	3 × 10
1b	Wall squat (hands on wall)	3 × 10	3 × 10	3 × 10
1c	Prone Y, T, I, W	3 × 10 each	3 × 10 each	3 × 10 each
2	Power clean	4 × 8	4 × 6-8	4 × 6
3	Back squat	4 × 8	4 × 6-8	4 × 6
4	Leg curl	4 × 8	4 × 6-8	4 × 6
5	Split squat	4 × 8 each	4 × 6-8 each	4 × 6 each
6	RDL	4 × 8	4 × 6-8	4 × 6
7a	Front plank	3 × 30 sec	3 × 30 sec	3 × 30 sec
7b	Half-kneeling stick chop	3 × 10 each	3 × 10 each	3 × 10 each
7c	Side plank with hip flexion	3 × 30 sec each	3 × 30 sec each	3 × 30 sec each

Tuesday: Upper Body

Order	Exercise	Sets × reps Week 7	Sets × reps Week 8	Sets × reps Week 9
1a	Thrower's 10	3 × 10 each	3 × 10 each	3 × 10 each
1b	Wrist ulnar and radial deviation	3 × 10	3 × 10	3 × 10
2	Bench press	4 × 8	4 × 6-8	4 × 6
3	One-arm DB row	4 × 8 each	4 × 6-8 each	4 × 6 each
4	Standing BB shoulder press	4 × 8	4 × 6-8	4 × 6
5	Seated row	4 × 8	4 × 6-8	4 × 6
6	Prone Y, T (use elastic band)	4 × 6 each	4 × 6 each	4 × 6 each
7a	Pull-up	4 × 6	4 × 6	4 × 6
7b	Wall hold	20 sec	20 sec	20 sec
8a	Superman	3 × 10	3 × 10	3 × 10
8b	MB wood chop	3 × 5	3 × 5	3 × 5
8c	Side crunch	3 × 10 each	3 × 10 each	3 × 10 each

Thursday: Lower Body

Order	Exercise	Sets × reps Week 7	Sets × reps Week 8	Sets × reps Week 9
1a	Trap bar jump (no weight)	3 × 10	3 × 10	3 × 10
1b	Battle rope slam	3 × 10	3 × 10	3 × 10
1c	Hurdle step over	3 × 10 each	3 × 10 each	3 × 10 each
2	Split squat	4 × 8 each	4 × 6-8 each	4 × 6 each
3	Stability ball leg curl	4 × 8	4 × 6-8	4 × 6
4	Two-arm KB swing	4 × 8	4 × 6-8	4 × 6

(continued)

Table 9.3 High School: Off-Season Microcycle 2, Maximum Strength (Training Age: 1-2 Years), Weeks 7-9 *(continued)*

Thursday: Lower Body

Order	Exercise	Sets × reps Week 7	Sets × reps Week 8	Sets × reps Week 9
5	Single-leg bridge	4 × 6 each	4 × 6 each	4 × 6 each
6	MB squat-to-press overhead	4 × 8-10	4 × 8-10	4 × 8-10
7a	MB seated twist	3 × 10 each	3 × 10 each	3 × 10 each
7b	Front plank	3 × 30 sec	3 × 30 sec	3 × 30 sec
7c	Side plank	3 × 30 sec each	3 × 30 sec each	3 × 30 sec each

Friday: Upper Body

Order	Exercise	Sets × reps Week 7	Sets × reps Week 8	Sets × reps Week 9
1a	Prone Y, T, I, W	3 × 10 each	3 × 10 each	3 × 10 each
1b	Wrist ulnar and radial deviation	3 × 10 each	3 × 10 each	3 × 10 each
2	DB bench press	4 × 8	4 × 6-8	4 × 6
3	Low pulley seated row	4 × 8	4 × 6-8	4 × 6
4	Standing DB shoulder press	4 × 8	4 × 6-8	4 × 6
5	DB pullover	4 × 8	4 × 6-8	4 × 6
6	MB chest pass	4 × 6	4 × 6	4 × 6
7a	Face pull	4 × 6	4 × 6	4 × 6
7b	Wall hold	20 sec	20 sec	20 sec
8a	Superman	3 × 10	3 × 10	3 × 10
8b	MB wood chop	3 × 5	3 × 5	3 × 5
8c	Side crunch	3 × 10 each	3 × 10 each	3 × 10 each

Table 9.4 High School: Off-Season Microcycle 2, Maximum Strength (Training Age: 3+ Years), Weeks 7-9

Monday: Lower Body

Order	Exercise	Sets × reps Week 7	Sets × reps Week 8	Sets × reps Week 9
1a	Overhead squat (use PVC bar)	3 × 10	3 × 10	3 × 10
1b	Wall squat (hands on wall)	3 × 10	3 × 10	3 × 10
1c	Prone Y, T, I, W	3 × 10 each	3 × 10 each	3 × 10 each
2	Power clean	4 × 6	4 × 4-6	4 × 4
3	Back squat	4 × 6	4 × 4-6	4 × 4
4	Leg curl	4 × 6	4 × 4-6	4 × 4
5	Split squat	4 × 6 each	4 × 4-6 each	4 × 4 each
6	RDL	4 × 6	4 × 4-6	4 × 4
7a	Front plank on hands	3 × 30 sec	3 × 30 sec	3 × 30 sec
7b	Half-kneeling stick chop	3 × 10 each	3 × 10 each	3 × 10 each
7c	Side plank with hip flexion	3 × 30 sec each	3 × 30 sec each	3 × 30 sec each

Tuesday: Upper Body

Order	Exercise	Sets × reps Week 7	Sets × reps Week 8	Sets × reps Week 9
1a	Thrower's 10	3 × 10 each	3 × 10 each	3 × 10 each
1b	Wrist ulnar and radial deviation	3 × 10 each	3 × 10 each	3 × 10 each
2	Bench press	4 × 6	4 × 4-6	4 × 4
3	One-arm DB row	4 × 6 each	4 × 4-6 each	4 × 4 each
4	Standing DB shoulder press	4 × 6	4 × 4-6	4 × 4
5	Seated row	4 × 6	4 × 4-6	4 × 4
6	Prone Y, T (use elastic band)	4 × 6 each	4 × 6 each	4 × 6 each
7a	Pull-up	4 × 6	4 × 6	4 × 6
7b	Wall hold	20 sec	20 sec	20 sec
8a	Superman	3 × 10	3 × 10	3 × 10
8b	MB wood chop	3 × 5	3 × 5	3 × 5
8c	Side crunch	3 × 10 each	3 × 10 each	3 × 10 each

Thursday: Lower Body

Order	Exercise	Sets × reps Week 7	Sets × reps Week 8	Sets × reps Week 9
1a	Trap bar jump (no weight)	3 × 10	3 × 10	3 × 10
1b	Battle rope slam	3 × 10	3 × 10	3 × 10
1c	Hurdle step over	3 × 10 each	3 × 10 each	3 × 10 each
2	Split squat	4 × 6 each	4 × 4-6 each	4 × 4 each
3	Stability ball leg curl	4 × 6	4 × 6	4 × 6
4	Two-arm KB swing	4 × 6	4 × 4-6	4 × 4
5	Single-leg bridge	4 × 6 each	4 × 6 each	4 × 6 each
6	MB squat-to-press overhead	4 × 8-10	4 × 8-10	4 × 8-10
7a	MB seated twist	3 × 10 each	3 × 10 each	3 × 10 each
7b	Front plank	3 × 30 sec	3 × 30 sec	3 × 30 sec
7c	Side plank	3 × 30 sec each	3 × 30 sec each	3 × 30 sec each

Friday: Upper Body

Order	Exercise	Sets × reps Week 7	Sets × reps Week 8	Sets × reps Week 9
1a	Prone Y, T, I, W	3 × 10 each	3 × 10 each	3 × 10 each
1b	Wrist ulnar and radial deviation	3 × 10 each	3 × 10 each	3 × 10 each
2	DB bench press	4 × 6	4 × 4-6	4 × 4
3	Low pulley seated row	4 × 6	4 × 4-6	4 × 4
4	Standing DB shoulder press	4 × 6	4 × 4-6	4 × 4
5	DB pullover	4 × 6	4 × 4-6	4 × 4
6	MB chest pass	4 × 6	4 × 6	4 × 6
7a	Face pull	4 × 6	4 × 6	4 × 6
7b	Wall hold	20 sec	20 sec	20 sec
8a	Superman	3 × 10	3 × 10	3 × 10
8b	MB wood chop	3 × 5	3 × 5	3 × 5
8c	Side crunch	3 × 10 each	3 × 10 each	3 × 10 each

Table 9.5 High School: Off-Season Microcycle 3, Power, Weeks 10-12

Monday: Lower Body

Order	Exercise	Sets × reps Week 10	Sets × reps Week 11	Sets × reps Week 12
1a	Overhead squat (use PVC bar)	3 × 10	3 × 10	3 × 10
1b	Wall squat (hands on wall)	3 × 10	3 × 10	3 × 10
1c	Prone Y, T, I, W	3 × 10 each	3 × 10 each	3 × 10 each
2	Hang clean	5 × 5	5 × 5	5 × 5
3	Front squat	5 × 5	5 × 5	5 × 5
4	Glute-hamstring raise	5 × 5	5 × 5	5 × 5
5	Step-up	5 × 5 each	5 × 5 each	5 × 5 each
6	RDL	5 × 5	5 × 5	5 × 5
7a	Front plank	3 × 30 sec	3 × 30 sec	3 × 30 sec
7b	Half-kneeling stick chop	3 × 10 each	3 × 10 each	3 × 10 each
7c	Side plank with hip flexion	3 × 30 sec each	3 × 30 sec each	3 × 30 sec each

Tuesday: Upper Body

Order	Exercise	Sets × reps Week 10	Sets × reps Week 11	Sets × reps Week 12
1a	Thrower's 10	3 × 10 each	3 × 10 each	3 × 10 each
1b	Wrist ulnar and radial deviation	3 × 10 each	3 × 10 each	3 × 10 each
2	Bench press	5 × 5	5 × 5	5 × 5
3	Lat pulldown	5 × 5	5 × 5	5 × 5
4	Push press	5 × 5	5 × 5	5 × 5
5	Inverted row	5 × 5	5 × 5	5 × 5
6	Prone Y, T (use elastic band)	5 × 5 each	5 × 5 each	5 × 5 each
7a	Seated row	5 × 5	5 × 5	5 × 5
7b	Wall hold	20 sec	20 sec	20 sec
8a	Superman	3 × 10	3 × 10	3 × 10
8b	MB wood chop	3 × 5	3 × 5	3 × 5
8c	Side crunch	3 × 10 each	3 × 10 each	3 × 10 each

Thursday: Lower Body

Order	Exercise	Sets × reps Week 10	Sets × reps Week 11	Sets × reps Week 12
1a	Trap bar jump (no weight)	3 × 10	3 × 10	3 × 10
1b	Battle rope slam	3 × 10	3 × 10	3 × 10
1c	Hurdle step over	3 × 10 each	3 × 10 each	3 × 10 each
2	Split squat	5 × 5 each	5 × 5 each	5 × 5 each
3	Stability ball leg curl	5 × 5	5 × 5	5 × 5
4	Two-arm KB swing	5 × 5	5 × 5	5 × 5
5	RDL	5 × 5	5 × 5	5 × 5
6	MB squat-to-press overhead	5 × 5	5 × 5	5 × 5
7a	MB seated twist	3 × 10 each	3 × 10 each	3 × 10 each
7b	Front plank	3 × 30 sec	3 × 30 sec	3 × 30 sec
7c	Side plank	3 × 30 sec each	3 × 30 sec each	3 × 30 sec each

Friday: Upper Body

Order	Exercise	Sets × reps Week 10	Sets × reps Week 11	Sets × reps Week 12
1a	Prone Y, T, I, W	3 × 10 each	3 × 10 each	3 × 10 each
1b	Wrist ulnar and radial deviation	3 × 10 each	3 × 10 each	3 × 10 each
2	Push-up	5 × 5	5 × 5	5 × 5
3	Low pulley seated row	5 × 5	5 × 5	5 × 5
4	DB front shoulder raise	5 × 5	5 × 5	5 × 5
5	Plate pullover	5 × 5	5 × 5	5 × 5
6	MB chest pass	5 × 5	5 × 5	5 × 5
7a	Face pull	5 × 5	5 × 5	5 × 5
7b	Wall hold	20 sec	20 sec	20 sec
8a	Superman	3 × 10	3 × 10	3 × 10
8b	MB wood chop	3 × 5	3 × 5	3 × 5
8c	Side crunch	3 × 10 each	3 × 10 each	3 × 10 each

Table 9.6   High School: Off-Season Microcycle 4, Power, Weeks 13-15

Monday: Lower Body

Order	Exercise	Sets × reps Week 13	Sets × reps Week 14	Sets × reps Week 15
1a	Overhead squat (use PVC bar)	3 × 10	3 × 10	3 × 10
1b	Wall squat (hands on wall)	3 × 10	3 × 10	3 × 10
1c	Prone Y, T, I, W	3 × 10 each	3 × 10 each	3 × 10 each
2	Power clean	5 × 5	5 × 5	5 × 5
3	Front squat	5 × 5	5 × 5	5 × 5
4	Leg curl	5 × 5	5 × 5	5 × 5
5	Split squat	5 × 5 each	5 × 5 each	5 × 5 each
6	Two-arm KB swing	5 × 5	5 × 5	5 × 5
7a	Front plank	3 × 30 sec	3 × 30 sec	3 × 30 sec
7b	Half-kneeling stick chop	3 × 10 each	3 × 10 each	3 × 10 each
7c	Side plank with hip flexion	3 × 30 sec each	3 × 30 sec each	3 × 30 sec each

Tuesday: Upper Body

Order	Exercise	Sets × reps Week 13	Sets × reps Week 14	Sets × reps Week 15
1a	Thrower's 10	3 × 10 each	3 × 10 each	3 × 10 each
1b	Wrist ulnar and radial deviation	3 × 10 each	3 × 10 each	3 × 10 each
2	Bench press	5 × 5	5 × 5	5 × 5
3	Lat pulldown	5 × 5	5 × 5	5 × 5
4	DB push press	5 × 5	5 × 5	5 × 5
5	Pull-up	5 × 5	5 × 5	5 × 5
6	Prone Y, T (use elastic band)	5 × 5	5 × 5	5 × 5
7a	One-arm DB row	5 × 5 each	5 × 5 each	5 × 5 each
7b	Wall hold	20 sec	20 sec	20 sec
8a	Superman	3 × 10	3 × 10	3 × 10
8b	MB wood chop	3 × 5	3 × 5	3 × 5
8c	Side crunch	3 × 10 each	3 × 10 each	3 × 10 each

(continued)

Table 9.6   High School: Off-Season Microcycle 4, Power, Weeks 13-15 *(continued)*

Thursday: Lower Body

Order	Exercise	Sets × reps Week 13	Sets × reps Week 14	Sets × reps Week 15
1a	Trap bar jump (no weight)	3 × 10	3 × 10	3 × 10
1b	Battle rope slam	3 × 10	3 × 10	3 × 10
1c	Hurdle step over	3 × 10 each	3 × 10 each	3 × 10 each
2	Forward step lunge	5 × 5 each	5 × 5 each	5 × 5 each
3	Stability ball leg curl	5 × 5	5 × 5	5 × 5
4	Two-arm KB swing	5 × 5	5 × 5	5 × 5
5	RDL	5 × 5	5 × 5	5 × 5
6	MB squat-to-press overhead	5 × 5	5 × 5	5 × 5
7a	MB seated twist	3 × 10 each	3 × 10 each	3 × 10 each
7b	Front plank	3 × 30 sec	3 × 30 sec	3 × 30 sec
7c	Side plank	3 × 30 sec each	3 × 30 sec each	3 × 30 sec each

Friday: Upper Body

Order	Exercise	Sets × reps Week 13	Sets × reps Week 14	Sets × reps Week 15
1a	Prone Y, T, I, W	3 × 10 each	3 × 10 each	3 × 10 each
1b	Wrist ulnar and radial deviation	3 × 10 each	3 × 10 each	3 × 10 each
2	DB bench press	5 × 5	5 × 5	5 × 5
3	One-arm DB row	5 × 5 each	5 × 5 each	5 × 5 each
4	One-arm DB push press	5 × 5 each	5 × 5 each	5 × 5 each
5	Plate pullover	5 × 5	5 × 5	5 × 5
6	MB chest pass	5 × 5	5 × 5	5 × 5
7a	Face pull	5 × 5	5 × 5	5 × 5
7b	Wall hold	20 sec	20 sec	20 sec
8a	Superman	3 × 10	3 × 10	3 × 10
8b	MB wood chop	3 × 5	3 × 5	3 × 5
8c	Side crunch	3 × 10 each	3 × 10 each	3 × 10 each

Table 9.7   College: Off-Season Microcycle 1, Hypertrophy/Strength Endurance, Weeks 1-4

Monday: Lower Body (Hinge Emphasis)

Order	Exercise	Sets × reps Week 1	Sets × reps Week 2	Sets × reps Week 3	Sets × reps Week 4
1a	DB or KB RDL	3 × 8	3 × 10	3 × 12	3 × 10
1b	Single-leg bridge with extended knee	3 × 10 each	3 × 10 each	3 × 10 each	3 × 10 each
2a	KB one-arm single-leg RDL	3 × 8 each	3 × 10 each	3 × 10 each	3 × 8 each
2b	Lateral lunge (with DB or KB)	3 × 10 each	3 × 10 each	3 × 10 each	3 × 10 each
3a	Step-up (with DB or KB)	3 × 8 each	3 × 8 each	3 × 8 each	3 × 6 each
3b	Starter rolling upper body*	3 × 5 each	3 × 5 each	3 × 5 each	3 × 5 each

Order	Exercise	Sets × reps	Sets × reps	Sets × reps	Sets × reps
		Week 1	**Week 2**	**Week 3**	**Week 4**
4a	Farmer's walk (with KB or DB)	3 × 50 yd (46 m)	3 × 50 yd (46 m)	3 × 50 yd (46 m)	3 × 30 yd (27 m)
4b	Forward and backward mini-band walk (band on ankles or above knees)	3 × 10 each	3 × 10 each	3 × 10 each	3 × 10 each

*Warm-ups: mobility and corrective exercise session options (see page 211)

Tuesday: Upper Body (Push Emphasis)

Order	Exercise	Sets × reps	Sets × reps	Sets × reps	Sets × reps
		Week 1	**Week 2**	**Week 3**	**Week 4**
1a	DB incline bench press	3 × 8	3 × 10	3 × 12	3 × 10
1b	T-spine rotation with reach*	3 × 10 each	3 × 10 each	3 × 10 each	3 × 10 each
2a	Half-kneeling one-arm cable chest press	3 × 8 each	3 × 10 each	3 × 10 each	3 × 8 each
2b	Cable row (side plank position)	3 × 10 each	3 × 12 each	3 × 12 each	3 × 10 each
3a	DB chest supported row (light)	3 × 4 (10 sec hold)	3 × 5 (10 sec hold)	3 × 6 (10 sec hold)	3 × 5 (10 sec hold)
3b	Side plank	3 × 30 sec each	3 × 30 sec each	3 × 30 sec each	3 × 30 sec each
4a	Bear crawl forward	3 × 10 yd (9 m)	3 × 15 yd (14 m)	3 × 20 yd (18 m)	3 × 15 yd (14 m)
4b	Tall kneeling hold anterior load with KB*	3 × 10 breaths	3 × 10 breaths	3 × 10 breaths	3 × 10 breaths

*Warm-ups: mobility and corrective exercise session options (see page 211)

Thursday: Lower Body (Squat Emphasis)

Order	Exercise	Sets × reps	Sets × reps	Sets × reps	Sets × reps
		Week 1	**Week 2**	**Week 3**	**Week 4**
1a	KB or DB split squat	3 × 6 each	3 × 8 each	3 × 10 each	3 × 8 each
1b	Half-kneeling hip flexor stretch*	3 × 10 each	3 × 10 each	3 × 10 each	3 × 10 each
2a	KB or DB walking lunge (rack position)	3 × 8 each	3 × 10 each	3 × 10 each	3 × 8 each
2b	Stability ball leg curl	3 × 10	3 × 10	3 × 10	3 × 10
3a	Hip thrust (banded or DB)	3 × 10	3 × 12	3 × 15	3 × 10
3b	Kneeling Pallof press	3 × 10 each	3 × 12 each	3 × 12 each	3 × 10 each
4a	One-arm farmer's walk (with one KB or DB)	3 × 50 yd (46 m) each	3 × 50 yd (46 m) each	3 × 50 yd (46 m) each	3 × 30 yd (27 m) each
4b	Lateral mini-band walk (band on ankles or above knees)	3 × 10 each	3 × 10 each	3 × 10 each	3 × 10 each

*Warm-ups: mobility and corrective exercise session options (see page 211)

(continued)

Table 9.7 College: Off-Season Microcycle 1, Hypertrophy/Strength Endurance, Weeks 1-4 *(continued)*

Friday: Upper Body (Pull Emphasis)

Order	Exercise	Sets × reps Week 1	Sets × reps Week 2	Sets × reps Week 3	Sets × reps Week 4
1a	Suspension trainer inverted row	3 × 8	3 × 10	3 × 12	3 × 10
1b	Brettzel 2.0*	3 × 5 each	3 × 5 each	3 × 5 each	3 × 5 each
2a	Cable kneeling lat pulldown	3 × 8	3 × 10	3 × 12	3 × 10
2b	Side plank with hip flexion	3 × 30 sec each	3 × 30 sec each	3 × 30 sec each	3 × 30 sec each
3a	Push-up (feet elevated)	3 × 10	3 × 12	3 × 15	3 × 12
3b	Quadruped T-spine rotation*	3 × 10 each	3 × 10 each	3 × 10 each	3 × 10 each
4a	Bear crawl backward	3 × 10 yd (9 m)	3 × 15 yd (14 m)	3 × 20 yd (18 m)	3 × 15 yd (14 m)
4b	KB tall kneeling head turns anterior load*	3 × 5 each	3 × 5 each	3 × 5 each	3 × 5 each

*Warm-ups: mobility and corrective exercise session options (see page 211)

Table 9.8 College: Off-Season Microcycles 2 and 3, Basic Strength, Weeks 5-12

NOTE: Weeks 5-8 are listed here. Weeks 9-12 repeat weeks 5-8.

Monday: Lower Body (Hinge Emphasis)

Order	Exercise	Sets × reps Week 5	Sets × reps Week 6	Sets × reps Week 7	Sets × reps Week 8
1a	BB RDL or deadlift	4 × 8	4 × 8	4 × 6	3 × 6
1b	Toe touch progression*	3 × 5 each	3 × 5 each	3 × 5 each	3 × 5 each
2a	KB or DB two-arm single-leg RDL	4 × 8 each	4 × 8 each	4 × 6 each	3 × 6 each
2b	KB or DB lateral lunge (feet in place or with step)	3 × 8 each	3 × 8 each	3 × 8 each	3 × 8 each
3a	Step-up (front rack position with BB, KB, or DB)	4 × 8 each	4 × 8 each	4 × 6 each	3 × 6 each
3b	Rolling upper body*	3 × 5 each	3 × 5 each	3 × 5 each	3 × 5 each
4a	Farmer's walk (with KB or DB)	3 × 30 yd (27 m)	4 × 30 yd (27 m)	4 × 30 yd (27 m)	3 × 30 yd (27 m)
4b	Single-leg bridge with extended knee	3 × 10 each	3 × 10 each	3 × 10 each	3 × 10 each

*Warm-ups: mobility and corrective exercise session options (see page 211)

Tuesday: Upper Body (Push Emphasis)

Order	Exercise	Sets × reps Week 5	Sets × reps Week 6	Sets × reps Week 7	Sets × reps Week 8
1a	DB bench press (simultaneous or alternating)	4 × 8	4 × 8	4 × 6	3 × 6
1b	Brettzel*	3 × 5 breaths each	3 × 5 breaths each	3 × 5 breaths each	3 × 5 breaths each

Order	Exercise	Sets × reps Week 5	Sets × reps Week 6	Sets × reps Week 7	Sets × reps Week 8
2a	Tall kneeling one-arm cable chest press	4 × 8 each	4 × 8 each	4 × 6 each	3 × 6 each
2b	Front-facing MB toss	3 × 6 each	3 × 6 each	3 × 6 each	3 × 6 each
3a	Suspension trainer one-arm inverted row	4 × 8 each	4 × 8 each	4 × 8 each	3 × 8 each
3b	Standing scapular wall slides with back on wall*	3 × 10	3 × 10	3 × 10	3 × 10
4a	Bear crawl forward (plate on back)	3 × 10 yd (9 m)	4 × 10 yd (9 m)	4 × 10 yd (9 m)	3 × 10 yd (9 m)
4b	Tall kneeling KB halo*	3 × 5 each	3 × 5 each	3 × 5 each	3 × 5 each

*Warm-ups: mobility and corrective exercise session options (see page 211)

Thursday: Lower Body (Squat Emphasis)

Order	Exercise	Sets × reps Week 5	Sets × reps Week 6	Sets × reps Week 7	Sets × reps Week 8
1a	BB front squat	4 × 8	4 × 8	4 × 6	3 × 6
1b	Half-kneeling rotations with dowel*	3 × 5 each	3 × 5 each	3 × 5 each	3 × 5 each
2a	KB or DB reverse or walking lunge (rack position)	4 × 8 each	4 × 8 each	4 × 6 each	3 × 6 each
2b	Stability ball single-leg curl	3 × 8 each	3 × 8 each	3 × 8 each	3 × 8 each
3a	BB hip thrust	4 × 8	4 × 8	4 × 6	3 × 6
3b	Kneeling stick chop	3 × 10 each	3 × 10 each	3 × 10 each	3 × 10 each
4a	One-arm farmer's walk (with one KB or DB)	3 × 30 yd (27 m) each	4 × 30 yd (27 m) each	4 × 30 yd (27 m) each	3 × 30 yd (27 m) each
4b	Single-leg bridge with leg extended	3 × 8 each	3 × 8 each	3 × 8 each	3 × 8 each

*Warm-ups: mobility and corrective exercise session options (see page 211)

Friday: Upper Body (Pull Emphasis)

Order	Exercise	Sets × reps Week 5	Sets × reps Week 6	Sets × reps Week 7	Sets × reps Week 8
1a	Low-pulley seated row	4 × 8	4 × 8	4 × 6	3 × 6
1b	Brettzel 2.0*	3 × 5 each	3 × 5 each	3 × 5 each	3 × 5 each
2a	Cable half-kneeling one-arm pulldown	4 × 8 each	4 × 8 each	4 × 6 each	3 × 6 each
2b	Side plank with hip abduction	3 × 30 sec each	3 × 30 sec each	3 × 30 sec each	3 × 30 sec each
3a	Suspension trainer push-up	4 × 8	4 × 8	4 × 8	3 × 8
3b	Child's pose breathing	3 × 3-5	3 × 3-5	3 × 3-5	3 × 3-5
4a	Bear crawl backward (plate on back)	3 × 10 yd (9 m)	4 × 10 yd (9 m)	4 × 10 yd (9 m)	3 × 10 yd (9 m)
4b	Kneeling Pallof press	3 × 30 sec each	3 × 30 sec each	3 × 30 sec each	3 × 30 sec each

*Warm-ups: mobility and corrective exercise session options (see page 211)

Table 9.9 College: Off-Season Microcycle 4, Maximum Strength, Weeks 13-16

Monday: Lower Body (Hinge Emphasis)

Order	Exercise	Sets × reps Week 13	Sets × reps Week 14	Sets × reps Week 15	Sets × reps Week 16
1a	BB or trap bar deadlift	4 × 8	4 × 6	4 × 4	3 × 4
1b	Assisted single-leg lowering*	3 × 10 each	3 × 10 each	3 × 10 each	3 × 10 each
2a	KB or DB one-arm single-leg RDL	4 × 8 each	4 × 6 each	4 × 4 each	3 × 4 each
2b	Half-kneeling stick lift	3 × 10 each	3 × 10 each	3 × 10 each	3 × 10 each
3a	One-arm KB or DB squat (rack position)	3 × 6 each	3 × 5 each	3 × 4 each	3 × 4 each
3b	Core control rolling with knee touch*	3 × 5 each	3 × 5 each	3 × 5 each	3 × 5 each
4a	Farmer's walk (with KB or DB rack position)	3 × 50 yd (46 m)	3 × 40 yd (37 m)	3 × 30 yd (27 m)	3 × 30 yd (27 m)
4b	Lateral mini-band walk (band on ankles or above knees)	3 × 10 each	3 × 10 each	3 × 10 each	3 × 10 each

*Warm-ups: mobility and corrective exercise session options (see page 211)

Tuesday: Upper Body (Push Emphasis)

Order	Exercise	Sets × reps Week 13	Sets × reps Week 14	Sets × reps Week 15	Sets × reps Week 16
1a	DB floor press	4 × 8	4 × 6	4 × 4	3 × 4
1b	Standing forearm wall slide*	3 × 10	3 × 10	3 × 10	3 × 10
2a	Standing one-arm cable chest press	3 × 10 each	3 × 8 each	3 × 6 each	3 × 6 each
2b	Lateral rotation MB shot put	3 × 6 each	3 × 6 each	3 × 6 each	3 × 6 each
3a	Staggered stance two-arm cable pulldown	3 × 12	3 × 10	3 × 8	3 × 8
3b	Trunk stability rotation with knees flexed*	3 × 10	3 × 10	3 × 10	3 × 10
4a	Turkish get-up to elbow or hand with hip lift	3 × 3-5 each	3 × 3-5 each	3 × 3-5 each	3 × 3-5 each
4b	Single-leg stance with core engagement (with cable system or Cook band)*	3 × 5 each	3 × 5 each	3 × 5 each	3 × 5 each

*Warm-ups: mobility and corrective exercise session options (see page 211)

Thursday: Lower Body (Squat Emphasis)

Order	Exercise	Sets × reps Week 13	Sets × reps Week 14	Sets × reps Week 15	Sets × reps Week 16
1a	BB front or back squat	4 × 8	4 × 6	4 × 4	3 × 4
1b	Active leg lowering to bolster*	3 × 10 each	3 × 10 each	3 × 10 each	3 × 10 each
2a	DB walking lunge (side hang)	4 × 8 each	4 × 6 each	4 × 5 each	3 × 5 each
2b	Single-leg RDL to chest pass with MB	3 × 6 each	3 × 6 each	3 × 6 each	3 × 6 each
3a	Two-arm KB swing	3 × 15	3 × 12	3 × 10	3 × 10
3b	Staggered stance stick chop	3 × 10 each	3 × 10 each	3 × 10 each	3 × 10 each
4a	One-arm farmer's walk (with one KB or DB in rack position)	3 × 50 yd (46 m) each	3 × 40 yd (37 m) each	3 × 30 yd (27 m) each	3 × 30 yd (27 m) each
4b	Double-leg bridge	3 × 10	3 × 10	3 × 10	3 × 10

*Warm-ups: mobility and corrective exercise session options (see page 211)

Friday: Upper Body (Pull Emphasis)

Order	Exercise	Sets × reps Week 13	Sets × reps Week 14	Sets × reps Week 15	Sets × reps Week 16
1a	DB chest supported row (heavy)	4 × 8	4 × 6	4 × 4	3 × 4
1b	Brettzel 2.0*	3 × 5 each	3 × 5 each	3 × 5 each	3 × 5 each
2a	One-arm cable row (standing)	3 × 10 each	3 × 8 each	3 × 6 each	3 × 6 each
2b	MB wood chop throw	3 × 6	3 × 6	3 × 6	3 × 6
3a	Push-up (band resisted)	3 × 8	3 × 10	3 × 12	3 × 10
3b	Child's pose breathing	3 × 3-5	3 × 3-5	3 × 3-5	3 × 3-5
4a	Bear crawl lateral	3 × 10 yd (9 m) each	4 × 10 yd (9 m) each	4 × 10 yd (9 m) each	3 × 10 yd (9 m) each
4b	Half-kneeling KB halo*	3 × 5 each	3 × 5 each	3 × 5 each	3 × 5 each

*Warm-ups: mobility and corrective exercise session options (see page 211)

Table 9.10 College: Off-Season Microcycle 5, Sport-Specific Power, Weeks 17-20

Monday: Lower Body (Hinge Emphasis)

Order	Exercise	Sets × reps Week 17	Sets × reps Week 18	Sets × reps Week 19	Sets × reps Week 20
1a	BB or trap bar deadlift	4 × 5	4 × 4	4 × 3	3 × 3
1b	Core control rolling with knee touch*	3 × 5 each	3 × 5 each	3 × 5 each	3 × 5 each
2a	KB or DB one-arm single-leg RDL	4 × 6 each	4 × 5 each	4 × 5 each	3 × 5 each
2b	Half-kneeling stick chop	3 × 10 each	3 × 10 each	3 × 10 each	3 × 10 each
3a	One-arm KB or DB squat (rack position)	3 × 6 each	3 × 5 each	3 × 4 each	3 × 4 each
3b	Rolling lower body*	3 × 5 each	3 × 5 each	3 × 5 each	3 × 5 each
4a	Farmer's walk backward (with KB or DB rack position)	3-4 × 30 yd (27 m)	3-4 × 30 yd (27 m)	3-4 × 30 yd (27 m)	3-4 × 30 yd (27 m)
4b	Alternating dead bug	3 × 10	3 × 10	3 × 10	3 × 10

*Warm-ups: mobility and corrective exercise session options (see page 211)

Tuesday: Upper Body (Push Emphasis)

Order	Exercise	Sets × reps Week 17	Sets × reps Week 18	Sets × reps Week 19	Sets × reps Week 20
1a	DB bench or floor press (2 sec pause at bottom)	4 × 5	4 × 4	4 × 3	3 × 3
1b	Seated scapular wall slide with back on wall*	3 × 10	3 × 10	3 × 10	3 × 10
2a	Staggered stance one-arm cable chest press	4 × 8 each	4 × 6 each	4 × 5 each	3 × 5 each
2b	Kneeling MB chest pass	3 × 6	3 × 6	3 × 6	3 × 6
3a	Squat position two-arm cable row (high to low)	4 × 8	4 × 8	4 × 8	4 × 8
3b	Quadruped T-spine rotation with lumbar locked*	3 × 10 each	3 × 10 each	3 × 10 each	3 × 10 each
4a	Turkish get-up to leg sweep	4 × 2 each	4 × 3 each	4 × 4 each	3 × 3 each
4b	90-90 breathing position*	3 × 5	3 × 5	3 × 5	3 × 5

*Warm-ups: mobility and corrective exercise session options (see page 211)

(continued)

Table 9.10 College: Off-Season Microcycle 5, Sport-Specific Power, Weeks 17-20 *(continued)*

Thursday: Lower Body (Squat Emphasis)

Order	Exercise	Sets × reps Week 17	Sets × reps Week 18	Sets × reps Week 19	Sets × reps Week 20
1a	BB front or back squat	4 × 5	4 × 4	4 × 3	3 × 3
1b	Open half-kneeling ankle mobility with KB*	3 × 10 each	3 × 10 each	3 × 10 each	3 × 10 each
2a	KB or DB forward to reverse lunge (side hang or rack position)	4 × 5 each	4 × 4 each	4 × 3 each	3 × 3 each
2b	Single-leg RDL to chest pass with MB	3 × 5 each	3 × 5 each	3 × 5 each	3 × 5 each
3a	Two-arm KB swing	4 × 10	4 × 8	4 × 6	4 × 6
3b	Staggered stance stick lift	3 × 10 each	3 × 10 each	3 × 10 each	3 × 10 each
4a	One-arm farmer's walk backward (with one KB or DB in rack position)	3 × 30 yd (27 m) each	4 × 30 yd (27 m) each	4 × 30 yd (27 m) each	3 × 30 yd (27 m) each
4b	Reverse abdominal crunch	3 × 10	3 × 10	3 × 10	3 × 10

*Warm-ups: mobility and corrective exercise session options (see page 211)

Friday: Upper Body (Pull Emphasis)

Order	Exercise	Sets × reps Week 17	Sets × reps Week 18	Sets × reps Week 19	Sets × reps Week 20
1a	One-arm DB row (knee supported)	4 × 8 each	4 × 6 each	4 × 4 each	3 × 4 each
1b	Brettzel 2.0*	3 × 5 each	3 × 5 each	3 × 5 each	3 × 5 each
2a	Staggered stance one-arm cable row (low to high pull)	4 × 8 each	4 × 6 each	4 × 5 each	3 × 5 each
2b	MB wood chop throw	3 × 6 each	3 × 6 each	3 × 6 each	3 × 6 each
3a	Push-up (knee to elbow)	3 × 8	3 × 10	3 × 12	3 × 10
3b	Standing forearm wall slide*	3 × 10	3 × 10	3 × 10	3 × 10
4a	Bear crawl forward to backward	3 × 10 yd (9 m) each	3 × 10 yd (9 m) each	3 × 10 yd (9 m) each	3 × 10 yd (9 m) each
4b	Tall kneeling hold posterior load with KB*	3 × 10 breaths	3 × 10 breaths	3 × 10 breaths	3 × 10 breaths

*Warm-ups: mobility and corrective exercise session options (see page 211)

Table 9.11 Professional: Off-Season Microcycle 1, Hypertrophy, Weeks 1-4

Monday: Total Body (Lower Emphasis)

Order	Exercise	Sets × reps Week 1	Sets × reps Week 2	Sets × reps Week 3	Sets × reps Week 4
1a	BB front squat	2 × 10	3 × 8	3 × 8	2 × 6
1b	Front plank	2 × 30 sec	3 × 30 sec	3 × 45 sec	2 × 30 sec
1c	Inverted row with suspension trainer	2 × 8	3 × 8	3 × 8	2 × 8
2a	DB reverse lunge	2 × 6 each	3 × 8 each	3 × 8 each	2 × 6 each
2b	Push-up	2 × 10	3 × 12	3 × 12	2 × 8
2c	Band bent-over lateral shoulder raise	2 × 12	3 × 12	3 × 12	3 × 12
3a	Half-kneeling stick lift	2 × 8 each	3 × 10 each	3 × 12 each	2 × 8 each
3b	KB or DB one-arm single-leg RDL	2 × 6 each	3 × 6 each	3 × 6 each	2 × 5 each

Wednesday: Total Body (Upper Emphasis)

Order	Exercise	Sets × reps Week 1	Sets × reps Week 2	Sets × reps Week 3	Sets × reps Week 4
1a	DB bench press (alternating arms)	2 × 8 each	3 × 8 each	3 × 8 each	2 × 6 each
1b	Lateral mini-band walk	2 × 10	3 × 10	3 × 10	2 × 10
1c	KB or DB lateral squat	2 × 6 each	3 × 8 each	3 × 8 each	2 × 6 each
2a	Seated row	2 × 8	3 ×	3 × 8	2 × 8
2b	Side plank	2 × 30 sec each	3 × 30 sec each	3 × 45 sec each	2 × 30 sec each
2c	Nordic hamstring curl	2 × 6	3 × 8	3 × 8	2 × 6
3a	Single-leg bridge	2 × 10 each	3 × 10 each	3 × 10 each	2 × 8 each
3b	Half-kneeling one-arm cable row	2 × 8 each	3 × 8 each	3 × 8 each	2 × 8 each

Friday: Total Body (Upper/Lower Emphasis)

Order	Exercise	Sets × reps Week 1	Sets × reps Week 2	Sets × reps Week 3	Sets × reps Week 4
1a	Trap bar deadlift	2 × 6 each	3 × 6 each	3 × 6 each	2 × 6 each
1b	Dead bug	2 × 8 each	3 × 10 each	3 × 12 each	2 × 8 each
2a	DB bent-over lateral shoulder raise	2 × 10	3 × 10	3 × 10	2 × 8
2b	DB single-leg squat	2 × 8	3 × 8	3 × 8	3 × 8
3a	Half-kneeling landmine press	2 × 8 each	3 × 8 each	3 × 8 each	2 × 8 each
3b	One-arm DB row	2 × 8 each	3 × 8 each	3 × 8 each	2 × 8 each
4a	Half-kneeling stick chop	2 × 10 each	3 × 10 each	3 × 12 each	2 × 8 each
4b	Prone Y, T (use elastic band)	2 × 10 each	3 × 10 each	3 × 10 each	2 × 10 each

Table 9.12 Professional: Off-Season Microcycle 2, Strength, Weeks 5-8

Monday: Total Body (Lower Emphasis)

Order	Exercise	Sets × reps Week 5	Sets × reps Week 6	Sets × reps Week 7	Sets × reps Week 8
1a	BB front squat	3 × 4	4 × 4	4 × 6	3 × 6
1b	Push-up shoulder tap	3 × 10	4 × 10	4 × 12	3 × 10
1c	Inverted row with suspension trainer	3 × 4	4 × 4	4 × 6	3 × 6
2a	Lateral step-up	3 × 5 each	4 × 5 each	4 × 5 each	3 × 5 each
2b	BB hip thrust	3 × 6	4 × 6	4 × 6	3 × 6
2c	Band bent-over lateral shoulder raise	3 × 5	4 × 5	4 × 5	3 × 5
3a	Half-kneeling stick lift	3 × 6 each	3 × 6 each	3 × 8 each	3 × 8 each
3b	Single-leg squat	3 × 8 each	3 × 8 each	3 × 8 each	3 × 8 each

(continued)

Wednesday: Total Body (Upper Emphasis)

Order	Exercise	Sets × reps	Sets × reps	Sets × reps	Sets × reps
		Week 5	Week 6	Week 7	Week 8
1a	DB bench press (alternating arms)	3 × 4 each	4 × 4 each	4 × 6 each	3 × 6 each
1b	Kneeling Pallof press	3 × 10	4 × 10	4 × 12	3 × 10
1c	KB or DB lateral squat	3 × 4 each	4 × 4 each	4 × 6 each	3 × 6 each
2a	Seated row	3 × 10	3 × 10	3 × 12	3 × 10
2b	DB lateral shoulder raise	3 × 6	3 × 6	3 × 6	3 × 6
2c	Nordic hamstring curl	3 × 5	3 × 5	3 × 5	3 × 5
3a	Half-kneeling stick chop	2 × 6 each	3 × 6 each	3 × 8 each	2 × 8 each
3b	Single-leg bridge	2 × 10 each	3 × 10 each	3 × 10 each	2 × 10 each

Friday: Total Body (Upper/Lower Emphasis)

Order	Exercise	Sets × reps	Sets × reps	Sets × reps	Sets × reps
		Week 5	Week 6	Week 7	Week 8
1a	BB or trap bar deadlift	3 × 4	4 × 4	4 × 6	3 × 6
1b	Dead bug	3 × 10	4 × 10	4 × 12	3 × 10
2a	DB bent-over lateral shoulder raise	3 × 6	4 × 6	4 × 6	3 × 6
2b	Reverse lunge	3 × 4 each	4 × 4 each	4 × 6 each	3 × 6 each
3a	Crossover step-up	3 × 6 each	4 × 6 each	4 × 6 each	3 × 6 each
3b	One-arm DB row	3 × 5 each	4 × 5 each	4 × 5 each	3 × 5 each
4a	Half-kneeling stick chop	3 × 6 each	3 × 6 each	3 × 8 each	3 × 8 each
4b	Prone Y, T (use elastic band)	3 × 8	3 × 8	3 × 8	3 × 8

Table 9.13   Professional: Off-Season Microcycle 3, Power, Weeks 9-12

Monday: Total Body (Lower Emphasis)

Order	Exercise	Sets × reps	Sets × reps	Sets × reps	Sets × reps
		Week 9	Week 10	Week 11	Week 12
1a	BB front squat	3 × 5	3 × 4	4 × 3	5 × 3
1b	Front plank	3 × 30 sec	3 × 30 sec	4 × 30 sec	5 × 30 sec
1c	Inverted row with suspension trainer	3 × 5	3 × 5	4 × 5	5 × 5
2a	DB reverse lunge	3 × 5 each	3 × 5 each	3 × 5 each	3 × 5 each
2b	Push-up	3 × 5	3 × 5	3 × 4	3 × 4
2c	DB front shoulder raise	3 × 5	3 × 5	3 × 5	3 × 5
3a	Half-kneeling stick lift	3 × 4 each	3 × 5 each	4 × 4 each	4 × 4 each
3b	Step-up	3 × 6 each	3 × 6 each	4 × 6 each	4 × 6 each

Wednesday: Total Body (Upper Emphasis)

Order	Exercise	Sets × reps Week 9	Sets × reps Week 10	Sets × reps Week 11	Sets × reps Week 12
1a	DB bench press (alternating arms)	3 × 5 each	3 × 4 each	4 × 3 each	5 × 3 each
1b	Lateral mini-band walk	3 × 5	3 × 5	4 × 5	5 × 5
1c	KB or DB lateral squat	3 × 6 each	3 × 6 each	4 × 6 each	5 × 6 each
2a	Lat pulldown	3 × 6	3 × 6	3 × 8	3 × 8
2b	Band bent-over lateral shoulder raise	3 × 6	3 × 6	3 × 6	3 × 6
2c	Nordic hamstring curl	3 × 5	3 × 5	3 × 6	3 × 6
3a	Half-kneeling one-arm cable row	3 × 5 each	3 × 5 each	4 × 4 each	4 × 4 each
3b	Double-leg bridge	3 × 10	3 × 10	4 × 10	4 × 10

Friday: Total Body (Upper/Lower Emphasis)

Order	Exercise	Sets × reps Week 9	Sets × reps Week 10	Sets × reps Week 11	Sets × reps Week 12
1a	BB or trap bar deadlift	3 × 5	3 × 4	4 × 3	5 × 3
1b	Dead bug	3 × 5 each	3 × 5 each	4 × 5 each	5 × 5 each
2a	One-arm cable pulldown	3 × 5 each	3 × 5 each	3 × 5 each	3 × 5 each
2b	DB single-leg squat	3 × 5 each	3 × 5 each	3 × 5 each	3 × 5 each
3a	Half-kneeling landmine press	3 × 4 each	3 × 4 each	3 × 5 each	3 × 5 each
3b	Face pull	3 × 5	3 × 5	3 × 5	3 × 5
4a	Half-kneeling stick chop	3 × 5 each	3 × 5 each	4 × 4 each	4 × 4 each
4b	DB lateral shoulder raise	3 × 10	3 × 10	4 × 10	4 × 10

Table 9.14   Professional: Off-Season Microcycle 4, Speed Strength, Weeks 13-16

Monday: Total Body (Lower Emphasis)

Order	Exercise	Sets × reps Week 13	Sets × reps Week 14	Sets × reps Week 15	Sets × reps Week 16
1a	BB front squat	4 × 4	5 × 4	5 × 3	5 × 2
1b	Yoga push-up	4 × 10	5 × 10	5 × 10	5 × 10
1c	Inverted row with suspension trainer	4 × 5	5 × 5	5 × 3	5 × 3
2a	Lateral step-up	3 × 5 each	3 × 5 each	3 × 5 each	3 × 5 each
2b	Band bent-over lateral shoulder raise	3 × 4	3 × 4	3 × 5	3 × 5
2c	Single-leg bridge	3 × 6 each	3 × 6 each	3 × 6 each	3 × 6 each
3a	Half-kneeling stick lift	3 × 6 each	3 × 6 each	3 × 8 each	3 × 8 each
3b	Single-leg squat	3 × 8 each	3 × 8 each	3 × 8 each	3 × 8 each

(continued)

Table 9.14 Professional: Off-Season Microcycle 4, Speed Strength, Weeks 13-16 *(continued)*

Wednesday: Total Body (Upper Emphasis)

Order	Exercise	Sets × reps Week 13	Sets × reps Week 14	Sets × reps Week 15	Sets × reps Week 16
1a	DB bench press (alternating arms)	4 × 4 each	5 × 4 each	5 × 3 each	5 × 2 each
1b	Lateral mini-band walk	3 × 10	5 × 10	5 × 10	5 × 10
1c	KB or DB split squat	4 × 5 each	5 × 5 each	5 × 3 each	5 × 3 each
2a	Lat pulldown	3 × 5	3 × 5	3 × 5	3 × 5
2b	Side plank	3 × 30 sec each	3 × 30 sec each	3 × 30 sec each	3 × 30 sec each
2c	Nordic hamstring curl	3 × 6	3 × 6	3 × 6	3 × 6
3a	DB front shoulder raise	3 × 6	3 × 6	3 × 8	3 × 8
3b	Single-leg bridge	3 × 8 each	3 × 8 each	3 × 8 each	3 × 8 each

Friday: Total Body (Upper/Lower Emphasis)

Order	Exercise	Sets × reps Week 13	Sets × reps Week 14	Sets × reps Week 15	Sets × reps Week 16
1a	Trap bar deadlift	5 × 4	5 × 3	5 × 3	5 × 2
1b	Dead bug	5 × 10	5 × 10	5 × 10	5 × 10
2a	One-arm DB row	4 × 5 each	4 × 5 each	4 × 3 each	4 × 3 each
2b	DB single-leg squat	4 × 5 each	4 × 5 each	4 × 5 each	4 × 5 each
3a	Face pull	3 × 4 each	3 × 4 each	3 × 5 each	3 × 5 each
3b	Half-kneeling landmine press	3 × 6 each	3 × 6 each	3 × 6 each	3 × 6 each
4a	DB lateral shoulder raise	3 × 6	3 × 6	3 × 8	3 × 8
4b	KB or DB one-arm single-leg RDL	3 × 8 each	3 × 8 each	3 × 8 each	3 × 8 each

Table 9.15 Resistance Training–Specific Rating of Perceived Exertion (RPE)

Rating	Description of Perceived Exertion
10	Maximum effort
9.5	No further repetitions but could increase the load
9	1 repetition remaining
8.5	1-2 repetitions remaining
8	2 repetitions remaining
7.5	2-3 repetitions remaining
7	3 repetitions remaining
5-6	4-6 repetitions remaining
3-4	Light effort
1-2	Little to no effort

Experimental scale for RPE for resistance exercise. Values in the "rating" column correspond to the repetitions in reserve (RIR) or perceived level of exertion indicated in the adjacent description column. Descriptions of perceived exertion are associated with the number of RIR.

Reprinted by permission from M. C. Zourdos et al., "Novel Resistance Training-Specific RPE Scale Measuring Repetitions in Reserve," *Journal of Strength and Conditioning Research* 30 (2016): 267-275.

10

PRESEASON PROGRAMMING

PATRICK MCHENRY (HIGH SCHOOL), CHRIS JOYNER (COLLEGE), JOE KESSLER (PROFESSIONAL)

The preseason resistance training program will focus on the sport- and position-specific demands needed to prepare the baseball player to be explosive on the field as well as maintain strength and decrease the potential for injury. Multi-joint primary exercises from the off-season and their variations are the focus so athletes can concentrate on baseball performance.

The preseason program outlined in this chapter includes the goals and objectives, length, structure, and organization of the preseason, and includes recommended exercises that are position and level specific for high school, college, and professional athletes. Additionally, this chapter will address intensity, volume, and exercise order for each level.

GOALS AND OBJECTIVES

The preseason training phase for baseball at all levels is often referred to as the "train to play" phase. It is designed to prepare athletes for a position on the team and endure the physical stress of a long season of competition. The preseason prepares the athletes for the large volume of physical effort required for fundamental skill work (hitting, throwing, pitching, fielding, and running). During the off-season, the resistance training focus was on qualities that make baseball players better athletes, including strength endurance, strength, and power. However, the physical gains made in the off-season will not assist baseball performance if they cannot be carried over to the field. Therefore, a major goal of the preseason at all levels of competition is to translate the strength gains made in the weight room during the off-season into improved and powerful on-field performance during the competitive season. During the preseason, the focus will also change from improving general movement to improving the baseball-specific movements and skills needed to enhance on-field performance. As the emphasis shifts toward on-field preparation, the volume and intensity of weight room training will be reduced to allow athletes to expend more energy in on-the-field activities and facilitate recovery between skill training and weight room workouts.

LENGTH, STRUCTURE, AND ORGANIZATION

The length, structure, and organization of the preseason program will depend on the level of play (high school, college, or professional), facilities, and geographic location. Although all professional teams and some colleges have access to relatively warm weather and excellent facilities during the preseason, some college and high school teams are in regions where the weather is not always conducive to optimal outdoor training, which can affect both the length and quality of preseason training workouts. In general, the structure for all levels of training includes a warm-up before resistance training begins. Page 243 shows various warm-up options that include mobility, corrective, active dynamic, and in-place flow stretch exercises that are recommended for athletes at the beginning of every resistance training session. Coaches should pick the most appropriate option for the specific training day. Some of these exercises are incorporated into the sample preseason programs for college and professional athletes.

High School

The high school baseball season generally starts at the end of February or the beginning of March, depending on the region, and ends at the conclusion of the school year in late May or playoffs in early June. Teams play two to three games per week, depending on the state in which they are located. This means that players must be in good enough condition to play 20 to 25 games—or 140 to 175 innings—per season. Preseason training is usually four weeks in length and runs from mid-January to mid-February. Based on this time frame, a single four-week microcycle with a loading pattern of low, medium, high, and unload will be implemented (2). The sample high school preseason program in this chapter is four days per week (tables 10.1 and 10.2). If a coach wants athletes to train three days per week, they should complete three training sessions that incorporate lower, upper, and total body exercises in one session. This phase incorporates resistance training as well as throwing, hitting, fielding, and speed work. Because throwing and hitting are multi-plane motions and many injuries occur during deceleration and change of direction, priority should be given to exercises that develop strength and power in all three planes of motion and improve the ability to reduce force and change direction under control.

The work in the weight room and on the field is designed to prepare the athletes for optimal performance in each of the 20 to 25 regular season games and playoffs. The goals of this phase are to transfer the strength and power gains developed in the off-season to explosive power and prepare the athlete to compete throughout the in-season. The high school athlete should have a solid base of strength developed from the off-season to the start of the preseason training phase.

College

During the off-season, athletes progressed through lower, upper, and total body primary exercises to improve strength and movement efficiency. Over the holiday break, which may be two to four weeks long, athletes may have completed a holiday resistance training program; coaches generally design multiple holiday programs that provide options for training two to four times per week. However, athletes do not always have the time or ability to train fully over the holidays.

For the preseason, the coach should design individualized and position-specific training programs that will transition to in-season training. These should include exercises the athlete is comfortable with and successful at performing. Not all athletes, for example, are comfortable or technically proficient at performing a barbell deadlift. For these athletes, the trap bar deadlift may be a better and safer option and still allows heavier loads to be performed. A similar case can be made for the back squat for those who prefer a front squat or another anteriorly loaded squat pattern. These decisions are collaborative between the athlete, strength and conditioning professional, and athletic trainer based on an athlete's training background, movement screen assessment, and medical history.

The college preseason starts when athletes return to school in January and extends through mid-February. The training priorities shift from strength, speed, and power to power, speed, and strength. The goal is to increase the ability of athletes to accelerate quickly, throw hard, and hit with power. The preseason training is divided into two three-week microcycles. At the beginning of the preseason, microcycle 1, team practice begins (table 10.3). During microcycle 2, intrasquad scrimmages occur before the competitive season begins (table 10.4).

During microcycle 1, position players and relief pitchers typically resistance train three times per week (table 10.5). One day will focus on total body training, whereas the other two days focus on upper and lower body separately. An optional fourth total body training day could be incorporated into the week if desired (table 10.3). For starting pitchers, resistance training days during microcycle 1 will be based on their live batting practice and bullpen sessions (table 10.3). Day 3 will focus on lower body training, day 4 will focus on upper body training after throwing a bullpen (post-bullpen), and day 6 will focus on total body training (tables 10.3 and 10.6).

During microcycle 2, position players will complete a total body resistance training session twice per week (table 10.4). Resistance training workouts will be scheduled around team practice and scrimmage schedules, and a scheduled off day will be included to facilitate recovery and mobility. Table 10.7 displays two sample total body resistance training sessions. The duration of each resistance training session will be 40 to 50 minutes. Because up to four intrasquad scrimmages are often scheduled during the week to prepare for the upcoming regular season, coaches must be mindful of athletes' demands on and off the field when scheduling resistance training sessions.

In general, relief pitchers, like position players, will train two days per week with total body training during microcycle 2 (table 10.7). However, their resistance training sequence is variable based on when they pitch. Relief pitchers who do not throw consistently during the week may be able to lift three times per week because they are not participating in scrimmage games as regularly as position players. If this is the case, relief pitchers could perform the training sessions in table 10.8 for starting pitchers. Starting pitchers will have a seven-day routine that will include lower body, upper body, and total body resistance training days between pitching starts (tables 10.4 and 10.8). Relief and starting pitcher routines will be based on individualized throwing programs, bullpen sessions, live batting practice sessions, and participation in scrimmage games. Drills that address footwork, speed, agility, and general conditioning will be implemented daily into team warm-ups and position-specific skill work such as baserunning for position players and interval runs for pitchers. Intensity and volume in resistance training and conditioning activities must be considered to balance the increase in throwing, hitting, and fielding against the need to recover.

Professional

The preseason for a professional athlete is called spring training. The goals in the weight room are two-fold: First, the athlete needs to transfer the gains made in the off-season to performance on the field. Second, the athletes, especially starting pitchers, need to develop, rehearse, and refine their in-season training routines. A typical spring training is six weeks in duration and is divided into two three-week microcycles (tables 10.9 and 10.10). In general, the loading pattern for weeks 1 to 3 is low, medium, and high, then weeks 4 to 6 are high, medium, and low. This means that preseason resistance training progresses to become the most demanding in weeks 3 and 4, then tapers down again before the baseball season begins. During spring training, the days are very long for the athletes. Coaches allow athletes to select the resistance training focus of the day (strength or power) based on how demanding the practice or scrimmage was. This provides autonomy for the athlete in addition to building the relationship between the coach and athlete. It is very important that the athlete knows that the coach is flexible and has the athlete's best interest in mind.

Traditionally, spring training starts with pitchers and catchers reporting to camp to begin their training activities approximately one week prior to the arrival of the position players. This additional week of training enables the pitchers to gradually increase arm strength, refine pitching mechanics, and pitch off the mound in a controlled environment before facing live batters. It also gives catchers time to gradually get their legs, arms, and hands in shape to catch multiple innings and days during the season.

Position players arrive in camp five to six days after the pitchers and quickly increase their running, throwing, fielding, and swinging volumes. Spring training games typically begin five to seven days after the position players arrive. Within the first day or two of spring training, pitchers are assigned a pitcher's fielding program (PFP) to improve defensive skills and a bullpen program to help prepare to throw live batting practice. The PFP, bullpen, and batting practice work progresses over a 9- to 10-day period and continues for the remainder of spring training as pitchers build arm strength and stamina. During this time, strength and conditioning work is adjusted to ensure recovery and help pitchers acclimate to an increase in baseball activity. This is accomplished by spreading out external load training, speed and agility movements, and conditioning.

During this period, a pitcher cycles through each training stimulus two to three times, after which he transitions to throwing live batting practice to position players. This will be the first time pitchers face live batters and vice versa. This progression simulates real game-play and allows pitchers to work on throwing accuracy and consistency while pitching to a batter. It also allows the pitcher to continue building arm strength with high-intensity pitches prior to pitching in games.

Once pitchers transition from live batting practice to pitching in games, the training schedule will be based on whether an athlete is a starter or relief pitcher. A starting pitcher's training is determined by their start day. During their five-day cycle, which consists of pitch (day 1), post-pitch (day 2), bullpen (day 3), two days from start (day 4), and pre-pitch (day 5), training activities are designed to complement the schedule. For example, a typical starting pitcher would complete two total body resistance training sessions, one on the post-pitch (day 2) day and one on two days from start (day 4). On the remaining three days of the five-day cycle, the pitcher will condition using both aerobic and anaerobic energy systems. Table 10.9 displays microcycle 1 with a loading pattern of low, medium, and high for weeks 1 to 3. Table 10.10 displays microcycle 2 with a loading pattern of high, medium, and low for weeks 4 to 6. This is very similar to the college preseason programming.

Relief pitchers will also have a minimum of two total body resistance training sessions per week on days that they are not scheduled to pitch (tables 10.9 and 10.10). The total number of resistance training sessions, however, may vary based on the number of relief appearances made by the athlete in a given week. A relief pitcher will also perform speed, agility, and conditioning work each day. These schedules are implemented for the duration of the preseason and carry over into the competitive season.

Position players have less time in camp than pitchers to prepare before the first game—typically, five to six days. After their arrival to spring training, position players place major emphasis on fielding and hitting progressions, with a large spike in the volume of fundamental skill work. During the week before games begin, position players complete high-speed, running-specific training on the bases to quickly acclimate to the angles of the basepaths and the force absorption of the bases. They will perform resistance training sessions two times per week. The loading pattern for the first week of training is low, with workout intensity and volume being light to moderate to help facilitate recovery. As position players progress through spring training and continue to play games, they will continue to resistance train two times per week on non-game days for the remainder of the preseason (tables 10.9 and 10.10). The loading pattern for weeks 2 and 3 of microcycle 1 will increase to medium and then high, then move from high to low through microcycle 2, weeks 4 to 6. The number of innings that position players play in games is also gradually increased; starting position players do not participate in back-to-back games until midway through spring training. Speed, agility, and conditioning drills are included in daily warm-ups prior to baseball activity.

The goal of the preseason is to improve the ability to adjust to the demands of increased position-specific fundamental work while preserving the levels of strength and power gained during off-season training. This requires a decrease in the volume, intensity, duration, and frequency of strength and conditioning work to ensure adequate recovery and prevent an overload of the central nervous system and skeletal muscles. This shift places a goal on recovery for the purpose of sustaining high levels of intensity during practice sessions and games, as well as the preservation of strength and power as playing time increases.

RECOMMENDED EXERCISES

The goal of the preseason training program is to prepare the athlete for the forthcoming season and potential playoffs.

Total Body Exercises

The total body exercises used during the preseason are consistent with those used in the off-season for high school, college, and professional athletes (see chapter 9). In this phase, for the high school athlete, power cleans will still be used early in the week for the athletes who have become proficient, regardless of training age; those who cannot power clean will continue with the midthigh clean pull, trap bar jump, and various medicine ball throws. This will help protect the shoulder from overuse and lessen the likelihood of an injury. High school athletes who were performing the standing or seated dumbbell shoulder press in the off-season will change to a push press or dumbbell push press. To improve rotational power, the landmine row to rotational press and rotational battle rope slam will be included in this phase.

College athletes will perform ground-based, total body exercises that provide stress throughout the kinetic chain to improve strength and power, such as the Turkish get-up and its variations in addition to bear crawl variations. Athletes will also use exercises that emphasize core stability, such as farmer's walk variations, and engage the core with resistance in rotational movement patterns, such as medicine ball rotational throws and tosses.

To maximize physical training and enhance performance for professional athletes during spring training, bilateral and unilateral lower and upper body exercises will be completed to correct individual deficiencies and improve strength and power. Because the athletes are practicing and playing every day, most total body exercises will not be performed. Certain total body exercises, such as the various medicine ball throws described in chapter 5, may be performed at times.

Lower Body Exercises

For the high school athlete, lower body exercises will include the back squat early in the week when intensity is higher and the step-up and single-leg squat later in the week when intensity is lower. Coaches should emphasize proper technique to ensure squat depth, shin and back angle, and foot placement are correct. The dumbbell forward step lunge and reach, reverse lunge, and trap bar deadlift are used to help develop strength in the legs and core. The incorporation of the dumbbell Romanian deadlift will occur early in the week, followed by the single-leg bridge and barbell hip thrust exercises later in the week.

At the college level, position players and relief pitchers will perform back, front, or goblet squats; trap bar deadlift with and without resistance bands; single-leg cable, dumbbell, or kettlebell RDL; and lateral lunge with plate press for lower body strength and power. Starting pitchers also perform the trap bar deadlift; single-leg RDL; back, front, or lateral squat; and reverse lunge.

For the professional athlete, bilateral and unilateral exercises are used to improve strength and power. Bilateral lower body exercises include the barbell or trap bar deadlift, squat variations, RDL, and bridges. Unilateral lower body exercises include step-up variations, lunge variations, the single-leg RDL, single-leg squat, and single-leg bridge.

Upper Body Exercises

For the high school athlete, the upper body will include two posterior pulling exercises for every anterior pushing exercise. The one-arm dumbbell row, lat pulldown, inverted row, neutral grip pull-up, and pullover variations will be performed during the preseason. The barbell bench press will be performed early in the week and variations of the dumbbell bench press will be performed later in the week. The dumbbell lateral shoulder raise will be performed throughout the week as well.

At the college level, position players and relief pitchers will perform dumbbell and alternating dumbbell bench presses from a stationary bench or the floor, as well as seated row, one-arm dumbbell row, and half-kneeling one-arm landmine press. Starting pitchers will also alternate the dumbbell bench press or dumbbell bench press from the floor, as well as kneeling cable two-arm pulldown.

To maximize physical training and enhance performance for professional athletes, bilateral and unilateral exercises will be used to maintain strength and power as well as correct individual deficiencies. Bilateral exercise examples are the seated row, inverted row, Pendlay row, and two-arm dumbbell bench press and its variations. Unilateral exercise examples are the one-arm dumbbell row and its variations, one-arm cable pulldown and rows from various positions, one-arm bench press, and one-arm landmine press.

Anatomical Core Exercises

For high school athletes, the anatomical core exercises are more explosive in the preseason phase to help develop power. When adding in a medicine ball with movement, the key will be to use a relatively light medicine ball (i.e., 2-4 kg [~5-10 lb]) to help ensure that form is not compromised and speed is emphasized. The main anatomical core exercises should include non-throwing and throwing medicine ball exercises. Non-throwing medicine ball exercises are the wood chop, diagonal wood chop, and the seated twist and its variations. Throwing medicine ball exercises include the twisting wood chop throw, front-facing toss across, diagonal wood chop throw, side toss, and seated partner overhead toss.

At the college level, position players and relief pitchers will focus on performing the dead bug exercise, child's pose breathing, farmer's walk variations, reverse abdominal crunch, kneeling Pallof press, and kneeling stick chops and lifts, whereas starting pitchers will focus on the Turkish get-up variations, farmer's walk variations, kneeling Pallof press, dead bug, and reverse abdominal crunch.

For the professional athlete, anti-rotation exercises, such as half-kneeling Pallof press, dead bug, plank variations, and half-kneeling stick chops and lifts and their body position variations will primarily be performed during the preseason. At times, medicine ball chops and throws will be implemented as well.

POSITIONAL ADJUSTMENTS

Positional adjustments will be made at all levels during the preseason phase. These adjustments will be based on specific needs, training age, and lifting ability. All forms of assessment data and performance testing are used to help determine an athlete's needs with regard to mobility, stability, strength, power, and adequate movement competency within fundamental movement patterns. These programming considerations should support the fundamental biomechanical efficiency of the player's position and ability. Although coaches may feel compelled to correct a movement pattern or deficiency, they must remember that the intervention should help support the athlete's mechanical efficiency. Coaches must be mindful not to create further dysfunction in the athlete's throwing, pitching, hitting, or fielding skills.

Pitchers (Starter, Middle Relief, Setup, and Closer)

At the high school level, pitchers may perform power cleans if their technique is good and the resistance is within 40% to 60% of the 1RM or estimated 1RM range. This range of resistance is appropriate because it will allow for triple joint extension and power development and reduce the risk of overloading the shoulders or back. There is no peer-reviewed scientific research on the relationship between the bench press and incidence of shoulder injury in baseball players, therefore high school pitchers may perform the barbell bench press provided they go through a full range of motion (i.e., touch the sternum with the bar), perform it at good speed (i.e., 1 repetition per second), and use a relatively light weight (40%-60% of the 1RM). However, it is recommended that pitchers perform the dumbbell bench press with a neutral grip if dumbbells are available. The Thrower's 10 exercises (4) are highly recommended as well.

At the college and professional level, however, most—if not all—forms of the barbell bench press, power clean, shrugs, upright row, and overhead presses are strongly discouraged by the medical team, strength and conditioning staff, and management due to the perceived risk. Light- to moderate-intensity dumbbell bench presses and incline dumbbell bench presses are approved by some college teams and professional organizations. All college and professional teams recommend push-ups. Additionally, pitchers require a high degree of arm care due to the high intensity, volume, and frequency of pitching. This can be accomplished, in part, by including upper body pulling movements such as bent-over rows, one-arm dumbbell rows, two- and one-arm pulldowns, and rotator cuff exercises. It is also highly recommended that college and professional pitchers perform T-spine, scapular, and anatomical core exercises.

It is highly recommended that pitchers perform unilateral lower body exercises because they will help develop functional strength that relates to the various positions of the pitching motion. These include, but are not limited to, the single-leg squat, the lunge and its variations, and the step-up and its variations.

Catchers

For catchers, some teams will switch from a back squat to a front squat to decrease the load on the lumbar spine due to bar and body position. Foot position may be wider than the squat stance to mimic the secondary stance receiving position of the catcher. The upper body exercises and core exercises for catchers are similar to those for other positions.

Catchers spend most of their time in a deep squat position. At the professional level, starting catchers will catch 120 to 140 games per season and squat over 140 times per game. The stress on the legs, hips, and low back are significant. As a result, additional weighted, bilateral, and unilateral squats may not be a necessary part of a catcher's resistance training program. Catchers may benefit more from hinge pattern movements, such as the Romanian deadlift and barbell hip thrust, aimed at strengthening the posterior chain, centering the pelvis, and lengthening the anterior hip. Most professional catchers do not perform power cleans or heavy squats during the preseason or in-season training phases.

Middle of the Field Positions (Shortstop, Second Base, and Center Field)

Position players that play up the middle—the shortstop, second baseman, and center fielder—must maintain their ability to react and accelerate. These athletes are often the fastest players on the team who must excel at reacting laterally, applying reactional forces to steal bases, and covering large portions of the field. They benefit from unilateral movements in the frontal and sagittal plane, such as the lunge, step-up, and single-leg squat.

Corner of the Field Positions (First Base, Third Base, Left Field, and Right Field)

Players that occupy the corner positions of the field such as the first baseman, third baseman, and left and right fielders are often power hitters who must create force and make hard contact with the ball while hitting. These athletes are often larger and are not required to cover as much defensive ground as middle fielders. Their ability to create rotational force, their added physical mass, and their overall strength allow for greater exit velocities. As a result, corner position players benefit from bilateral, high-intensity strength and power movements such as squatting, pressing, and medicine ball throws.

INTENSITY

Because the preseason requires a decrease in volume, frequency, and intensity of training, the goal for the strength and conditioning professional is to continue developing athletes' power, strength, and movement competency without overloading the body and causing additional stress. During the preseason, training consistency, communication, and monitoring become vital. If a coach does not require athletes to resistance train during the preseason on a regular basis, the inconsistency does not allow for continued muscle adaptation, which can result in increasing soreness. At this point, communication between athlete and coach becomes necessary in order to adjust the frequency of training and intensity of external loads. For athletes to train for power, they must use external loads that allow for higher bar velocity and appropriate rest time for recovery while decreasing time under tension. The monitoring of loads through assessment, external load tracking, and weight room attendance provides information for coaches to intervene should they see the athlete's fatigue levels increase.

Training for power can be accomplished by completing a limited number of repetitions (6 or less) while using moderate- to high-intensity (50%-85% of the 1RM) loads for the multi-joint primary exercises (1, 3). If a coach wants athletes to train for muscular strength or endurance, the repetitions can range from 5 to 15 per set (1, 3).

Besides selecting intensity from a tested 1RM or an estimated 1RM for back squat or bench press, a coach could use the athlete's resistance exercise–specific rating of perceived exertion (RPE) for lower and upper body exercises. This resistance training–specific RPE scale (see table 9.15 on page 232) provides the athlete with a practical verbal rating that describes, from 1 to 10, how intense it was to complete the repetitions for an exercise (5). During the first week of MLB spring training, it is recommended that athletes train at a resistance training–specific RPE of 6 to 7 (moderate intensity), which means the athlete could actually perform 3 to 5 more repetitions before failure.

Another option to determine intensity is to create a new, adjusted submaximal 1RM for the athlete by using 90% to 95% of the tested 1RM. This can be calculated by multiplying the athlete's 1RM (e.g., 300 pounds [136 kg]) by 0.90 and 0.95. The new, adjusted 1RM range would be 270 to 285 pounds (122-129 kg) for that exercise. Both methods could be used by a coach for lower and upper body primary exercises if they did not want to use the athlete's tested 1RM or estimated 1RM for training.

Similarly, assistance exercises do not need to be performed under maximal load or to failure. Instead, the load should allow for the proper execution of exercise form. Athletes performing assistance exercises with improper form due to heavy loads should be instructed to perform the exercise correctly with a resistance training–specific RPE of 7 to 8 (see table 9.15 on page 232), which means they could complete 2 to 3 more repetitions before failure. Working at lower intensities allows for reclamation of strength and power training stimuli while performing increased loads of baseball skill work. Because athletes will be building their playing volume and frequency once games begin, this allows intensity and duration to increase in a progressive manner. Furthermore, this provides an opportunity to plan training sessions when athletes' game load is low.

VOLUME

During the high school and college preseason, the **volume load** (the total number of sets multiplied by the number of repetitions per set, then multiplied by the weight lifted per repetition) is reduced from the off-season because athletes are practicing and scrimmaging most days of the week (3). For high school, there will be a four-week microcycle that slightly increases in volume from weeks 1 to 3 followed by an unloading week before the season begins (2). Sets will range from 3 to 4; repetitions will range from 3 to 6 for the primary exercises and 5 to 12 for assistance exercises. For the college baseball player, there will be two three-week microcycles. Microcycle 1 will increase the volume from week 1 to week 3. Microcycle 2 will decrease volume from week 4 to week 6 before the season begins. Sets will range from 3 to 4; repetitions will range from 4 to 10.

For the professional athlete, the first 10 days of spring training for pitchers and catchers are designed to focus on acclimating to the volume and frequency of baseball fundamentals, such as throwing, fielding, hitting, and even wearing spikes while practicing every day. As a result, the total volume of external load weight training, including both conditioning and resistance training, must be reduced. This should be reflected in conditioning, as well as strength training. This decrease in volume allows for a linear progression of training at its fundamental level. The beginning of the preseason should be limited to 2 sets of low repetitions for lower body primary exercises and 2 sets of moderate repetitions for upper body movements. The acclimation for position players is done in a similar fashion, but on an accelerated timeline because they have fewer days until live game activity. The sets and repetitions used during the preseason for the primary exercises will be 2 to 3 sets of 4 to 6 repetitions. Assistance exercises will include 2 to 3 sets of 6 to 12 repetitions.

EXERCISE ORDER

For the high school baseball player, the number of resistance training days will determine the exercise order. To train the athletes four days per week, the coach will implement a four-day split routine—two combined total and lower body days and two upper body days. The total and lower body day will begin by having the athletes perform an appropriate warm-up before doing rotator cuff and scapula stabilization exercises. The sidebar after the conclusion includes five example warm-up options. Coaches should pick the most appropriate option for the specific training day. After the warm-up and shoulder exercises are completed, the exercise order is total body explosive lifts, such as the power clean and its variations, followed by multi-joint lower body push and pull exercises. On the upper body day, athletes will perform multi-joint upper body push and pull exercises. When the multi-joint exercises are completed on any of the training days, anatomical core exercises conclude the resistance training session.

For the college athlete, the exercise order during the preseason depends on the microcycle. For microcycle 1, position players, relief pitchers, and starting pitchers will have training days that are total body, lower body, and upper body. In general, exercise order will be a multi-joint primary exercise combined with an anatomical core stability, mobility, or corrective exercise whether the daily emphasis is total, lower, or upper body. During microcycle 2, position players and relief pitchers will have two total body training days, whereas starting pitchers will perform three resistance training sessions (lower body, upper body, and total body) based on when they pitch in intrasquad scrimmages. Total body exercise order will basically follow the same sequencing as microcycle 1. The total body days will have a multi-joint lower or upper body exercise combined with an anatomical core stability, mobility, or corrective exercise. Starting pitchers will perform various lower body push and pull exercises combined with an anatomical core stability, mobility, or corrective exercise. In general, the upper body exercises will be multi-joint and one-arm exercises combined with an anatomical core stability, mobility, or corrective exercise.

For the professional athlete, the exercise order is designed to maximize training efficiency by combining three exercises before advancing to the next group of three exercises. In general, athletes will perform lower body, upper body, and anatomical core strengthening exercises one after the other before beginning the next set. This allows for a greater volume of work to be completed in a shorter period of time and allows all muscle groups involved a chance to recover between sets.

CONCLUSION

The preseason resistance training program is important to enhance explosiveness and prepare baseball athletes for the competitive season. The preseason resistance training program must meet each athlete's specific needs to be most effective, especially because the athletes are on the field for longer periods of time. This means that the coach must select the appropriate training frequency, exercises, intensity, and volume to achieve the desired goals. Because of these considerations, the sample programs in this chapter provide sound guidelines for the high school, college, and professional baseball player; however, they can and should be modified for each athlete and training facility as needed.

Warm-Ups: Mobility, Corrective, Active Dynamic, and In-Place Flow Stretch Exercises

Choose the most appropriate warm-up option based on the specific training day.

OPTION 1

Foam roll, activation, and movement-based warm-up

- T-spine rotation with reach (3 × 10 each arm) or trunk stability rotation with knees flexed (3 × 10)
- Starter rolling upper body (3 × 5 each side) or rolling upper body (3 × 5 each arm)
- Standing scapular wall slide with back on wall (3 × 10)
- Half-kneeling hip flexor stretch (3 × 10 each leg)
- Toe touch progression (3 × 5 each)
- Single-leg stance with core engagement with cable system or Cook band (3 × 5 each leg)
- Tall kneeling hold anterior load (3 × 10 breaths) or tall kneeling hold anterior load with optional head turn or head and shoulder turn (3 × 5 each side)

OPTION 2

Foam roll, activation, and movement-based warm-up

- Quadruped T-spine rotation or quadruped T-spine rotation lumbar locked (3 × 10 each arm)
- Rolling lower body (3 × 5 each leg)
- Standing forearm wall slide (3 × 10)
- Half-kneeling rotation with dowel (3 × 5 each side)
- Assisted single-leg lowering (3 × 10 each leg)
- Tall or half-kneeling kettlebell halo (3 × 5 each direction)
- 90-90 breathing position (3 × 5)

(continued)

(continued)

OPTION 3

Foam roll, activation, and movement-based warm-up

- Brettzel (3 × 5 breaths each side) or Brettzel 2.0 variation (3 × 5 each side)
- Core control rolling with knee touch (3 × 5 each side)
- Seated scapular wall slide with back on wall (3 × 10)
- Open half-kneeling ankle mobility with KB (3 × 10 each leg)
- Active leg lowering to bolster (3 × 10 each leg)
- Deep squat assisted with Functional Movement Trainer (FMT) (3 × 10)
- Tall kneeling hold posterior load (3 × 10 breaths) or tall kneeling hold posterior load with optional head turn or head and shoulder turn (3 × 5 each side)

OPTION 4

Activation and dynamic warm-up

Activation

- Lateral mini-band walk (1 × 12 each leg)
- Forward and backward mini-band walk (1 × 12 each leg)
- Double-leg bridge (1 × 15)
- Supine single-leg lowering with full exhale (1 × 8 each leg)
- Quadruped opposite arm and leg reach with full exhale (1 × 8 each leg)
- Yoga push-up with full exhale (1 × 5)
- Bear crawl forward and backward (1 × 10 yards or meters each)

Dynamic warm-up (1 × 10 yards or meters for each movement)

- Walking knee hug
- Walking quad stretch with overhead reach
- Walking leg cradle
- Walking toe touch
- Walking RDL with reach
- World's greatest stretch
- Forward lunge with rotation
- Lateral shuffle lunge and reach
- Lateral shuffle
- Carioca high knee
- Butt kick
- A-skip
- Lateral A-skip
- Backward run with reach
- Lateral shuffle to sprint acceleration

OPTION 5

In-place flow stretch (each movement flows into the next)

Cluster 1

- Squat to stand
- World's greatest stretch (alternate legs × 3 each leg)

Cluster 2

- Inchworm
- Yoga push-up
- Half-kneeling hip flexor stretch (alternate legs × 3 each leg)

Activate (done independently)

- Butterfly bridge (1 × 15)
- Lateral plank on knees with abduction (1 × 30 seconds each side)
- Turkish get-up (1 × 3 each side)

Note: The mobility and corrective exercises can be found online at https://functionalmovement.com/exercises.

Interpreting the Sample Program Tables

BB = Barbell

BW = Body weight

DB = Dumbbell

MB = Medicine ball

KB = Kettlebell

RDL = Romanian deadlift

Side hang = Holding BB, DB, or KB with the arms hanging down, palms facing legs, and elbows extended

Rack position = Holding BB, DB, or KB in the catch or rack position on the anterior shoulder

Goblet = Holding DB or KB with both hands below the chin and elbows pointed out to the side in the midline of the body.

Order = Performing one set of each exercise (1a, 1b, 1c) in the group one after the other. After the first set is completed, go back to the first exercise in the group and do the second set of each exercise. If certain exercises call for fewer sets than others in the group, perform those sets on the back end of the grouping. For example, if exercise 1a calls for 4 sets and exercise 1b calls for 3 sets, perform exercise 1b during sets 2 through 4 of exercises 1a.

Each = Each side (arm or leg), direction, or exercise.

Table 10.1 High School Pitcher: Preseason Microcycle, Power, Weeks 1-4

Day 1: Lower Body

Order	Exercise	Sets × reps Week 1	Sets × reps Week 2	Sets × reps Week 3	Sets × reps Week 4
1a	Hip circle forward/backward	3 × 20 sec	3 × 25 sec	3 × 30 sec	3 × 15 sec
1b	World's greatest stretch	3 × 6 each	3 × 8 each	3 × 10 each	3 × 5 each
1c	Thrower's 10 (choose 4)	3 × 10 each	3 × 12 each	3 × 14 each	3 × 8 each
2	Midthigh clean pull*	4 × 4	4 × 5	4 × 6	4 × 3
3	Back squat	4 × 4	4 × 5	4 × 6	4 × 3
4	DB RDL	4 × 6	4 × 8	4 × 10	4 × 5
5	DB forward step lunge and reach	4 × 6 each	4 × 8 each	4 × 10 each	4 × 5 each
6	Step-up**	4 × 6 each	4 × 8 each	4 × 10 each	4 × 5 each
7a	MB BLOB throw	3 × 6	3 × 8	3 × 10	3 × 5
7b	MB twisting wood chop throw	3 × 6 each	3 × 7 each	3 × 8 each	3 × 5 each
7c	MB BLSU throw	3 × 6	3 × 8	3 × 10	3 × 5

*Trained pitcher will perform power clean.

**Trained pitcher will perform trap bar deadlift.

Day 2: Upper Body

Order	Exercise	Sets × reps Week 1	Sets × reps Week 2	Sets × reps Week 3	Sets × reps Week 4
1a	Thrower's 10 (choose 4)	3 × 10 each	3 × 12 each	3 × 14 each	2 × 10 each
1b	Push-up plus	3 × 10	3 × 12	3 × 14	2 × 10
2	DB bench press	4 × 4	4 × 5	4 × 6	4 × 3
3	Lat pulldown*	4 × 4	4 × 5	4 × 6	4 × 3
4	MB chest pass	4 × 8	4 × 10	4 × 12	4 × 6
5	Face pull	4 × 8	4 × 10	4 × 12	4 × 6
6	Neutral grip pull-up	3 × 6	3 × 8	3 × 10	3 × 5
7a	Superman	3 × 10	3 × 12	3 × 15	3 × 8
7b	Curl-up with leg extension	3 × 10	3 × 12	3 × 15	3 × 8
7c	Side crunch	3 × 15 each	3 × 20 each	3 × 25 each	3 × 12 each

*Trained pitcher will perform EZ-bar pullover.

Day 3: Lower Body

Order	Exercise	Sets × reps Week 1	Sets × reps Week 2	Sets × reps Week 3	Sets × reps Week 4
1a	Walking lunge	3 × 6 each	3 × 7 each	3 × 8 each	3 × 5 each
1b	Rotational battle rope slam	3 × 15 sec	3 × 20 sec	3 × 25 sec	3 × 10 sec
1c	Lateral mini-band walk	3 × 10	3 × 12	3 × 14	3 × 8
2	DB forward lunge and reach	4 × 4 each	4 × 5 each	4 × 6 each	4 × 3 each
3	Leg curl*	4 × 6	4 × 8	4 × 10	4 × 5
4	MB squat-to-press throw	4 × 6	4 × 8	4 × 10	4 × 5
5	BW single-leg squat**	4 × 8 each	4 × 10 each	4 × 12 each	4 × 6 each
6a	Standing trunk rotation toss	3 × 6 each	3 × 8 each	3 × 10 each	3 × 5 each
6a	Front-facing MB toss across	3 × 6 each	3 × 8 each	3 × 10 each	3 × 5 each
6c	Diagonal wood chop throw	3 × 6 each	3 × 8 each	3 × 10 each	3 × 5 each

*Trained pitcher will perform BB hip thrust.

**Trained pitcher will perform step-up.

Day 4: Upper Body

Order	Exercise	Sets × reps	Sets × reps	Sets × reps	Sets × reps
		Week 1	Week 2	Week 3	Week 4
1a	Prone Y, T, I, W	3 × 8 each	3 × 10 each	3 × 12 each	3 × 6 each
1b	Forearm pronation and supination	3 × 8 each	3 × 10 each	3 × 12 each	3 × 6 each
1c	Wrist ulnar and radial deviation	3 × 8 each	3 × 10 each	3 × 12 each	3 × 6 each
2	Push-up*	4 × 15	4 × 20	4 × 25	4 × 10
3	One-arm DB row	4 × 4 each	4 × 5 each	4 × 6 each	4 × 3 each
4	DB lateral shoulder raise	4 × 8	4 × 10	4 × 12	4 × 6
5	DB pullover	4 × 8	4 × 10	4 × 12	4 × 6
6	Inverted row	4 × 8	4 × 10	4 × 12	4 × 6
7a	Seated partner MB overhead toss	3 × 8	3 × 10	3 × 12	3 × 6
7b	Kneeling Pallof press	3 × 8 each	3 × 10 each	3 × 12 each	3 × 6 each
7c	Stability ball cable rotation	3 × 8 each	3 × 10 each	3 × 12 each	3 × 6 each

*Trained pitcher will perform DB bench press alternating arms.

Table 10.2 High School Position Player: Preseason Microcycle, Power, Weeks 1-4

Day 1: Lower Body

Order	Exercise	Sets × reps	Sets × reps	Sets × reps	Sets × reps
		Week 1	Week 2	Week 3	Week 4
1a	Hip circle forward/backward	3 × 20 sec	3 × 25 sec	3 × 30 sec	3 × 15 sec
1b	World's greatest stretch	3 × 6 each	3 × 8 each	3 × 10 each	3 × 5 each
1c	Thrower's 10 (choose 4)	3 × 10 each	3 × 12 each	3 × 14 each	3 × 8 each
2	Power clean	4 × 4	4 × 5	4 × 6	4 × 3
3	Back squat*	4 × 4	4 × 5	4 × 6	4 × 3
4	DB RDL	4 × 6	4 × 8	4 × 10	4 × 5
5	Reverse lunge**	4 × 6 each	4 × 8 each	4 × 10 each	4 × 5 each
6	Trap bar deadlift	4 × 6	4 × 8	4 × 10	4 × 5
7a	MB BLOB throw	3 × 6	3 × 8	3 × 10	3 × 5
7b	MB twisting wood chop throw	3 × 6 each	3 × 7 each	3 × 8 each	3 × 5 each
7c	MB BLSU throw	3 × 6	3 × 8	3 × 10	3 × 5

*Catcher will perform back or front squat with feet wide.

**Catcher will perform lateral lunge.

Day 2: Upper Body

Order	Exercise	Sets × reps	Sets × reps	Sets × reps	Sets × reps
		Week 1	Week 2	Week 3	Week 4
1a	Thrower's 10 (choose 4)	3 × 10 each	3 × 12 each	3 × 14 each	2 × 10 each
1b	Push-up plus	3 × 10	3 × 12	3 × 14	2 × 10
1c	Rotational battle rope slam	3 × 15 sec	3 × 20 sec	3 × 25 sec	2 × 15 sec
2	Bench press	4 × 4	4 × 5	4 × 6	4 × 3
3	EZ-bar pullover*	4 × 4	4 × 5	4 × 6	4 × 3
4	DB push press	4 × 4	4 × 5	4 × 6	4 × 3
5	Neutral grip pull-up	4 × 6	4 × 8	4 × 10	4 × 5

(continued)

Table 10.2 High School Position Player: Preseason Microcycle, Power, Weeks 1-4 *(continued)*

Day 2: Upper Body *(continued)*

Order	Exercise	Sets × reps	Sets × reps	Sets × reps	Sets × reps
		Week 1	**Week 2**	**Week 3**	**Week 4**
6	Face pull	4 × 8	4 × 10	4 × 12	4 × 6
7a	Superman	3 × 10	3 × 12	3 × 15	3 × 8
7b	Curl-up with leg extension	3 × 10	3 × 15	3 × 15	3 × 8
7c	Side crunch	3 × 15 each	3 × 20 each	3 × 25 each	3 × 12 each

*Catcher will perform lat pulldown.

Day 3: Lower Body

Order	Exercise	Sets × reps	Sets × reps	Sets × reps	Sets × reps
		Week 1	**Week 2**	**Week 3**	**Week 4**
1a	Walking lunge	3 × 6 each	3 × 7 each	3 × 8 each	3 × 5 each
1b	Battle rope slam	3 × 15 sec	3 × 20 sec	3 × 25 sec	3 × 10 sec
1c	Lateral mini-band walk	3 × 10 each	3 × 12 each	3 × 14 each	3 × 8 each
2	Landmine row to rotational press	4 × 4 each	4 × 5 each	4 × 6 each	4 × 3 each
3	BB hip thrust*	4 × 6	4 × 8	4 × 10	4 × 5
4	MB squat-to-press throw	4 × 6	4 × 8	4 × 10	4 × 5
5	Step-up**	4 × 6 each	4 × 8 each	4 × 10 each	4 × 5 each
6	Single-leg bridge	4 × 8 each	4 × 10 each	4 × 12 each	4 × 6 each
7a	Standing trunk rotation toss	3 × 6 each	3 × 8 each	3 × 10 each	3 × 5 each
7b	Front-facing MB toss across	3 × 6 each	3 × 8 each	3 × 10 each	3 × 5 each
7c	Diagonal wood chop throw	3 × 6 each	3 × 8 each	3 × 10 each	3 × 5 each

*Catcher will perform leg curl.
**Catcher will perform BW single-leg squat.

Day 4: Upper Body

Order	Exercise	Sets × reps	Sets × reps	Sets × reps	Sets × reps
		Week 1	**Week 2**	**Week 3**	**Week 4**
1a	Prone Y, T, I, W	3 × 8 each	3 × 10 each	3 × 12 each	3 × 6 each
1b	Forearm pronation and supination	3 × 8 each	3 × 10 each	3 × 12 each	3 × 6 each
1c	Wrist ulnar and radial deviation	3 × 8 each	3 × 10 each	3 × 12 each	3 × 6 each
2	DB bench press	4 × 4	4 × 5	4 × 6	4 × 3
3	One-arm DB row	4 × 4 each	4 × 5 each	4 × 6 each	4 × 3 each
4	DB lateral shoulder raise	4 × 8	4 × 10	4 × 12	4 × 6
5	DB pullover	4 × 8	4 × 10	4 × 12	4 × 6
6	Inverted row	4 × 8	4 × 10	4 × 12	4 × 6
7a	Seated partner MB overhead toss	3 × 8	3 × 10	3 × 12	3 × 6
7b	Kneeling Pallof press	3 × 8 each	3 × 10 each	3 × 12 each	3 × 6 each
7c	Stability ball cable rotation	3 × 8 each	3 × 10 each	3 × 12 each	3 × 6 each

Table 10.3   College: Preseason Microcycle 1, Example Schedule, Weeks 1-3

Day	Position players	Relief pitchers	Starting pitchers (seven-day routine; Friday night starter)
Monday	Recovery/mobility*	Total body	Day 4: Bullpen: Upper body (post-bullpen)
Tuesday	Total body	Mobility*	Day 5: Recovery/mobility*
Wednesday	Recovery/mobility*	Live batting practice (versus hitters)	Day 6: Total body
Thursday	Upper body	Lower body	Day 7: Mobility*
Friday	Lower body	Upper body	Day 1: Live batting practice (versus hitters)
Saturday	Recovery/mobility*	Mobility*	Day 2: Light BW/metabolic focused
Sunday	Total body (optional)	Bullpen	Day 3: Heavy lower body

*Warm-ups: mobility and corrective exercise session options (see page 243)

Table 10.4   College: Preseason Microcycle 2, Example Schedule, Weeks 4-6

Day	Position players and relief pitchers*	Starting pitchers (seven-day routine; Tuesday starter)
Monday	Total body	Day 7: Mobility**
Tuesday	Intrasquad scrimmage	Day 1: Game
Wednesday	Recovery/mobility**	Day 2: Light BW/metabolic focused
Thursday	Total body	Day 3: Heavy lower body
Friday	Intrasquad scrimmage	Day 4: Bullpen: Upper body (post-bullpen)
Saturday	Intrasquad scrimmage	Day 5: Recovery/mobility**
Sunday	Intrasquad scrimmage	Day 6: Total body

*Relief pitchers' schedule is not listed because their resistance training routine is based on the days they participate in scrimmage games, number of pitches/innings thrown, and availability to pitch the next day, if necessary.

**Warm-ups: mobility and corrective exercise session options (see page 243)

Table 10.5   College: Preseason Microcycle 1, Position Player and Relief Pitcher, Weeks 1-3

Day 1: Total Body

Order	Exercise	Sets × reps Week 1	Sets × reps Week 2	Sets × reps Week 3
1a	BB front or back squat	3 × 5	4 × 4	4 × 5
1b	Half-kneeling hip flex or stretch*	3 × 10 each	4 × 8 each	4 × 10 each
2a	Kneeling two-arm cable pulldown	3 × 6	3 × 8	4 × 6
2b	MB chest pass (alternating step)	3 × 8	3 × 10	4 × 10
3a	KB or DB reverse lunge (one- or two-arm side hang)	3 × 5 each	3 × 6 each	4 × 5 each
3b	Turkish get-up to elbow or hand position hold	3 × 5 each	3 × 6 each	4 × 5 each
4a	One-arm farmer's walk (with one KB or DB in rack position)	3 × 30 yd (27 m) each	3 × 35 yd (32 m) each	3 × 40 yd (37 m) each
4b	Bear crawl lateral	3 × 10 yd (9 m) each	3 × 15 yd (14 m) each	3 × 20 yd (18 m) each

*Warm-ups: mobility and corrective exercise session options (see page 243)   *(continued)*

Table 10.5 College: Preseason Microcycle 1, Position Player and Relief Pitcher, Weeks 1-3 (*continued*)

Day 2: Upper Body

Order	Exercise	Sets × reps Week 1	Sets × reps Week 2	Sets × reps Week 3
1a	Seated row (pronated wide grip)	3 × 6	3 × 8	4 × 6
1b	MB side toss	3 × 5 each	3 × 6 each	4 × 6 each
2a	DB flat or incline bench press	3 × 6	3 × 8	4 × 6
2b	Rolling upper body*	3 × 5 each	3 × 6 each	4 × 5 each
3a	One-arm DB row (hand supported on bench)	3 × 6 each	3 × 8 each	4 × 6 each
3b	Landmine row to rotational press	3 × 6 each	3 × 8 each	4 × 8 each
4a	Tall kneeling KB halo*	3 × 4 each	3 × 6 each	3 × 8 each
4b	Child's pose breathing	3 × 3	3 × 4	3 × 5

*Warm-ups: mobility and corrective exercise session options (see page 243)

Day 3: Lower Body

Order	Exercise	Sets × reps Week 1	Sets × reps Week 2	Sets × reps Week 3
1a	Trap bar deadlift (band resisted)	3 × 6	4 × 5	4 × 6
1b	Assisted single-leg lowering*	3 × 10 each	4 × 10 each	4 × 10 each
2a	KB or DB goblet squat	3 × 6	3 × 8	3 × 10
2b	Rolling lower body*	3 × 5 each	3 × 6 each	3 × 7 each
3a	Single-leg cable RDL	3 × 6 each	3 × 8 each	4 × 6 each
3b	Lateral lunge with plate press	3 × 5 each	3 × 6 each	4 × 6 each
4a	Farmer's walk (with KB or DB)	3 × 30 yd (27 m)	3 × 35 yd (32 m)	3 × 40 yd (37 m)
4b	90-90 breathing position*	3 × 5	3 × 6	3 × 7

*Warm-ups: mobility and corrective exercise session options (see page 243)

Table 10.6 College: Preseason Microcycle 1, Starting Pitcher, Weeks 1-3

Day 1: Lower Body

Order	Exercise	Sets × reps Week 1	Sets × reps Week 2	Sets × reps Week 3
1a	Trap bar deadlift (band resisted)	3 × 6	4 × 5	4 × 6
1b	Assisted single-leg lowering*	3 × 10 each	4 × 8 each	4 × 10 each
2a	BB front or back squat	3 × 5	4 × 4	4 × 5
2b	Half-kneeling hip flex or stretch*	3 × 10 each	4 × 8 each	4 × 10 each
3a	Single-leg cable RDL	3 × 6 each	3 × 8 each	4 × 6 each
3b	Lateral lunge with plate press	3 × 5 each	3 × 6 each	4 × 6 each
4a	KB or DB reverse lunge (one- or two-arm side hang)	3 × 5 each	3 × 6 each	4 × 5 each
4b	Kneeling Pallof press	3 × 8 each	3 × 10 each	4 × 10 each
5a	Farmer's walk (with KB or DB)	3 × 30 yd 27 m)	3 × 35 yd (32 m)	3 × 40 yd (37 m)
5b	90-90 breathing position*	3 × 3	3 × 4	3 × 5

*Warm-ups: mobility and corrective exercise session options (see page 243)

Day 2: Upper Body

Order	Exercise	Sets × reps	Sets × reps	Sets × reps
		Week 1	Week 2	Week 3
1a	Kneeling two-arm cable pulldown	3 × 6	3 × 8	4 × 6
1b	Brettzel 2.0*	3 × 5 each	3 × 6 each	4 × 5 each
2a	DB flat or incline bench press	3 × 6	3 × 8	4 × 6
2b	Rolling upper body*	3 × 5 each	3 × 6 each	4 × 5 each
3a	One-arm DB row (hand supported on bench)	3 × 6 each	3 × 8 each	4 × 6 each
3b	Turkish get-up to elbow or hand position hold	3 × 5 each	3 × 6 each	4 × 5 each
4a	Tall kneeling KB halo*	3 × 4 each	3 × 6 each	3 × 8 each
4b	Child's pose breathing	3 × 3	3 × 4	3 × 5

*Warm-ups: mobility and corrective exercise session options (see page 243)

Day 3: Total Body

Order	Exercise	Sets × reps	Sets × reps	Sets × reps
		Week 1	Week 2	Week 3
1a	Band hip thrust	3 × 6	3 × 8	3 × 10
1b	Turkish get-up to elbow or hand with hip lift	3 × 3 each	3 × 4 each	3 × 5 each
2a	Suspension trainer inverted row	3 × 8	3 × 10	3 × 12
2b	MB chest pass (alternating step)	3 × 8	3 × 10	3 × 12
3a	KB or DB goblet squat	3 × 6	3 × 8	3 × 10
3b	Rolling lower body*	3 × 5 each	3 × 6 each	3 × 7 each
4a	One-arm farmer's walk (with one KB or DB)	3 × 30 yd (27 m) each	3 × 35 yd (32 m) each	3 × 40 yd (37 m) each
4b	Bear crawl lateral	3 × 10 yd (9 m) each	3 × 15 yd (14 m) each	3 × 20 yd (18 m) each

*Warm-ups: mobility and corrective exercise session options (see page 243)

Table 10.7   College: Preseason Microcycle 2, Position Player and Relief Pitcher, Weeks 4-6

Day 1: Total Body

Order	Exercise	Sets × reps	Sets × reps	Sets × reps
		Week 4	Week 5	Week 6
1a	BB RDL	4 × 6	4 × 5	3 × 6
1b	Single-leg stance with core engagement (with cable system or Cook band)*	4 × 6 each	4 × 5 each	3 × 5 each
2a	Alternating DB bench or floor press	4 × 6 each	3 × 8 each	3 × 6 each
2b	T-spine rotation with reach*	4 × 10 each	3 × 10 each	3 × 8 each
3a	KB or DB lateral step-up (goblet position)	4 × 5 each	3 × 6 each	3 × 5 each
3b	Kneeling Pallof press	4 × 12 each	3 × 10 each	3 × 8 each
4a	One-arm seated cable row	4 × 6 each	3 × 8 each	3 × 6 each
4b	Bear crawl hold (alternating opposite arm and opposite leg in place)	4 × 8 each	3 × 6 each	3 × 5 each
5a	One-arm farmer's walk backward (with one KB or DB in rack position)	3 × 40 yd (37 m) each	3 × 30 yd (32 m) each	3 × 25 yd (27 m) each
5b	Elevated single-leg bridge	3 × 10 each	3 × 8 each	3 × 6 each

*Warm-ups: mobility and corrective exercise session options (see page 243)   *(continued)*

Table 10.7 College: Preseason Microcycle 2, Position Player and Relief Pitcher, Weeks 4-6 *(continued)*

Day 2: Total Body

Order	Exercise	Sets × reps	Sets × reps	Sets × reps
		Week 4	Week 5	Week 6
1a	KB two-arm squat (rack position)	4 × 5	4 × 4	3 × 5
1b	Half-kneeling rotation with dowel*	4 × 5 each	4 × 4 each	3 × 5 each
2a	DB chest supported row	4 × 6	3 × 8	3 × 6
2b	Lateral rotation MB shot put	4 × 8 each	3 × 8 each	3 × 6 each
3a	DB or BB hip thrust	3 × 10	3 × 8	3 × 6
3b	Turkish get-up to leg sweep (or full get-up)	3 × 3 each	3 × 2 each	3 × 1 each
4a	Push-up (band resisted)	3 × 10	3 × 8	3 × 6
4b	Suspension trainer one-arm inverted row	3 × 10 each	3 × 8 each	3 × 6 each
5a	Farmer's walk backward (with KB or DB)	3 × 40 yd (37 m)	3 × 30 yd (32 m)	3 × 25 yd (27 m)
5b	Reverse abdominal crunch	3 × 20	3 × 15	3 × 10

*Warm-ups: mobility and corrective exercise session options (see page 243)

Table 10.8 College: Preseason Microcycle 2, Starting Pitcher, Weeks 4-6

Day 1: Lower Body

Order	Exercise	Sets × reps	Sets × reps	Sets × reps
		Week 4	Week 5	Week 6
1a	BB RDL	4 × 6	4 × 5	3 × 6
1b	Single-leg stance with core engagement (with cable system or Cook band)*	4 × 6 each	4 × 5 each	3 × 5 each
2a	Two-arm KB squat (rack position)	4 × 5	4 × 4	3 × 5
2b	Half-kneeling rotation with dowel*	4 × 5 each	4 × 4 each	3 × 5 each
3a	Two-arm KB single-leg RDL	4 × 6 each	3 × 8 each	3 × 6 each
3b	Lateral squat (KB or DB)	4 × 6 each	3 × 8 each	3 × 6 each
4a	KB or DB lateral step-up (goblet position)	4 × 5 each	3 × 6 each	3 × 5 each
4b	Side plank with hip flexion	4 × 30 sec each	3 × 30 sec each	3 × 25 sec each
5a	Farmer's walk backward (with KB or DB)	3 × 40 yd	3 × 30 yd	3 × 25 yd
5b	Reverse abdominal crunch	3 × 20	3 × 15	3 × 10

*Warm-ups: mobility and corrective exercise session options (see page 243)

Day 2: Upper Body

Order	Exercise	Sets × reps	Sets × reps	Sets × reps
		Week 4	**Week 5**	**Week 6**
1a	Tall kneeling one-arm cable pulldown	4 × 6 each	3 × 8 each	3 × 6 each
1b	Brettzel 2.0*	4 × 5 each	3 × 6 each	3 × 5 each
2a	Alternating DB bench or floor press	4 × 6 each	3 × 8 each	3 × 6 each
2b	T-spine rotation with reach*	4 × 10 each	3 × 10 each	3 × 8 each
3a	Seated row (pronated wide grip)	4 × 6	3 × 8	3 × 6
3b	Half-kneeling landmine press	4 × 8 each	3 × 8 each	3 × 6 each
4a	Tall kneeling hold anterior load with KB*	3 × 10 breaths	3 × 8 breaths	3 × 6 breaths
4b	Alternating dead bug	3 × 10 each	3 × 8 each	3 × 6 each

*Warm-ups: mobility and corrective exercise session options (see page 243)

Day 3: Total Body

Order	Exercise	Sets × reps	Sets × reps	Sets × reps
		Week 4	**Week 5**	**Week 6**
1a	DB or BB hip thrust	3 × 10	3 × 8	3 × 6
1b	Turkish get-up to leg sweep (or full get-up)	3 × 3 each	3 × 2 each	3 × 1 each
2a	Suspension trainer one-arm inverted row	3 × 10 each	3 × 8 each	3 × 6 each
2b	Lateral rotation MB shot put	3 × 8 each	3 × 6 each	3 × 5 each
3a	Deep squat assisted with FMT*	3 × 10	3 × 8	3 × 6
3b	Trunk stability rotation knees flexed*	3 × 10	3 × 8	3 × 6
4a	One-arm farmer's walk backward (with one KB or DB in rack position)	3 × 40 yd (37 m) each	3 × 30 yd (27 m) each	3 × 25 yd (23 m) each
4b	Bear crawl hold (alternating opposite arm and opposite leg in place)	3 × 8 each	3 × 6 each	3 × 5 each

*Warm-ups: mobility and corrective exercise session options (see page 243)

Table 10.9 Professional: Spring Training Microcycle 1, Strength/Power, Weeks 1-3

Day 1: Total Body

Order	Exercise	Sets × reps	Sets × reps	Sets × reps
		Week 1	**Week 2**	**Week 3**
1a	BB or trap bar deadlift	2 × 6	3 × 5	3 × 4
1b	One-arm landmine press	2 × 6 each	3 × 5 each	3 × 4 each
1c	Dead bug	2 × 5 each	3 × 5 each	3 × 6 each
2a	Nordic hamstring curl	2 × 6	3 × 5	3 × 6
2b	One-arm DB row	2 × 8 each	3 × 8 each	3 × 6 each
2c	DB bent-over lateral shoulder raise	2 × 12	3 × 12	3 × 10
3a	Lateral lunge	2 × 6 each	3 × 8 each	3 × 6 each
3b	Half-kneeling one-arm pulldown	2 × 8 each	3 × 8 each	3 × 6 each
3c	MB wood chop throw	2 × 6	3 × 6	3 × 8

(continued)

Table 10.9 Professional: Spring Training Microcycle 1, Strength/Power, Weeks 1-3 (continued)

Day 2: Total Body

Order	Exercise	Sets × reps Week 1	Sets × reps Week 2	Sets × reps Week 3
1a	Reverse lunge	2 × 5 each	3 × 5 each	3 × 4 each
1b	DB bench press (alternating arms)	2 × 6 each	3 × 6 each	3 × 8 each
1c	Half-kneeling Pallof press	2 × 8 each	3 × 8 each	3 × 10 each
2a	One-arm single-leg RDL	2 × 6 each	3 × 5 each	3 × 6 each
2b	One-arm cable row (staggered stance)	2 × 8 each	3 × 6 each	3 × 8 each
2c	Prone Y raise	2 × 12	3 × 10	3 × 12
3a	Crossover step-up with reach	2 × 6 each	3 × 5 each	3 × 6 each
3b	Half-kneeling one-arm pulldown	2 × 8 each	3 × 6 each	3 × 8 each
3c	Half-kneeling stick lift	2 × 10 each	3 × 8 each	3 × 10 each

Table 10.10 Professional: Spring Training Microcycle 2, Strength/Power, Weeks 4-6

Day 1: Total Body

Order	Exercise	Sets × reps Week 4	Sets × reps Week 5	Sets × reps Week 6
1a	BB or trap bar deadlift	3 × 4	3 × 5	2 × 6
1b	One-arm landmine press	3 × 4 each	3 × 5 each	2 × 6 each
1c	Dead bug	3 × 6 each	3 × 5 each	2 × 5 each
2a	Nordic hamstring curl	3 × 6	3 × 5	2 × 6
2b	One-arm DB row	3 × 6 each	3 × 8 each	2 × 8 each
2c	DB bent-over lateral shoulder raise	3 × 10	3 × 12	2 × 12
3a	Lateral lunge	3 × 6 each	3 × 8 each	2 × 6 each
3b	Half-kneeling one-arm pulldown	3 × 6 each	3 × 8 each	2 × 6 each
3c	MB wood chop throw	3 × 8	3 × 6	2 × 6

Day 2: Total Body

Order	Exercise	Sets × reps Week 4	Sets × reps Week 5	Sets × reps Week 6
1a	Reverse lunge	3 × 4 each	3 × 5 each	2 × 5 each
1b	DB bench press (alternating arms)	3 × 8 each	3 × 6 each	2 × 6 each
1c	Half-kneeling Pallof press	3 × 10 each	3 × 8 each	2 × 8 each
2a	One-arm single-leg RDL	3 × 6 each	3 × 5 each	2 × 6 each
2b	One-arm cable row (staggered stance)	3 × 8 each	3 × 6 each	2 × 8 each
2c	Prone Y raise	3 × 12	3 × 10	2 × 12
3a	Crossover step-up with reach	3 × 6 each	3 × 5 each	2 × 6 each
3b	Half-kneeling one-arm pulldown	3 × 8 each	3 × 6 each	2 × 8 each
3c	Half-kneeling stick lift	3 × 10 each	3 × 8 each	2 × 10 each

IN-SEASON PROGRAMMING

PATRICK MCHENRY (HIGH SCHOOL), CHRIS JOYNER (COLLEGE), JOE KESSLER (PROFESSIONAL)

After completing a preseason resistance training program to prepare athletes for the demands of the competitive season, in-season resistance training should be continued to help them maintain strength and power so they can perform at their best. This chapter provides goals and objectives as well as the length, structure, and organization of in-season resistance training for high school to professional athletes. Recommended exercises for the various levels of play and positions will be discussed (note that many of the in-season exercises will be the same ones implemented during the preseason to prepare athletes for the competitive season). Additionally, appropriate intensity, volume, and exercise order will be described. Finally, sample in-season resistance training programs are provided for each level of play.

GOALS AND OBJECTIVES

In-season resistance training is often referred to as the "train to win" phase. Athletes at all levels have just completed preseason training and their power, strength, and strength endurance are at their highest levels. The main focus during the competitive season is on performance, and the primary goal is to win as many games as possible. The training objects are to improve performance, reduce the risk of injury, enhance recovery between games and across the season, and to maintain the improvements in strength, speed, and power developed during the off- and preseason training.

High School

The objective for in-season training is to maintain the athlete's strength, explosiveness, and range of motion while allowing for recovery throughout the entire competitive season. In high school, the season runs from March to May, when the playoffs start, and usually includes two to three games a week. This allows for two total body resistance training sessions to be completed on non-game days. Resistance training sessions begin with a warm-up that focuses on mobility and arm care before beginning the primary exercise routine. Following those exercises, each session ends with various anatomical core exercises.

College

With up to 56 regular season games in college baseball, the training focus is to maintain the gains in strength and power that were made in the off-season and preseason while aiming to peak in time for the postseason. Managing fatigue due to the frequency and number of games and applying strategies to aid in recovery are therefore considerations the coach must take into account when designing an in-season resistance training program. If a team is fortunate enough to make it to the College World Series, the total number of games played could exceed 70, and will ultimately define when the postseason microcycle will begin.

Professional

The transition from preseason to in-season for the professional athlete allows for baseball fundamental work and game volume, intensity, and frequency to increase on a progressive scale. Although the focus shifted from resistance training in the off-season to baseball-related activities and games in the preseason, the in-season focus continues to remain on fundamental skill work and game preparation. The goals for the in-season are to support athlete health, aid in recovery, and assist in physical development for improved performance.

Because a professional baseball season consists of 162 games in a six-month period, an athlete's off days for recovery are limited. As athletes' total work volume accumulates, fatigue becomes a large factor. This is when consistency and accountability are key. Because athletes are expected to play, as well as practice, almost every day of the week, the redundancy can begin to feel overwhelming. Taking ownership of their routines is necessary for athletes to battle this fatigue. Although routines vary among athletes based on their physical restrictions, game demands, and overall training, the more an athlete can maintain personal consistency, the more quickly and efficiently he can recover.

LENGTH, STRUCTURE, AND ORGANIZATION

Regardless of the level of play, the in-season has the potential to be the longest training period of the baseball training year. The resistance training program has to be frequent and intense enough to allow athletes to maintain strength, speed, and power without producing performance-inhibiting fatigue or soreness. Page 266 shows various warm-up options that include mobility, corrective, active dynamic, and in-place flow stretch exercises that are recommended for athletes at the beginning of every resistance training session. Coaches should pick the most appropriate option for the specific training day. Some of these exercises are incorporated into the sample in-season programs for college and professional athletes.

High School

For most high school teams, in-season training will be 8 to 10 weeks long, depending on whether the team makes the postseason. The regular in-season will be divided into two four-week microcycles during which athletes will perform two total body sessions per week. In the first four-week microcycle for pitchers (table 11.1) and position players (table 11.2), there will be a "hard" workout day and a "light" workout day. In the second four-week microcycle (not represented by additional tables in this chapter because the exercises are the same), athletes will have a "moderate" day and a "light" day. The loading pattern for both four-week microcycles will be low, medium, high, and unload (6a). If a coach does not know the 1RM or estimated 1RM for specific primary exercises for athletes, repetitions completed can be used for programming. The hard day can be based on the number of repetitions that an athlete can perform with a given load for a given exercise and not a percentage of the 1RM. The load will be reduced and the number of repetitions performed will be increased on moderate and light days. However, if a coach has 1RM or estimated 1RM values for the power clean, back squat, bench press, and one-arm dumbbell row, for example, percentages and repetitions can be used to control the intensity. Because athletes are competing two to three days per week and practicing four to five days per week, light and moderate training sessions are included in the in-season resistance training program to help reduce fatigue, decrease the risk of overtraining, and diminish the chances of injury. These variations in training intensity over the course of the competitive season should allow athletes to perform at their best during the playoffs.

The resistance training schedule will vary depending on the game schedule. When the schedule calls for a game on Monday and Wednesday, for example, athletes will lift on Tuesday and Friday and use Thursday as a recovery day. The Friday workout should be the hard day because the athlete will have two days to recover before they play again. Tuesday will be the light day. If the games are played on Tuesday and Thursday, athletes will lift on Monday and Friday and use Wednesday as a recovery day. The Friday workout should be the hard day, with two days of recovery before the light Monday workout.

College

The college in-season resistance training mesocycle, which is 16 to 20 weeks long, begins with the first week of regular season games in mid-February and runs through May or June depending on the team's success during the regular season. In general, this mesocycle can be divided into four or five repeated four-week microcycles. The loading pattern for the four-week microcycles will be low, medium, high, and unload (6a).

There are many factors to consider when planning the in-season mesocycle, compared to previous training cycles that allowed for a more consistent training schedule with little or no baseball requirements. These include, but are not limited to, the athletes' class and practice schedules, number of games played per week, off days, travel schedule, academic calendar, and NCAA regulations. When the team is playing at home, the training schedules are typically easier to follow and equipment availability is certain. However, when the team goes on the road, careful planning is needed to help ensure that routines are minimally affected. When competing away from home, the daily on-field workout and weight room schedules may change, and there may be limited access to training equipment. Sometimes the strength and conditioning professional has to coordinate a site in which the athletes can train (hotel, local gym, or the home team's facility). At other times, the coach will travel with portable training equipment (foam rollers, bands, tubing, suspension trainer, medicine balls, and kettlebells).

College teams typically play four to five games per week. Midweek games occur on Tuesday or Wednesday (or both), and the weekend series is Thursday through Saturday or Friday through Sunday. Planning training days can also require a difficult balance between the travel schedule and the various classroom responsibilities of the student-athletes.

The resistance training goals for a position player and relief pitcher during a week would be total body sessions that include multi-joint exercises on Monday and Thursday with one recovery/mobility session on Wednesday (table 11.3). (Note: A relief pitcher's program is similar to that of a position player rather than a starting pitcher because he participates in games more frequently than a starting pitcher.) Relative to the loading pattern for a respective week within the four-week microcycle, Monday's training intensity is hard after a weekend series, but it can be modified by the coach to moderate intensity if the starting position players are fatigued from an unusually long weekend of play. Thursday's training intensity is either light or moderate as athletes head into a three-game weekend series where all athletes need to be at their best and fully recovered (table 11.4). Readers should notice that day 2 includes two options. Option 1 begins with an upper body pulling and lower body hinge sequence, whereas option 2 begins with a lower body squat and upper body pulling sequence. Coaches can use the most appropriate program for each athlete. In general, option 1 could be used for a moderate intensity day and option 2 could be used for a light intensity day based on the included primary exercises; however, a coach can control the intensity of either option based on resistance prescribed to the athlete.

Because they only play one game per week, starting pitchers will be on a seven-day routine that includes more resistance training sessions than position players (table 11.3). The focus for day 3 will be lower body, for day 4 it will be upper body after throwing a bullpen session, and for day 6 it will be total body. A sample in-season starting pitcher's program can be found in table 11.5.

Professional

The ultimate goal of professional in-season training is to encourage quick recovery and complement the athlete's performance and overall health. Athletes must have a routine that allows them to remain consistent with their training and preparation while also allowing for modifications as necessary. Specific factors must be taken into consideration, such as travel, game times, the number of games played, and the overall duration of individual games, including rain delays and extra innings. The testing assessments done in the off-season or during the preseason (spring training) should also continue to drive specific program needs. These results can then be formatted in a total body routine that emphasizes lower and upper body primary pushing and pulling exercises, lower and upper body assistance exercises, and anatomical core exercises.

The program should be designed to allow for load progressions per cycle and account for alterations in exercise selection and intensity without changing joint angles, which can promote soreness. A cycle progression during the in-season consisting of three weeks of progressive overload (low, medium, and high loading pattern), followed by an unload week, will allow the athlete to maintain preseason strength and power while competing at an elite level (6a). A coach can use the four-week microcycle approach, modified as needed throughout the competitive season. Performing total body workouts twice a week on consistent days provides a level of accountability and allows the athlete to acclimate to the stimulus, focus on skill-related needs, and complete regular recovery routines. A sample in-season resistance training program for professionals can be found in table 11.6.

As these training routines are established and practiced, it becomes easier to understand the athlete's needs and the program considerations that must be addressed. For instance, many workouts are best performed prior to baseball activities because of the benefit of neuromuscular activation with external load training and post-game recovery strategies. The duration of each workout should complement the athlete's preparation with any necessary skill work to be completed prior to the game. A training session, which includes a warm-up, resistance training, and post-workout recovery, should last no longer than 30 minutes. Ideally, the resistance training–specific rating of perceived exertion (RPE) should be no more than 7 (moderate intensity), which means the athlete could complete 3 more repetitions with a given load for a respective set (13). See table 9.15 on page 232 for the resistance training–specific RPE scale.

RECOMMENDED EXERCISES

An athlete's in-season resistance training program should not change a great deal from the preseason. Programmed exercises should complement the athlete's athleticism, address their positional needs and skills associated with pitching and hitting, and be formulated based on assessments. Similar multi-joint lower and upper body primary pushing and pulling exercises, as well as anatomical core exercises, will be performed at all levels. Furthermore, exercises for the rotator cuff muscles will be implemented into the athlete's programming. Because of the long competitive season and differences in age, training experience, and history of injury, exercise selection should stay relatively consistent throughout the regular season. Introducing new exercises into an athlete's program could cause soreness that could negatively affect on-the-field performance.

TOTAL BODY EXERCISES

Total body exercises for the athlete could include Olympic-style lifts, such as the power clean and its variations, trap bar jump, medicine ball throw, kettlebell swing, battle rope slam, Turkish get-up, bear crawl, and various landmine exercises. For each level of play, the types of total body exercises presented in this chapter will vary.

High School

The power clean will be the main total body exercise for position players on hard days, whereas pitchers will perform the medicine ball squat-to-push overhead, which will reduce any additional stress on the shoulders, elbows, and wrists. If a position player performed high pulls or midthigh clean pulls during the preseason phase, he will continue to do so during the in-season. On light days all athletes will perform the two-arm kettlebell swing for their total body exercise. However, the coach should consider the pitch count for the week as well as upcoming games and substitute a two-arm kettlebell goblet squat as needed for pitchers experiencing throwing arm soreness.

College

College athletes will perform ground-based, total body exercises that provide stress throughout the kinetic chain to improve strength and power. Total body exercises, such as the Turkish get-up and its variations, two-arm kettlebell swing, and bear crawl variations, will be performed by position players and pitchers.

Professional

To maximize physical training and enhance performance during the professional baseball season, individual athletes will perform bilateral and unilateral lower and upper body exercises as well as mobility and corrective exercises. Although certain total body exercises, such as the various medicine ball throws described in chapter 5, may be performed at times during the in-season, most will not be performed at this time due to the frequency of game-play and travel.

LOWER BODY EXERCISES

Recommended lower body exercises will include single- and multi-joint pushing and pulling exercises performed in the sagittal, frontal, and transverse planes. For each level of play, the exercises used will vary based on resistance training experience, time, and equipment availability (9).

High School

The lower body exercises implemented in the high school in-season require different stances, such as the normal squat stance, staggered stance, and single-leg stance. The lower body primary pushing exercises are the back squat, forward step lunge, and crossover step-up. It is preferred for athletes to use dumbbells instead of the barbell because dumbbells require more focus on body posture to avoid leaning if the rhomboids, trapezius, rear deltoids, and latissimus dorsi are not engaged; however, if coaches do not have a variety of dumbbells, barbells can be used. Pulling exercises for the lower body during the in-season are the single-leg RDL, single-leg curl, and double- and single-leg bridge.

College

At the collegiate level, athletes will perform multi-joint lower body pushing exercises such as the back, front, or goblet squat with barbell, dumbbells, or kettlebells; reverse lunge; step-up; trap bar deadlift with and without resistance bands; and lateral lunge with plate press. Lower body pulling exercises that will be performed are the single-leg cable, dumbbell, or kettlebell RDL and double- and single-leg bridge.

Professional

For the professional athlete, bilateral and unilateral exercises are used to maintain strength and power during the in-season. Bilateral lower body exercises include the barbell or trap bar deadlift, squat variations that are low stress on the lumbar spine, RDL, and double-leg bridge. Unilateral lower body exercises include the step-up, lunge variations, single-leg RDL, single-leg squat, split squat, single-leg bridge, and single-leg curl.

UPPER BODY EXERCISES

Upper body exercises will emphasize single- and multi-joint pulling and pushing exercises that safely achieve the goal of maintaining power and strength without compromising the athlete's throwing shoulder. In general, the recommended upper body exercises will be consistent for each level of play.

High School

Upper body pushing and pulling exercises will use barbells, dumbbells, bands, and medicine balls. Early in the week, on the hard day, the bilateral dumbbell bench press will be performed; later in the week, on the light day, athletes will change to the alternating or one-arm dumbbell bench press. Push-ups will also be incorporated into the in-season program. For the pulling exercises, the one-arm dumbbell row and neutral grip pull-up will be performed. Additional upper body exercises will include rotator cuff exercises, such as the Thrower's 10 and prone Y, T, I, W, as well as forearm and wrist exercises.

College

To allow for greater freedom of movement and range of motion in upper body pushing exercises, dumbbell and cable press exercises are recommended over a barbell to protect the shoulder joint. One-arm pushing and pulling exercises that simulate more sport-specific movement and challenge stability in various positions while executing the loaded pattern should also be included. For example, half-kneeling and staggered stance pushing and pulling variations challenge hip and shoulder separation as well as thoracic spine mobility, which are essential to hitting and throwing. The multi-joint upper body primary pushing and pulling exercises are dumbbell bench or floor press, medicine ball chest pass, one-arm cable or dumbbell shoulder press, one-arm cable row, lat pulldown, seated row, and suspension trainer inverted row. Additional upper body exercises will include rotator cuff exercises, such as the Thrower's 10 and prone Y, T, I, W. Tables 11.4 and 11.5 do not display these exercises because they are generally performed with the athletic trainer in a separate session. However, if a coach would like to incorporate these exercises into the athlete's resistance training sessions, it is recommended to perform them after warm-ups and before primary exercises for position players and relief pitchers and on days 4 and 6 for starting pitchers.

Professional

To maintain strength and power for professional athletes during the in-season, bilateral and unilateral upper body exercises will be used. Bilateral exercise examples are the seated row, suspension trainer inverted row, half-kneeling lat pulldown, Pendlay row, push-up variations, and two-arm dumbbell bench press and its variations. Unilateral exercise examples are the one-arm dumbbell row (on a bench and chest supported), one-arm cable pulldowns and rows from various positions, one-arm bench press, one-arm landmine press, standing one-arm dumbbell shoulder press, and dumbbell bent-over lateral shoulder raise. Additional upper body exercises will include rotator cuff exercises, such as the Thrower's 10 and prone Y, T, I, W. Table 11.6 does not display these exercises because they are generally performed with the athletic trainer in a separate session. However, if a coach would like to incorporate these exercises into the athlete's resistance training sessions, it is recommended to perform them after warm-ups and before primary exercises on days 1 and 2.

ANATOMICAL CORE EXERCISES

Recommendations of anatomical core exercises may vary based on the philosophy, knowledge, and experience of those administering the resistance training program. For the in-season, athletes should perform a range of anatomical core exercises from the various movement and exercise categories described in chapter 8. Recommendations for high school, college, and professional athletes will be included in this section.

High School

The anatomical core exercises will be very similar to those in the preseason phase. When adding a medicine ball with movement, the key will be to use a light medicine ball (i.e., 2-4 kg [~5-10 lb]) so that form is not compromised and speed is emphasized. The main anatomical core exercises will include throwing and non-throwing exercises, such as the seated stability ball cable rotation, medicine ball diagonal wood chop throw, twisting wood chop throw, seated trunk rotation toss, and seated partner medicine ball overhead toss. Traditional anatomical core exercises, such as curl-up, side crunch, and superman, in addition to anti-rotation exercises, such as front to side plank, will also be performed.

College

Because athletes are swinging and throwing at very high volumes and intensities, in-season anatomical core exercises are primarily anti-rotation, anti-flexion, and anti-extension. Being able to maintain proximal stability and proper pelvic alignment is essential to sport performance and injury prevention. Examples of anti-rotation exercises include the half-kneeling stick chop and lift, side plank, and Pallof press variations. Examples of anti-flexion and anti-extension exercises include the kneeling hold and farmer's walk variations. A rotational exercise included in the in-season program is the medicine ball twisting wood chop throw.

Professional

For the professional athlete, anti-rotation exercises, such as Pallof press, kneeling stick chops and lifts from various positions, plank variations, and dead bug will primarily be performed during the in-season. At times, medicine ball chops and throws will be implemented as well. Additionally, many of the upper body exercises that are performed from a half-kneeling position indirectly recruit the anatomical core muscles to provide stability.

POSITIONAL ADJUSTMENTS

The in-season training program at all levels will be similar to the preseason—information taken from assessments should continue to drive the selection of primary exercises, while assistance exercises will be adjusted to complement the athlete's position requirements. Catchers, for example, have one of most demanding positions in the game of baseball, thus their resistance training program must meet their needs and allow for recovery between games (8). Pitchers also must have a program that is functional and position specific (3, 10). The use of unilateral exercises for pitchers and up-the-middle position players helps develop lateral and linear efficiency and acceleration. Corner position players can use more bilateral exercises for increased strength and power development associated with increased external load.

Pitchers (Starter, Middle Relief, Setup, and Closer)

Pitchers should perform single-leg exercises that are specific to the various phases of the pitching motion (1). For example, the dumbbell forward step lunge and reach, crossover step-up, and step-up with leg lift will be performed instead of back or front squats. The dumbbell bench press, push-up, or medicine ball chest press can be performed in place of the barbell bench press. The Thrower's 10 and Y, T, I, W exercises should be performed for rotator cuff muscles (4, 12).

Catchers

Catchers can perform various squats with a barbell or a dumbbell using a squat stance or wider to activate the muscles that will be used in their catching stance (6). High school catchers can perform a midthigh clean pull instead of a power clean to generate triple extension power without catching the bar. Throwing from the knees is a movement pattern that requires great arm and torso strength (7); therefore, Thrower's 10 and Y, T, I, W exercises will be performed in addition to throwing and non-throwing rotational medicine ball exercises to maintain stability, strength, and power (12).

Infielders and Outfielders

Infielders and outfielders will perform multi-joint total body exercise sessions that address anterior and posterior musculature for a balanced program. Lateral squats or lunges in the frontal plane could be incorporated in addition to sagittal plane lower body exercises. All the athletes will perform the Thrower's 10 and Y, T, I, W exercises and a hip mobility warm-up on the field before practice (12).

INTENSITY

For the high school position player who has previously tested 1RM or estimated 1RM, the intensity during microcycle 1 of the in-season program will be 40% to 80% of the 1RM (5, 9). For example, intensity for weeks 1 to 4, following the low, medium, high, and unload loading pattern (6a), would be 70%, 75%, 80%, and 65% of the 1RM on the hard day (day 1) and 60%, 65%, 70%, and 55% of the 1RM on the light day (day 2). If 1RM or estimated 1RM testing values were not available or completed, and a coach wants to control intensity without percentages of 1RM, the load can be increased each week from weeks 1 to 3. For example, athletes could increase the load by 15 pounds (6.8 kg) for bilateral lower body exercises and 10 pounds (4.5 kg) for bilateral upper body exercises from weeks 1 to 3. If the load on the bar for a back squat (bilateral lower body exercise) was 210 (95 kg) pounds for week 1, then the load would be 225 pounds (102 kg) for week 2 and 240 pounds (109 kg) for week 3. Then the athlete would decrease the week 3 load by 45 pounds (20 kg) for a bilateral lower body exercise and 30 pounds (14 kg) for a bilateral upper body exercise for week 4. For the back squat example provided, this would mean that the athlete would use 195 pounds (88 kg) for week 4.

The intensity for microcycle 2 (not shown in table format in this chapter because it uses the same exercises as microcycle 1) is reduced 5% each week compared to microcycle 1 to decrease chances of fatigue during the second half of the season. For position players, the intensity will be 35% to 75% of the 1RM. For example, weeks 5 to 8 would be 65%, 70%, 75%, and 60% of the 1RM on the moderate day (day 1) and 55%, 60%, 65%, and 50% of the 1RM on the light day (day 2). If a coach does not have 1RM or estimated 1RM values, the same increase or decrease in load discussed for microcycle 1 should be implemented. Both in-season microcycles will focus on power.

Pitchers will be using medicine balls, bands, and dumbbells so the load will be a weight that allows them to perform the exercise explosively and with good form. However, if pitchers were tested previously for 1RM or estimated 1RM, the same percentages described for position players can be used for those exercises. If testing values for 1RM are not available, then coaches can use the same increase or decrease in load described for position players. All medicine ball work, regardless of position, will be 2 pounds (0.9 kg) or lighter for one-arm work, 6 pounds (2.7 kg) or lighter for two-arm throwing or rotational throwing work, and 10 pounds (4.5 kg) or lighter for total body throws (11).

For the college resistance training program, it is recommended to use moderate to hard intensity of 85% to 93% of the 1RM at low to moderate volumes for multi-joint bilateral lower and upper body exercises to maintain strength and power (5). Additionally, the percentages of the 1RM or load increases or decreases listed for the high school athlete can be used during heavy game schedules because these intensities allow the athlete to perform exercises explosively without fatigue (5, 9).

For the professional athlete, the in-season resistance training program should continue to focus on performance and health as its foundational objective. In effort to achieve these goals, each session should be performed with intensity and intent. Using the resistance training–specific RPE scale in table 9.15 on page 232 is recommended and allows coaches to determine load and progression for the athlete (13). Best resistance training practices should allow the athlete to report having a perceived exertion no more than 8 on the Cleveland Clinic RPE scale in table 11.7 (2). A score equal to or lower than 8 (very heavy) means that the athlete should have enough energy for continued training or game-play. If RPE values for either scale are greater than the range or score listed above, the coach should reduce the athlete's training loads (intensity).

VOLUME

During the high school in-season resistance training program, athletes will complete 3 sets for all the primary exercises. In microcycle 1 for position players, the repetitions will be 4 to 10 for tested primary exercises, such as the power clean, back squat, bench press, and one-arm dumbbell row (table 11.2). In microcycle 2, which does not have a table in this chapter, the repetitions will be 5 to 12 for tested primary exercises. In general, the number of repetitions for a specific percentage will be cut in half. For example, if an athlete uses 80% of the 1RM for a tested primary exercise like the back squat during week 3 of microcycle 1, 4 repetitions should be completed instead of 8 (9). If a coach does not have tested or estimated 1RM values, the loads recommended in the Intensity section of this chapter can be used. The key is to complete all the repetitions with proper technique and explosiveness.

For the college in-season resistance training program, if athletes have been previously tested for 1RM or estimated 1RM, it is recommended to use low to moderate volumes with 2 to 5 sets of 3 to 6 repetitions for multi-joint primary exercises on hard days (5). However, some exercises will have repetitions that range from 5 to 7 on a moderate day and 6 to 10 on a light day when the load or percentage of 1RM is lower. If a coach does not have tested or estimated 1RM values, the loads recommended in the Intensity section of this chapter can be used. If a coach uses a four-week microcycle that repeats multiple times, the volume for week 1 will be low, week 2 will be medium, week 3 will be high, and week 4 will be low to very low, respectively.

For the professional resistance training program, a training intensity that is moderate to moderately hard, or 6 to 7 on the resistance training–specific RPE scale (table 9.15, page 232), is recommended to allow the athlete to maintain an appropriate volume, remain consistent with training, encourage neuromuscular activation prior to baseball activity, and allow for proper recovery. However, in order for the progression of training phases to continue, the volume of training must be kept to an appropriate and effective dose, given that fatigue-related variables accumulate through game-play. The Cleveland Clinic RPE scale in table 11.7 allows athletes to report their RPE or fatigue, which provides the coach with some insight into how the athlete should train that day. If a coach modifies a training program because they listened to how the athlete is feeling, the athlete knows and trusts that the coach has the athlete's best interest in mind.

The number of repetitions and sets performed will vary, depending on where the player is in the season. After an athlete reports his recovery status from the previous day's practice or game, a decision can be made regarding the number of sets and repetitions. For example, an athlete who reports a 1 through 5 on the Cleveland Clinic RPE scale is determined to be "fresh," whereas an athlete who reports a 10 is exhausted (2). The fresh athlete will complete a workout with a relative intensity of moderate to moderately hard (resistance training–specific RPE scale of 6 to 7) with limited repetitions. The athlete who reports a 6 or 7 (very heavy) on the Cleveland Clinic RPE scale prior to training will be given a workout with minimal sets and light to moderate intensity (3 to 5 on the resistance training–specific RPE scale) (13). Finally, if an athlete reports an 8 or higher on the Cleveland Clinic RPE scale prior to training, which means the athlete has "very heavy" perceptions of exertion or fatigue, he will be counseled to use recovery strategies such as dynamic mobility, stretching and activation, or passive recovery with a massage therapist or athletic trainer (2).

To further regulate volume during the in-season, the total number of repetitions performed for a single- or multi-joint bilateral lower body exercise (e.g., the back squat during week 3) will not exceed 13. Athletes who perform a unilateral lower body primary exercise (e.g., the reverse lunge) during hard intensity training should complete 10 or fewer repetitions. This might include 2 sets of 5 repetitions on day 2 of week 1, or 3 sets of descending repetitions, such as 4, 3, and 2, on day 2 of week 3 (table 11.6). Furthermore, it is important to know that the resistance will increase for each working set of the back squat when an athlete performs 6, 4, and 2 repetitions on day 1 of week 2, and 6, 4, and 3 repetitions on day 1 of week 3, for example, in table 11.6. The same progressive increase in resistance should be understood for the reverse lunge on day 2 during weeks 2 and 3 in table 11.6. When the athlete self-reports a Cleveland Clinic RPE scale of 7 (very heavy) before training, a workout can be modified to reflect an intensity of "moderate to light" on the resistance training–specific RPE scale, which means the athlete will complete at least 4 to 6 fewer repetitions than he could complete for a given load (2, 13). An exercise prescription using these repetitions and intensity regulates the load and time under tension throughout the working sets of the exercise.

Due to their limited throwing volume, a progressive, linear approach can be used for pitchers during the first several microcycles of in-season training. Furthermore, relief pitchers will seldom be asked to pitch three or more days in a row, therefore they tend to recover more quickly than position players. A progression from 2 to 3 sets on all exercises during weeks 1 and 3 in table 11.6, for example, allows the athlete to acclimate to stressors (game time, game location, travel, playing volume, and in-game situations) during the initial month of the season.

By capping the total number of sets in an exercise, pitchers continue to develop strength as they build game volume. As pitchers' workout microcycles progress through the season, volume decreases while intensity continues to build. Once pitchers have reached the second half of the season, a non-linear approach, similar to the position players, is implemented to further promote recovery while maintaining their ability to move heavy loads at a lower volume.

EXERCISE ORDER

For high school athletes, exercise order for the total body sessions will include the hip circle, world's greatest stretch, and rotator cuff exercises at the beginning of the resistance training program, followed by multi-joint, lower, upper, and total body primary exercises (1). The end of the program will include a mixture of throwing and non-throwing rotational and non-rotational anatomical core exercises, as well as anti-rotation and traditional anatomical core exercises (1). Tables 11.1 and 11.2 display sample in-season programs for high school athletes.

For the college athlete, exercise order during the in-season will differ based on position. Position players and relief pitchers will complete two total body resistance training sessions consisting of a multi-joint lower and upper body primary exercise combined with an anatomical core stability, mobility, or corrective exercise (10). Starting pitchers will complete three resistance training sessions (lower body, upper body, and total body) based on when they pitch. The lower body day will incorporate a multi-joint pushing or pulling exercise combined with an anatomical core stability, mobility, or corrective exercise (10). The upper body day will incorporate a multi-joint and one-arm pushing or pulling exercise combined with an anatomical core stability, mobility, or corrective exercise (10). The total body day will have a multi-joint lower or upper body pushing and pulling exercise combined with an anatomical core stability, mobility, or corrective exercise. Tables 11.4 and 11.5 show the sample in-season training programs for college athletes.

For the professional athlete, the exercise order during the in-season is designed to maximize training efficiency in a relatively short period of time by combining two or three exercises. In general, the first and second sequence of exercises on days 1 and 2 combine three exercises. There is a multi-joint lower body primary exercise performed first, a multi-joint upper body exercise completed second, and an anatomical core strengthening or rotator cuff/scapula stability exercise performed last. The third sequence of exercises is the pairing of an anatomical core exercise with a half-kneeling pulling exercise. Table 11.6 displays a sample in-season training program for the professional athlete.

CONCLUSION

In-season resistance training is vital to success on the field. If strength and conditioning professionals plan and implement an effective program, athletes should be able to maintain strength and power as well as decrease the chances of injury. This will provide the opportunity for all athletes to perform at their best for the duration of the season. Because this is often the longest phase in the resistance training program and the busiest time of the baseball player's year, it is crucial that the in-season programs are appropriate and based on evidence-based principles. However, coaches must also be willing and able to make modifications as needed due to the unpredictability of the competitive season.

Warm-Ups: Mobility, Corrective, Active Dynamic, and In-Place Flow Stretch Exercises

Choose the most appropriate warm-up option based on the specific training day.

OPTION 1

Foam roll, activation, and movement-based warm-up

- T-spine rotation with reach (3 × 10 each arm) or trunk stability rotation with knees flexed (3 × 10)
- Starter rolling upper body (3 × 5 each side) or rolling upper body (3 × 5 each arm)
- Standing scapular wall slide with back on wall (3 × 10)
- Half-kneeling hip flexor stretch (3 × 10 each leg)
- Toe touch progression (3 × 5 each)
- Single-leg stance with core engagement with cable system or Cook band (3 × 5 each leg)
- Tall kneeling hold anterior load (3 × 10 breaths) or tall kneeling hold anterior load with optional head turn or head and shoulder turn (3 × 5 each side)

OPTION 2

Foam roll, activation, and movement-based warm-up

- Quadruped T-spine rotation or quadruped T-spine rotation lumbar locked (3 × 10 each arm)
- Rolling lower body (3 × 5 each leg)

- Standing forearm wall slide (3 × 10)
- Half-kneeling rotation with dowel (3 × 5 each side)
- Assisted single-leg lowering (3 × 10 each leg)
- Tall or half-kneeling KB halo (3 × 5 each direction)
- 90-90 breathing position (3 × 5)

OPTION 3

Foam roll, activation, and movement-based warm-up

- Brettzel (3 × 5 breaths each side) or Brettzel 2.0 variation (3 × 5 each side)
- Core control rolling with knee touch (3 × 5 each side)
- Seated scapular wall slide with back on wall (3 × 10)
- Open half-kneeling ankle mobility with KB (3 × 10 each leg)
- Active leg lowering to bolster (3 × 10 each leg)
- Deep squat assisted with Functional Movement Trainer (FMT) (3 × 10)
- Tall kneeling hold posterior load (3 × 10 breaths) or tall kneeling hold posterior load with optional head turn or head and shoulder turn (3 × 5 each side)

OPTION 4

Activation and Dynamic Warm-Up

Activation

- Lateral mini-band walk (1 × 12 each leg)
- Forward and backward mini-band walk (1 × 12 each leg)
- Double-leg bridge (1 × 15)
- Supine single-leg lowering with full exhale (1 × 8 each leg)
- Quadruped opposite arm and leg reach with full exhale (1 × 8 each leg)
- Yoga push-up with full exhale (1 × 5)
- Bear crawl forward and backward (1 × 10 yards or meters each)

Dynamic warm-up (1 × 10 yards or meters for each movement)

- Walking knee hug
- Walking quad stretch with overhead reach
- Walking leg cradle
- Walking toe touch
- Walking RDL with reach
- World's greatest stretch
- Forward lunge with rotation
- Lateral shuffle lunge and reach
- Lateral shuffle
- Carioca high knee
- Butt kick
- A-skip
- Lateral A-skip

(continued)

(continued)
- Backward run with reach
- Lateral shuffle to sprint acceleration

OPTION 5

In-place flow stretch (each movement flows into the next)

Cluster 1
- Squat to stand
- World's greatest stretch (alternate legs × 3 each leg)

Cluster 2
- Inchworm
- Yoga push-up
- Half-kneeling hip flexor stretch (alternate legs × 3 each leg)

Activate (done independently)
- Butterfly bridge (1 × 15)
- Lateral plank on knees with abduction (1 × 30 seconds each side)
- Turkish get-up (1 × 3 each side)

Note: The mobility and corrective exercises can be found at https://functionalmovement.com/exercises.

Interpreting the Sample Program Tables

BB = Barbell

BW = Body weight

DB = Dumbbell

KB = Kettlebell

MB = Medicine ball

RDL = Romanian deadlift

SB = Stability ball

Side hang = Holding BB, DB, or KB with the arms hanging down, palms facing legs, and elbows extended.

Rack position = Holding BB, DB, or KB in the catch or rack position on the anterior shoulder.

Goblet = Holding DB or KB with both hands below the chin and elbows pointed out to the side in the midline of the body.

Order = Performing one set of each exercise (1a, 1b, 1c) in the group one after the other. After the first set is completed, go back to the first exercise in the group and do the second set of each exercise. If certain exercises call for fewer sets than others in the group, perform those sets on the back end of the grouping. For example, if exercise 1a calls for 4 sets and exercise 1b calls for 3 sets, perform exercise 1b during sets 2 through 4 of exercises 1a.

Each = Each side (arm or leg), direction, or exercise.

Table 11.1   High School Pitcher: In-Season Microcycle 1, Weeks 1-4

Day 1: Total Body (Hard)

Order	Exercise	Sets × reps	Sets × reps	Sets × reps	Sets × reps
		Week 1	Week 2	Week 3	Week 4
1a	Hip circle forward/backward	2 × 20 sec	2 × 25 sec	2 × 30 sec	2 × 15 sec
1b	World's greatest stretch	2 × 4 each	2 × 5 each	2 × 6 each	2 × 3 each
1c	Thrower's 10 (choose 4)	2 × 10 each	2 × 12 each	2 × 14 each	2 × 8 each
2	MB squat-to-push overhead	3 × 10	3 × 8	3 × 6	3 × 5
3	DB forward step lunge	3 × 10 each	3 × 8 each	3 × 6 each	3 × 5 each
4	Double-leg bridge	3 × 10	3 × 8	3 × 6	3 × 5
5	Push-up	3 × 12	3 × 15	3 × 20	3 × 10
6	One-arm DB row	3 × 10 each	3 × 8 each	3 × 6 each	3 × 5 each
7a	MB BLOB throw	2 × 8	2 × 7	2 × 6	2 × 5
7b	MB twisting wood chop throw	2 × 8 each	2 × 7 each	2 × 6 each	2 × 5 each
7c	Front to side plank	2 × 20 sec each	2 × 25 sec each	2 × 30 sec each	2 × 15 sec each

Day 2: Total Body (Light)

Order	Exercise	Sets × reps	Sets × reps	Sets × reps	Sets × reps
		Week 1	Week 2	Week 3	Week 4
1a	Prone Y, T, I, W	2 × 10 each	2 × 12 each	2 × 14 each	2 × 8 each
1b	Push-up plus	2 × 10	2 × 12	2 × 14	2 × 8
1c	Forearm pronation and supination	2 × 8 each	2 × 10 each	2 × 12 each	2 × 6 each
2	DB crossover step-up	3 × 10 each	3 × 8 each	3 × 6 each	3 × 5 each
3	DB single-leg RDL	3 × 10 each	3 × 8 each	3 × 6 each	3 × 5 each
4	Two-arm KB swing	3 × 10	3 × 8	3 × 6	3 × 5
5	Neutral grip DB bench press	3 × 10	3 × 8	3 × 6	3 × 5
6	Neutral grip lat pulldown	3 × 10	3 × 8	3 × 6	3 × 5
7a	Superman	3 × 10	3 × 12	3 × 15	2 × 10
7b	Curl-up with leg extension	3 × 10	3 × 12	3 × 15	2 × 10
7c	Side crunch	3 × 10 each	3 × 12 each	3 × 15 each	2 × 10 each

Table 11.2 High School Position Player: In-Season Microcycle 1, Weeks 1-4

Day 1: Total Body (Hard)

Order	Exercises	Sets × reps	Sets × reps	Sets × reps	Sets × reps
		Week 1	**Week 2**	**Week 3**	**Week 4**
1a	Hip circle forward/backward	3 × 20 sec	3 × 25 sec	3 × 30 sec	3 × 15 sec
1b	World's greatest stretch	3 × 5 each	3 × 6 each	3 × 7 each	3 × 4 each
1c	Thrower's 10 (choose 4)	3 × 10 each	3 × 12 each	3 × 14 each	3 × 8 each
2	Power clean*	3 × 6	3 × 5	3 × 4	3 × 6
3	Back squat**	3 × 6	3 × 5	3 × 4	3 × 6
4	SB single-leg curl***	3 × 10 each	3 × 8 each	3 × 6 each	3 × 5 each
5	DB bench press	3 × 10	3 × 8	3 × 6	3 × 5
6	One-arm DB row	3 × 10 each	3 × 8 each	3 × 6 each	3 × 5 each
7a	MB BLOB throw	3 × 7 each	3 × 6 each	3 × 5 each	3 × 4 each
7b	MB twisting wood chop throw	3 × 7 each	3 × 6 each	3 × 5 each	3 × 4 each
7c	Front to side plank	3 × 20 sec each	3 × 25 sec each	3 × 30 sec each	3 × 15 sec each

*Catchers will perform midthigh clean pull.

**Catchers will perform back squat with wide stance.

***Catchers will perform double-leg bridge.

Day 2: Total Body (Light)

Order	Exercises	Sets × reps	Sets × reps	Sets × reps	Sets × reps
		Week 1	**Week 2**	**Week 3**	**Week 4**
1a	Prone Y, T, I, W	3 × 10 each	3 × 12 each	3 × 14 each	3 × 8 each
1b	Forearm pronation and supination	3 × 8 each	3 × 10 each	3 × 12 each	3 × 6 each
1c	Wrist ulnar and radial deviation	3 × 8 each	3 × 10 each	3 × 12 each	3 × 6 each
2	Two-arm KB swing	3 × 10	3 × 8	3 × 6	3 × 5
3	DB forward step lunge	3 × 10 each	3 × 8 each	3 × 6 each	3 × 5 each
4	DB single-leg RDL	3 × 10 each	3 × 8 each	3 × 6 each	3 × 5 each
5	DB bench press (alternate arm)	3 × 10	3 × 8	3 × 6	3 × 5
6	Neutral grip pull-up	3 × 10	3 × 8	3 × 6	3 × 5
7a	Seated partner MB overhead toss	3 × 12	3 × 10	3 × 8	3 × 6
7b	Seated trunk rotation toss	3 × 8 each	3 × 7 each	3 × 6 each	3 × 5 each
7c	Seated SB cable rotation	3 × 8 each	3 × 7 each	3 × 6 each	3 × 5 each

Table 11.3 College: In-Season Maintenance, Example Weekly Schedule

Day	Position players and relief pitchers	Starting pitchers (seven-day routine; Friday night starter)
Monday	Total body (hard)	Day 4: Bullpen: upper body (post-bullpen: moderate)
Tuesday	Game	Day 5: Recovery/mobility*
Wednesday	Recovery/mobility*	Day 6: Total body (light to moderate)
Thursday	Total body (light or moderate)	Day 7: Mobility*
Friday	Game	Day 1: Game
Saturday	Game	Day 2: Light BW/metabolic focused
Sunday	Game	Day 3: Lower body (hard)

*Warm-ups: mobility and corrective exercise session options (see page 266)

Table 11.4 College: In-Season Microcycle 1, Position Player and Relief Pitcher, Weeks 1-4

Day 1: Total Body (Hard)

Order	Exercise	Sets × reps Week 1	Sets × reps Week 2	Sets × reps Week 3	Sets × reps Week 4
1a	Trap bar deadlift	3 × 6	4 × 5	4 × 4	3 × 6
1b	Open half-kneeling ankle mobility with KB*	3 × 10 each	4 × 8 each	4 × 10 each	3 × 8 each
2a	DB flat or incline bench press	3 × 6	4 × 5	4 × 4	3 × 6
2b	Quadruped T-spine rotation*	3 × 10 each	4 × 8 each	4 × 10 each	3 × 8 each
3a	KB or DB reverse lunge or step-up (rack position)	3 × 8 each	3 × 7 each	3 × 6 each	3 × 5 each
3b	Standing Pallof press	3 × 8 each	3 × 9 each	3 × 10 each	3 × 6 each
4a	Suspension trainer inverted row	3 × 6	3 × 8	3 × 10	3 × 5
4b	Double-leg bridge	3 × 5 breath hold	3 × 5 breath hold	3 × 5 breath hold	3 × 5 breath hold
5a	Farmer's walk (with KB or DB)	3 × 25 yd (23 m)	3 × 30 yd (27 m)	4 × 30 yd (27 m)	3 × 20 yd (18 m)
5b	Toe touch progression*	3 × 5 each	3 × 5 each	4 × 5 each	3 × 5 each

Day 2: Total Body (Option 1: Moderate)

Order	Exercise	Sets × reps Week 1	Sets × reps Week 2	Sets × reps Week 3	Sets × reps Week 4
1a	Lat pulldown or seated row	3 × 8	4 × 7	4 × 6	3 × 8
1b	Rolling upper body*	3 × 5 each	4 × 5 each	4 × 5 each	3 × 5 each
2a	Single-leg RDL (with BB, KB, or DB)	3 × 8 each	3 × 6 each	4 × 6 each	3 × 8 each
2b	Half-kneeling stick chop or lift	3 × 8 each	3 × 10 each	4 × 10 each	3 × 6 each
3a	Cable or DB staggered stance shoulder press (one-arm)	3 × 8 each	3 × 7 each	3 × 6 each	3 × 8 each
3b	Side plank	3 × 20 sec each	3 × 25 sec each	3 × 30 sec each	3 × 15 sec each
4a	KB one-arm squat (rack position)	2 × 8 each	2 × 7 each	2 × 6 each	2 × 8 each
4b	Lateral mini-band walk (band on ankles or above knees)	2 × 10 each	2 × 12 each	2 × 15 each	2 × 8 each
5a	Bear crawl (forward, backward, or lateral)	3 × 10 yd (9 m)	3 × 15 yd (14 m)	3 × 20 yd (18 m)	2 × 10 yd (9 m)
5b	Tall kneeling hold anterior load with head and shoulder turn*	3 × 5 each	3 × 5 each	3 × 5 each	2 × 5 each

*Warm-ups: mobility and corrective exercise session options (see page 266)

(continued)

Table 11.4   College: In-Season Microcycle 1, Position Player and Relief Pitcher, Weeks 1-4 *(continued)*

Day 2: Total Body (Option 2: Light)

Order	Exercise	Sets × reps Week 1	Sets × reps Week 2	Sets × reps Week 3	Sets × reps Week 4
1a	Front squat (BB, or KB or DB goblet)	3 × 8	4 × 6	4 × 5	3 × 8
1b	Half-kneeling hip flex or stretch*	3 × 10 each	4 × 10 each	4 × 10 each	3 × 10 each
2a	Cable staggered stance one-arm row (high to low pull)	3 × 8 each	4 × 7 each	4 × 6 each	3 × 8 each
2b	Kneeling MB chest pass	3 × 8	4 × 10	4 × 10	3 × 6
3a	Two-arm KB swing	3 × 10	3 × 8	3 × 6	3 × 6
3b	Turkish get-up to hand with hip extension	3 × 3 each	3 × 4 each	3 × 5 each	3 × 2 each
4a	MB twisting wood chop throw	3 × 5 each	3 × 6 each	3 × 7 each	3 × 4 each
4b	Quadruped T-spine rotation*	3 × 10 each	3 × 10 each	3 × 10 each	3 × 10 each
5a	One-arm farmer's walk (side hang or rack position with KB or DB)	3 × 20 yd (18 m) each	3 × 25 yd (23 m) each	3 × 30 yd (27 m) each	3 × 15 yd (14 m) each
5b	Forward and backward mini-band walk (band on ankles or above knees)	3 × 8 each	3 × 10 each	3 × 12 each	3 × 6 each

*Warm-ups: mobility and corrective exercise session options (see page 266)

Table 11.5   College: In-Season Microcycle 1, Starting Pitcher, Weeks 1-4

Day 3: Lower Body (Hard)

Order	Exercise	Sets × reps Week 1	Sets × reps Week 2	Sets × reps Week 3	Sets × reps Week 4
1a	Trap bar deadlift	3 × 6	4 × 5	4 × 4	3 × 6
1b	Open half-kneeling ankle mobility with KB*	3 × 10 each	4 × 10 each	4 × 10 each	3 × 10 each
2a	Front squat (BB, or KB or DB goblet)	3 × 6	4 × 5	4 × 4	3 × 6
2b	Half-kneeling hip or stretch*	3 × 10 each	4 × 10 each	4 × 10 each	3 × 10 each
3a	Single-leg RDL (with BB, KB, or DB)	3 × 6 each	3 × 5 each	4 × 4 each	3 × 6 each
3b	Half-kneeling stick chop or lift	3 × 8 each	3 × 10 each	4 × 10 each	3 × 6 each
4a	KB or DB reverse lunge or step-up (rack position)	3 × 10 each	3 × 8 each	3 × 6 each	3 × 10 each
4b	Rolling upper body*	3 × 5 each	3 × 5 each	3 × 5 each	3 × 5 each
5a	Farmer's walk (one or two-arm variations with KB or DB)	3 × 25 yd (23 m)	3 × 30 yd (27 m)	4 × 30 yd (27 m)	3 × 20 yd (18 m)
5b	Toe touch progression*	3 × 5 each	3 × 5 each	4 × 5 each	3 × 5 each

*Warm-ups: mobility and corrective exercise session options (see page 266)

Day 4: Upper Body (Moderate)

Order	Exercise	Sets × reps Week 1	Sets × reps Week 2	Sets × reps Week 3	Sets × reps Week 4
1a	Lat pulldown or seated row	3 × 8	4 × 7	4 × 6	3 × 8
1b	Brettzel 2.0*	3 × 5 each	4 × 5 each	4 × 5 each	3 × 5 each
2a	DB bench or floor press	3 × 8	3 × 7	4 × 6	3 × 8
2b	Quadruped T-spine rotation*	3 × 8 each	3 × 10 each	4 × 10 each	3 × 8 each
3a	Cable staggered stance one-arm row (high to low pull)	3 × 8 each	4 × 7 each	4 × 6 each	3 × 8 each
3b	Rolling lower body*	3 × 5 each	4 × 5 each	4 × 5 each	3 × 5 each
4a	Cable or BB landmine reverse lunge to press	3 × 10 each	3 × 8 each	4 × 6 each	3 × 10 each
4b	Turkish get-up to elbow or hand position hold	3 × 5 breaths each	3 × 5 breaths each	4 × 5 breaths each	3 × 5 breaths each
5a	Bear crawl (forward, backward, or lateral)	3 × 10 yd (9 m)	3 × 15 yd (14 m)	3 × 20 yd (18 m)	2 × 10 yd (9 m)
5b	Half-kneeling rotation with dowel*	3 × 5 each	3 × 5 each	3 × 5 each	2 × 5 each

*Warm-ups: mobility and corrective exercise session options (see page 266)

Day 6: Total Body (Light)

Order	Exercise	Sets × reps Week 1	Sets × reps Week 2	Sets × reps Week 3	Sets × reps Week 4
1a	Two-arm KB swing	3 × 10	3 × 8	3 × 6	3 × 5
1b	Turkish get-up to leg sweep	3 × 2 each	3 × 3 each	3 × 4 each	3 × 2 each
2a	MB twisting wood chop throw	3 × 5 each	3 × 6 each	3 × 7 each	3 × 4 each
2b	Active leg lowering to bolster*	3 × 10 each	3 × 10 each	3 × 10 each	3 × 10 each
3a	Suspension trainer inverted row	3 × 6	3 × 8	3 × 10	3 × 5
3b	Side plank	3 × 20 sec each	3 × 25 sec each	3 × 30 sec each	3 × 15 sec each
4a	KB one-arm squat (rack position)	2 × 8 each	2 × 7 each	2 × 6 each	2 × 8 each
4b	Lateral mini-band walk (band on ankles or above knees)	2 × 8 each	2 × 10 each	2 × 12 each	2 × 6 each
5a	Tall kneeling hold anterior load with head and shoulder turn*	3 × 5 each	3 × 6 each	3 × 7 each	3 × 4 each
5b	90-90 breathing position*	3 × 5	3 × 5	3 × 5	3 × 5

*Warm-ups: mobility and corrective exercise session options (see page 266)

Table 11.6 Professional: In-Season Microcycle 1, Weeks 1-4

Day 1: Total Body

Order	Exercise	Sets × reps Week 1	Sets × reps Week 2	Sets × reps Week 3	Sets × reps Week 4
1a	Back squat	2 × 5	× 6, × 4, × 2*	× 6, × 4, × 3*	2 × 4
1b	Suspension trainer inverted row	2 × 8	3 × 8	3 × 10	2 × 6
1c	Dead bug	2 × 8 each	3 × 8 each	3 × 10 each	3 × 5 each
2a	One-arm single-leg RDL	2 × 6 each	3 × 6 each	3 × 6 each	2 × 6 each
2b	Standing one-arm DB shoulder press	2 × 8 each	3 × 8 each	3 × 10 each	2 × 6 each
2c	Prone T raise	2 × 12	3 × 10	3 × 12	2 × 10
3a	Half-kneeling stick chop	2 × 10 each	3 × 10 each	3 × 12 each	2 × 8 each
3b	Half-kneeling cable row (high)	2 × 8 each	3 × 8 each	3 × 10 each	2 × 6 each

*Increase the resistance for each working set of the back squat when an athlete performs 6, 4, and 2 repetitions on day 1 of week 2 and 6, 4, and 3 repetitions on day 1 of week 3.

Day 2: Total Body

Order	Exercise	Sets × reps Week 1	Sets × reps Week 2	Sets × reps Week 3	Sets × reps Week 4
1a	Reverse lunge	2 × 5 each	× 4, × 2, × 1* each	× 4, × 3, × 2* each	2 × 4 each
1b	Half-kneeling one-arm DB row	2 × 8 each	3 × 8 each	3 × 10 each	2 × 6 each
1c	Push-up shoulder tap	2 × 8 each	3 × 8 each	3 × 10 each	2 × 6 each
2a	Leg curl	2 × 8	3 × 8	3 × 10	2 × 6
2b	Push-up	2 × 10	3 × 10	3 × 12	2 × 8
2c	DB bent-over lateral shoulder raise	2 × 10	3 × 10	3 × 12	2 × 8
3a	Half-kneeling stick lift	2 × 10 each	3 × 10 each	3 × 12 each	2 × 8 each
3b	Half-kneeling lat pulldown	2 × 8 each	3 × 8 each	3 × 10 each	2 × 6 each

*Increase the resistance for each working set of the reverse lunge when an athlete performs 4, 2, and 1 repetition (for each leg) on day 2 of week 2 and 4, 3, and 2 repetitions (for each leg) on day 1 of week 3.

Table 11.7 Cleveland Clinic Rated Perceived Exertion (RPE) Scale

Rating	Description of perceived exertion
0	Nothing at all
0.5	Just noticeable
1	Very light
2	Light
3	Moderate
4	Somewhat heavy
5	Heavy
6	
7	Very heavy
8	
9	
10	Very, very heavy
**	Maximal

12

POSTSEASON PROGRAMMING

PATRICK MCHENRY (HIGH SCHOOL), CHRIS JOYNER (COLLEGE), JOE KESSLER (PROFESSIONAL)

The postseason, sometimes referred to as the "active rest and restoration" phase, begins once the baseball season has officially ended and generally lasts no more than four weeks (1, 9). When the season technically ends differs for the high school and college baseball player compared to the professional. In high school and college, the end of the school-related competitive baseball season is late May or early June if the team advances to the playoffs. However, the competitive season typically continues immediately or shortly after, because the summer season runs from late May to the first week of August. The professional baseball player, on the other hand, plays a 142-game minor-league or 162-game major-league season until October, which is much longer than the high school and college seasons. However long the season, it is highly recommended that these athletes take some time off from playing and training to rest and recover both physically and mentally before they begin the next annual training cycle (3, 4, 5, 9).

This chapter includes goals and objectives, length, structure, and organization of the postseason training as well as recommended exercises. Additionally, intensity, volume, and exercise order for high school, college, and professional athletes will be described. Finally, sample postseason training programs are provided for each level of play.

GOALS AND OBJECTIVES

The postseason begins with a time to rest and recover physically and psychologically from the competitive season (9). During this initial time when the athlete is intentionally not training, which may be two weeks or more, detraining will occur. This is to be expected, but it is a much-needed time for athletes to remove themselves from the daily physical and mental grind of the game. Once this recovery time is completed, the postseason transitions to a time of general activity and retraining at low intensities and volumes (9). This section will discuss the goals and objectives for the high school, college, and professional postseason.

High School and College

The combined number of games played during a high school or college season plus the games played during summer league has been attributed to the increase in baseball-related injuries (2). Because of this, two of the three main goals of the postseason are to mentally and physically recover from the competitive baseball season. The third goal is to begin preparing to transition into the off-season. If an athlete sustained an injury during the season, this is an excellent time to rest, recover, and rehabilitate. This is also a good time to get away from the game and stay active by engaging in recreational activities or light resistance training exercises that the athlete enjoys. Additionally, this would be an outstanding time to work on flexibility and mobility if those are areas of need. Finally, the postseason is a good time to work on exercise technique with no or light resistance.

Professional

The rigors of competition during the major- and minor-league season take a toll on athletes, both physically and mentally. Athletes are expected to remain competitive for 162 games at the professional level while also practicing each day and training several times a week. Once the competitive season has come to an end, athletes must allow themselves time to recover their minds and bodies prior to beginning their off-season training.

During the competitive season, many athletes develop chronic compensations, largely due to the duration of the season, rotational elements of hitting and throwing, extensive travel, and schedule of game start times. This accumulated effect of fatigue makes recovery the first priority. As the athletes transition from the competitive season to the postseason, there must be an immediate period of training inactivity to allow the athletes to shift their mindset back to a focus on physical development. The length of this phase will vary by individual needs and personal obligations. This is an important opportunity for athletes to reconnect with family and friends and to step away from the structure of a long season. Many athletes will begin to slowly add active recovery activities that can be incorporated into vacations, hobbies, or general downtime.

Once athletes have had the much-needed downtime, they will begin active recovery, which focuses on primary foundational movements, gross asymmetries, mobility, stability, and general cardiovascular fitness. Due to the absence of baseball skill work, this is an opportunity to become a more symmetrical and functional athlete and to prepare for the added external load that will be used in the off-season. The inclusion of organized, low-impact workouts, such as yoga and Pilates, can also provide a productive primary focus in the beginning stages of the off-season. After the postseason has been completed, the athlete will progress to more rigorous strength and power training in the off-season.

It should be noted that the postseason has a very different meaning for teams that are playing in the MLB playoffs. For these teams, the postseason presents an interesting challenge, due to the uncertainty of each series. These teams must push beyond the boundaries of an already exhausting MLB season schedule to continue competing in an emotionally charged environment at the highest level of the game. For playoff teams, the routines established during the competitive season should remain in place during postseason play. However, though training should continue, the volume of training should be significantly decreased. Workout duration is decreased through exercise elimination while working at a lower intensity. Training should continue to complement performance, but in a much more limited capacity, to compensate for the high levels of exhaustion athletes face by this point in the season.

LENGTH, STRUCTURE, AND ORGANIZATION

The postseason generally lasts four weeks. It is designed to help the athlete rest and recover while incorporating low intensity circuit and restoration training; however, the length of the postseason depends on the level of play. The postseason should be considered a preparatory period for the off-season training. The structure and organization for high school to professional athletes will be addressed in this section.

High School and College

For the high school and college athlete, the postseason may occur at different times. If an athlete is finished playing with the school team and not playing on a summer or travel team, he will start the postseason program in June. This allows for a four-week postseason program before the athlete starts the general preparation phase for the more demanding off-season training program. However, most high school athletes go right into summer ball, which begins in late May and ends in early August at the beginning of the school year. In this situation, the athlete may have four weeks or less before starting fall baseball or another fall sport. A summer team does not have to follow the National Federation of High School Coaches or NCAA rules, so they can play as many games or tournaments that they want. Some teams may compete in 12 tournaments of two to three games each over a three-month summer period.

Due to the long summer playing schedule, a postseason program is critical for active recovery and restoration. The sample postseason programs in this chapter for high school and college athletes both last four weeks. At the high school level, athletes will train two days a week with total body circuit training routines (table 12.1), with the third day used for recovery with foam rolling, an ice bath, or other appropriate recovery options. The warm-up options on page 283 can also be used for recovery. During this time, a certified athletic trainer should evaluate any areas that are sore, tender, or swollen. Athletes should follow any appropriate medical treatment prescribed to aid recovery. The strength and conditioning professional can perform a functional movement assessment to identify any areas of mobility or flexibility that need to be addressed (7, 8).

At the collegiate level, athletes will train three days a week with a total body focus restoration program (table 12.2). Mobility and corrective exercises are incorporated into the training sessions after completing a primary exercise. The loading pattern for the high school and college athlete's four-week postseason program is low, medium, high, and unload (10).

Professional: Playoff Teams

Because of the uncertainty of how long a playoff team's postseason run will last, this period does not allow for any form of progression. Instead, a continued implementation of the phases used in the latter half of the season are most appropriate during the playoffs. The postseason typically includes scheduled off days that many teams use for travel or practice. These days are perfect for any external load training, done in a limited capacity. The workout program should not deviate a great deal from what the athletes performed in-season. In general, each training session (workouts A and B in table 12.3) is organized with three combined exercises: multi-joint lower body pushing and upper body pulling exercises (1a and 1b), multi-joint lower body pulling and upper body pushing exercises (2a and 2b), and two anatomical core exercises combined (3a and 3b).

Professional: Non-Playoff Teams

The structure of the postseason when the season is over should attempt to address movement efficiency and aerobic capacity while progressing the athlete's metabolic work capacity prior to beginning the off-season. This microcycle typically consists of four weeks of training with three to four exercise sessions per week. General movement patterns of squatting, lunging, crawling, and hinging can be included with body-weight exercise progressions. This progression is first incorporated as a primary movement sequence focused on length, stability, and mobility of musculature, a process used by yoga and Pilates programs. The flow of each movement from one position to the next should progressively speed up to increase heart rate. Aerobic activity can also be included to solidify a general physical foundation for subsequent training phases. Workouts A and B can be rotated each working day to provide stimulus and variety while addressing multiple movement patterns and progressions. The first two weeks typically include three exercise sessions (A, B, and A followed by B, A, and B), then increase to four exercise sessions during the second two weeks of the cycle (A, B, A, and B repeated).

In general, each exercise session for the professional athlete is organized as a total body circuit training session with one exercise performed after the other with minimal rest, followed by two to three minutes of rest at the end of the circuit. Multi-joint lower body pushing and pulling exercises, multi-joint upper body pushing and pulling exercises, total body exercises, and anatomical core exercises are all incorporated into the 16-exercise circuit training program. The loading pattern for this four-week cycle is low, medium, high, and unload (table 12.4) (10).

RECOMMENDED EXERCISES

The postseason resistance training program includes a variety of total body, lower body, upper body, and anatomical core exercises. Recommendations for high school to professional athletes will be discussed in this section.

High School

It is highly recommended that athletes perform a warm-up before training. One of the five warm-up options starting on page 283 can be selected based on the option that is the most appropriate for the respective training day. After the warm-up, athletes should complete a total body circuit training session comprising predominantly multi-joint lower and upper body pushing and pulling exercises. During this time of the annual training year, exercises with barbells or machines do not necessarily need to be part of the athlete's program. However, if a coach wants to incorporate light resistance or work on an athlete's exercise technique for some of the more technical exercises, such as Olympic-style lifts, this would be an excellent time to do it. Table 12.1 displays the postseason total body circuit training program for the high school athlete.

College

As with the high school athlete's program, it is highly recommended that collegiate athletes perform a warm-up before training using the most appropriate option (see page 283). After the warm-up, the athlete will perform multi-joint lower and upper body pushing and pulling exercises that have a total body focus and are integrated with mobility or corrective exercises. Exercise selection for the postseason may vary, but coaches should incorporate exercises that athletes are familiar with.

Professional: Playoff Teams

Exercise selection during the playoffs should remain consistent with the athlete's in-season program and include multi-joint lower and upper body exercises. This is not the time to make changes. The alteration of joint angles under load can promote muscle fatigue and soreness. Because this is arguably the most important time of the season, exercise selection should focus on consistency for the athlete.

Professional: Non-Playoff Teams

Postseason exercise selection when the competitive season has ended will vary. For example, bilateral movements, such as the body-weight and band squat, push-up and its variations, and inverted row will be incorporated into the postseason programming. Unilateral movements in the sagittal and frontal planes, such as the lunge, step-up, split squat, bridge, one-arm pulldown, and face pull, and total body exercises such as the bear crawl and Turkish get-up variations, will also be included in the postseason programming.

Total Body Exercises

If a high school or college athlete has poor power clean technique or has not previously performed power cleans or other Olympic-style lifts, this is a good time for the athlete to work on exercise technique with the coach. To focus on the mechanics of the power clean, the athlete should use a PVC bar or aluminum bar during this cycle of training. If an athlete has any shoulder issues, rest and recovery is recommended before performing exercises that could put additional stress on the shoulder joint. Table 12.1 for the high school athlete and table 12.2 for the college athlete do not include the power clean or its progressions; however, if a coach wants the athlete to perform these types of exercises, they should be completed with light resistance when the athlete is not fatigued.

In table 12.2, college athletes will perform total body exercises such as the Turkish get-up and bear crawl. These exercises allow for controlled total body movement patterns. The professional athlete will not perform total body exercises during the playoffs; however, when the competitive season has ended, athletes will perform the Turkish get-up and its variations as well as bear crawl variations.

Lower Body Exercises

The postseason for the high school athlete is a great time to work on squat range of motion. The athlete can perform a full squat below parallel, focusing on foot, knee, and torso position. The entire movement can be evaluated by the athlete and coach because no weight or light weight is being used. High school athletes will also perform single-leg and double-leg bridge exercises with no weight for the hamstrings.

The college athlete will perform the deadlift with body weight or light equipment (BB, DB, or KB) so the athlete can work on exercise technique and patterning. Various lunges and step-ups are also performed as multi-joint pushing exercises. The single-leg RDL and hip thrust are performed as multi-joint primary pulling exercises.

The professional athlete will perform the back squat or other squat variations, deadlift, and split squat for multi-joint pushing exercises in addition to the single-leg RDL during the playoffs. When the competitive season is over, the professional athlete will perform the back squat with a band, split squat, crossover step-up, band deadlift, and various lunges as well as the single-leg glute bridge, single-leg RDL, and double-leg bridge.

Upper Body Exercises

Shoulder muscle imbalance and posterior tightness can be a problem for baseball players because they perform a chronic, repetitive throwing motion. Like other training seasons during the year, the postseason is a time when foam rolling, stretching, and rotator cuff exercises can be implemented to help improve range of motion and attempt to prevent shoulder imbalances. Implementing the Thrower's 10 program, prone Y, T, I, W exercises, or other rotator cuff and scapula stabilization exercises will benefit the athlete (12). High school and college athletes will perform various types of push-ups and pulling exercises, such as the lat pulldown, one-arm dumbbell row, inverted row, and chin-up. For the professional athlete during the playoffs, push-ups, inverted rows, and seated rows will be performed. When the competitive season is over, like the high school and college athletes, professional athletes will perform various forms of push-ups and pulling exercises, such as the inverted row, one-arm band pulldowns, and face pulls.

Anatomical Core Exercises

The postseason is an excellent time to introduce anatomical core exercises that athletes might not be familiar with performing. Chapter 8 includes eight categories of anatomical core exercises that are designed to help athletes learn how to control their breathing while performing core function exercises. They are categorized as educational re-patterning, core strengthening, repositioning, traditional, isometric, medicine ball, throwing, and functional. Readers are encouraged to practice performing exercises they have not done before in order to teach the athlete how to perform them correctly. These exercises, for example, educational re-patterning, core strengthening, and repositioning, can be substituted for any of the anatomical core exercises in the various tables in this chapter.

Tables 12.1 to 12.4 include such exercises as various planks, dead bug, side crunch, various curl-ups, superman, various types of Pallof presses, half-kneeling stick chops and lifts, farmer's walk, and medicine ball chopping exercises. All of these exercises provide variations from the movement and exercise categories described in chapter 8. They will develop a well-rounded foundation for the athlete to build on for the next training year.

INTENSITY

For the high school athlete, the postseason intensity will be body weight as well as relatively light bands and dumbbells (5 pounds [2.3 kg] or less) or a barbell. This period is designed to help with recovery and teach technique. The college athlete will use body weight as well as relatively light to moderate loads or percentages (35%-75% of the 1RM) (1, 11). The desired outcome is to prepare the athlete for the upcoming off-season. For the professional athlete during the playoffs, the training needed to maintain strength and power can be performed at a moderate intensity level, which is based on the athlete's resistance training–specific RPE of 6 to 7 displayed in table 9.15 on page 232 (13). Strength and power have been developed or maintained all season, so continuing a high-intensity program is no longer needed. When the competitive season is over, the professional athlete's exercise intensity is light, which is a resistance training–specific RPE of 3 to 5, focusing on time under tension (13). Exercises are performed using body weight, bands, dumbbells, kettlebells, or cable machines.

VOLUME

The postseason training phase begins to set the foundation for the off-season training phase. Because athletes will be coming off a long competition season, the volume for the postseason will be low and then gradually progress to help prepare the athletes for the high training volume off-season. The volume for high school to professional athletes will be discussed in this section.

High School and College

Most of the repetitions for primary exercises during the postseason are between 6 and 20 for the high school athlete and between 8 and 15 for the college athlete. Some exercises will be performed for a certain amount of time or distance and not a specific number of repetitions. There will be 2 to 3 sets depending on the week. This will be the lowest volume of the entire annual program.

Professional: Playoff Teams

For the athlete to recover quickly, the volume of each exercise session for each of the four weeks during the playoffs should stay consistent. The sets and repetitions for the first primary exercise for workout A (back squat) and B (deadlift) has five options based on how the athlete is feeling that day. Option 1 is 5 sets of 2 repetitions. Option 2 is 3 sets of 3 repetitions. Option 3 is 1 set of 5 repetitions, 1 set of 3 repetitions, and 1 set of 2 repetitions. Option 4 is 2 sets of 5 repetitions. Option 5 is 1 set of 4 repetitions, 1 set of 2 repetitions, and 1 set of 1 repetition. All these options have a total amount of 9 or 10 repetitions completed for that specific exercise. The other exercises listed in table 12.3 are limited to 2 sets of 5 to 12 repetitions depending on the type of exercise. In general, an overall resistance training–specific RPE moderate intensity of 6 to 7, displayed on page 232 in table 9.15, should be maintained for the working sets (13). However, resistance training–specific RPE can be modified based on how the athlete feels that day. The athlete's perception of exertion before training can be monitored with the Cleveland Clinic RPE scale, which is displayed on page 247 in table 11.7 (6).

Professional: Non-Playoff Teams

The assigned sets and repetitions for the postseason increase weekly from weeks 1 to 3 and then decrease in the fourth week. To increase time under tension, exercises progress in the number of repetitions and sets rather than external load. Weeks 1 and 2 include 2 sets, but progress by repetitions, time, or distance (table 12.4). Weeks 3 and 4 include 3 sets for each exercise, then decrease in repetitions, time, or distance during week 4 (table 12.4). An overall resistance training–specific RPE light intensity of 3 to 5 should be maintained for the working sets (13).

EXERCISE ORDER

The exercise order during the postseason is relatively similar for high school to professional athletes. In general, the entire body will be trained with a variety of multi-joint lower and upper body exercises, and, at times, total body exercises will be added.

High School

In general, the exercise order for the high school athlete's postseason program is a total body circuit consisting of four general exercise categories. The first four exercises are a multi-joint lower body pushing exercise, a multi-joint upper body pushing exercise, an anatomical core exercise, and a rotator cuff/scapula stabilization exercise. The second four exercises are a multi-joint lower body pulling exercise, a multi-joint upper body pulling exercise, an anatomical core exercise, and a rotator cuff/scapula stabilization exercise. A coach could also add a third group of four exercises similar to the ones provided in table 12.1, but it would be recommended to decrease the number of sets to 2.

College

Each of the training sessions for the collegiate athlete is organized by combining two exercises (e.g., 1a and 1b) before moving on to the next two exercises (e.g., 2a and 2b). In general, the first exercise will be a multi-joint lower body pulling exercise followed by a multi-joint lower body pushing exercise, then a multi-joint upper body pushing exercise followed by a multi-joint upper body pulling exercise. Finally, the athlete will perform a variation of a farmer's walk. All of these exercises will be combined with a mobility, corrective, or anatomical core exercise. At times, total body exercises are integrated into the exercise combinations. Table 12.2 displays college postseason restoration training sessions.

Professional

For the professional athlete that is in the playoffs, each training session is generally three exercises that are each combined with another exercise. For example, the athlete may perform a multi-joint lower body pushing and upper body pulling exercise combined, then a multi-joint lower body pulling and upper body pushing exercise combined, and finally two anatomical core exercises combined (table 12.3).

For the professional athlete that is not in the playoffs, each training session is organized as a total body circuit with one exercise performed after the other with minimal rest, followed by two to three minutes of rest before starting the next circuit. Multi-joint lower body pushing and pulling exercises, multi-joint upper body pushing and pulling exercises, total body exercises, and anatomical core exercises are all incorporated into the 16-exercise total body circuit training program (table 12.4).

CONCLUSION

Although it is the shortest of the training seasons, the postseason is an important part of the annual program because it allows the athlete to mentally and physically recover from the competitive season with low-intensity, low-volume active recovery and restoration training. It is also a time that allows the coach to evaluate and reflect on the previous year, then plan and design programming for the next training year. The training sessions presented in this chapter are examples of what could generally be performed at each level of play, but coaches can modify the exercise selections based on their facility and equipment. Ultimately, the goal of the postseason is to refresh the athletes and prepare them for the next year's off-season training plan.

Warm-Ups: Mobility, Corrective, Active Dynamic, and In-Place Flow Stretch Exercises

Tables 12.1 through 12.4 include the most appropriate warm-up option at the beginning of each workout.

OPTION 1

Foam roll, activation, and movement-based warm-up

- T-spine rotation with reach (3 × 10 each arm) or trunk stability rotation with knees flexed (3 × 10)
- Starter rolling upper body (3 × 5 each side) or rolling upper body (3 × 5 each arm)
- Standing scapular wall slide with back on wall (3 × 10)
- Half-kneeling hip flexor stretch (3 × 10 each leg)
- Toe touch progression (3 × 5 each)
- Single-leg stance with core engagement with cable system or Cook band (3 × 5 each leg)
- Tall kneeling hold anterior load (3 × 10 breaths) or tall kneeling hold anterior load with optional head turn or head and shoulder turn (3 × 5 each side)

OPTION 2

Foam roll, activation, and movement-based warm-up

- Quadruped T-spine rotation or quadruped T-spine rotation lumbar locked (3 × 10 each arm)
- Rolling lower body (3 × 5 each leg)
- Standing forearm wall slide (3 × 10)
- Half-kneeling rotation with dowel (3 × 5 each side)
- Assisted single-leg lowering (3 × 10 each leg)
- Tall or half-kneeling KB halo (3 × 5 each direction)
- 90-90 breathing position (3 × 5)

OPTION 3

Foam roll, activation, and movement-based warm-up

- Brettzel (3 × 5 breaths each side) or Brettzel 2.0 variation (3 × 5 each side)
- Core control rolling with knee touch (3 × 5 each side)
- Seated scapular wall slide with back on wall (3 × 10)
- Open half-kneeling ankle mobility with KB (3 × 10 each leg)
- Active leg lowering to bolster (3 × 10 each leg)
- Deep squat assisted with Functional Movement Trainer (FMT) (3 × 10)
- Tall kneeling hold posterior load (3 × 10 breaths) or tall kneeling hold posterior load with optional head turn or head and shoulder turn (3 × 5 each side)

OPTION 4

Activation and Dynamic Warm-Up

Activation

- Lateral mini-band walk (1 × 12 each leg)
- Forward and backward mini-band walk (1 × 12 each leg)

(continued)

(continued)

- Double-leg bridge (1 × 15)
- Supine single-leg lowering with full exhale (1 × 8 each leg)
- Quadruped opposite arm and leg reach with full exhale (1 × 8 each leg)
- Yoga push-up with full exhale (1 × 5)
- Bear crawl forward and backward (1 × 10 yards or meters each)

Dynamic warm-up (1 × 10 yards or meters for each movement)

- Walking knee hug
- Walking quad stretch with overhead reach
- Walking leg cradle
- Walking toe touch
- Walking RDL with reach
- World's greatest stretch
- Forward lunge with rotation
- Lateral shuffle lunge and reach
- Lateral shuffle
- Carioca high knee
- Butt kick
- A-skip
- Lateral A-skip
- Backward run with reach
- Lateral shuffle to sprint acceleration

OPTION 5

In-place flow stretch (each movement flows into the next)

Cluster 1

- Squat to stand
- World's greatest stretch (alternate legs × 3 each leg)

Cluster 2

- Inchworm
- Yoga push-up
- Half-kneeling hip flexor stretch (alternate legs × 3 each leg)

Activate (done independently)

- Butterfly bridge (1 × 15)
- Lateral plank on knees with abduction (1 × 30 seconds each side)
- Turkish get-up (1 × 3 each side)

Note: The mobility and corrective exercises can be found at https://functionalmovement.com/exercises.

Interpreting the Sample Program Tables

BB = Barbell

BW = Body weight

DB = Dumbbell

KB = Kettlebell

MB = Medicine ball

RDL = Romanian deadlift

Side hang = Holding BB, DB, or KB with the arms hanging down, palms facing legs, and elbows extended.

Rack position = Holding BB, DB, or KB in the catch or rack position on the anterior shoulder.

Goblet = Holding DB or KB with both hands below the chin and elbows pointed out to the side in the midline of the body.

Order = Performing one set of each exercise (1a, 1b, 1c, 1d) in the group one after the other. After the first set of all exercises are completed, go back to the first exercise in the group and do the second set of each exercise. If certain exercises call for fewer sets than others in the group, perform those sets on the back end of the grouping. For example, if exercise 1a calls for 4 sets and exercise 1b calls for 3 sets, perform exercise 1b during sets 2 through 4 of exercises 1a.

Each = Each side (arm or leg), direction, or exercise.

Table 12.1   High School: Postseason, Circuit Training, Weeks 1-4

Day 1: Total Body

Order	Exercise	Sets × reps	Sets × reps	Sets × reps	Sets × reps
		Week 1	**Week 2**	**Week 3**	**Week 4**
	Warm-up: Option 4*				
1	BW squat	3 × 12	3 × 15	3 × 20	2 × 12
2	Push-up with neutral hand position	3 × 12	3 × 15	3 × 20	2 × 12
3	Side plank	3 × 20 sec each	3 × 25 sec each	3 × 30 sec each	2 × 20 sec each
4	Bent-over I and Y	3 × 10	3 × 12	3 × 15	2 × 10
5	Single-leg bridge	3 × 10 each	3 × 12 each	3 × 15 each	2 × 10 each
6	Chin-up	3 × 6	3 × 8	3 × 10	2 × 6
7	Side crunch	3 × 10 each	3 × 15 each	3 × 20 each	2 × 10 each
8	Bent-over T and W	3 × 10 each	3 × 12 each	3 × 15 each	2 × 10 each

*Warm-ups: mobility and corrective exercise session options (see page 283)

(continued)

Table 12.1 High School: Postseason, Circuit Training, Weeks 1-4 *(continued)*

Day 2: Total Body

Order	Exercise	Sets × reps Week 1	Sets × reps Week 2	Sets × reps Week 3	Sets × reps Week 4
	Warm-up: Option 1, 2, or 3*				
1	Overhead squat with PVC or BB	3 × 12	3 × 15	3 × 20	2 × 12
2	Push-up plus	3 × 8	3 × 10	3 × 12	2 × 8
3	Front plank	3 × 20 sec	3 × 25 sec	3 × 30 sec	2 × 20 sec
4	External and internal shoulder rotation at 90 degrees	3 × 10 each	3 × 12 each	3 × 15 each	2 × 10 each
5	Double-leg bridge	3 × 10	3 × 12	3 × 15	2 × 10
6	Inverted row	3 × 10	3 × 12	3 × 15	2 × 10
7	Superman	3 × 10	3 × 12	3 × 15	2 × 10
8	Scaption with external rotation	3 × 10	3 × 12	3 × 15	2 × 10

*Warm-ups: mobility and corrective exercise session options (see page 283)

Table 12.2 College: Postseason, Restoration, Weeks 1-4

Monday (Day 1): Total Body

Order	Exercise	Sets × reps Week 1	Sets × reps Week 2	Sets × reps Week 3	Sets × reps Week 4
	Warm-up: Option 1*				
1a	Deadlift (BW, band, BB, DB, or KB)	2 × 8	2 × 10	3 × 10	3 × 8
1b	Open half-kneeling ankle mobility with KB*	2 × 8 each	2 × 10 each	3 × 10 each	3 × 8 each
2a	Lateral lunge (BW, DB, or KB)	2 × 10 each	2 × 12 each	3 × 12 each	3 × 10 each
2b	Half-kneeling rotation with dowel*	2 × 6 each	2 × 8 each	3 × 8 each	3 × 6 each
3a	Push-up (feet elevated)	2 × 12	2 × 15	3 × 15	3 × 10
3b	Side plank	2 × 30 sec each	2 × 45 sec each	3 × 45 sec each	3 × 30 sec each
4a	Inverted row (BB or suspension trainer)	2 × 12	2 × 15	3 × 15	3 × 12
4b	Turkish get-up to elbow or hand position hold	2 × 5 breaths each	2 × 6 breaths each	3 × 6 breaths each	3 × 5 breaths each
5a	Farmer's walk (with KB or DB rack position)	2 × 30 yd	2 × 40 yd	3 × 40 yd	3 × 30 yd
5b	Bear crawl hold (alternating opposite arm and opposite leg in place)	2 × 6 each	2 × 8 each	3 × 8 each	3 × 6 each

*Warm-ups: mobility and corrective exercise session options (see page 283)

Wednesday (Day 2): Total Body

Order	Exercise	Sets × reps Week 1	Sets × reps Week 2	Sets × reps Week 3	Sets × reps Week 4
	Warm-up: Option 2*				
1a	Single-leg RDL (BW, BB, DB, or KB)	2 × 8 each	2 × 10 each	3 × 10 each	3 × 8 each
1b	Elevated single-leg bridge	2 × 10 each	2 × 12 each	3 × 12 each	3 × 10 each
2a	Deep squat assisted with FMT*	2 × 10	2 × 12	3 × 12	3 × 10
2b	Half-kneeling hip flex or stretch*	2 × 8 each	2 × 10 each	3 × 10 each	3 × 8 each
3a	Turkish get-up to leg sweep	2 × 3 each	2 × 5 each	3 × 5 each	3 × 3 each
3b	Front plank	2 × 45 sec	2 × 60 sec	3 × 60 sec	3 × 45 sec
4a	Half-kneeling one-arm row (with band or cable)	2 × 10 each	2 × 12 each	3 × 12 each	3 × 10 each
4b	Core control rolling with knee touch*	2 × 5 each	2 × 8 each	3 × 8 each	3 × 5 each
5a	One-arm farmer's walk (with one KB or DB)	2 × 30 yd (27 m) each	2 × 40 yd (37 m) each	3 × 40 yd (37 m) each	3 × 30 yd (27 m) each
5b	Standing Pallof press overhead	2 × 5 each	2 × 6 each	3 × 6 each	3 × 5 each

*Warm-ups: mobility and corrective exercise session options (see page 283)

Friday (Day 3): Total Body

Order	Exercise	Sets × reps Week 1	Sets × reps Week 2	Sets × reps Week 3	Sets × reps Week 4
	Warm-up: Option 3*				
1a	Hip thrust (banded, DB, or BB)	2 × 10	2 × 12	3 × 12	3 × 10
1b	Assisted single-leg lowering*	2 × 8 each	2 × 10 each	3 × 10 each	3 × 8 each
2a	Step-up or lateral step-up (BW, DB, or KB)	2 × 10 each	2 × 12 each	3 × 12 each	3 × 10 each
2b	Toe touch progression*	2 × 5 each	2 × 8 each	3 × 8 each	3 × 5 each
3a	Push-up plus or push-up shoulder tap	2 × 8	2 × 10	3 × 10	3 × 8
3b	Turkish get-up to hand with hip extension	2 × 3 each	2 × 5 each	3 × 5 each	3 × 3 each
4a	Half-kneeling two-arm pulldown (with band or cable)	2 × 10	2 × 12	3 × 12	3 × 10
4b	MB diagonal wood chop	2 × 10 each	2 × 12 each	3 × 12 each	3 × 10 each
5a	Farmer's walk (with KB or DB)	2 × 30 yd (27 m)	2 × 40 yd (37 m)	3 × 40 yd (37 m)	3 × 30 yd (27 m)
5b	Bear crawl (forward, backward, or lateral)	2 × 10 yd (9 m)	2 × 15 yd (14 m)	3 × 15 yd (14 m)	3 × 10 yd (9 m)

*Warm-ups: mobility and corrective exercise session options (see page 283)

Table 12.3 Professional: Postseason (Playoffs), Maintenance, Weeks 1-4

Workout A: Total Body

Order	Exercise	Sets × reps Week 1	Sets × reps Week 2	Sets × reps Week 3	Sets × reps Week 4
	Warm-up: Option 4*				
1a	Back squat	Option 1: 5 × 2 Option 2: 3 × 3 Option 3: 1 × 5, 1 × 3, 1 × 2 Option 4: 2 × 5 Option 5: 1 × 4, 1 × 2, 1 × 1	Option 1: 5 × 2 Option 2: 3 × 3 Option 3: 1 × 5, 1 × 3, 1 × 2 Option 4: 2 × 5 Option 5: 1 × 4, 1 × 2, 1 × 1	Option 1: 5 × 2 Option 2: 3 × 3 Option 3: 1 × 5, 1 × 3, 1 × 2 Option 4: 2 × 5 Option 5: 1 × 4, 1 × 2, 1 × 1	Option 1: 5 × 2 Option 2: 3 × 3 Option 3: 1 × 5, 1 × 3, 1 × 2 Option 4: 2 × 5 Option 5: 1 × 4, 1 × 2, 1 × 1
1b	Inverted row (supinated grip)	2 × 8	2 × 8	2 × 8	2 × 8
2a	Single-leg RDL	2 × 5 each	2 × 5 each	2 × 5 each	2 × 5 each
2b	Push-up	2 × 10	2 × 10	2 × 10	2 × 10
3a	Pallof press	2 × 12 each	2 × 12 each	2 × 12 each	2 × 12 each
3b	Half-kneeling one-arm row (high)	2 × 8 each	2 × 8 each	2 × 8 each	2 × 8 each

*Warm-ups: mobility and corrective exercise session options (see page 283)

Workout B: Total Body

Order	Exercise	Sets × reps Week 1	Sets × reps Week 2	Sets × reps Week 3	Sets × reps Week 4
	Warm-up: Option 5*				
1a	Deadlift	Option 1: 5 × 2 Option 2: 3 × 3 Option 3: 1 × 5, 1 × 3, 1 × 2 Option 4: 2 × 5 Option 5: 1 × 4, 1 × 2, 1 × 1	Option 1: 5 × 2 Option 2: 3 × 3 Option 3: 1 × 5, 1 × 3, 1 × 2 Option 4: 2 × 5 Option 5: 1 × 4, 1 × 2, 1 × 1	Option 1: 5 × 2 Option 2: 3 × 3 Option 3: 1 × 5, 1 × 3, 1 × 2 Option 4: 2 × 5 Option 5: 1 × 4, 1 × 2, 1 × 1	Option 1: 5 × 2 Option 2: 3 × 3 Option 3: 1 × 5, 1 × 3, 1 × 2 Option 4: 2 × 5 Option 5: 1 × 4, 1 × 2, 1 × 1
1b	Half-kneeling one-arm landmine press	2 × 8 each	2 × 8 each	2 × 8 each	2 × 8 each
2a	Split squat	2 × 5 each	2 × 5 each	2 × 5 each	2 × 5 each
2b	Seated row	2 × 10	2 × 10	2 × 10	2 × 10
3a	Dead bug	2 × 12 each	2 × 12 each	2 × 12 each	2 × 12 each
3b	Half-kneeling stick chop	2 × 8 each	2 × 8 each	2 × 8 each	2 × 8 each

*Warm-ups: mobility and corrective exercise session options (see page 283)

Table 12.4 Professional: Postseason (No Playoffs), Circuit Training, Weeks 1-4

Workout A: Total Body

Order	Exercise	Sets × reps Week 1	Sets × reps Week 2	Sets × reps Week 3	Sets × reps Week 4
1	Warm-up: Option 1 or 2*				
2	Single-leg glute raise	2 × 15 each	2 × 20 each	3 × 25 each	3 × 15 each
3	Side plank	2 × 30 sec each	2 × 45 sec each	3 × 60 sec each	3 × 30 sec each
4	MB wood chop	2 × 12	2 × 15	3 × 20	3 × 12
5	Push-up shoulder tap	2 × 8 each	2 × 10 each	3 × 12 each	3 × 8 each
6	Back squat with bands	2 × 12	2 × 15	3 × 20	3 × 12
7	Push-up	2 × 10	2 × 15	3 × 20	3 × 10
8	Inverted row	2 × 10	2 × 15	3 × 20	3 × 10
9	Dead bug	2 × 8 each	2 × 10 each	3 × 12 each	3 × 8 each
10	Step-up	2 × 8 each	2 × 10 each	3 × 12 each	3 × 8 each
11	Bear crawl	2 × 10 yd (9 m)	2 × 15 yd (14 m)	3 × 20 yd (18 m)	3 × 10 yd (9 m)
12	One-arm band pulldown	2 × 8 each	2 × 10 each	3 × 12 each	3 × 8 each
13	Pallof press	2 × 8 each	2 × 10 each	3 × 12 each	3 × 8 each
14	Split squat	2 × 8 each	2 × 10 each	3 × 12 each	3 × 8 each
15	Push-up with feet elevated	2 × 8	2 × 10	3 × 12	3 × 8
16	Face pull	2 × 15	2 × 20	3 × 25	3 × 15
17	Curl-up with leg extended	2 × 8	2 × 10	3 × 12	3 × 8

*Warm-ups: mobility and corrective exercise session options (see page 283)

Workout B: Total Body

Order	Exercise	Sets × reps Week 1	Sets × reps Week 2	Sets × reps Week 3	Sets × reps Week 4
	Warm-up: Option 3*				
1	Double-leg bridge	2 × 20	2 × 25	3 × 30	3 × 20
2	Side plank	2 × 30 sec each	2 × 45 sec each	3 × 60 sec each	3 × 30 sec each
3	Crossover step-up	2 × 12 each	2 × 15 each	3 × 20 each	3 × 12 each
4	Superman with opposite arm and leg hold	2 × 15 sec each	2 × 30 sec each	3 × 45 sec each	3 × 15 sec each
5	Band deadlift	2 × 8	2 × 10	3 × 12	3 × 8
6	Yoga push-up	2 × 8	2 × 10	3 × 12	3 × 8
7	One-arm band pulldown	2 × 8 each	2 × 10 each	3 × 12 each	3 × 8 each
8	Turkish get-up (shoe on fist)	2 × 3 each	2 × 5 each	3 × 5 each	3 × 3 each
9	Reverse lunge	2 × 8 each	2 × 10 each	3 × 12 each	3 × 8 each
10	Push-up shoulder tap	2 × 6 each	2 × 8 each	3 × 10 each	3 × 6 each
11	One-arm single-leg RDL	2 × 8 each	2 × 10 each	3 × 12 each	3 × 8 each
12	Kneeling Pallof press	2 × 8 each	2 × 10 each	3 × 12 each	3 × 8 each
13	Lateral lunge	2 × 8 each	2 × 10 each	3 × 12 each	3 × 8 each
14	Lateral bear crawl	2 × 10 yd (9 m) each	2 × 15 yd (14 m) each	3 × 15 yd (14 m) each	3 × 10 yd (9 m) each
15	Dumbbell lateral shoulder raise	2 × 8	2 × 12	3 × 15	3 × 8
16	Abdominal curl-up	2 × 12	2 × 15	3 × 20	3 × 12

*Warm-ups: mobility and corrective exercise session options (see page 283)

Chapter 1

1. Baker, D. Improving vertical jump performance through general, special, and specific strength training: A brief review. *J Strength Cond Res* 10:131-136, 1996.

2. Camp, CL, Dines, JS, van der List, JP, Conte, S, Conway, J, Altchek, DW, Coleman, SH, and Pearle, AD. Summative report on time out of play for Major and Minor League Baseball: An analysis of 49,955 injuries from 2011 through 2016. *Am J Sports Med* 7:1727-1732, 2018.

3. Carter, J, and Greenwood, M. Complex training reexamined: Review and recommendations to improve strength and power. *Strength Cond J* 36(2): 11-19, 2014.

4. Conte, S, Camp, CS, and Dines, JS. Injury trends in Major League Baseball over 18 seasons: 1998-2015. *Am J Orthop* 45(3):116-123, 2016.

5. DeRenne, C, Ho, KW, and Murphy, JC. Effects of general, special, and specific resistance training on throwing velocity in baseball. *J Strength Cond Res* 15:148-156, 2001.

6. DeWeese, BH, and Nimphius, S. Program design and technique for speed and agility. In *Essentials of Strength Training and Conditioning*. 4th ed. Haff, GG, and Triplett, NT, eds. Champaign, IL: Human Kinetics, 521-557, 2016.

7. Draper, JA, and Lancaster, MG. The 505 test: A test for agility in the horizontal plane. *Aust J Sci Med Sport* 17:15-18, 1985.

8. Escamilla, RF, Speer, KP, Fleisig, GS, Barrentine, SW, and Andrews, JR. Effects of throwing overweight and underweight baseballs on throwing velocity and accuracy. *Sports Med* 29:259-272, 2000.

9. Fleck SJ, and Falkel, JE. Value of resistance training for the reduction of sports injuries. *Sports Med* 3(1):61-68, 1986.

10. French, D. Adaptations to anaerobic training programs. In *Essentials of Strength Training and Conditioning*. 4th ed. Haff, GG, and Triplett, NT, eds. Champaign, IL: Human Kinetics, 87-113, 2016.

11. Gabbett, TJ. Debunking the myths about training load, injury and performance: Empirical evidence, hot topics and recommendations for practitioners. *Br J Sports Med* 54(1):58-66, 2018.

12. Gambetta, V. How much strength is enough? *Strength Cond* 17(4):46-49, 1995.

13. Haff, GG. Periodization. In *Essentials of Strength Training and Conditioning*. 4th ed. Haff, GG, and Triplett, NT, eds. Champaign, IL: Human Kinetics, 583-604, 2016.

14. Harrison, AJ, ed. Biomechanical factors in sprint training—where science meets coaching. In *XXVIII International Symposium of Biomechanics in Sports,* July 2010. Marquette, MI: 38, 2010.

15. Lauersen, JB, Bertelsen, DM, and Andersen, LB. The effectiveness of exercise interventions to prevent sports injuries: A systematic review and meta-analysis of randomised controlled trials. *Br J Sports Med* 48(11):871-877, 2014.

16. McBride, JM. Biomechanics of resistance exercise. In *Essentials of Strength Training and Conditioning*. 4th ed. Haff, GG, and Triplett, NT, eds. Champaign, IL: Human Kinetics, 19-42, 2016.

17. Powers, SK, and Howley, ET, eds. Common measurements in exercise physiology. In *Exercise Physiology: Theory and Application to Fitness and Performance.* 10th ed. New York: McGraw-Hill, 16-37, 2018.

18. Powers, SK, and Howley, ET, eds. The physiology of training: Effect on VO$_2$ Max, performance, and strength. In *Exercise Physiology: Theory and Application to Fitness and Performance.* 10th ed. New York: McGraw-Hill, 293-323, 2018.

19. Sheppard, JM, and Young, WB. Agility literature review: Classifications, training, and testing. *J Sports Sci* 24:919-932, 2006.

20. Suchomel, TJ, Nimphius, S, and Stone, MH. The importance of muscular strength in athletic performance. *Sports Med* 46:1419-1449, 2016.

21. Szymanski, DJ. Effects of various resistance training methods on overhand throwing power athletes: A brief review. *Strength Cond J* 34(6):61-74, 2012.

22. Szymanski, DJ. Physiology of baseball pitching dictates specific exercise intensity for conditioning. *Strength Cond J* 31(2): 41-47, 2009.

23. Szymanski, DJ, DeRenne, C, and Spaniol, FJ. Contributing factors for increased bat swing velocity. *J Strength Cond Res* 23(4): 1338-1352, 2009.

24. Szymanski, DJ, and Fredrick, GA. Baseball (Part II): A periodized speed program. *Strength Cond J* 23(2):44-52, 2001.

25. Verkhoshansky, Y, and Siff, M. *Supertraining*. 6th ed. Rome: Verkhoshansky, 1, 2009.

26. Young, WB, James, R, and Montgomery, R. Is muscle power related to running speed with changes in direction? *J Sports Med Phys Fitness* 42:282-288, 2002.

Chapter 2

1. Bushnell, BD, Anz, AW, Noonan, TJ, Torry, MR, and Hawkins, RJ. Association of maximum pitch velocity and elbow injury in professional baseball pitchers. *Am J Sports Med* 38(4):728-732, 2010.

2. Coleman, AE. *52-week baseball training*. Champaign, IL: Human Kinetics, 2000.

3. Clamp, J. An introduction to strength and strength training. https://simplifaster.com/articles/introduction-strength-training. Accessed April 8, 2020.

4. Edwards, J. Pitching velocity and injury: Is throwing less hard worth it? 2018. https://community.fangraphs.com/pitch-velocity-and-injury-is-throwing-less-hard-worth-it. Accessed April 8, 2020.

5. Ellis, S. Pitching speeds. www.thecompletepitcher.com/pitching_speeds.htm. Accessed April 8, 2020.

6. Go Big Recruiting. www.gobigrecruiting.com/recruiting101/baseball/positional_guidelines. Accessed April 8, 2020.

7. Hammami, R, Behm, DG, Chtara, M, Othman, AB, and Chaouachi, A. Comparison of static balance and the role of vision in elite athletes. *J Human Kinetics* 41(1):33-41, 2014.

8. Herda, TJ, and Cramer, JT. Bioenergetics of exercise and training. In *Essentials of Strength Training and Conditioning*. 4th ed. Haff, GG, and Triplett, NT, eds. Champaign, IL: Human Kinetics, 43-63, 2016.

9. Hoffman, JR, Vazquez, J, Pichardo, N, and Tenenbaum, G. Anthropometric and performance comparisons in professional baseball players. *J Strength Cond Res* 23(8):2173-2178, 2009.

10. Major League Baseball Statcast Leaderboard. http://m.mlb.com/statcast/leaderboard. Accessed April 8, 2020.

11. McGuigan, M. Principles of test selection and administration. In *Essentials of Strength Training and Conditioning*. 4th ed. Haff, GG, and Triplett, NT, eds. Champaign, IL: Human Kinetics, 316, 2016.

12. Perfect Game. Top event performers. www.perfectgame.org/Records/statrankings.aspx. Accessed April 8, 2020.

13. Rossow, LM, Fukuda, DH, Fahs, CA, Lonneke, JP, and Stout, JR. Natural bodybuilding competition preparation and recovery: A 12-week study. *Int J Sports Physio Perform* 8(5):582-592, 2013.

14. Runge, CF, Shupert, CL, Horak, FB, and Zajac, FE. Role of vestibular information in initiation of rapid postural responses. *Experimental Brain Res* 122(4):403-412, 1998.

15. Ryan, N. *Nolan Ryan's Pitcher's Bible*. New York, NY: Simon and Schuster, 1991.

16. Sabesan, V, Prey, B, Smith, R, Lombardo, DJ, Borroto, WU, and Whaley, JD. Concussion rates and effects on player performance in Major League Baseball players. Open access *J Sports Med* 9:253-260, 2018.

17. Savant Statcast Search. https://baseballsavant.mlb.com/statcast_search. Accessed April 8, 2020.

18. Stodden, DF, Campbell, BM, and Moyer, TM. Comparison of trunk kinematics in trunk training exercise and throwing. *J Strength Cond Res* 22(1):112-118, 2008.

19. Szymanski, DJ, McIntyre, JS, Szymanski, JM, Molloy, JM, Madsen, NH, and Pascoe, DD. Effect of wrist and forearm training on linear bat-end,

center of percussion, and hand velocities and on time to ball contact of high school baseball players. *J Strength Cond Res* 20(1):231-240, 2006.

20. Szymanski, DJ, Szymanski, JM, Schade, RL, Bradford, TJ, McIntyre, JS, DeRenne, C, and Madsen, NH. The relation between anthropometric and physiological variables and bat velocity of high-school baseball players before and after 12 weeks of training. *J Strength Cond Res* 24(11):2933-2943, 2010.

21. Valle, C. Why sport-specific training is a red herring. https://simplifaster.com/articles/sport-specific-training-debate. Accessed April 8, 2020.

22. Veronique, LB. Interval training for performance: A scientific and empirical practice. Special recommendations for middle- and long-distance running. Part I: Aerobic interval training. *Sports Med* 31(1):13-31, 2001.

23. Wade, MG, and Jones, G. The role of vision and spatial orientation in the maintenance of posture. *Phys Ther* 77(6):619-628, 1997.

Chapter 3

1. Earle, RW. Weight training exercise prescription. In *Essentials of Personal Training Symposium Workbook*. Lincoln, NE: NSCA Certification Commission, 3-39, 2006.

2. Harman, EA, Rosenstein, MT, Frykman, PN, Rosenstein, RM, and Kraemer, WJ. Estimation of human power output from vertical jump. *J Appl Sport Sci Res* 5(3):116-120, 1991.

3. Hoffman, J. *Norms for Fitness, Performance, and Health*. Champaign, IL: Human Kinetics, 5, 6, 38, 2006.

4. Hoffman, JR, Vazquez, J, Pichardo, N, and Tenenbaum, G. Anthropometric and performance comparisons in professional baseball players. *J Strength Cond Res* 23(8):2173-2178, 2009.

5. Lehman, G, Drinkwater, EJ, and Behm, DG. Correlation of throwing velocity to the results of lower-body field tests in male college baseball players. *J Strength Cond Res* 27(4):902-908, 2013.

6. Mangine, GT, Hoffman, JR, Fragala, MS, Vazquez, J, Krause, MC, Gillett, J, and Pichardo, N. Effect of age on anthropometric and physical performance measures in professional baseball players. *J Strength Cond Res* 27(2):375-381, 2013.

7. Mathiowetz, V, Weber, K, Volland, G, and Kashman, N. Reliability and validity of grip and pinch strength evaluations. *J Hand Surg [Am]* 9A(2):222-226, 1984.

8. McGuigan, M. Administration, scoring, and interpretation of selected tests. In *Essentials of Strength Training and Conditioning*. 4th ed. Haff, GG, and Triplett, NT, eds. Champaign, IL: Human Kinetics, 259-316, 2016.

9. Sayers, SP, Harachiewicz, DV, Harman, EA, Frykman, PN, and Rosenstein, MT. Cross-validation of three jump power equations. *Med Sci Sport Exerc* 31(4):572-577, 1999.

10. Sheppard, JM, and Triplett, NT. Program design for resistance training. In *Essentials of Strength Training and Conditioning*. 4th ed. Haff, GG, and Triplett, NT, eds. Champaign, IL: Human Kinetics, 439-469, 2016.

11. Spaniol, FJ. Baseball athletic test: A baseball-specific test battery. *Strength Cond J* 31(2):26-29, 2009.

12. Spaniol, FJ. Striking skills: Developing power to turn. *Strength Cond J* 34(6):57-60, 2012.

13. Swanson, S, Alfred, B, Ivan, BM, and Groot, D. The strength of hand. *J Assoc Child Pros Ortho Clin* 13:1-8, 1974.

14. Szymanski, DJ, Albert, JM, Reed, JG, Hemperley, DL, Moore, RM, and Walker, JP. Effect of over-weighted forearm training on bat swing and batted-ball velocities of high school baseball players. *J Strength Cond Res* 22(6):109-110, 2008.

15. Szymanski, DJ, Albert, JM, Reed, JG, and Szymanski, JM. Relationships between anthropometric and physiological variables and sport-specific skills of collegiate baseball players. *Med Sci Sport Exerc* 43(5):S596, 2011.

16. Szymanski, DJ, Beiser, EJ, Bassett, KE, Till, ME, Medlin, GL, Beam, JR, and DeRenne, C. Effect of various warm-up devices on bat velocity of intercollegiate baseball players. *J Strength Cond Res* 25(2):287-292, 2011.

17. Szymanski, DJ, Beiser, EJ, Bassett, KE, Till, ME, and Szymanski, JM. Relationship between sports performance variables and bat swing velocity of collegiate baseball players. *J Strength Cond Res* 25(3):122, 2011.

18. Szymanski, DJ, DeRenne, C, and Spaniol, FJ. Contributing factors for increased bat swing velocity. *J Strength Cond Res* 23(4):1338-1352, 2009.

19. Szymanski, D, Donahue, T, Tolbert, W, Stover, B, Elumalai, A, and Greenwood, M. Effect of weighted implement training on bat velocity of high school baseball players: A pilot study. *J Strength Cond Res* 27(10):S78, 2013.

20. Szymanski, D, Fairbanks, B, Light, T, and Szymanski, J. Relationship of anthropometric and performance variables to offensive statistics of

collegiate baseball hitters over two years. *J Strength Cond Res* 30(1):S142-143, February 2016.

21. Szymanski, DJ, McIntyre, JS, Szymanski, JM, Bradford, TJ, Schade, RL, Madsen, NH, and Pascoe, DD. Effect of torso rotational strength on angular hip, angular shoulder, and linear bat velocities of high school baseball players. *J Strength Cond Res* 21(4):1117-1125, 2007.

22. Szymanski, DJ, McIntyre, JS, Szymanski, JM, Molloy, JM, Madsen, NH, and Pascoe, DD. Effect of wrist and forearm training on linear bat-end, center of percussion, and hand velocities, and time to ball contact of high school baseball players. *J Strength Cond Res* 20(1):231-240, 2006.

23. Szymanski, D, and Porche, B. Relationships of anthropometric and performance variables to offensive statistics of college baseball hitters. *J Strength Cond Res* 27(4):S71, 2013.

24. Szymanski, D, Qiao, M, Singh, V, and Szymanski, J. Correlation of power to fastball velocity of collegiate baseball pitchers. *J Strength Cond Res* 35(4):e3-e288, 2021.

25. Szymanski, DJ, Szymanski, JM, Albert, JM, Beam, JR, Hsu, HS, Reed, JG, and Spaniol, FJ. Physiological and anthropometric characteristics of college baseball players over an entire year. *J Strength Cond Res* 24(Suppl. 1):1, 2010.

26. Szymanski, DJ, Szymanski, JM, Brooks, KA, Braswell, MT, Britt, AT, Hsu, HS, Lowe, HE, Taylor, EG, and Weil, KL. The relationship between power and lean body mass to sport-specific skills of college baseball players. *Med Sci Sports Exerc* 41(5):307-308, 2009.

27. Szymanski, DJ, Szymanski, JM, Molloy, JM, and Pascoe, DD. Effect of 12 weeks of wrist and forearm training on high school baseball players. *J Strength Cond Res* 18(3):432-440, 2004.

28. Szymanski, DJ, Szymanski, JM, Schade, RL, and Bradford, TJ. Relationship between physiological variables and linear bat swing velocity of high school baseball players. *Med Sci Sports Exerc* 40(5):S422, 2008.

29. Szymanski, DJ, Szymanski, JM, Schade, RL, Bradford, TJ, McIntyre, JS, DeRenne, C, and Madsen, NH. The relation between anthropometric and physiological variables and linear bat swing velocity of high school baseball players before and after 12 weeks of training. *J Strength Cond Res* 24(11):2933-2943, 2010.

30. Szymanski, JM, Szymanski, DJ, Albert, JM, Reed, JG, Hemperley, DL, Hsu, HS, Moore, RM, Potts, JD, and Winstead, RC. Relationship between physiological characteristics and baseball-specific variables of high school baseball players. *J Strength Cond Res* 22(6):110-111, 2008.

31. Szymanski, JM, Szymanski, DJ, Britt, AT, and Cicciarella, CF. Effect of preseason over-weighted medicine ball training on throwing velocity. *J Strength Cond Res* 25(3):64, March 2011.

Chapter 4

1. Cronin, J, Lawton, T, Harris, N, Kilding, A, and McMaster, DT. A brief review of handgrip strength and sport performance. *J Strength Cond Res* 31(11):3187-3217, 2017.

2. DeFroda, SF, Goyal, D, Patel, N, Gupta, N, and Mulcahey, MK. Shoulder instability in the overhead athlete. *Current Sports Med Rep* 17(9):308-314, 2018.

3. Dechant, Z. Baseball and the Olympic Lifts. www.zachdechant.com/baseball/baseball-and-the-olympic-lifts. Accessed March 3, 2020.

4. Ebben, WP, Hintz, MJ, and Simenz, CJ. Strength and conditioning practices of Major League Baseball strength and conditioning coaches. *J Strength Cond Res* 19(3):538-546, 2005.

5. Haff, GG. Periodization. In *Essentials of Strength Training and Conditioning.* 4th ed. Haff, GG, and Triplett, NT, eds. Champaign, IL: Human Kinetics, 483-603, 2016.

6. Haff, GG, and Nimphius, S. Training principles for power. *Strength Cond J* 34(6):2-12, 2012.

7. Hammer, E. Preseason training for college baseball. *Strength Cond J* 31(2):79-85, 2009.

8. Kibler, WB. The role of the scapula in athletic shoulder function. *Am J Sports Med* 26(2):325-337, 1998.

9. Morrissey, MC, Everett, HA, and Johnson, MJ. Resistance training modes: Specificity and effectiveness. *Med Sci Sport Exerc* 27:648-660, 1995.

10. Reuter, BH, and Dawes, JJ. Program design and technique for aerobic endurance training. In *Essentials of Strength Training and Conditioning.* 4th ed. Haff, GG, and Triplett, NT, eds. Champaign, IL: Human Kinetics, 559-582, 2016.

11. Ribiero-Alvares, JB, Marques, VB, Vaz, MA, and Baroni, BM. Four weeks of Nordic hamstring exercise reduce muscle injury risk factors in young adults. *J Strength Cond Res* 32(5):1254-1262, 2017.

12. Sforzo, GA, and Touey, PR. Manipulating exercise order affects muscular performance during a resistance exercise training session. *J Strength Cond Res* 10(1):20-24, 1996.

13. Sheppard, JM, and Triplett, NT. Program design for resistance training. In *Essentials of Strength Training and Conditioning*. 4th ed. Haff, GG, and Triplett, NT, eds. Champaign, IL: Human Kinetics, 439-470, 2016.

14. Suchomel, TJ, and Sato, K. Baseball resistance training: Should power clean variations be incorporated? *J Athl Enhancement* 2:2, 2013.

15. Unholz, C. Force-velocity: Relationship and application. www.trainwithpush.com/blog/want-to-get-the-most-out-of-your-training-get-ahead-of-the-curve-the-force-velocity-curve-that-is. Accessed April 21, 2020.

Chapter 5

1. Dawes, J, and Lentz, D. Methods of developing power to improve acceleration for the non-track athlete. *Strength Cond J* (34)6:44-51, 2012.

2. Ebben, WP, Hintz, MJ, and Simenz, CJ. Strength and conditioning practices of Major League Baseball strength and conditioning coaches. *J Strength Cond Res* 19(3):538-546, 2005.

3. Magrini, M, Dawes, J, Spaniol, F, and Roberts, A. Speed and agility training for baseball/softball. *Strength Cond J* (40)1:68-74, 2018.

4. Soriano, MA, Suchomel, TJ, and Comfort, P. Weightlifting overhead pressing derivatives: A review of the literature. *Sports Med* 49:867-885, 2019.

5. Suchomel, TJ, and Sato, K. Baseball resistance training: Should power clean variations be incorporated? *J Athl Enhancement* 2:2, 2013.

6. Szymanski, DJ, Szymanski, JM, Bradford, TJ, Schade, RL, and Pascoe, DD. Effect of twelve weeks of medicine ball training on high school baseball players. *J Strength Cond Res* 21(3):894-901, 2007.

7. Wallace, B, and Janz, J. Implications of motor unit activity on ballistic movement. *Int J Sports Sci Coach* 4(2):285-292, 2009.

Chapter 6

1. Bartelink, DL. The role of abdominal pressure in relieving the pressure on the lumbar intervertebral discs. *J Bone Joint Surg Br* 39-B:718-725, 1957.

2. Hackett, DA, and Chow, CM. The Valsalva maneuver: Its effect on intra-abdominal pressure and safety issues during resistance exercise. *J Strength Cond Res* 27:2338-2345, 2013.

3. McBride, JM. Biomechanics of resistance exercise. In *Essentials of Strength Training and Conditioning*. 4th ed. Haff, GG, and Triplett, NT, eds. Champaign, IL: Human Kinetics, 19-42, 2016.

Chapter 7

1. Wilk, KE, Arrigo, C, and Andrews, JR. Rehabilitation of the elbow in the throwing athlete. *J Orthop Sports Phys Ther*, 17(6):305-317, 1993.

2. Wilk, KE, Yenchak, AJ, Arrigo, C, and Andrews, JR. The advanced throwers ten exercise program: A new exercise series for enhanced dynamic shoulder control in the overhead throwing athlete. *Phys Sportsmed*, 39(4):90-97, 2011.

3. Wilk, KE. Rehabilitation of the shoulder. In *Injuries in Baseball*. Philadelphia: Lippincott-Raven Publishers, 451-467, 1998.

Chapter 8

1. Boyle, M. *Advances in Functional Training: Training Techniques for Coaches, Personal Trainers and Athletes*. Santa Cruz, CA: On Target Publications. 39, 2010.

2. Clare, F, Kobesova, A, and Kolar, P. Dynamic neuromuscular stabilization and sports rehabilitation. *Int J Sports Phys Ther* 8(1):62-73, 2013.

3. Haff, GG, Berninger, D, and Caulfield, S. Exercise technique for alternative modes and nontraditional implement training. In *Essentials of Strength Training and Conditioning*. 4th ed. Haff, GG, and Triplett, NT, eds. Champaign, IL: Human Kinetics, 409-438, 2016.

4. Houglum, D. Asymmetrical posture and common related pain syndromes. www.posturalrestoration.com/_resources/dyn/files/75332407zd7eb9eb9/_fn/NATA+2015+presentation+-+Dan+Houglum.pdf. Accessed May 14, 2020.

5. McGill, S. *Ultimate Back Fitness and Performance*. 6th ed. Waterloo, Ontario: Wabuno Publishers, 2017.

6. Smith, S. Top 5 reasons why PRI integration for baseball is as good as it gets. www.posturalrestoration.com/resources/dyn/files/1309705z667f9803/_fn/PRI+Integration+for+Baseball+Review+by+Steve+Smith.pdf. Accessed May 14, 2020.

7. Szymanski, DJ. Collegiate baseball in-season training. *Strength Cond J* 29(4):68-80, 2007.

8. Szymanski, DJ. General, special, and specific core training for baseball players. *NSCA's Perform Train J* 9(5):13-16, 2010.

9. Szymanski, DJ, and Fredrick, GA. College baseball/softball periodized torso program. *Strength Cond J* 21(4):42-47, 1999.

10. Szymanski, DJ, Szymanski, JM, Bradford, TJ, Schade, RL, and Pascoe, DD. Effect of 12 weeks

of medicine ball training on high school baseball players. *J Strength Cond Res* 21(3):894-901, 2007.

Chapter 9

1. Bompa, TO, and Carrera, MC. *Periodization Training for Sports.* 2nd ed. Champaign, IL: Human Kinetics, 163-222, 2005.

2. Cho, CY, Hwang, YS, and Cherng, RJ. Musculoskeletal symptoms and associated risk factors among office workers with high workload computer use. *J Manipulative Physiol Ther* 35(7):534-540, 2012.

3. Cook, G. *Athletic Body in Balance: Optimal Movement Skills and Conditioning for Performance.* Champaign, IL: Human Kinetics, 2003.

4. Fleck, SJ, and Kraemer, WJ. *Designing Resistance Training Programs.* 4th ed. Champaign, IL: Human Kinetics, 1-62, 179-296, 2014.

5. Haff, GG. Periodization. In *Essentials of Strength Training and Conditioning.* 4th ed. Haff, GG, and Triplett, NT, eds. Champaign, IL: Human Kinetics, 583-604, 2016.

6. Janda, V. Muscles and motor control in cervicogenic disorders. In *Physical Therapy of the Cervical and Thoracic Spine.* Grant R, ed. St. Louis, MO: Churchill Livingstone, 182-199, 2002.

7. Page, P. Shoulder muscle imbalance and subacromial impingement syndrome in overhead athletes. *Intern J Sports Phys Ther* 6(1):51-58, 2011.

8. Sheppard, J, and Triplett, NT. Program design for resistance training. In *Essentials of Strength Training and Conditioning.* 4th ed. Haff, GG, and Triplett, NT, eds. Champaign, IL: Human Kinetics, 439-470, 2016.

9. Verkhoshansky, J. The skills of programming the training process. *Journal New Studies in Athletics* 14(4):44-54, 1999.

10. Wilk, KE. Rehabilitation of the shoulder. In *Injuries in Baseball.* Philadelphia: Lippincott-Raven Publishers, 451-467, 1998.

11. Zourdos, MC, Klemp, A, Dolan, C, Quiles, JM, Schau, KA, Jo, E, Helms, E, Esgro, B, Duncan, S, Garcia Merino, S, and Blanco, R. Novel resistance training-specific rating of perceived exertion scale measuring repetitions in reserve. *J Strength Cond Res* 30(1):267-275, 2016.

Chapter 10

1. Bompa, TO, and Carrera, MC. *Periodization Training for Sports.* 2nd ed. Champaign, IL: Human Kinetics, 171-222, 2005.

2. Plisk, SS, and Stone, MH. Periodization strategies. *Strength Cond J* 25(6):19-37, 2003.

3. Sheppard, J, and Triplett, NT. Program design for resistance training. In *Essentials of Strength Training and Conditioning.* 4th ed. Haff, GG, and Triplett, NT, eds. Champaign, IL: Human Kinetics, 439-470, 2016.

4. Wilk, KE. Rehabilitation of the shoulder. In *Injuries in Baseball.* Philadelphia: Lippincott-Raven Publishers, 451-467, 1998.

5. Zourdos, MC, Klemp, A, Dolan, C, Quiles, JM, Schau, KA, Jo, E, Helms, E, Esgro, B, Duncan, S, Garcia Merino, S, and Blanco, R. Novel resistance training–specific rating of perceived exertion scale measuring repetitions in reserve. *J Strength Cond Res* 30(1):267-275, 2016.

Chapter 11

1. Brumitt, J, Meira, E, and Davidson, G. In-season functional shoulder training for high school baseball pitchers. *Strength Cond J* 27(1):26-32, 2005.

2. Cleveland Clinic. Rated Perceived Exertion (RPE) Scale. https://my.clevelandclinic.org/health/articles/17450-rated-perceived-exertion-rpe-scale. Accessed November 25, 2020.

3. Coleman, AE. Training the power pitcher. *Strength Cond J* 31(2):48-58, 2009.

4. Escamilla, R, Ionno, M, Demhay, S, Gleisig, G, Wilk, K, Yamashiro, K, Mikla, T, Paulos, L, and Andrews, J. Comparison of three baseball-specific 6-week training programs on throwing velocity in high school baseball players. *J Strength Cond Res* 26(7):1767-1781, 2012.

5. Haff, GG. Periodization. In *Essentials of Strength Training and Conditioning.* 4th ed. Haff, GG, and Triplett, NT, eds. Champaign, IL: Human Kinetics, 583-604, 2016.

6. Peng, YC, Lo, KC, and Wang, LH. Lower extremity muscle activation and kinematics of catchers when throwing using various squatting and throwing postures. *J Sports Sci Med* 14(3):484-493, 2015.

6a. Plisk, SS, and Stone, MH. Periodization strategies. *Strength Cond J* 25(6):19-37, 2003.

7. Plummer, H, and Oliver, GD. Descriptive analysis of kinematics and kinetics of catchers throwing to second base from their knees. *J Electromyogr Kinesiol* 29:107-112, 2016.

8. Plummer, H, and Oliver, GD. Quantitative analysis of kinematics and kinetics of catchers throwing to second base. *J Sports Sci* 31(10):1108-1116, 2013.

9. Sheppard, JM, and Triplett, NT. Program design for resistance training. In *Essentials of Strength Training and Conditioning.* 4th ed. Haff, GG, and Triplett, NT, eds. Champaign, IL: Human Kinetics, 439-469, 2016.

10. Szymanski, D. Collegiate baseball in-season training. *Strength Cond J* 29(4):68-80, 2007.

11. Szymanski, D. Effects of various resistance training methods on overhand throwing power athletes: A brief review. *Strength Cond J* 34(6):61-74, 2012.

12. Wilk, KE. Rehabilitation of the shoulder. In *Injuries in Baseball*. Philadelphia: Lippincott-Raven Publishers, 451-467, 1998.

13. Zourdos, MC, Klemp, A, Dolan, C, Quiles, JM, Schau, KA, Jo, E, Helms, E, Esgro, B, Duncan, S, Garcia Merino, S, and Blanco, R. Novel resistance training-specific rating of perceived exertion scale measuring repetitions in reserve. *J Strength Cond Res* 30(1):267-275, 2016.

Chapter 12

1. Bompa, TO, and Haff, GG. *Periodization: Theory and Methodology of Training*. 5th ed. Champaign, IL: Human Kinetics, 1-424, 2009.

2. Borrelli, A. Engineering a strong pitching elbow: An off-season training plan. *Strength Cond J* 31(2):64-73, 2009.

3. Charniga, A, Gambetta, V, Kraemer, W, Newton, H, O'Bryant, HS, Palmieri, G, Pedemonte, J, Pfaff, D, and Stone, MH. Periodization: Part 1. *NSCA J* 8(5):12-22, 1986.

4. Charniga, A, Gambetta, V, Kraemer, W, Newton, H, O'Bryant, HS, Palmieri, G, Pedemonte, J, Pfaff, D, and Stone, MH. Periodization: Part 2. *NSCA J* 8(6):17-24, 1986.

5. Charniga, A, Gambetta, V, Kraemer, W, Newton, H, O'Bryant, HS, Palmieri, G, Pedemonte, J, Pfaff, D, and Stone, MH. Periodization: Part 3. *NSCA J* 9(1):16-26, 1987.

6. Cleveland Clinic. Rated Perceived Exertion (RPE) Scale. https://my.clevelandclinic.org/health/articles/17450-rated-perceived-exertion-rpe-scale. Accessed November 25, 2020.

7. Cook, G, Burton, L, Hoogenboom, BJ, and Voight, M. Functional movement screening: The use of fundamental movements as an assessment of function—part 1. *Int J Sport Phys Ther* 9(3):396-409, 2014.

8. Cook, G, Burton, L, Hoogenboom, BJ, and Voight, M. Functional movement screening: The use of fundamental movements as an assessment of function—part 2. *Int J Sport Phys Ther* 9(4):549-563, 2014.

9. Haff, GG. Periodization. In *Essentials of Strength Training and Conditioning*. 4th ed. Haff, GG, and Triplett, NT, eds. Champaign, IL: Human Kinetics, 583-604, 2016.

10. Plisk, SS and Stone, MH. Periodization Strategies. *Strength Cond J* 25(6):19-37, 2003.

11. Sheppard, JM, and Triplett, NT. Program design for resistance training. In *Essentials of Strength Training and Conditioning*. 4th ed. Haff, GG, and Triplett, NT, eds. Champaign, IL: Human Kinetics, 439-469, 2016.

12. Wilk, KE. Rehabilitation of the shoulder. In *Injuries in Baseball*. Philadelphia: Lippincott-Raven Publishers, 451-467, 1998.

13. Zourdos, MC, Klemp, A, Dolan, C, Quiles, JM, Schau, KA, Jo, E, Helms, E, Esgro, B, Duncan, S, Garcia Merino, S, and Blanco, R. Novel resistance training-specific rating of perceived exertion scale measuring repetitions in reserve. *J Strength Cond Res* 30(1): 267-275, 2016.

INDEX

Note: The italicized *f* and *t* following page numbers refer to figures and tables, respectively.

The National Strength and Conditioning Association (NSCA) is the world's leading organization in the field of sport conditioning. Drawing on the resources and expertise of the most recognized professionals in strength training and conditioning, sport science, performance research, education, and sports medicine, the NSCA is the world's trusted source of knowledge and training guidelines for coaches and athletes. The NSCA provides the crucial link between the lab and the field.

ABOUT THE EDITORS

A. Eugene ("Gene") Coleman, EdD, RSCC*E, is professor emeritus in the Exercise and Health Science Program at University of Houston-Clear Lake. He served as a strength consultant for the Texas Rangers from 2013-2020, and is currently the content editor for the Professional Baseball Strength and Conditioning Society website. Coleman was the first strength and conditioning professional in Major League Baseball (MLB) and worked with the Houston Astros from 1978-2012. He was also the first strength and conditioning professional invited to the MLB All-Star game in 2012, the same year in which he earned the NSCA Lifetime Achievement Award.

David J. Szymanski, PhD, CSCS,*D, RSCC*E, FNSCA, is the department chair and a professor of kinesiology at Louisiana Tech University in Ruston, Louisiana. He is the director of baseball performance for the Louisiana Tech baseball team and formerly served as the head strength and conditioning coach and as an assistant baseball coach for that team as well as at Auburn University and Texas Lutheran University.

William E. Amonette, PhD, CSCS, is an associate professor and the executive director of the Health and Human Performance Institute (HHPI) at the University of Houston–Clear Lake, where he leads an interdisciplinary team of scientists, engineers, and practitioners striving to empower individuals through leading-edge testing, research, and technology development to overcome barriers that limit human performance. Previously, Amonette served as a strength conditioning and rehabilitation specialist for astronauts

at NASA's Johnson Space Center, a strength and conditioning coach for the Houston Rockets and China's Olympic basketball team, and a sport science consultant to the Texas Rangers professional baseball organization.

Jay Dawes, PhD, CSCS,*D, NSCA-CPT,*D, TSAC-F, FNSCA, is an associate professor of applied exercise science at Oklahoma State University (OSU) and the codirector of the OSU Tactical Fitness and Nutrition Lab. He has conducted research and testing and has served as a consultant to numerous baseball clubs ranging from the youth sport level to the professional level.

Rigo Febles, CSCS, RSCC, has spent the entirety of his career as a strength and conditioning coach in professional baseball. He began his career with the Cincinnati Reds in 2010, and he joined the New York Yankees in 2016 to become their player development strength and conditioning coordinator. Febles earned his bachelor's degree in exercise physiology from the University of Florida in 2009. He resides in Tampa, Florida, with his wife, Louise, and two sons, Maximo and Rocco.

Paul Fournier, ATC, CSCS, RSCC*E, is presently in his 27th year in professional baseball and currently the head major league strength and conditioning coach for the Philadelphia Phillies. Prior to joining the Phillies, Fournier spent 9 years as the head major league strength and conditioning coach for the Florida Marlins and 7 years with the Montreal Expos, first as a minor league athletic trainer and then as coordinator of strength, athletic training, and rehabilitation. Fournier has been awarded the Montreal Expos'

John McHale Award for outstanding service in player development. He was part of the 2003 World Series Champion Florida Marlins, and he was the National League strength and conditioning coach for the 2014 All-Star Game.

Zach Gjestvang, MS, CSCS, RSCC*D, spent 16 seasons in the Cincinnati Reds organization; his most recent position with the club was as assistant director of strength and conditioning. Gjestvang also spent 9 years as a minor league affiliate strength coach and 4 years as minor league strength and conditioning coordinator. He completed his bachelor's degree at Minnesota State University–Moorhead and his master's degree at California University of Pennsylvania. Gjestvang lives in Cincinnati with his wife and two children.

Chris Joyner, CSCS, RSCC, is the strength and conditioning coach for the Auburn University baseball team and has held the position since 2019, when the Tigers made their first College World Series appearance in 22 years. Joyner arrived at Auburn University with 16 years of experience in professional baseball, most recently serving as the major league strength and conditioning coordinator for the Toronto Blue Jays (2014-2017). He also held the same position with the Milwaukee Brewers (2007-2010). Joyner broke into professional baseball as a minor league strength and conditioning intern for the Blue Jays in 2002 and worked his way into a permanent role with the organization the following season.

Joe Kessler, MS, CSCS, RSCC*D, is has been the strength and conditioning coach for the Cleveland Indians since 2009. He was named MLB Strength Coach of the Year by his MLB peers at the 2018 winter meetings, and he served as the American League strength and conditioning coach at the 2019 All-Star Game. Kessler's previous experience includes two years as the director of athletic development for Oak Athletic Development in Bourbonnais, Illinois, and spent two seasons (2005-2007) as a strength and conditioning assistant with the Indianapolis Colts and with the Chicago Bears in 2004. Kessler is a graduate of Illinois State University, where he majored in kinesiology with a concentration in exercise science. He also hold a master's degree in leadership and organizational development.

Matthew Krause, MA, ATC, CSCS,*D, RSCC*E, is the president of the Professional Baseball Strength and Conditioning Coaches Society. Previously, he served six seasons (2014-2019) as the New York Yankees' director of strength and conditioning and 11 seasons (2003-2013) with the Cincinnati Reds, including 9 seasons (2005-2013) as its major league strength and conditioning coordinator. Krause earned his master's degree in physical education and wellness from Central Florida in 1999 and his bachelor's degree in exercise and sport science from East Carolina University in 1997. He is a certified athletic trainer and holds the National Strength and Conditioning Association (NSCA) designations of certified strength and conditioning specialist with distinction and registered strength and conditioning coach emeritus. Krause was honored as the MLB's Medical Staff of the Year in 2012 and the NSCA's Professional Strength and Conditioning Coach of the Year in 2018. In 2013, he was honored with the Nolan Ryan Award which recognizes an outstanding strength and conditioning coach in professional baseball whose accomplishments, in the opinion of peers, reflect an exemplary dedication to strength and conditioning.

Brad Lawson, MEd, CSCS, RSCC, is the major league strength and conditioning coach for the San Francisco Giants. The year 2021 marked his 10th year with the Giants organization and 13th year in professional baseball, having also worked with the Chicago Cubs and Washington Nationals. Lawson earned a dual degree in kinesiology (BKin) and education (MEd) from the University of New Brunswick in Canada, and he holds the National Strength and Conditioning Association designations of certified strength and conditioning specialist and registered strength and conditioning coach. He resides in Scottsdale, Arizona, with his wife, Kristen; daughter, Layla; and son, Jackson.

Sean Marohn, MS, CSCS,*D, RSCC*D, SFG1, FMS1, has been a professional strength coach for over 20 years. Marohn served as the director of strength and conditioning for the Cincinnati Reds major league baseball club. He also served as a strength and conditioning coach for minor league affiliates of the Reds, Pirates, and Brewers. While earning his master's degree at the University of Tennessee, Knoxville. Marohn served as part of the strength and conditioning staff. He speaks regularly at conferences and clinics all over the country and has published articles on topics ranging from training young athletes to promoting health in the fire service.

Patrick McHenry, MA, CSCS,*D, RSCC, has 32 years of experience as an educator and strength coach, with 20 of those years as a director of strength and conditioning in the high school setting. He earned a master's degree in physical education, with an emphasis in kinesiology, from the University of Northern Colorado. McHenry holds the National Strength and Conditioning Association (NSCA) designations of certified strength and conditioning specialist with distinction and registered strength and conditioning coach. He was named regional Strength Coach of the Year by *American Football Monthly* in 2003, and he was the recognized as the NSCA's High School Strength and Conditioning Coach of the Year in 2005. McHenry served two consecutive terms on the NSCA board of directors, and he is an international presenter, speaking at conferences and Olympic training centers around the world.

Nate Shaw, ATC, CSCS,*D, RSCC, is in his 19th year (since 2002) in professional baseball and is the major league strength and conditioning coach for the Arizona Diamondbacks. His first season with the Diamondbacks was in 2006, after three seasons (2003-2005) with the Tampa Bay Rays organization. Shaw was the minor league strength coordinator in 2004 through 2005 and was an athletic trainer the for the Hudson Valley Renegades in 2003. He attended the University of Florida, where he majored in exercise and sport science, with a specialization in athletic training.

Derek Somerville, MS, LMT, CSCS, RSCC, is in his seventh season as a strength and conditioning coach in professional baseball, including two seasons with the San Francisco Giants, and currently is in his fifth season with the Arizona Diamondbacks. Somerville is originally from Minot, North Dakota, and attended the University of Mary in Bismarck, North Dakota, where he studied exercise science and competed in collegiate baseball. He attended Liberty University to complete a master's of science degree program in exercise science. Most recently, Somerville obtained his massage therapy license through the Cortiva Institute.

Jose Vazquez, MPT, RSCC, has been a major league strength coach for 20 years and is currently the strength coach for the Texas Rangers major league team. Previously, he was the assistant strength and conditioning coordinator for the New York Mets (2002-2004) and a sports physical therapist for the Therapy Center in Knoxville, Tennessee (1998-2001). Vazquez earned All-American honors at the University of Tennessee in 1992 and was selected in the 42nd round of the 1992 June draft by the St. Louis Cardinals. He graduated with a BS degree from the University of Tennessee and received his MPT degree from Nova Southeastern University. He coauthored *Total Fitness for Baseball* (published by Coaches Choice) and "Effect of Age on Anthropometric and Performance Measures in Professional Baseball Players" (*Journal of Strength and Conditioning Research*). Vazquez was recognized with the Nolan Ryan Award as MLB strength coach of the year in 2014. He attended the MLB Scouting Bureau scouting development program in October 2014, and he has earned a black belt in Brazilian jiujitsu.

TAKE THE
NEXT
STEP

A continuing education course
is available for this text.
Find out more.